There
and Then

ALSO, BY DANIEL T. CHAPMAN

Be Not Forgot'

Messages from Vallarta

Poetic Justice

War Torn

There and Then

A SUMMER TO REMEMBER

DANIEL T. CHAPMAN

ISBN: 978-1-957203-80-5 (sc)
ISBN: 978-1-957203-81-2 (hc)
ISBN: 978-1-957203-82-9 (e)

Because of the dynamic nature of the Internet, any web addresses or links contained in this book may have changed since publication and may no longer be valid. The views expressed in this work are solely those of the author and do not necessarily reflect the views of the publisher, and the publisher hereby disclaims any responsibility for them.

THE EWINGS
PUBLISHING

One Galleria Blvd., Suite 1900, Metairie, LA 70001
1-888-421-2397

To: BARBARA ADAMSON,
my sister, whose recollections
and support helped encourage this story.

To: KELLY ESPOSITO,
my other sister, whose generous guidance
and assistance helped manage this story.

To: Michael Chapman,
my son, whose computer knowledge and kind services
made my online and word-processing efforts much easier.

"I am forever grateful for our lives shared
and lasting friendships."
Daniel T. Chapman

Summer of '66 Europe Travel Map

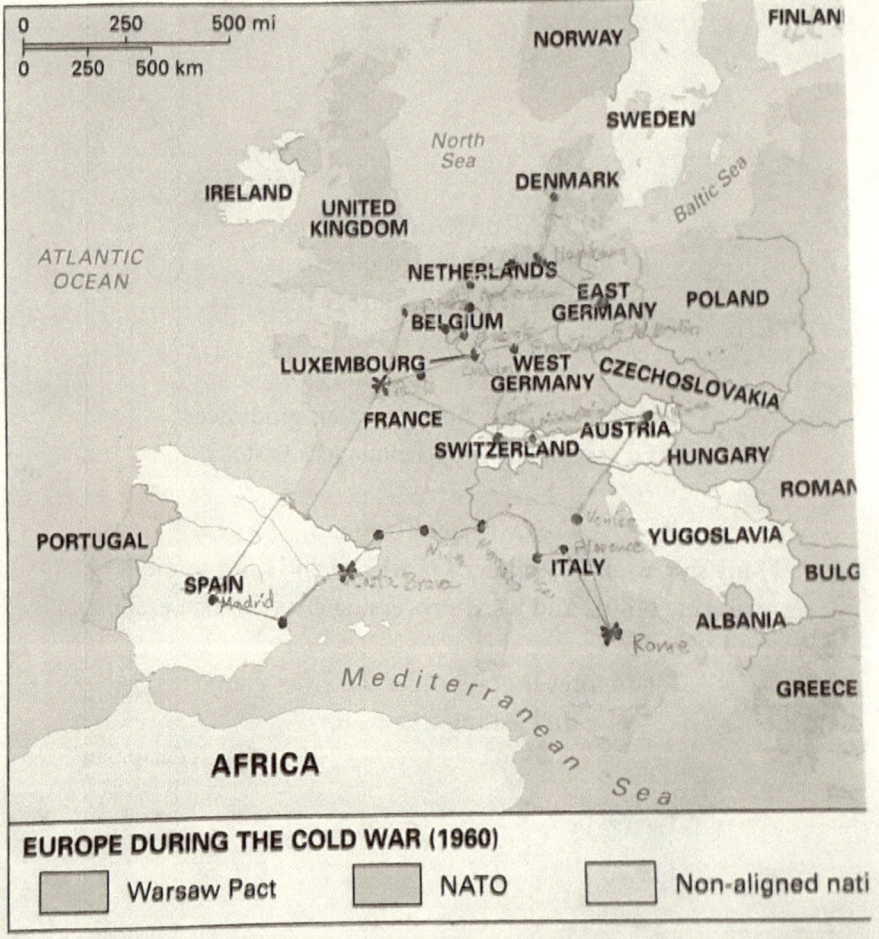

EUROPE DURING THE COLD WAR (1960)

Warsaw Pact   NATO   Non-aligned nati

50 Nights (*) With beds and longer stays in *Paris*, France, *Costa Brava*, Spain, *Rome*, Italy

24 Nights (.) On the road overnighters

Summer '66 Road Overnighter Records

Location	Inside (w/Bed)	Outside (w/Other)	Accommodations
Paris, France	3		Hotel Left Bank
Calais, France		1	Ground (Storage shed)
Roeselare, Belgium		1	Ground (Flower field)
Brussels, Belgium	2		Brussels Youth Hostel
Netherlands	1		Ground (Under bridge)
Amsterdam, Netherlands	2		SF Friend's Hotel
Netherlands		1	Ground (Under Carport)
Germany		1	Ground (Grove of trees)
Denmark		3	Ground (Groves of trees)
Hamburg, W. Germany	2		Hamburg Youth Hostel
West Berlin, E. Germany	1		West Berlin Youth Hostel
Frankfurt, W. Germany		1	Frankfurt Train Station
Frankfurt, W. Germany	1		Frankfurt Youth Hostel
Luxembourg		1	Ground (Forest creek side)
France (Outside Paris)		1	Walking (all night)
Paris, France	3		Hotel Left Bank
Madrid, Spain	2		Madrid Youth Hostel
Valencia, Spain		1	Ground (Haystack)
Barcelona, Spain		1	Beach (Lounge chair)
Costa Brava, Spain	9		Costa Brava Youth Hostel
Montpellier, France		1	Beach (Lounge chair)
Nice, France	1		Nice Apartment
Monaco, Monaco		1	Monaco (Yacht harbor)
Pisa, Italy		1	Ground (Flower meadow)
Florence, Italy	1		Florence Hotel
Rome, Italy	10		Youth Hostel

Location	Nights w/beds	Nights w/otherwise	Place
Venice, Italy		2	Ground (Grove of trees)
Vienna, Austria	2		Ingrid's Family Home
Liechtenstein		1	Ground (Forest grove)
Zurich, Switzerland		1	Swiss Round-trip train
Paris, France		2	Orly Airport
Paris, France		1	Central City Jail
Paris, France	8		Hotel Left Bank
Paris, France		4	Orly Airport
	48 **Nights w/beds**	**26** **Nights w/ otherwise**	

CONTENTS

PART THREE: TRAVELS WITH "CAESAR"

PART FOUR: GOING HOME

PREFACE

....

In virtually every society the world over, there are varying, yet all relevant and significant, measures and/or steps by which boys are measured as having grown into socially accepted placements among men. In some more tribal cultures, there can be very drastic rites-of-passage required of boys to successfully pass-through channels into manhood recognition. Some of these *rites* may include circumcision, beatings, torture, masculinity challenges, daredevil feats of courage, fierce hunting skills tests, long periods of isolation, impregnating females, achieving significant work and income levels, and countless other means to gain *passage.*

In most modern, democratic societies, on-the-other-hand, *manhood* is typically associated with elements such as minimal age, formal schooling ended, and workplace affiliations. Other recognized and often accepted standards touted may be marriage, fatherhood and child-rearing, military enlistment, advanced academic studies, adult incarceration, adult sports achievement, adult levels of finance or business acumen, and a myriad of other possibilities deserving proposed *manhood* credibility.

As a student, teacher, traveler, and author, I have always been interested in social and anthropological studies. From readings, studies, travels, and observations, I have become mesmerized, if not awed, while learning about cultures with such extreme measures some boys are forced or challenged to perform in order to prove their worthiness of *manhood* status. To many outsiders some of those complicated tasks may seem nearly impossible to perform successfully.

Personally, within our Western cultures I am grateful, for example, that circumcisions, when performed at all, usually occur right after birth or during infancy. To have had to wait until my teens, as in some primitive cultures, and then go through the procedure as some ritualistic act would have likely denigrated me to tears and *sissyhood*. Well, perhaps not, but I probably would likely have cringed, if not screamed, and not liked it one bit.

Even still, I enjoy reading commentaries from <u>National Geographic</u> magazine's socio-anthropological articles. Its studies about worldwide cultural differences and uniquely varying, value-system structures are always fascinating. Among its countless research topics have been riveting stories of various rites-of-passage cases. One particularly favorite report was about the Australian Aboriginal person's system of boys-to-men rituals, referred to as the *Walkabout*. In that culture, once a tribe's elders accept an older boy as mentally prepared and physically fit for their *ritual*, a subjected boy is sent out all alone into the remote Outback Wilderness. For five months he must survive by fending for himself and living off the land, thereby proving his manhood's worth.

As a youth, that system or method for displaying manhood prowess would have seemed gratefully acceptable to me. Having been raised in the lower mountain country of Northern California, it was pleasing to take multi-night treks into the woods earning self-anointed accolades for living-off nature. Of course, I usually had a rifle, fishing pole, pots, utensils, a sleeping bag, and a tent to aid my adventure. So sure, it was likely that using the *isolation* scheme as my own manhood challenge would have been easier than for one of those Aboriginal boys. No doubt, my case would have been much different had I disappeared into those high mountainous forests with only a pocket-knife to serve me. And for five months? No thanks, and I shall remain eternally gratified for our own Western Civilization practices.

However, many of those other accepted standards of manhood initiation are universally accepted. In interesting research studies of *rites-of-passage* by Arnold Van Gennep and Anthropologist Lambert, they explain much in studies about youth merging into manhood. In Lambert's *universal models of ideal societies*, there is the model of an *ideal free man*. In those models, a young man achieves *manhood* when he is considered to be strong, determined, and willing and able to do what is necessary to maintain his honor. He must also be believed to be level-headed and reasonable. He uses his strength and determination to exact compensation required to maintain his honor, and no more. Furthermore, he does not rush to avenge wrongs done to him, nor does he use his strength to dishonor opponents...

Lambert's thought-provoking research also suggests that worthy *manhood* candidates of these *ideal manhood models* are careful not to impose obligations on others. They accept responsibility for all their own actions, paying compensation when it is right, and they "...are not so hot-headed and self-indulgent as to engage in reckless acts which may compel family to bail (them) out." A proper *man* is strong, determined and "... exercises restraint because of his commitment to the ideal of a community of free men who respect one another's honor." Therefore, *universal laws of manhood* promote *distinct construction of masculinity, yet are ones specifically tinged by social responsibility.*

Regarding my own youthful vision and dream of proving self-reliance, independence, and worthiness of *manhood status*, I developed a somewhat vague mental attitude which combined Lambert's *universal model of an ideal man* with a sort of modernized, or civilized, social adaptation of an Aboriginal male's *walkabout*, or lost-in-the-wilderness challenge. As a young man wishing to prove his *manhood*, I wanted the opportunity to travel far away from home all by myself, survive on my own merits, and do so without contact or additional assistance from family.

Thus, analogous to Lambert's model of *ideal manhood* and the Aboriginal youth's *solo challenge* in the wilds, throughout my travels I planned to show my adaptability skills living within various unique cultures while moving freely and satisfyingly among them. Additionally, I would always behave with appropriate manners which championed ideal qualities of caring, sharing, and humility. In essence, I saw myself as a sort of *ambassador-at-large*, so-to-speak, who sought camaraderie and understanding with those international characters with whom I might come in contact. While doing so, I recognized a need to communicate positive images of America and American manhood.

Therefore, sharing now with my readers that summerlong mental exercise, and often dramatic physical experiment, thus became the focus of this book. It is, of course, *autobiographical* in nature. Throughout the story, I have attempted recalling and explaining pent-up emotions and sensitivities felt during so many interactive relationships and personal experiences encountered. This is the tale, therefore, of a young, boy-man's struggles, adventures, and survival while traveling through distant, unfamiliar cities and countryside all rushing by in vivid, countless details while filling his adventures with valuable life lessons and meanings of becoming a man and mature adult. Henceforward, it is this author's own personal saga and accounting of: **There and Then:** *A Summer to Remember.*

The Author

PART ONE

Getting There

CHAPTER 1

FANTASY FLIGHT

Taking Off

The amazing, TWA Boeing 727 Passenger Airliner, called the Tri-jet for its three engines, touched down smoothly onto the generous runway of Orly International Airport. Its direct flight from San Francisco, California had been a wild and bumpy, but otherwise uneventful, ride throughout the previous stormy night. The plane had taken a unique route saving airtime and flight distance by traveling up and over the Arctic Circle and then dropping back down southward to its destination just outside *Paris,* France. Even still, the long trip had lasted nearly twelve hours having departed in late afternoon the previous day. With time zone changes of nine additional hours reconfiguring any schedule, it was already a late morning arrival there in France. I was tired from the flight, exhausted actually from lack of any sleep, but the newness of everything offered plenty of adrenaline to keep me charged and eager to go.

For myself, though, that long flight had been sensually entertaining and exciting from start to finish. Wide-eyed and awestruck, once inside the sleek, long, narrow but roomy aircraft, I had easily, though excitedly, found my assigned window seat toward the rear of the plane. There were six comfortable cloth seats to each row with three on either side of the center aisle, and I felt lucky and privileged to be designated next to a window with spectacular viewing of the outside. Quickly, I introduced myself and met the passengers assigned to seats next to me. With glee and youthful enthusiasm, I had no problems with new greetings.

Flighty Friends

"Hi, my name is Daniel," I proudly boasted, "and this is my first ride in an airplane. I'm going to *Paris*, France first and then traveling all over Europe."

"Well, congratulations, young man," the somewhat startled flight companion seated beside me replied. "My husband and I are going to *Paris* for a holiday," the woman continued while her eyes glanced around finally settling back on my earnest gaze. "Where's your family?" she quizzed curiously.

"Oh, no," I quickly responded grinning broadly, "I'm traveling solo. I'm on my own this whole summer. I have eight and a half weeks to hitchhike around and see what I can, before going back home for college, that is."

"My goodness, I do declare that's a long time! And hitchhike all alone?" The surprised woman responded. "What will you do if you have any problems over there?"

I just laughed and declared, "Ah, no, I heard everybody does it. Besides, if I get in trouble, well then, I'll just have to become a Frenchman. I've heard that they've already got plenty of problems. One more won't hurt 'em much!"

Laughing heartily along with my slightly awkward but amiable passenger friends, I quickly and soberly reflected aloud a timely amusement, "We can laugh now, but my jokes may not be considered too funny in *Paris*, do you think?"

But my genial new friends seemed pleased with my sense of humor, and wishing me well, I felt assured that they would help make the entire flight more agreeable and pleasant. In fact, throughout that afternoon and long night's ride, both of the husband/wife couple had even thoughtfully offered me snack items from their own flight meals. No doubt they were wishing to help reduce a teenager's considerable appetite. I gratefully accepted their gestures appreciating both my new acquaintances. I also considered how far a few extra snacks, like cookies and pretzels, could go in developing heartfelt bonds between new contacts.

"Cookies sure go a long way in making friends," I remember thanking my associates. Then, suddenly I laughed aloud recognizing my own double-entendre: *Cookies making friends and also traveling faraway.*

"That's *two* long ways," I teased while holding up my counting fingers. "One, in making friends, and two, going clear to *Paris!*" Then I chuckled aloud as my passenger friends joined in with laughter, "And the joke should still count even when the cookies are in my stomach!"

Truthfully, the entire incredible flight to *Paris*, France had been spectacular from start to finish for my memorable *first* flight. Initially, there had been the thrilling takeoff, itself. The modern, streamlined 727's own smooth taxiing approaching the take-off runway had been precise and well-rehearsed while following the paths of previous flights. Then its jet's engines had begun roaring to life, apparently evaluating their endurance, it had felt. Next, just as the sturdy thunderous aircraft had barely hinted at instantly shaking and bursting apart at its seams, brakes were released, and the otherwise horizontal rocket began leaping and hurtling forward faster and faster down the seemingly endless runway.

With me shoved firmly back into the recesses of my chair by sheer force of the airplane's take-off, and even though I was tightly seat-belted and sitting upright, I twisted my outstretched body toward the window's view. Grasping my small, ten"X12" window frame by my palms, and with squinting eyes hard pressed against the thick plexiglass, I gawked wildly as distant terminal buildings were swiftly left behind and frantic tarmac rushed past underneath in seeming desperation. Ultimately, with the ocean easily sighted dead ahead, closing rapidly, and with airport runway about to disappear, suddenly the jet's wing flaps raised up, bent to their extreme, and the brightly painted, aluminum bird tipped its nose skyward. Without hesitation thereafter, the thrill-giving aircraft gently yet forcefully lifted its enormous body upwards and charged headlong toward the giant and puffy, cumulous cloudy heavens.

Then came the amazing climb into the clear blue sky as the plane circled and soared higher and higher northward with endlessly stunning views below. Multi-colored, beautifully textured countryside, with its marvelous geometric layouts of land shapes and borders, were seen far down and as distant as sight allowed. From my advantageous window seat, I could make out multiple cities, towns, and a variety of rural farmhouse communities. Those were often surrounded by vast arrangements of crisscrossing roads and highways, immense valleys, and gigantic mountains with their generous forests. As the plane continued to ascend, I also recognized nature's and man-made scatterings of many magnificently shaped lakes often feeding, or fed by, multiple wandering and snaking rivers.

Finally, giving up the brilliant scenery below, the Boeing aircraft eventually and swiftly climbed up and through a thick, heavy crowding of ominous looking, cumulous clouding. Still climbing further into and above a thick and dense stratospheric level of cloud cover, the surrounding sky steadily evolved into dark, thick, and ominous wrappings of storming nimbus billows. Fighting through fierce rain and angry winds as they pounded against the hardy airplane's fuselage, a temporary nervousness was no doubt spread about amongst the passengers. Even though awestruck at the dark, dangerous looking view, and becoming momentarily uneasy myself, I quickly recovered.

"This is just great!" I mused quietly but joking aloud to myself. "My first, big adventure finally gets started, and WHAM! Just like that it suddenly ends up crash landing and lost forever by some mountain storm. Well, isn't that just swell!"

My seat mates probably did not appreciate my grisly, teenager humor. Instead, they both simply smiled curtly while sitting tensely still and likely focusing on their own thoughts. The wife then just sheepishly offered reassurances, "Don't worry, Daniel. This is not bad at all. It will be fine."

But then I couldn't resist the opportunity and, instead, shook my faking but morbidly imagining mind, and grinning again, I cupped my hands to my mouth and whispered loudly, "But, I suppose it could be worse. We could be over the ocean, ha! And I'll tell you, I'd rather crash in the hills any day, and be forced to live off the woods, than land in that big, ugly, cold Pacific Ocean and have to tread water until I finally drowned."

Stormy Weather

Why I behaved so ominously only a teenager, or a psychologist, knows for sure; however, my background explained some things. I knew virtually nothing about the ocean. Yet, please understand, I was a country boy who was extremely comfortable with hiking, hunting, and camping in the woods. Perhaps, that was another special reason I was excited about my summer getaway. As a really young boy, I had always loved living in my family's very rural country home in Northern California. Once I began attending high school far down in the valley below in our county seat, a large city of 8,000 plus residents, however, I became enthralled with big city lights and urban sophistication's suggestive societal advancements.

Even back then I remember being emotionally awestruck by a high school English class study of the Greek poet Ovid whose famously paraphrased line read, "The grass is always greener on the other side of the fence." Conceivably, that often-analyzed quote has influenced much of my own life's expressive contemplations and visual desires. Maybe that's why I developed my explorational drive, or curiosity's courage for challenging status-quo, or my get-up-and-go to keep trying to jump fences, so-to-speak. I suppose I have always wanted to find out what's on the other side of the mountain. Or, in this case, *the other side of the ocean...*

But alas, though my mind often wandered aimlessly, still I simply had to acknowledge and accept a truth about myself: Ever since I was quite young, I became a *Culture Vulture.* From my appreciated, deep-mountain roots to those magnetically fascinating, bright-flowering city lights, I just felt drawn toward and destined, I believed, not to just see the world, but feel, taste, smell, and even hear all its magnificence too...

Return to Normal

Finally, though, my thoughts began settling down just as the plane's course seemed to calm. Eventually, the pilots had managed to steer the aircraft further upwards and mostly above the sky-high maelstrom. Afterwards, the Boeing 727 remained above and out of sight of Earth for nearly the entire balance of the flight. Below us continued to lay a frighteningly immense, endless, and everlasting blanket of billowing, cloud-cover blending dark, ominous, and deceptively looking grays into more gentle appearing soft white edges.

Ultimately, however, the plane was required, and thus forced, to drop back down roughly and return into another active storm. Pushing through that next tormenting storm's churning mass, our plane was once again lifted up, shoved down, jerked sideways, and whipped about to a frenzy. Most of the plane's passengers, and probably some of the flight attendants, had been agitated into equally frantic alarms. After a seemingly eternal few minutes, though, the pilots managed to slip, slide, and lower our aircraft beneath that angry, overhead frenzy and prepare it for an eventual full descent.

Considering all, to be sure, the flight had provided an overwhelming barrage of visual and sensory data for my inexperienced but eager, information-consuming mind. Next, and only slightly later, came the airplane's ear-popping drop and descent over the English Channel. Thereafter, while crossing over Northern France for the brief remaining distance to *Paris*, my tiny window views once again came vividly alive. They were refilled with so many wonderful, similarly amazing, graphically detailed, and vibrant pictorial images as had awed me during our initial ascent over Northern California.

My mind raced to comprehend, embrace, and relate to our entire flight's experience and meaning: *To be uplifted, raised, and removed from Earth and its familiar, homeland-comfort zone had been, in itself, curious and splendidly breathtaking. Then to be jettisoned, far separated, and transported over a defined range of distance, yet through unusual portals of time, was at best confusing and uncertain. And finally, to be lowered back, returned but transferred, and then reconnected to a completely different and uniquely faraway part of the world was, in itself, both minds boggling and inspiring...*

The whole flight experience had been an exciting, joyful, fascinating, and intriguing puzzle which unexpectedly and effectively had initiated my *traveler's* imagination. I began to really sense and appreciate how I had indeed been physically transported to a distant and forward time zone into an unfamiliar world. I was now approaching a new land, and indeed an entire continent, of uncertainty with their own unique cultural differences to experience. I started imagining my future encounters correlating with some of those outlandish adventures described in another favorite book of mine, Mark Twain's: <u>A Connecticut Yankee in King Arthur's Court</u>. Well, perhaps so, if I actually made it to England and had been clubbed upside the head or fallen out of a tree rather than out of the sky. But for there and then, I actually did begin recognizing certain necessary, personal, and psychological transformations that I was undergoing.

For one thing, by then I began appreciating that I was truly on my own; my adventure had absolutely begun. Furthermore, I also started understanding conscious changes necessary with relocating into a new, temporary life and independent style for myself. On that special day with that *transformative landing*, I was surely celebrating my independence. It was to be an *independence* from all else. I was virtually alone for the first time in my life and completely *dependent* upon myself and no one else. I clearly recognized an issue: *From that flight on, I would need to keep-my (proverbial)-wits-about-me.*

In fairness though, regarding the actual overseas flight itself, I had really enjoyed the sometimes-shuddering ride, and especially the jolting and bouncy part through those rip-roaring and rip-snorting, northern storms. In fact, during some especially heavy jostling of the plane, I had once needed to use the bathroom. When finished, I actually remained standing in the rear of that Boeing 727 near the attendant's quarters during the most active part of the plane's violent jarring reactions to the storm. While thrillingly laughing-off those often, fierce-shaking motions, but still holding firmly onto a passenger seat's backing for stability, some stewardesses had even become somewhat unnerved themselves. They even fretfully asked if I didn't wish to sit down and buckle-up. But I just shook my head and laughed them off joking in my mediocre French about our pilots' well-being, and that the bouncing around was the best part of flying.

One sweet, concerned, and obviously French stewardess even politely asked me twice, first in English then French "Sir, don't you want your own seat? Monsieur, ne voulez-vous pas vous asseoir?"

Fortunately, three years of decent high school French classes came in handy. Smiling broadly, I laughed and blurted back with delight, "Non merci. Si les pilotes vont bien, moi aussi. C'est la partie la plus amusante du vol!" *No, thank you. If the pilots are okay, so am I. This is the funnest part of the whole flight!*

Eventually, the storm died down, or the plane flew beneath it and calmed itself, and I did reluctantly take my own seat again for the flight's remaining course. It was an exciting start for my summer adventure, though, and uniquely special because the flight was my *first* time ever on an airplane. Maybe I behaved comically dismissive of potential danger during our flight because I had nothing prior for which to compare it, so it was simply typical for me, and *far safer than driving an automobile*, proud advertisements bragged. Thus, my excursion's beginning was stimulating, to-be-sure, for a young, audacious traveler. Yet, at that particular time, I hardly understood or was aware that my *first*, exciting flight experience was only to be the start of many *firsts* to come.

Even still, as I excitedly exited the airplane that late morning, I respectfully recalled my place, time, and circumstances. From then on,

I promised myself that I would remember how important it was to make good impressions. After all, I believed that in an informal way, of course, I was sort of like an ambassador for America. How I might be seen overseas, or anywhere for that matter, was how Americans anywhere might be perceived. I would never allow myself to be identified as just another *Ugly American(s)* like those depicted in Burdick and Lederer's novel that I had read in my US History class.

Sure, that story had depicted embarrassing descriptions from Southeast Asia during the pre-Vietnam War era's early beginnings and pertained to America's image failures there at that time. But it was still relevant everywhere. Ideally, and hopefully, I was sure that good manners would always go a longer way assisting me. *Good manners* and maybe even cookies! At least that seemed an important and viable part of my own journey's plan.

Therefore, as I left the plane to cross the tarmac and enter the terminal building, I found myself smiling charmingly while politely bowing slightly as I passed by each pretty stewardess. Struggling a bit to avoid any sudden and embarrassing giggling outbursts, I casually saluted the girls while proffering my best French accented, "Merci beaucoup et au revoir."

I couldn't help but notice, too, that the ladies' smiles and slightly rosy-blushed cheeks suggested surprise and delight at having been affably charmed. I knew that kindness and good manners did make me feel surprisingly good and were almost always received congenially. Therein, it became like a trademark for me. Smiles, "Please," and "Thank you" were to become permanent parts of my behavior and speech. Besides, what a waste, I thought, to be rude and then unwelcomed, and especially in a foreign country where I may likely depend on kindly and welcoming receptions. So, with a big, easy smile and alert, gawking eyes I headed into the terminal building.

Once inside the enormous French terminal, I recall giving myself a quick reality check by reflecting once more upon that *transformative* flight. I laughed nervously to myself at the prospect of that plane ride becoming only the beginning of a potentially long, *rocky ride* throughout my entire upcoming and unknown summer. But regardless, I was all smiles. I firmly assured myself that my lively airplane ride from America to Europe had actually just been the beginning of a rush of excitement to come. It was but the tip-of-the-(old) iceberg, so to say, and hopefully, not with a sunken, Titanic-like outcome...

Besides, I was simply an eager, thrilled, and very recent high school graduate on the lookout for both some unusually unique experiences and a little summer fun too. Come-hell-or-high-water, I was determined to make that summer's adventure become filled with exciting, decent, and memorable encounters. After all, I had worked hard and earned rights for that special excursion to happen.

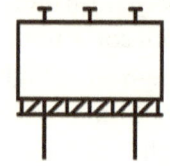

CHAPTER 2

....

THE PLAN

Friendly Contacts

Essentially, the trip had been a reward for my successes at school. It was to be a sort of congratulatory *rite-of-passage,* or a welcoming into adulthood. At least I was being handed a great deal of trust, I knew. I had been given the gift, or opportunity, to travel alone throughout Europe, and all on-my-own, for eight and one-half weeks (60 days) during that life changing summer of 1966. Where I went, what I did, and how I spent my limited funds would be up to me; however, my challenge always remained making my journey worthwhile. My decisions were to be my own, and I would have to exercise good judgement and frugality to successfully travel throughout Europe over the two, potentially long, summer months ahead.

Having considered the possibility of visiting friends or acquaintances during my travels, I had brought along with me two special addresses of people I knew would be in Europe at that same time as me. Finding and visiting with any of them might be difficult, but if accomplished, they would probably be my only useful contacts with any known acquaintances. One of those connections I hoped to make could be with three adult, fellows that I had met a couple of months previously. They were to be vacationing that summer in *Amsterdam*, Netherlands, way up north from *Paris*. My tentative and loosely planned itinerary had allowed for a potential visit with those guys early on during my trip. Basically, after visiting *Paris*, my loose-laid plans were to work my way up north to *Amsterdam* and try to find them.

Earlier that spring, I had been introduced to the trio by my trip-sponsoring Aunt Jean and her roommate, Phyllis, whom I also considered an aunt, but which neither preferred being called "Aunt." Together, though, they both had purposefully arranged a meeting a couple of months earlier for me with the men at the threesome's home in the San Francisco Castro District. During that visit, it had been suggested that while hitching rides around Europe, and in the unlikely circumstance that I should manage to get that far up north to *Amsterdam*, and within a generally specified period of time, the three companions, Ron, Dick, and Dwayne, could tentatively expect my arrival and provide temporary lodging. In my own mind, the guys had been suggested as good contacts to check-in with for greetings, travel tips, or possible updates from home. Additionally, they could deliver messages of my safety to family back home. It seemed nice and decent of them to offer their assistance.

My other contact was to be with a young lady from high school, Ingrid, who had been my high school's foreign-exchange student, and whom by then would have returned back to her own home in Vienna, Austria. We had become friends during our senior year together having shared several classes. Toward the end of our school term, I had vaguely mentioned to Ingrid that I planned to travel around Europe that summer. Later, during emotional, graduation party good-byes, I had even made awkward, uncertain promises to sure look her up when traveling there.

"Oh, yes, please do visit!" was Ingrid's natural, feigned-excitement response; however, I imagined that her true, private inner reaction had followed with a disbelieving, "Yeah, sure!... I'll bet you will... NOT!"

"Oh, ye of such little faith!" I laughed to myself. No matter, I had no idea what to expect, but I did have every intention to find, surprise, and visit both contacts. I had said that I would, and even promised. It was my intension and challenge to keep my word.

Dudley Do-Right

After the summer break had ended, my European trek had finished, and following my triumphant return home in late-August, heading off for college was definitely planned. That, however, had not always been the case. Earlier that April of 1966, I had received goal-crushing, and incredibly disappointing news of denied acceptance into the US Air Force Military Academy due to poor eyesight. Up until that cruel, *denial* letter had actually arrived, all my life and plans for my future had been totally focused on fulfilling an US Army military career after graduating from West Point Military Academy.

During Spring of '66, my father, an ex-army veteran from pre-WWII, but avid airplane enthusiast, pulled me aside and convinced me that the future was in the air. He believed I should go to the Air Force Academy, instead. So, at the last-minute, and while heeding his advice, I changed my dreams and applied to the USAF Academy at Colorado Springs, CO instead. Unfortunately, I failed the eye exam and was turned down. "Pilots do not wear corrective lenses," I was indirectly informed.

I was not prepared for that sudden *denial*, and it took a period of time to mentally adjust to that life-changing letter. That was actually when the summertime alternative, a European getaway, really became an ideal option. Why, I would simply run away, instead! If the USAF Academy didn't want me, then I would just forget them all and run off to Europe and *play* in its place.

Regardless, I still had another alternative: A back-up, scholarship awaited me to attend Sacramento State College. No doubt, both those factors, the *denial,* and the *scholarship*, had influenced my parents' acceptance and agreement for my summer escapade. Yet, my European trip was also sympathetic compensation for having had my summer freed up. Suddenly, an unpredictable entire summer's three months had become available.

Furthermore, my future, long-term goals and plans were also effective pressures on my parents' judgement. Wanting to become a teacher one day, I also considered that world travel would be a purposeful experience to share with future, potential students. Whatever I did and however I presented myself would be worth sharing. But regarding the next sixty days, I also impressed my parents that I wanted the opportunity to explore myself too. I felt that the chance to be alone, thereby discovering any strengths and weaknesses of my own mind, heart, and character, would be an exciting challenge to face.

Concurrently, I looked forward to seeing and learning about the fascinating vastness of an entire foreign continent's unique lands, people, languages, cultures, and governments. Sure, I could have taken a good old-fashioned, road-trip adventure throughout the USA, but my fascination for European history and culture, from my own basic roots and heritage, by-the-way, was far more appealing. To me, Europe simply had so much more potential historical learning and adventure to offer, and its variety of uniquely exclusive *cultures* would wet any *vulture's* appetite!

Anyway, it was to be my privilege, challenge, and responsibility, I understood, not to just travel but also to see and do as much as was remotely possible during my summer's timeframe, and within my limited budget. As a graduation gift, my Aunt Jean had sponsored my journey by paying the incredible fee of $560 for my TWA, round-trip airplane tickets. That was a lot of money in 1966. Additionally, my parents had skimped, saved, and struggled to provide $250 dollars cash for me to exchange for local currencies in order to cover my summer's necessary living and travel expenses. I knew how that sum had been a real hardship for them to dole out for my private, summer trek, and I was never to take their pressured contribution lightly.

Furthermore, it had not been an easy decision in the first place for my folks to agree. Allowing me to leave on a trip of that magnitude ultimately alone, besides helping finance my escapade, required serious consideration. After all, even if my two friends were supposedly to go along, being away for two months while wandering around in foreign lands together was still a risky lot to ask. In fact, during that earlier, parental *permission/discussion* stage which had started late that April, essentially right after the "so sorry" USAF letter had arrived, I realized that it would require time and energy to convince my parents of my trip's value. I also understood that a great deal of persuasion would be necessary from both me and Aunt Jean to reassure my folks and finalize my plans...

CHAPTER 3

··

THE PLEA

Dinner Conversations

During April, and after my potential, summertime-military obligation was canceled, leaving three months open for new possibilities, was when I had first spoken about my new situation with Jean. I had called her about prospects of once more living with her over the summer and working again for her and Phyllis, something I had done nearly all preceding summers since I was young enough to be away from home.

Therefore, giving initial credit to Jean was when the two of us first discussed the possibility of me traveling to Europe for the summer instead. Around that same time was also when my aunt arranged a meeting for me with her friends in San Francisco whom she had already learned would be in Europe for that coming summer. Thus, utilizing those basic beginning terms, the two of us began concocting a general parental plea for my journey. We had both agreed that it would be no simple task to convince my parents of my trip's value. Cost? Yes, that would be relatively easy to prove and potentially depress them, especially my dad. But the intrinsic worth of such a journey would be even more difficult. Definitely, we decided that we would need to join forces in order to persuade my mother, and then father, into allowing such an overseas venture to occur.

Even though I was already eighteen years of age, demanding anything from my parents was not wise. Nor did I believe that sort of tactic would work anyway. I needed both their moral support and their financial assistance. Either of them could say no to my plan, or they could simply refuse to help pay for it. That would nullify the experience right off, and, therefore, I knew that I was going to have to be clever and suave with any *persuasive* techniques. After all, just to get started I also needed them to take me to the distant airport in San Francisco. That was also where and when they would hug me, say goodbyes, and wave as I vanished for two months into oblivion. Thus, I needed them both *wishing me well, giving me money,* and then *providing me a getaway ride.* A lot to ask, to be sure.

I would need to find just the right time and place to properly *plant* my "conceptual seed." Therefore, during that fateful springtime, I began applying my own specialized, creative, yet perfunctory, and often confounding, persuasive techniques upon my parents. Those *techniques,* however, had often transpired with conflicted results.

Columbus Analogy

For example, there was that one time. . . It was during a mid-spring evening when I finally had an opportunity to address both my parents simultaneously and hopefully receive vocal encouragement from my younger siblings at the same time. Finally, a weekend had arrived, and our dad was home from his distant construction job for a couple of days. With my parents and sibs all gathered at the kitchen table for an infrequently special, Saturday-dinner meal, I remember snatching a highly unusual, but ideal, moment of silence from our dinner conversations.

Gaining immediate attention, I boldly declared, "Mom and Dad, don't you know that *every* great adventure *has* to start *somewhere.* . . And it only needs a dream, an idea, if you know what I mean. Not even much of a plan either. Just desire, to get it going!"

My parents, who were momentarily startled by my curious and disconnected comments, stopped eating long enough to lower their dining utensils in unison, look over at me together, and provide desired, full attention. Both stared quizzically while waiting for a typical punchline or joke to follow which would close my supposed sudden outburst of attempted humor. However, that initial comment about ". . . great adventures starting somewhere . . ." was precisely what I had spiritly pronounced that evening. Unfortunately, I instantly became excited and immediately lost my verbal direction, vocal balance, and found myself pleading:

"Folks," I cried out, "I really honestly want to go to Europe this summer after school ends!"

I then began fiercely defending my previous vaguely proposed, upcoming-summer journey by launching enthusiastically into an eager cross-examination challenging my own arguments.

"I know you must be worried about plans I have for my trip," I began, "but just ask yourselves, 'How do people get anywhere when they don't even know where they're going?'"

I quickly noted the confused faces of my suddenly bewildered, and by then oppositional, parents. "Here he goes again!" my parents surmised while both shaking their heads adamantly in union.

"Pass me the potatoes," my father said as he side-stepped my upcoming proposed scheme and deliberately ignored my squirrely questioning and absurd wishes.

Yet, with even more determination encouraging my anxiously eager voice, I continued with my case. "I'll tell you *how they do it*," I burst forth with unqualified but gleefully weak evidence, "They just get out there and go!"

"They what?" came their mutually muddled reactions at this point.

I foresaw my apparently desperate, wannabe adventure plans to be quickly fading, if not utterly dissolving or crumbling. At least it seemed so at that moment due to sheer lack of enthusiasm on the faces of my unfocused audience of two. My siblings, however, were quietly sitting by, curiously watching, and listening attentively while trying to assess the potentially arising, dinner-table conflict. Quickly, I mentally changed gears by displaying my typically winning smile of grinning ear-to-ear with natural exuberance. Then becoming anxiously wound-up with my own self-generated excitement, once more I attempted strengthening my weakened defensive case.

Pleading directly to my somewhat confused, yet stoic parents, I blabbered-out my next bold exclamation: "Don't you agree that the greatest adventurer of all time was Christopher Columbus?"

My folks, both well-read history enthusiasts, were nonetheless noticeably caught off-guard by my sudden proclamation. But sensing their sudden and notable attention, I determined that I was on a precipitously positive roll, so I immediately resumed my vigorous oratory.

Continuing, I asserted, "You see, Folks, Columbus had a dream... and he had a plan too! And he really tried to see them both through."

Was *my plan* working? I quickly studied the faces of my then curiously amused parents. At least it seemed they were both attentive to my fuzzy dinnertime lecture. That appeared to be a good time for me to make my point. Greedily controlling my symbolic moment, I lowered my voice while gradually increasing its volume as I completed my testimony.

"Oh, sure," I began again, "in the end Columbus died broken-hearted and impoverished because he never realized his actual plan of finding a shortcut to India. But, in the beginning, though, he really *did* follow his *dream!*"

Studying both parents' confused faces closely, I sought out any cheerful outlook or behavior shifts. Were either one of their opinions being swayed? Were either my loving, smiling, but seemingly worried mother or my caring, frowning, but unenthusiastic father moved? Yes! My dad was *moved*. He was done eating and wanted to *move* from the kitchen table and go relax in his living room armchair to smoke and watch "Gunsmoke," his favorite show, or something.

Uh, oh! I knew that I was going to have to try harder and think of something quick. My parents really needed some compelling convincing. So, staring imploringly and directly into their eyes, I excitedly continued with my loosely prepared Columbus analogy.

"Folks, do you also realize," I earnestly quipped, "that in the beginning, eventually Christopher got straight-up *permission and allowance* from the King and Queen of Spain to practically commit *royally sanctioned suicide* just for their own greedy profiteering?"

My parents, suddenly aghast with mild shock, nearly bolted upright in their dining chairs and stared queasily and uneasily at me. Practically in unison they both queried, "Where in God's name are you going with this ridiculous and confusing babble?"

Of course, at that very same instant came my own spontaneous and embarrassed reflection. "Oh, crap!" I cursed myself. "That was really stupid! Why the heck did (you) go and say, 'died broken-hearted,' and 'suicide' and 'greedy profiteering?'" Bad moves.

For the following brief and uneasy moments, I squirmed and flinched like roly polies lying on their backs. I had immediately recognized my foolish, literal-blunder comments. I also recognized that I must quickly try to restrain my parents' shock by refocusing my plea with some kind of a quick diversion.

Therefore, suddenly from my kitchen chair, I began flailing my right arm in broad, sweeping strokes. With an extended hand still clutching my dinner fork, I started waving my arm all around in wide, distracting circles attempting to regain my folks' attention again. Also, I was dubiously struggling to demonstrate the vastness of my upcoming conceptualization. I knew too that my visual theatrics had to be quickly explained, so I promptly staged my next supportive argument.

"Chris's idea was huge, Folks!" I cried out with emphasis while desperately waving my pointing arm upwards.

Regrettably, however, once more I thoughtlessly backstepped by persisting with that same foolish and mis-calculated, *death-and-dying* historical theme. Charging headlong into yet another nightmarish, potential-persuasion disaster, once again I crowed quizzically with a new misaimed approach.

Recklessly continuing, "Did you know that on his first voyage attempting to sail over a deadly and unknown sea, almost everyone else in Europe also believed Chris was going to kill himself and his crews? They didn't believe his round world theory of reaching Asia by sailing west. In fact, both Italy and Portugal had already turned him down flat!

"Ha! Ha! Get it? *Flat*, just like their *world view*!" At first, I was noticeably amused with my homonymic humor, but my parents' frowns suggested annoyance instead. "Oh, crud! Dang my stupid mouth, anyway!" I groaned internally.

Immediately, I recognized a need to change my defense tactics and get off that morbidly fruitless talk. I had used another stupid, "end-of-life" remark again, and I knew I had to cease with that corny, death-obsessed humor at once.

"'Bad defense, Dummy,' my parents internally shouted," I remember mumbling to myself.

While silently cursing myself, my eyes squinting tightly as I gritted my teeth, I can remember ridiculing my worthless debating skills. Nonetheless, though embarrassed, I still understood that I had to regroup and reenergize myself once again. Returning to my eternally optimistic ploy of grinning ear-to-ear, I leaned slightly toward my now mulish parents and continued with my obvious Columbus fetish.

Searching beseechingly into both their faces, I carefully started again, "Mom, Dad, the point is that Christopher Columbus did have a dream, a wild unproven theory, a crazy plan. Why, in fact, he had an even *weaker* plan than me! And look at what he accomplished. *Here we are!*"

Finally surging with pride at my initial accomplished detail, and while still grinning, I suddenly pointed upwards again with my extended fork still in hand raising my right arm toward an imaginary sky, our kitchen ceiling, naturally. Once more, I began play-acting again. That time as a demonstrably defensive character emphatically attempting to dramatize an imagined Chris Columbus with his victoriously persuasive speech to the King and Queen of Spain.

As eloquently as I could muster up, I bridled forth, "'Your Highnesses,' Chris said to his Spanish majesties, 'The world is NOT a flat surface! It has bumps, and dips, and curves, and is round like my head!'"

I chuckled again admiring my silly analogy and assessing momentarily that a bit of humor right then might just help ease any tension. Then I persisted with my version of Columbus's illusory appeal using my best, corny Italian accent.

"You see," I began clarifying, "Christopher explained to King Ferdinand and Queen Isabella, 'Ju see, ifa I jus filla-upa foura cheapo boatsa wit' enougha fooda to lasta little while, anda I keepa sailin' righta into da sunset, why, I'ma sure gonna bumpa into somethin' before longa. An' thena Ima gonna returna homa wit jour fortunes anda my owna fame an'a glory!'"

My pathetic, Italian-laced drawl nearly caused my humor riddled dialogue to collapse from my own nearly hysterical self-amusement. But with tireless comedic strategy, I quickly added, "And do you know what? Those Spanish Majesties said, 'Si, Si, Senor! For cryin'-out-loudo, go! Ando hurryo backo witho ouro goldo and spiceso!'"

I remember being so amused back then at my own cleverly referenced Italian "a's" and Spanish "o's" at word endings to emphasize language differences. Back then I really loved theatrical comedy and always got A's in English, history, and drama classes partly because I was an active and popular member of the high school's Drama Club. Whenever possible, I loved mixing dramatic arts with other classes' assignments for inimitable emphasis. Teachers always enjoy being entertained by students.

Also, many kitchen table mealtimes had been previously filled with my loud, obtrusive theatrics. That particular dinnertime was no exception either. Having sat listening throughout my overly melodramatic, though bewildering, rhetoric, I was at least assured that my younger sisters and brother were entertained and amused. Still, I concerned myself primarily with my parents' reactions and worried over their possibly unamused anxieties.

Yet, so typical of my thought processing, however, my mind wandered momentarily as I reflected on Columbus's own possibly anxious thoughts while quietly muttering to himself, "Yeah, and if I'm wrong and the world is not round, then I'll probably get eaten by sea monsters, drown in some terrible storm, or fall off the edge of the world! But at least I tried. Ugh!"

But quickly shaking my derailing head, I regained composure by wisely warning myself, "Don't go there! You'll screw-up everything!"

Thus fortunately, though temporarily, my mindless wandering ceased and I managed refocusing my thoughts once again. Quickly back-on-trac, I then tried softening my approach.

"Oh, sure," I gently continued pleading applying my haphazard argument, "Mom, Dad, I suppose you're worried, and that's okay, but you have to admit that some wonderful adventures can happen with just a little support and encouragement."

I studied my parents' puzzled yet perhaps somewhat amused faces. Finally, a good sign, I believed. A little humor won't hurt. I took in a deep breath and began my closing argument.

"But the good ones," I said smiling, "the *adventures* of lifetimes, are ones that really count, Mom and Dad. They all begin with having open minds and simply basic plans. And I've got one, a really good one that's even better than Columbus's!"

At that point, I recall feeling slightly desperate. So, excitedly I exclaimed with sheer determination and righteous reasoning: "You see, I already *know where I want to go!* I *know* where Europe is; I've studied it on maps for so long now. And I can fly straight there, travel everywhere easily, and see everything over the summer to my heart's delight and wit's end."

At that point it appeared like I had perhaps sparked a glint of interest or curiosity from my parents. Well, at least my mother. I decided to pursue that line of defense with her.

Remembering my mom's church ties, her having pushed my older brother and me years earlier into becoming altar boys for our local Catholic church, I cleverly and quickly added, "And I'll be sure and visit all the Catholic Cathedrals and churches everywhere too, Mom, so God will watch out for me. . . And He'll probably make sure I see them all. Then I can fly straight back home before school begins and bring pictures of *Notre Dame* and souvenirs of all my travels! I'll have lots of pictures too of the *Sistine Chapel*, and we'll all become rich and famous!"

My mother actually smiled, yet she still looked hesitantly, first from Dad and then to my imploring eyes, and meekly parried, "Two months traveling around Europe? But I would worry so much for you, Daniel. I'm just not sure."

However, Mom's reaction was just the positive sign I was looking for. She had obviously softened from her original stance weeks earlier: "Are you nuts?" she had exclaimed. "Don't be silly. Ha! I know this is my sister Jean's idea. You two have probably been plotting this scheme for some time. Get this ridiculous, idea out-of-your-head right now!"

On-the-other-hand, though, and on a parallel but independent vein, my father was more serious and pragmatic in his posture. He just scornfully laughed at the idea while blurting out to his wife, "Of course it's his hair-brained aunt's idea! Your sister and he don't even have enough common sense between them to come-in-out-of-the-rain!"

Then, dramatically pointing his finger at me to center his accusations, he sneeringly added, "Are you dense, Boy? Have you lost your mind? You want to fly clear over to Europe, and wander all around those idiotic, foreign lands for the whole summer and all by yourself? Why, you'll probably get lost at the airport and starve to death! Forget about it!"

Not reacting to my dad's insulting remarks was wise. It was obvious to me that he was going to be a bit harder nut-to-crack, so-to-speak. "But what-the-heck?" I chuckled to myself, "Nuts run in the family, and they're all cracked-up already!"

With self-discipline at least momentarily improving, I continued keeping my mouth shut while allowing my parents to simmer down and then hopefully regret the harsh way they were treating their nearly grown and graduating, honor-student son. However, internally I mumbled, "How dare they talk to me that way?" while continuing to smile feebly, yet agonizingly.

Then continuing with my self-indulging humor and laughing again inside my head, I reflected, "I'm winning Mom over. I can feel it. Besides, Mom rules-the-roost, and she'll say, 'Yes!' I just know it."

Yep, I knew that *when* I won my mother over to the idea, my father would assuredly, even if begrudgingly, fall-in-line. After all, like the hilariously true, household-humor line went, "When it comes to home and family matters, Dads are absolutely *Captains* of those ships. And if you don't believe it, just ask Moms, the *Admirals!*"

My pops might bellow out, "No way in Hell! Forget about it!" But then he'd pause, look sheepishly toward his wife (and my mom) and query indecisively, "Honey, what do you think?"

In other words, I mentally philosophized, "Win Moms over, and Dads were sure to follow!" Mothers all over were truly the shepherds of the world, and fathers and kids were the sheep. Baaaa! Just follow along and do what moms say. That really seems the way-of-the-world, I thought to myself smiling.

"My mother, and then father soon, thereafter, would agree," I reflected positively; however, I could not do all the convincing alone. So, who else could I depend on for support and aid in helping to promote my little dream of a summer's Adventurous Crusade?

Sibling Support

There was no doubt that my one-year older brother, David, although far away, would be an ally and a supporter. He was only nineteen and had already been in the US Navy for two years, including a tour already to Vietnam on the <u>USS Midway</u> and scheduled for yet another on the <u>USS Kitty Hawk</u>. He would back me up for sure. That aspect even griped me a little too.

"Oh, sure," I recall complaining to myself regularly, "we send our young men off to fight in dangerous, illegal wars far overseas, but let just one younger fella want to take a fun, little summer vacation, and 'No, that's unacceptable!'"

"Alright, but be careful with that argument," I admonished myself.

My older brother's absence was due to military service, and it could be useful, but I would need to tread softly. David's travels were during wartime and he was in the navy. My mother might just burst out sobbing woefully over losing yet another son for a voyage far away. Furthermore, being summertime with my other siblings at home, that factor could be much more noticeable to her . . . and everyone, for that matter. "Back-off," I wisely instructed myself.

And sure, my one-year younger sister Barbara, almost always sitting right beside me at the dinner table, might be helpful with my defense. In fact, she could really come-in-handy encouraging my trip by suggesting gratefulness for my absence. Actually, she'd likely support my leaving because she would then automatically inherit natural rein and control of our family's child kingdom. Finally, she could personally and singly take command of the younger ones by displaying her own limitless talents and prowess for ruling over our kiddie realm.

"Okay," Barbara would tease and taunt, "I'll watch over you (children) at the swimming hole like Mom wants, but you have to do everything I say. Get it?" That's what she'd say, for sure. I *got* it, but her helpfulness could be useful. Sis Barbara was a natural babysitter, and she loved her younger siblings, especially our littlest sister.

Speaking of the youngest ones, I smiled to myself while mentally and lovingly embracing my early teen, kid-brother Kerry and my eight-year-old sister, Sissy Kelly. They would both probably fake misty tears over my potential absence snickering, "If you're gone this summer, who's going to drive us to the swimming hole and chase us around the yard?"

To be honest, though, by that time I understood, kid-brother Kerry probably hardly missed his elder brothers much. Truth be told, eldest Brother David had been long gone by then, and I was, myself, already absent so much of the time. For me, it was because of my living-away during my senior year on weekdays due to study demands at our distant high school and for all my afterschool-related activities. Besides, Kerry was growing up with his own friends now and didn't need us much anymore. And just like his older brothers before him, he could walk, run, hike, or hitchhike almost anywhere in those country hills, all by himself.

He didn't really need any of my help except for infrequent rides somewhere or on brother-bonding treks down to the big city of Marysville, California to visit its bright lights and maybe take-in a movie sometimes. But Kerry was mostly happy for my potential summer trip and surely envious as he likely patiently waited for his own turn for some adventurous campaigns. However, his brotherly loyalty and support would still be useful, I figured.

The wee one, Sissy Kelly, might be a concern, however. I loved to tease the heck out of her whenever I was home. She might whimper way too much at the prospect of my summer-long absence if she were brought into the conversation. After all, eight weeks to an eight-year-old was practically a lifetime. I knew I'd have to bribe her with all kinds of homecoming-gift promises to keep her quiet and supportive.

"Kelly-Nelly," as I affectionately cooed teasingly, "I'll bring you dollies from every country I visit. Okay? Now don't cry, and just beg Mom and Dad to let me go. Deal?" I trusted that I could get that *agreement* sealed. She was lovingly spoiled but a little sweetheart.

Parental Backgrounds

Then came some real hope for confirming my summer adventure. Besides my father, and myself, of course, the closest other persuasive person in the whole world for my mother was Jean McCord, her eldest sister, and my potential trip's sponsor. Over the years, I had heard bits and pieces of dramatic stories from both Mom and Jean of their own young lives together. They both had shared some wild times and pretty daring situations while traveling and hitchhiking around the country before and during WWII. In fact, a potential footnote detail is the fact that during my mother's final years with us all, out of respect, I even authored a novel, War Torn, honoring her own young life and wild escapades. She had a special adventurous spirit all her own, for sure.

When young, both she and her sister Jean had run-off together hitch-hiking and romping all over the countryside, even eventually doing so as welders of *Rosie-the-Riveters* fame. It was during WWII that just the two of them, with thumbs-out and all smiles, caught rides to each next, uncertain, and cross-country destination. And my mother, at that time, was even younger than me. Surely, Jean could remind my mother of her own, past adventuresome spirit and desire to travel. Actually, I even considered that my mother should be reminded of her still present *need* to seek adventure. That *need* was surely in her own blood and, therefore, in mine too... She should be made to remember and appreciate that.

Aunt Jean could also help reassure my mom and ease my father's trepidations. Jean would stress those life lessons that I would learn, and she could advise them regarding important values of independence and self-reliance such a voyage could teach a young man my age. And she would emphasize that I had earned the summer's trip with all my schooling achievements. After all, I had been a successful student throughout school with all sorts of accolades and awards coming to me at school's end, and I even had a full scholarship to college for the upcoming year at Sacramento State. For those factors alone, she might argue, I deserved my "trip" and their trust; I had earned both.

Also, my two best buddies, Jimmy, and Jack, who had initially agreed to join me, were planning to go along that summer for company and safety-in-numbers. We had all even teasingly referred to ourselves as the *Jimbo-Jack-Daniels-Escapade* in our youthful exuberance, giving humorous reference to ourselves and popular whiskies. When my mother had first heard about us three guys potentially traveling as a trio, she had been somewhat relieved, that factor being a reassuring selling point to her. Helping persuade my dad, though, Jean went to the heart of the issue with him. She had agreed to finance the entire airfare, all $560 of it, for me. That was a small fortune to my folks, and her generosity was nothing to quibble over.

Additionally, according to Jean's advisement to my parents with her being a world-class traveler, herself, European nations were decades ahead of America with social acceptances and inner-nation travel welcoming all youth. According to her, young students were traipsing all over Europe during summers. Jean would inform, comfort, and relieve my parents' anxieties by explaining about various transportation modes available such as the widely used Eurail Pass system, a vast network of inexpensive railway usage geared toward traveling students, plus buses and hitchhiking.

Jean would also mention about supportive Youth Hostels that were scattered effectively throughout European cities and towns as very inexpensive sites for overnight and brief stays. Just as I had already read and learned, she would likely explain that most hostels were uniquely student and youth-focused facilities. They had varying natures, structures, architectures, and designs like hotels, adapted schools, and mansions, and such as were explained in travelogues. They were almost always helpful guide stops for typical student travelers and were useful places for youth connecting with each other, hooking up, and sharing highlights and tips from each other's experiences.

Also, if push-came-to-shove, I figured that Jean could also remind my dad, her beloved and respected brother-in-law, that he himself had actually run away from an unhappy home at fifteen years of age. Barely over a year after that, she could also emphasize, Guy had even lied about his age to the Recruiter's Office and had joined the US Army at barely seventeen-years of age. True, it had been during a different and difficult period of the mid-1930's Great Depression Era and several years before WWII. Regardless, though, he too had been so young during his own youthful adventures. I hoped that my dad's past, with its own powerful imagery, would remind and urge him into acquiescent consent,... once my mother, the *Admiral*, agreed, that is.

CHAPTER 4

THE ARRIVAL

Made in America

After that difficult beginning of parental discussions determining the feasibility of my summer trek throughout Europe, the fact remained that ultimately they had not only agreed but had also financed my trek too. Finally, I had landed, and then I was actually there. In that early June of 1966, and after all the pleadings, debates, yelling, begging, promises, and assurances, my flight had at last dashed away from San Francisco with me onboard. Disembarking into *Paris*, France, therefore, made this passenger absolutely ecstatic about arriving.

Having already been filled with awe by the flight itself, I was nervously anticipating the immediate rush I would feel upon touchdown. I found myself stepping off the plane and entering headlong into my new life, even if only temporary for that summer. I tried fathoming how the next couple of months would have me surviving in all those foreign countries, each with their own language, unique cultures, and customs.

My journey, however, having definitely begun had by then already been slightly modified. A few minor glitches had actually occurred prior to my departure. For one matter, my two best friends' minds had changed. Although the flight dates had been accepted, initial transportation agreements had been verbally arranged and, finally, round-trip tickets had been pre-purchased for my own flight by Jean, nevertheless, the "Jimbo-Jack-Daniels-Escapade" collapsed in nature and substance.

With my buddies' excuses ranging from "wanting summer work instead" to "needing to save money for fall school expenses," both my friends, and supposed, future-travel mates, cancelled-out at the last minute. If I were to go, then it would have to be definitely all on my own.

Upon listening to both my friend's lame excuses, I just shunned them off, saying briskly, "No? Too bad. Oh, well, don't need either of you. I'll just go alone." And I did.

At first, I felt like *The Lone Ranger*, though, but without his *Tonto* sidekick{s}, or better yet, one of *The Three Stooges* without the other two. However, I considered myself to be a real trooper who would still get by simply fine on my own. Besides, I would find new friends to travel with at the Youth Hostels if I wanted. And I believed firmly in myself and in my good decision-making capabilities. I assured my parents that I would still be alright. To my credit, it was probably my determination, grit, and self-confidence that relieved my parents, more-than-anything else, into still allowing and supporting their son's *solo venture*. . . It was that, or else they had tricked me all along and were actually glad to have gotten rid of me so cheaply, and for the whole summer too. Ha! No, just kidding... It wasn't that cheap!

Anyway, another compromising factor was the unfortunate circumstance of any desired, additional funds not materializing to help finance my summer trek. Where I had hoped for extra donated money from other extended family or friends, nothing arrived. Instead, I was sent-off on my sixty-day venture clutching only my parents' obliged $250 to cover my entire summer's journey. I was mostly unaware and ignorant of various, typical cost outlays toward necessary food, shelter, and transportation expenses. Plus, I didn't even consider or include potential fees for any desired activities such as museum visits and other pricey experiences while traveling.

Nevertheless, I did understand that prudent budgeting was going to be a necessity. When doing basic math, I easily calculated that spending daily over sixty days averaging twenty-nine dollars a week might potentially become a hardship. How to live on four dollars a day would challenge even the thriftiest and most prudent travelers.

But, in all honesty, with my parents' generous financing stashed safely inside my front jeans pocket, I felt comfortably well-off at that moment of my arrival in *Paris*, France. Besides, I had already thought of a hopefully clever plan to assist with my fiscal needs. While still in flight, I had heard a notification over the loudspeaker system advising any interested passengers to quickly buy certain *Tax-Free* items from the flight crew without paying typical additional fees. With that information to consider, I suddenly concocted my *first*, brilliantly bright idea.

Although not a smoker, myself, I excitedly determined that by buying a couple of cartons of Salem cigarettes (a menthol brand my aunt smoked) from the stewardesses for two dollars each, I could create a clever way to make some extra cash. Two bucks a carton and tax-free figured to be cheap and profitable. Quickly calculating, I figured, therefore, that meant twenty cents per pack. Thus, later on during my travels, as circumstances permitted or necessitated, I could then sell the smokes pack-by-pack at huge price increases to desperately wanting Europeans for nifty profits. Minimal initial costs would likely generate tons of useful extra revenues helping to finance my travels.

"Of course," my inexperienced, non-smoker's mind surmised, "Europeans must be pleading for *American* cigarettes, just like all things "American." And after all, aren't the best cigarettes in the world *Made In America*? Didn't everyone everywhere who smoked crave them? And won't they willingly pay high prices to get some?"

In fact, I had seen such build-ups in theatre movies with desperate foreigners crying, "Yes! Yes! Thank you, so much. Ahhh, American cigarettes? Oh, how wonderful!"

Then the films' foreign actors would gratefully fondle the pack, open it, retrieve a cigarette, light it, inhale, and finally slump back in delighted pleasure. My idea was sure fire to be a *sure-fire* money maker. I was sure...

Refocusing, once off the plane, I fetched my two Salem cigarettes cartons, found my way to *Baggage Claim,* and retrieved my single piece of luggage, a large, navy sea bag which had been given to me by my older brother. I then tucked those two Salems cartons deep inside that bag. Confidently throwing the sea bag over my shoulder, I headed for the Custom's Gate. Still pondering, I considered how my fruitful plan would involve retrieving individual packs, as requested, and reselling them.

"What a creative business mind I had," so I figured. With visions of generous riches and grandeur, excess money bulging in my pockets, I imagined how my initial, small investment would be guaranteeing me such large returns.

At least those were my naïve, initial plans during the outset of my journey. There was much to learn and experience for that yet unlearned and inexperienced traveler...

PART TWO

....

Being There

CHAPTER 5

VIVE' PARIS!

Parlez-vous francais?

Walking through the passageways to the Custom's Gate, I felt a little nervous, to be sure, being uncertain of so much yet to happen, but I felt like there was little to lose. After all, my rather light sea bag had all my necessary belongings in it, and that wasn't much: A couple changes of underwear and socks, another nice shirt, two additional T-shirts, two pair of shorts, another pair of pants, an extra light jacket, swimming trunks, and a blanket. Accessories included a camera, extra film, and a towel, including personal items wrapped inside like soap, comb, and toothbrush with toothpaste.

Oh, yes, also inside my sea bag was a copy of my favorite book, Moby Dick, to help pass any needed time, and a map of Europe to mark my travels. Of course, now from the flight, there were also two cartons of Salem cigarettes. Considering all, it seemed like a lot, but it really wasn't that heavy. Fact is, once that sea bag was tossed over my shoulder, it was very manageable. It made me think of my older, sailor brother, and that pleased me. Eventually, I was to find out just how handy that bag came in too. All was fine with me . . . at *first*.

Tossing that big bag around was easy for me also, and that was necessary all the time. There at *Paris Orly Airport* and then going through Customs was no problem. I understood some of what was said to me by the officials, but just my willingness in handing over my USA Passport and smiling a lot made clearances seem simpler. Lots of "Merci, beaucoups" and "S'il vous plaits," helped too. Nearly everyone everywhere appreciates smiles, good manners, and kindness. I noticed, too, that the French seemed very appreciative, or else expectant, of my attempts to communicate in their language. They seemed not to speak any English. My French classes helped.

Thinking back now, I swear I must have appeared so innocent too. Clean-cut, well groomed, young, harmless, and so naïve looking may have drawn more negative attention than I knew, deserved, or wanted. Yet, my potential gullibility coupled with decent manners and frequent smiles practically rushed me through many otherwise obstacles, including my *first* deliberate conversational exchange. Right away, I needed French money, francs, for my immediate travels.

"S'il vous plait, j'ai besoin de francs, merci. Changer pour des dollars, s'il vous plait." Please, *I need francs*, thanks. *Change for dollars* (heavy on the *thank you* and *please*, too).

It worked like a charm, though, and a kind, airport agent pointed out an exchange booth to me. The transaction was easily dealt with, and soon I found myself outside the Orly International Airport Terminal Building facing oncoming, passing traffic, and counting my new money. Quickly, I learned that a French franc was worth about twenty cents, in American money. My initial, exchanged twenty-dollar bill brought me almost one hundred francs. I almost felt like I was getting richer already. "I love this country even more!" I grinned. And I did...

A quick study of available bus routes showed my immediate choice. *Route 1* bus went into *Central Paris*, about ten miles away, or rather fifteen kilometers. I had to start thinking metric from then on, which I liked. A much easier system or method to mentally process; every unit was measured in factors of ten. Meters, grams, or liters (Distances, mass, or liquids). Go up or down by units of ten. A way better and easier system to use than our complicated and confusing yards, pounds, or gallons system. The rest of the world's methods were so much simpler to learn, understand, and use. I supposed American leaders thought we citizens were too simple-minded to comprehend the metric system, or too impatient to accept converting to its use. That, or they are . . . Of course, being American I am also humored by the twisted thought, "I just can't understand why the rest of the whole world is wrong!"

Anyway, *Route 1* had the only stop on it that I recognized, la tour Eiffel, *the Eiffel Tower.* I knew I could spot that tourist site easily and then figure my way anywhere from there. I was heading for the *Left Bank* area designated on a city map I had picked up inside *Orly Airport Terminal.* During preparations for my trip, I had been informed by my aunt that the famous *Left Bank* zone was supposed to be an inexpensive area for thrift-minded travelers to find shelter.

In only a few minutes, a *Route 1* bus arrived. I hoisted my sea bag up and climbed aboard greeting the driver with my new standard, "Bon jour y merci beaucoup."

I held out my hand with many francs showing, and the driver looked at me and held up two fingers. Transaction completed, and I easily found an open seat. It had cost me two francs (forty cents!), and grinning ear-to-ear, quickly I was on my way into *Paris*, the *City of Love,* my *first* layover and a curiously friendly, though sometimes not-so-friendly, but beautiful and romantic place on Earth.

Route 1 Bus

The brief bus ride into the city of *Paris* was scenic and exciting. We passed so many typical and similar advertising billboards along *Route 1* offering such delights as exotic perfumes, delicious restaurant foods, classy hotels, and all sorts of other human needs, wants, pleasures, or interests. It seemed I might have been approaching any city in the world. The differences were the exotic French language on the advertisements and the thrilling sensations welling up inside me with each closing mile, or kilometer, that is. As our bus got closer to the metropolitan zone, I became filled with an exhilarating feeling of *Vive' Paris!*

I could easily make out the highway ads with their advertised products. I could also grasp the identifying names of many of the surrounding buildings that we passed. And I could even recognize meanings and purposes of most of the international highway signs instructing drivers and travelers what to do or where to go. Turnoffs and advertisements for *The Palace of Versailles, The Fontainebleau Palace, Norte-Dame de Paris, The Louvre Museum*, and many other city favorites filled one's eyes with tantalizing recommendations. However, I was looking for the one attraction that would set me off on my footpath officially beginning my hiking and hitchhiking journey: *La Tour Eiffel.*

I eagerly watched for that easily recognizable structure and soon spotted it far off in the distance, just as I had pictured in my mind. It lay alongside the famous Seine River and would be walking distance, hopefully, from my first night's quarters in the *Left Bank* section of the city. The streets were zigzagging all over the place in all sorts of curves and angles, but it was manageable to determine direction and distances on my map. After an impressive and included mini tour of so many favorite tourist attractions, my bus pulled over right near the *Eiffel Tower* for my stop.

"Je vous remercie. Merci beaucoup et bonne journe'e!" I hollered at the driver while practically leaping from the rear exit of the bus *thanking him and wishing him a wonderful day.*

And there I was . . . right smack in the middle of one of the most famous and romantic cities in the world, *Paris*, France! *The Eiffel Tower* lay directly before me within a beautiful parklike setting, and the *Seine River* was just beyond in near proximity. Shuddering internally, I sensed untethered freedom with my journey laying ahead. I was momentarily breath taken; however, I quickly gained my composure knowing full well that immediate lodging for the night was my primary and necessary goal.

The cheap hotel zone destination was off to my left. After some easy map calculations, I figured to have about a mile, or around one and a half kilometers, to walk and find a place for my first night's lodging. So, I hoisted my sea bag up and over my shoulder and off I went crossing boulevards and hiking along some industrious, pleasant enough, and remarkably busy streets with their hustling, bustling pedestrians and hurried, noisy, late-afternoon traffic.

Accidental Walk

And *Voila*! There and then came my very *first* and noticeably unique impression of *Paris*. During my brief, one hour or more walk through those *Parisian* streets and boulevards to my sought after *Left Bank* area, I actually couldn't help but begin keeping count of the number of auto accidents I personally observed happening directly before me. I was an actual eyewitness to multiple collisions, mishaps, and even pedestrian/automobile accidents.

Cars were suddenly swerving to the left or right and thereby side-swiping other vehicles. Short-sighted or rushed tailgaters were slow reacting, thus rear-ending autos in front of them after sudden stops. Hurried drivers were racing too late through intersections causing themselves to pile into other, unforeseen cars passing through, or turning left, or right. And the craziest and worst of all were those drivers who gave zero right-of-way to street-crossing pedestrians. The *first* of those ambushes involved a vehicle's driver absent-mindedly smacking right into a person stepping off an intersection's curb at a crossing, and on a green light for the pedestrian, to boot. Crazy!

I mean to say that my entire walk, a measly twelve blocks or so, were *accidentally* odd sights to behold. I actually personally witnessed six accidents occur over my brief one-mile course. It was almost absurd, it seemed. I'd walk awhile, and then right there before me would be two cars colliding. Then the two involved drivers would get out of their cars, walk over to each other, and sometimes even shake hands. They would talk momentarily and soon exchange pieces of paper, which I assumed had names and insurance companies on them. After that, they would seem to wave at each other, walk back to their respective cars, and drive off, if possible, almost pleasantly.

Even two accidents involving pedestrians seemed agreeably treated as merely casual incidents with apologies and information exchanges, when necessary. Afterwards, both parties involved simply left the scene and apparently went on about their business with hardly any fuss. It was amazing. I suppose I was so shocked because of having been so impressed by American TV shows and movies' scenes with highly different reactions to similar events.

Typical responses that I imagined would have been like those New York City scenes with pedestrians pounding fists on driver's car hoods and screaming, "Hey, I'm walkin' here!" Lots of yelling and angry words and middle fingers waving about pointing accusations at each other with angry challenges of righteousness or guilt. Not in *Paris*, however. The *city of love*, I supposed.

They were accidents, which was all. No one's actual fault. No problems. Let insurance companies dicker-out appropriate solutions. Once the initial shock on my part began to ease after observing yet another mishap incident, and then another, I began to shrug-off those events as *C'est la vie!* Heck, maybe those were standard responses for all fender-benders throughout *Paris*, and even all of France; maybe even all of Europe!

Anyway, with my first eye-witnessing, I was shocked and surprised at how calmly and pleasantly all those incidents were managed. After a few more, I became almost curiously humored. By the end of my *accidental walk* and final inadvertent *mishap* observation, I was just shrugging-off those incidents like no big deals. Fact was that the last accident had actually involved another pedestrian. That time a fellow on the opposite side of a large boulevard was in the middle of making a street crossing when he was hit by a car quickly turning right too widely and without even giving right-of-way to the pedestrian at the intersection.

I couldn't claim who was to blame; the lights may have been red for both of them, but it had not mattered. Each party had offered jovial manners while exchanging personal information, and then the driver simply vanished, speeding off on his way while the pedestrian continued on across the street limping toward his own destination. Weird. I wondered, "If someone walking had been paralyzed or killed by a moving vehicle, would the driver have simply pinned a note to their victim's chest with all appropriate insurance information and then continued on their way?" Oh, well, that was *Paris*, apparently, I supposed and chuckled as I ever-so-carefully continued on my own way.

Left Bank

Nonetheless, it wasn't long afterward that I found my way into and entered the desired, less-expensive *Left Bank* area. After some simple searching, I found a very modest looking hotel with a small, discreet sign advertising vacancies. I entered, sought out the desk clerk and we quickly yet awkwardly arranged accommodations for me. It was my next serious attempt at conversational French, and I cannot say that it went well. The maître-de refused to speak English, and my French was really put to the test.

"Bon jour," I said . "Avez-vous des chambres, s'il vous plaît?" *Hello, do you have any rooms?*

I didn't fully understand his curt reply, "Tu n'as pas vu dehors? Il dit que oui." But it sounded like, "Didn't you see the sign outside, Asshole? Yes, we do. What's the matter? Are you blind, or just an imbecile, or something?"

I was very embarrassed, "Je suis desole', mais mon francais es tres pauvre." *I am sorry, but my French is poor.* Then I asked again, "Mais une chamber bon marche,' s'il vous plaît?" *But, a cheap room, please,* I hoped.

I didn't know why he seemed not to like me. After all, I was so polite, and kind, and apologetic, and at least attempting French. He probably disliked his job, or Americans, or just me, or whatever. Nevertheless, he merely shoved a large book to me, and I understood it was a register for which to sign-in. So, I did, and he then told me, "Dix francs, par nuit a l'advance chaque pour." He had said, "Ten francs per night in advance each day."

Two bucks American! I attempted a somewhat casual demeanor, but I was so shocked, yet pleased. I quickly did some mental math and determined that at that rate, my lodgings' expense could last me my whole trip if I just stayed right there. That sum would stretch to about half of all my money for an entire summer's lodging. But then, I realized, that I'd see little else with only *Paris* to talk about . . . which might be okay under different circumstances. Too bad, though, I had a lot more planned to see and even more to do.

Nevertheless, I happily handed over ten francs to the lethargic, bored, or upset clerk, took a key from him, and headed to the elevator. A couple minutes later, I was in my *first,* very own, private room with my very own spectacular, sixth-floor view of the hotel's small, grungy, empty courtyard, and another similar building directly across the way with its own rear viewings. Okay, it wasn't the Presidential Suite, but it was my suite, and a sweet suite, at that: A twin bed, a desk with a chair and lamp, a mirror, a closet, and a window with a shade. Each floor's double, communal bathrooms and showers were gender separated and lockable, and the single, public phone on each floor was commonly shared at a mid-hallway point. But that was okay, too. After all, I had grown up in the country using an outhouse and a six, family-line phone service. I was used to sharing and interruptions.

"Hey, close the door! I'm in here! Go away!" At least that's what another family member would say to me practically each time. Or, after sneakily listening in on shared, phone-line calls, somebody would interrupt and say, "Hey, you mind hurrying up? Somebody else needs to make a call." So, that hotel's system presented no issues for me. I would easily be prepared for any intrusions by me or from someone else. No problems. Besides, I would be gone most of the time and likely using outside toilet facilities. Also, I had no plans to make any calls and no extra money for expensive overseas phoning, anyway.

Regardless, it seemed like my favorite, or most often used, phrase was, "Oh, je suis vraiment desole'!" *Oh, I am so sorry.* Quickly, I had added two new words to my constantly attended French vocabulary. Before, it was mostly just "S'il vous plait," and "Merci." *Please and thank you.* Now, it was those plus "Je suis vraiment desole" and "Mes excuses," or "Excusez-moi. *I am so sorry, my apologies, or excuse me...*

At *first*, "Je suis desole', mes excuses, excusez-moi, s'il vous plait, and pardonne-moi" *forgive me* were my most useful, common, and trusted French vocabulary. In the beginning, I was full-of-it! I mean begging pardons. It seemed like I was pleading forgiveness or apologizing so much of the time, yet l usually kept right on smiling. Maybe that was just to throw anyone off balance by either disarming them or to keep 'em guessing.

No matter, though, I was hungry after registering and reviewing my accommodations. Plus, I was ready for some exploring. So, once I dropped off my belongings in my own, private-palatial space and mildly cleaned up, I was out the door and off for my *first* adventure. In no time, I was wandering alongside the *Seine River,* or what *Parisians* affectionately called *la Seine,* and could see both *la Tour Eiffel* off to my right and to my left a wonderful yet smaller but exact replica of our own Statue of Liberty in New York City. I was surprised to see it sitting there on a little isle in the middle of the river, having seen our own special statue when I was quite young.

I learned that, in fact, after we received our "Statue of Liberty" from the French government in 1886, we had reciprocated with a smaller version in 1889 which was placed in the middle of *la Seine* in a place called *Pont de Grenelle.* No offense meant but having seen the original in NYC at the ripe old age of seven years, I was still more impressed back then, it seemed. *La Statue de la liberte de Paris* exchange was nice, however. It offered a pleasant reminder of home while providing a small connection to the exciting and romantic city of *Paris.*

La Tour Eiffel was off at a distance, and I was absolutely going to visit that grand sight, but not just then. I wanted at least half a day to plan for that, and right then I wanted food. Plus, right away I learned another *first*: Eighteen years was the legal drinking age in France, and all over Europe for that matter. Of course, I had to ask *first,* and I learned more about that rule right away.

"Puis-je avoir du vin, s'il vous plait?" *Can I have some wine, please?* I mentioned earlier that I was a quick learner. Well, actually it wasn't until I had noticed some other young guys walk out of a shop holding some wine and didn't even seem to be sneaking around with it. Go for it, I thought!

I made my way across the street and entered the same liquor store that I had noticed the other guys leaving. Once inside the store and after *first* asking, the nonchalant attendant just pointed to the varietal, wine-selection wall giving me free reign to determine and snag what I wanted. At *first*, being so wide-eyed astonished at all the legally fabulous possibilities, I didn't want to seem cheap. But after a few minutes and some quick calculations, I gave in to the fact that, well, yes, I was cheap, by necessity, not character. So, I didn't care after that. Stranger in a strange land... It didn't matter.

I just looked for something that only cost a few francs. As soon as I found a pretty bottle with a nice rose flower on the label and which was really cheap, I grabbed it. Then I quickly snatched up some other complimentary necessities, like cookies and chips, and practically rushed to the counter. Trying to hide my deviously sneaky and embarrassingly *cheapened* smile, I attempted instead to suggest a confident air of aloofness and matter-of-fact smugness. Still, I promptly paid my five francs debt, "Merci, beaucouped" the clerk, clutched my loot, and was out the door in a *Parisian* minute. By then I was chuckling freely to myself over my good fortune and grinning up a storm at all my loot and (otherwise delinquent) success.

La Seine Riverwalk was a really delightful stretch that wandered far in either direction following beside the river. I had come upon the river at a particularly pleasing point because off in one distance, I could see the *la Tour Eiffel* standing famously tall with its unique Erector Set image; to the other direction was that actual smaller *la Statue de la Liberte' de Paris* replica.

I laughed while humming to myself and projecting into my future: "Oh, Paris, here I am! Wow! If I make it here, I can make it anywhere! Look out! Here I come!"

No matter. This city was unique too, though. Their *Statue de la liberte de Paris* was placed out on the tip of a long, narrow, man-made, parklike island right in the middle of *la Seine* and approachable at either end by special bridge crossings which allowed for foot traffic. The statue's placement point was called *Pont du Grenelle* and was open to the public. From my advantage point, both were especially meaningful recognizing each's unique structure as visible tourist attractions: *The Eiffel Tower,* far upriver to my right; and the *Statue of Liberte.* off to my left. They both made me feel giddy and excited.

In fact, I learned there that at about the same time as our USA reciprocated, *Liberty Statue* replica model from 1889 was set up, the famous *Tour Eiffel* was being constructed not far away. It made for spectacular views, and I could only assume they were what made that particular area I was in so popular. Artists from around the world gathered in the vicinity to paint, draw, sketch, and etch the magnificent surroundings.

The towering tourist objects, the interesting people, the fascinating architecture of the older and newer buildings and homes, the massive and vibrant river, and all the lovely parks provided endless suggestions for artists' subject matter. I also appreciated the fact too that less than a hundred years earlier, famous painters like Monet, Van Gogh, Gauguin, Picasso, Dali, Renoir, Cezanne, and scores of others had likely endeavored their special skills and masterful talents right there where I stood alongside *la Seine* as they created masterpieces of similarly enchanting views that I was right there and then also observing.

Even that very day, as I strolled beside *la Seine* through its parklike setting, dozens of new artists were scattered aimlessly about the walkway absorbing and studying the brilliant views and likely pressing their brushes to canvas in the same way as the old masters. However, many of those present, and notably eccentric, artists seemed equally caught up in their own notoriety as they unsubtly flashed their pallets and brush strokes about while dressed in amusingly wild regalia. They were enjoying receiving as much attention for their own extravagant caricatures as for their own unique, artistic creations. Some, no doubt, even more so. No matter, it made my stay seem all the more charming while passing through that flamboyant and imaginative area. The artists with their colorful artistic flairs for both personal and canvas effects were memorable and welcoming for my *first* local visit. I just knew, however, that there was still so much more to discover there in *Paris,* and everywhere else too.

Obviously, the world famous <u>la Seine</u> was still an apparent, celebrated gathering spot for artists everywhere to come and highlight their talents and their bravado. They visited one another, commented, and critiqued each other's works, drank, smoked, bragged about themselves, and, oh, yes, also even painted a little of the lovely scenery surrounding the river, too. I could imagine that in those older 1800's days, all the bars, pubs and cafes along the side streets had been packed nightly with rabble rousing artists and show-offs shouting imprudent obscenities, claiming personal stardom, and offering subtle, facetious compliments or criticism to one another while drunkenly entertaining themselves. Probably, it was still the same that day too, I acknowledged.

After casually ambling up the river walk wandering past others, I admired, gawked, and took in the wonderful aesthetics of the area while many artists continued remaining scattered everywhere up and down _la Seine_ displaying their talents and peculiar charm to all passersby. And actually, the painters' views were wonderful. The river, itself, was a fairly clean, greenish blue current that was both flatly calm yet actively moving. It ran from southeast to northwest in a long bend past oddly elegant mixtures of centuries old structures to more modern classic buildings all aligning either riverside, but also stretched along the opposite side's busy thoroughfare lying directly beside _la Seine_.

All sorts of commercial cargo boats, plus lively and imaginative watercraft, casually meandered up and down the waterway offering needed products and quaint aesthetics for viewers and artists. Highly curved, creative bridge crossings, off in either direction, seemed artistically acceptable and appropriate while allowing for both the shipping and recreational craft to pass underneath as reasonable foot and some vehicle traffic passed overhead across and back. I also realized from my _Paris_ map _that_ there were well over twenty-five bridge crossings of _la Seign_ throughout _Paris_. I assumed there had to be great commercial and personal needs to get back and forth across that busy river...

Happy Drunk

Then during my pleasant walk alongside the river, eventually I came to a lovely grassy and wooded park area available for picnickers which offered shade, relaxation, and simple enjoyment of the gratifying surroundings. And it was there that I found an empty bench for my very _first_ early-evening meal that became a pleasing, relaxing, and yes, an intoxicating bit of self-overindulgence and satisfying entertainment. The cheap wine turned out to be more than I could barely manage with my inexperienced alcohol palate. By the end of my late afternoon snack, and the bottle of wine, I was snockered.

In a short time, however, I was likely becoming a little obnoxious to observers. So, after my goofy silliness on the park bench began blundering into sloppy giddiness, I vaguely recall stuffing the remainder of my edible goods into my pocket and once again with bottle in hand continuing my trek. Though by then slightly staggering, I ventured still further up the beautiful *la Seine* walkway ever smiling and ever so polite to all bystanders, artists, and questioning onlookers. With my wine jug gleefully, but firmly, gripped and waved rashly about, I cheerfully stumbled, fumbled, and graciously greeted everyone with flamboyant charity and an overabundance of congeniality that perhaps only a young, drunken American tourist might display. Or maybe some of those *la Seine* artists too, I considered. However, "Remember your manners, Daniel," I chided myself. "Don't forget to be a polite and *handsome* American, not an *ugly* one!"

"Bonjour! Bonjour! Merci beaucoup! Comment allez-vous? Comment ca va? Je vais bien! Je suis fantastique! Ne t'inquiete pas, je vais bien et heureux!"" *Hello! Hello! Thank you very much! How are you? How's it going? I am fantastic! Don't worry, I am fine and happy.* Oh, yes, I was pleased with myself, thankful, and filled with good manners and joyful feelings. And not to worry, I was feeling good too. . .

A happy drunk, I was filled with love for all humanity and offering friendly verbal gestures to all observers and listeners. Although, I was a bit overfilled with liquor too. It was definitely my *first* time officially getting drunk, and all by myself at that, and though it was not to be my only intoxicating spree during that special summer, that *la Seine* experience was certainly my most pleasant, entertaining, harmless enough, and memorable. Hopefully, it was for all my noticing onlookers also.

At some point, though, I recall crossing *la Seine* for an alternate or opposing view of my surroundings. With the *Eiffel Tower* still standing tall and off in the distance, however, I remember not wanting to hike too far toward it that *first* evening for fear of forgetting what direction I came and ending up wasting my night's lodging and having to sleep on some nearby park bench. Besides, I wasn't sure I could find anything once it became dark. So, I nonchalantly strolled back across the river at the next bridge crossing and proceeded further up the riverfront boulevard still toward *la Tour Eiffel*. Yet, I kept looking back over my shoulder to remind myself of whence I came.

Eventually, I understood that I was obviously staggering far too much, so I attempted feebly to maintain my dignity. Turning about I sought a welcomed, homeward-bound route, and I found my temporary home with only occasional outbursts of pure joy. The return to my hotel was filled and accented by obnoxious but innocent and delightfully intoxicated laughter.

Finally finding my way back, and once arrived, I discovered a nice and reasonable café just around the corner of my hotel. After ordering and devouring an inexpensive meal of soupe aux legumes, *vegetable soup*, along with the remainder of my rose' and bread, I spent the rest of the evening relaxing outside that café. I just sat watching the locals as they passed by while contemplating my afternoon's activities. Two observational viewpoints I determined and agreed upon: First, city people the world over all seemed to behave the same; and second, *Parisian* life seemed vibrantly beautiful...

Some folks strolled right on down the boulevard so comfortably and seemingly stress and care-free while enjoying the evening air with a friend, a pet, or both, and not. Others rushed up and down the streets so hurriedly trying to get where they were anxiously going. There were those who appeared oblivious to everything else, nature and man, while a few others suspiciously watched everyone and everything else, including their shadows. Just city life, I imagined, and for a moment I sensed my *first* moment of nostalgia for my quiet, country-home lifestyle.

Then, as I browsed over the café menu again, but barely recognizing or understanding much of what I read, due to so many new and unusual words, I took a chance and ordered a cup of coffee for two francs. A haughty waiter with a smug look brought my order served in a small cup and saucer. As I "*Merci* ed" him, I even saw him chuckling while leaving. I chuckled too; no tip for him!

The drink was awful, though. I gagged on my first sip. That's why the clown waiter laughed; he knew. My beverage was a thick, syrupy Turkish brew that practically held my spoon straight up when I stirred it. Strong too. It required plenty of sugar and took a long time to finish but finish it I did. However, I learned something new, another *first*: Yuuck! Never buy that stuff again!

Even still the remainder of that evening was very pleasing as I sat back all stretched out at that relaxing sidewalk table and watched the passing locals. The unintended, but jubilant alcohol buzz, I had received earlier from that tasty bottle of rose' had mellowed me down quite a bit and especially after my dinner. It helped me to settle in nicely for a warm and comfortable twilight. Off in the distance, I could hear some smooth and easy saxophone jazz playing from yet another really talented *Parisian* artist performing for passers-by and other street people.

All-in-all, that casual mixture of city-life movements of sounds, café smells, my beverage and food delights, and the many other local aesthetics made for a memorable and comfortable *first* night in *Paris*. The artful promenade, enjoyable and entertaining meals, curious but fascinating city culture, and finally the soothing, pleasant jazz music were much to pleasingly absorb that *first* day in *Paris* for me. For a young country kid all alone, and thousands of miles from home in a foreign land, my journey was starting-off on a surprisingly good note.

La Tour Eiffel

The next two days in *Paris* were filled with a wanderer's lust for visual stimulation. Every street seemed stunning, impressive, and inspirational. Each morning, I awoke early, cleaned-up and dressed, then headed out for a light, continental breakfast from a local store usually consisting of fruit, a juice drink, more cheese, bread, and small piece of meat like salami or pepperoni. The bread was delicious and inexpensive. Grocery shops everywhere placed barrels out front of their establishments on sidewalks and filled them with fresh new loaves. For twenty cents, one franc, it was a real meal deal. With a loaf in hand, I eagerly strode up the streets each day, munching away, but remained comfortably relaxed while stopping as often as I chose to enjoy sights before me.

The next couple of mornings I had general destinations in mind, but I paced myself too. I knew that I could see a lot but not afford to pay for much. That was okay, though, because just being there was the special attraction. A few sights were easy and free to see such as *Notre Dame Cathedral*, *la Arc de Triomphe*, and the wonderful and abundant statue-filled parks, spectacular architecture everywhere, and of course, <u>*la Seine*</u>. One longer evening walk included a delightful stroll down the world-famous commercial street, *Champs-Elysees Avenue,* which connects the impressive *Place de la Concorde* on one end to the glorious *Arc de Triomphe* at the other end.

La Place de la Concorde, a major public square in Paris, is a monumental display originally intended to glorify King Louis XV. Throughout the French revolution around 1787-1799, however, it became famous as a place of royal executions, including Louis XVI. In modern times, it also became famous for the *Luxor Obelisk*, an enormous 3,300-year-old Egyptian artifact, placed there in the 1830's. Of course, at the other end of the grand avenue, the extremely popular visit site of *la Arc de Triomphe* is the famous tributary monument to Napoleon's victories during the French Revolution. That leisurely round-trip saunter down the *Champs-Elysees*, though, was over four kilometers in itself. But the marvelous shops, wonderful restaurants and cafes with sidewalk tables, and those famous hotels along the avenue made for entertaining, interesting, and relaxing strolls.

Also, I have always enjoyed waterways like lakes, rivers, creeks, and streams. So, that wonderful *la Seine* right in the middle of the city, and always close to me, was genuinely pleasant to be nearby. Although it hooks, winds, and meanders all around *Paris*, and France for that matter, the areas in *Paris* that I did visit, and of which splintered off from the *Left Bank* zone, were developed alongside *la Seine*'s one long, slight citywide curve. With so many bridge connections, though, walks were encouraged with many easy crossings.

Several other interesting sights around town were visually stunning from outside but also required tickets to enter and fully enjoy. Examples were the *Eiffel Tower*, the *Louvre Museum*, and the famous *Catacombes* deep underneath the city. Plus, even within my limited walking stretches, *Paris* overflowed with so many other art museums, historical structures, and popular tourist sights. But, I simply did not have time or money to see them all.

Yet, it seemed that no matter what direction I took off walking from my hotel each morning, I kept coming upon wonderful, historic buildings, statue-filled artistic parks, and special exhibits. Unfortunately, my modest budget only allowed me to enjoy what special attractions I could locate and afford in a day's hike. Thus, I limited myself to only a few unique, but pricey, sights such as those mentioned above. But I made a promise, though, to see whatever else I could still afford at the end of summer when I returned a final time before my flight back home...

What can I say, though? What I did see during those next two days was spectacular and wonderful. Of course, *la Tour Eiffel* was *first*. I had gotten so close after stepping off the bus from the airport, and then again while staggering nearby the day before. Plus, it was the *first* recognizable sight that I had noticed of *Paris*. So, it was natural to be my *first* paid visit. After another nice, poetic walk past all the early-riser artists setting up their easels, canvasses, and colorful pallets for their own day's adventures, I arrived at the enormous base of the tower.

Fortunately, I was still energized for the ascent ahead and above. Visitors had the option of taking an elevator or using stairs, so I naturally chose the climb. There were 674 steps to the *Esplanade*, the first viewing level, and it was a little challenging to any who dared. Of course, for an energetic and excited young fellow, I excitedly bound up the easy stairways stopping only to check writings, photos, and views of the tower's history, construction stages, timely pictures of past *Parisian* sights, and views of *Paris* that morning. *Incroyable et amusant!*

Fortunately, a required elevator hoisted me the rest of the way to the upper, tower-viewing level, and I did not complain. Like the paraphrased song, from there, literally, and musically, "I could see for *kilometres et kilometres!*" And there were plenty of signs pointing out wonderful city views all around. After a nice visit at the top viewing level, though, I physically submitted to taking the elevator all the way down past the *Esplanade* to the ground floor trying to conserve energy. There was still a lot more walking ahead and sights to see that day...

Les Catacombes de Paris

Les Catacombs de Paris was my next visit that day and an absolute necessity for a young fellow obsessed with the macabre, anything of death and dying fantasies, and mysticisms of the afterlife. The entrance was only about a mile and a half away, about two and a half kilometers, so I nearly sprinted to get there with enough time for a tour and underground visitation. It was worth it too. The catacombs are multi-level floors located deep beneath the surface of *Paris* and were originally a vast labyrinth of underground quarries dug for their high-demand minerals. In the late 1700's, when most of *Paris's* cemeteries were overfilled with France's dearly departed, *Paris* officials began relating and connecting many of the city's health issues to *Paris's* vast array of unsanitary cemeteries.

Around the same time, so much of the underground quarries started collapsing causing great fear and anxiety for the city's dwellers. A governmental decision was made to literally transfer countless grave remains into the abandoned and collapsed mining tunnels, or ossuaries, deep below the city's surface. Essentially, the nearly empty and neglected mines were turned into graveyards for over six million, relocated French deceased. Literally millions of bones, fragments, and skeletal corpse remains were basically shoved and piled everywhere into viewing galleries. It was a little gory and ghoulish but just the sort of visual aids necessary to tantalize midnight dreams, or nightmares. Of course, the English-speaking tour guide tried to make each gruesome scene even more morbid and macabre, and from all the crowd's *oohs, aahs,* and *shuuudders,* including mine, he succeeded. Definitely worth the fare, though.

After the tour's end, however, I had the ghastly company of all those morbid scenes occupying my mind for the walk back to my hotel room. With still another decent trek ahead to my hotel, though, I hoped that my dinner and ideally another relaxing evening would clear my head. After that day, I needed to shake all the bones loose, pun intended, for the following day's memorable and famous exercises. I'd need my rest too because the next day would be another long walk for my final two *Parisian* attractions and, expectedly, the best of all: *The Louvre Museum* and *Notre Dame Cathedral.* Plus, later on, I added another unexpected evening stroll down the *Champs-Elysees.*

La musee du Louvre

or

Mona Lisa's *Moustache*

The previous evening and next morning's inexpensive meals reenergized me for more upcoming, long city hikes necessary for my day's touring. But talk about worth it. . . My first stop was *The Louvre,* and it was a magnificent structure spread out beyond a huge and wonderful, park-like setting emphasizing its splendid glamour. I knew I was really denting my budget, but some things just deserve the cost. *La musee' du Louvre* was incredible, and even for an untrained eye, and still an unsophisticated visitor, the museum's exhibits simply took my breath away.

So many great works from centuries old, famous artists, sculptures, and countless other brilliant creators were exhibited there. Granted, at my age I had not learned much from school about most of *la Louvre's* exhibits, nor little about the exhibited artists. As a result, at that time in my life

I didn't really understand or fully appreciate all the exquisite aspects of those many, famous-displayed works of artists' skills and talents. Yet, I could certainly feel and sense which art objects sensitized my emotions, and I confess that *la Louvre* practically shook me with giddy pleasures and enjoyment. I remember teasing myself, "I may not know much about art, but I know what I like!"

Other's use of that phrase was a considerable annoyance to my high school art teacher. She would scoff at students' lack of artistic appreciation while instructing us to study all fine arts: Painting, drawing, sculpture, classical music, opera, dance, theatre, literature, film, etc.. "You students," she would say, "need to study the enduring efforts of artists, composers, musicians, singers, choreographers, actors, authors, and directors, to truly learn how to appreciate fine talent, skill, and effort that goes into any creative subject-matter."

Well, I'm sure she had a point, but at seventeen-eighteen, all I ever wanted to do in art class was make macramé plant hangers, hope to get a chance to draw nude females someday, read all sorts of literature, or climb on a stage and overact a character in some dramatic or comedic role's dialog before a large, adulating audience. I didn't understand *good* or *bad* regarding art. I just did what I could and allowed others to review and decide on quality. "One man's favorite was another's butt of some joke," I laughed. But I did listen to others and, regardless, thoughtfully considered their subjective opinions.

Yet, I did learn to appreciate, even love, and support all forms of art and especially due to my trip-sponsoring aunts', Jean McCord and Phyllis Manley, influences. As an author, herself, a semi-popular Bay Area personality, and advocate of all the fine arts, Jean, always encouraged my introductions to the art world. Along with her roommate, Phyllis, herself a successful artist painter, continuously took me to view everything artistic, including foreign films without subtitles. "You don't need subtitles," they would insist, "Just watch! Observe! Study! Learn from the acting and voice intonations!" Okay, fine, I thought, but most of the time, however, I went along for the bag of popcorn that came with my sacrificial observations.

However, fact is, having mentioned Jean's roommate, Phyllis Manley, before, I should emphasize that over the years, she had become a rather successful California artist with annual, Berkeley and Southern California art gallery and private exhibitions of her paintings for sale. Phyllis had her very own, unique mixture of styles that other people either liked, or did not. Yet, she always sold everything she painted at her celebrity-attended showcases, and Hollywood stars filled their homes with her expensive, popularized works.

Of course, Phyllis also laughed while telling me how many Southern California banks were filled with her art too. She said it was because "*Movie folks* would pay much for her paintings and then enormously inflate their paintings' values before donating them to various institutions, like banks for incredible tax write-offs!" Go figure.

Anyway, I can proudly state that out of twenty-three nephews and nieces of Jean McCord, *I was the only "true" supporter of the arts.* At twelve years of age, I became the single, only relative to ever pose nude for one of Phyllis's paintings. Naturally, many years later, when Phyllis was nearing her life's end, I amusingly bragged to her about posing over several days for her only nude, child-subject masterpiece, while curiously wondering aloud what wall-in-the-world that painting of me may actually still be hanging on somewhere. Her response was disappointing, though. She stared at me oddly and simply denied any culpability, "Oh, really? I don't remember that at all."

Sign of our present times, I suppose. Maybe she thought I was trying to initiate a child pornography lawsuit against her estate. And all I really wanted was appreciation for my contribution to her artistic success and then travel to Southern California to find that painting *hanging* somewhere . . . hanging loose. Or maybe I'd bring along some crayons and attempt exaggerating the *hanging* part. I don't know. At that early time in my life, however, I hadn't fully rationalized, or humorized, that part yet.

But, I really enjoyed Phyllis's art, and I was always immensely proud of her accomplishments. Heck, who knows? Maybe I'm actually *hanging* somewhere in *la musee du Louvre* as a prime illustration of modern art. More likely, though, I'm logged-jammed in a crowded basement somewhere in an obscure museum of abstract art. Ah, but what do they know? "They only like what they know about," *and they don't know me!* I also wondered about those who had viewed the painting. Did any of them wonder about me, and if so, what did they think? "Oh, my, what a generously fortunate little boy!" Or else, "Oh, that young pervert! How disgusting he is." Or, maybe just, " Oh, my!"

Anyway, back to *la musee du Louvre* and, naturally, my favorite exhibit was Leonardo da Vinci's <u>Mona Lisa</u>. She was absolutely stunning, both mysterious and beautiful. But for the life of me, I could not understand why that world-famous painting was placed up there on its modest wall space, shoulder high, and so close to viewers. She looked so fragile and unguarded. A simple, two-posted, enclosure of protective rope was all that protected that majestic painting, with merely a meter's separation distance, from any questionable public's potentially damaging or thieving hands.

Yet, I would be dishonest and remiss about those _Mona Lisa_ moments, way back there and then at the _Louvre,_ if I didn't admit something typical of a teenage boy's mischievous, vandalistic thoughts. While standing there all alone, directly before da Vinci's masterpiece, and practically secluded from any other observers, my mind began wandering again and vegetating, I suppose I couldn't help but momentarily contemplate slipping right underneath that casual and careless protective rope surrounding _Mona Lisa_, stepping right up to that beautiful portrait, and quickly sketching a heavy, dark moustache on her. It would have served the museum authorities right for trusting the public so much, and me in particular. Plus, for my own artistic contribution that day, if found accountable, I may actually have gone down in history as a future example, and criminalistic model, of some pretty darned good, and perhaps even famously deviant, graffiti.

Yes. Yes. Alright, I get it! I understand. . . You readers are all probably cringing and screaming, "Blasphemy! Heretic! Where's the guillotine? Off with his head!" But don't worry, I only had a pencil on hand, so merely an eraser would have been all that was necessary to correct my aberrant delinquency.

Nevertheless, after my immaturely conflicted, but thoughtfully impressed, encounters with _Mona,_ and my entire _Louvre_ visit, corrections were made and rules changed. Apparently, my criminally oppositional sympathies may still have actually exhibited their own positive effects. Perhaps, transmissions of my negative-minded thoughts sent vibrations which eventually subconsciously alerted museum security to better protect _The Louvre's_ valuables. In fact, I have heard these days, and even seen on You Tube, that _Mona Lisa_ is now protected from incorrigible hands by thick, plate-glass shields completely surrounding it. No camera flashes are allowed now, nor even human breath either, to touch upon and potentially infect her gloriously sensitive, yet always _mysteriously_ smiling and oily, face. And definitely, no pencils or crayons.

So, to all _la Louvre_ world visitors I mentally and emotionally apologize for your now obstructed views; however, nevertheless, you're welcome. Unfortunately, perhaps my devious, mental lapse did ultimately taint your viewings, but do not be concerned; _Mona Lisa_ really was a gorgeous close-up view, I guarantee you. At least, however, no scoundrels have ever jumped over the ropes and viciously drawn tattoos or sketched beards upon her bewitched and beguiling, smiling face. That would have been disgusting with the culprits deserving guillotine beheadings, or even shootings-by-firing-squad, or maybe drawing-and-quartering, and, and their bloody parts hung on tall fenceposts for public display in the now demolished _Place de la Bastille,..._ or, or all of the above...

Cathedrale Notre-Dame

Next stop, _Cathedrale Notre-Dame de Paris._ It would make for another long stroll getting there and then an extra-long walk back to the hotel. However, that visit was to be for my mother's sake, as well as my own. And, besides, who has never heard of _Notre Dame_? Why, we even have a popular college football team in the USA named after it. Plus, everyone knows about _Quasimodo,_ the deformed bellringer of the church, with his anxious desire to be accepted. Well, I just figured that I had to find him and tell him that he was loved and welcomed by many, after all. It was that, or ring the bells myself, and maybe stop inside, bow down low, and say a little prayer asking forgiveness for my foolish mental transgressions defacing _Mona Lisa_. Then I could beg for some protection for my future travels. Mom would have liked that.

Cathedrale Notre-Dame de Paris was an enormous and spectacular example of French Gothic architecture. So much ornately carved stone siding with its spectacular, gigantic spires awed all spectators. Inside, glorious statues and art treasures were everywhere with magnificently stained glass illuminating the entire nave throughout. Even its famous, most precious, and most venerated relic, the _Crown of Thorns,_ believed to have been placed on the head of our crucified Jesus Christ, was there for public viewing and inspirational tribute.

It took almost two hundred years (1163-1345) to build _Notre Dame Cathedrale de Paris,_ and it was worth all the effort and waiting to see its stupendous glory. Filled with myriads of priceless relics and art treasures, including massive centuries old paintings and wonderful marble statues, the cathedral represents all the past and present splendor, wealth, and power of the Catholic Church. Probably little else compares to its majesty besides maybe the *Sistine Chapel* in Vatican City within Rome, Italy.

As it turned out, though, it was not a long visit at *Cathedrale Notre-Dame* for me that late afternoon. Perhaps, I was just so overwhelmed by all the grand, artistic beauty I had absorbed that day. Also, I was definitely tiring from such long walks to, and then through, *la Louvre's* many rooms, halls, levels, and galleries. Next had come the lengthy trek to *Notre Dame Cathedral* for its magnificent, though brief and exhausting, visit. Plus, I still had another hefty hike getting myself back to my hotel in the *Left Bank*. However, as exhausted both physically and emotionally as I was getting, I still managed to slip a few blocks over to the impressive *Place de la Concorde* and take a magnificent stroll up the charming *Avenue des Champs Elysees* to the magnificent *Arc de Triomphe* before finally returning back to my hotel again.

Another terrific morning, afternoon, and early evening, though, but I still needed to make plans for the following day's extra-long hike. With my sea bag then shouldered, I would be crossing over the entire city to its far northern edge. The next day I'd be leaving *Paris* and heading north by hitchhiking. My goal was to eventually reach *Amsterdam*, Netherlands for my next destination and a roughly scheduled, somewhat surprise visit. My recently made friends from San Francisco were supposedly still staying there who may, or may not, *still* be expecting me. Besides, I also wanted to shock and impress them anyway. . .

Early the next morning, therefore, I was up, bathed and cleaned-up from the communal showers. Then I dressed, packed, and practically rushed out the hotel's Exit door with snide goodbyes to the same stiff, hotel clerk who had checked me in when I had first arrived. Courteously sliding my room key over the counter to him, the gruff, non-attentive attendant hardly even bothered looking up from the book he was pretending to read. Apparently, I was disturbing his faked concentration.

Perhaps he was simply and deliberately ignoring my early morning enthusiasm and cheerfulness. Maybe, though, my French was simply so intolerable to him. Oh, well, sorry, 'bout that. At least, I was trying. No matter. Leave politely, anyway. After all, it was his country and his language that I was probably defiling. *Forgeef me. I jam soo sorrie.* (Just try to say that without spitting or grinning!)

Nevertheless, *grinning* up-a-storm I laid my *adieus* on pretty thick, "Au revoir et merci beaucoup pour votre incroyable hospitalite." While simpering up a broad smile I had said to the rude clerk, "*Goodbye and thank you for your incredible hospitality.*"

Right around the corner, once more I bid farewell as I purchased another typical, continental breakfast of fruit, juice, cheese, and bread. That time, however, I spent a couple more francs and bought a large chunk of salami to carry along. My map showed a long walk ahead to get out of town for the highway heading north. So, hoisting my bag upon my shoulder, and while munching away at my meat n' cheese breakfast, off I hiked northward toward the far side of town.

My early morning trek was made a little more pleasant because I repeated my *Champs Elysees* walk once again. That departure route, however, only allowed me to half-circle the *Arc de Triomphe* on my route. I was heading for a major thoroughfare which would supposedly take me to the northwestern part of France. Once there, I was to come upon its ocean shore town of *Calais*, directly across the *English Channel* from Great Britain and closely bordering Belgium, my next visiting country...

Au revoir, mesdames

It wasn't too long before I was meandering along various streets turning and twisting this way and that while seeking the main highway leading north out of town. As I sauntered up the slim sidewalks still enjoying the morning air, after a bit I began noticing that streets became narrower and were heavily lined with parked cars on both sides. Medium tall structures, one after another, were jammed together as residential dwellings. Crowded, city-apartment buildings, I decided. Yet, it was during that peaceful, early-morning walk that I pleasantly encountered some reassuring human connections reminding me of humanity's good graces and demeanor, or at least French, or *Parisian* decency, anyway.

It was while passing through those many solid blocks of tall, multi-level, brick apartment buildings that I also noticed so many of the upper-floor apartment windows opened wide to the morning's gentle breezes, and many even had their simple, plain, and typically drab curtains pulled back. No matter. In just a few moments after my neighborhood entrance, many of those open windows became filled right away with pretty, young women all waving and hollering salutations to me from their respective windowsills...

"Salut beaute'. Venez me voir, pourquoi pas vous?" one attractive, young girl called out. I had to think twice about what I heard, but I was fairly certain she had shouted something like, "Hi, handsome. Why don't you come up and see me?"

I was immediately taken by surprise at the young lady's unwarranted and abrupt friendliness, but I just smiled heartily and waved back. Furthermore, just considering stopping and visiting with any of those nice ladies gave me a slight guilt complex. After all, my sweetheart back home had encouraged me to travel but would hardly have approved of any chitchatting with strange girls, no matter how kind and friendly they were.

No, I needed to mind my manners and think about dutifully plodding on ahead, remaining focused, and being content just missing my girlfriend back home. Continuing my saunter up the slim city sidewalk on that calm and somewhat cool morning, however, couldn't help but make me feel quite pleased and comforted with myself. Warm feelings for my love back home helped me enjoy and appreciate the brisk morning air even more, and that odd but kind greeting having pleasantly floated down from above, made me truly feel special. Somehow, I really felt welcome and content.

Then, right away another pretty girl hollered, followed closely by still yet another who began wolf-whistling and bellowing, "He', mon gars, tu n'es pas seul?" and "Bonjour, beau. Venez me voir et je vous ferai sentir comme chez vous."

I could hardly believe my ears. I had to rethink my hearing and challenge my French translation skills. Did those ladies just shout out asking, "Hey, young fellow, aren't you lonely?" with the other offering something like, "Come on up, and I'll make you feel at home."

My French was weak, but I could understand most of what they were saying. And I just couldn't get over how kind, welcoming, and generous those French girls were. In my mind, I was already admiring and toasting the French, "Well, golly, how about that?" I cheered. "Here's to the nicest, friendliest ladies anywhere!"

Progressing on up the street even further, more sociable, and outgoing girls, some leaning outrageously far out over their barren windowsills, began waving vigorously and calling out to me with even more energy as they practically pleaded for me to stop, and come up to visit. And they were persistent too. It was as though nearly all those upper-level, apartment ladies were attempting to usher me upstairs. Each was welcoming me to their own, personal habitats just so they could greet me, a total stranger to them, just to visit.

They all actually wished to make me feel more comfortable and *at home*. I was really touched. All I could imagine was that those kind, sweet ladies were either abundantly friendly or maybe just lonely too. I became sensitive to their potential seclusion and thus behaved even more graciously and humble at all their boisterously cooing requests.

Yet, I didn't know what the day ahead held, so I really couldn't stay and lollygag. Thus, I kept right on trekking through that delightfully friendly neighborhood waving back sincerely after each greeting but then shrugging my shoulders and apologizing for my obvious but unmeant rudeness. I would have enjoyed visiting with each of them, one by one, or even all of them at one place and one time, but I had not planned or scheduled for these kind, selfless and decent strangers. So, I simply pointed to my wristwatch exclaiming politely, "Je suis vraiment desole'. Merci pour votre aimable offres, mais pas de temps. Dois y aller." *"So sorry, thank you very much for your offers, but no time. Gotta go!"*

My easy carrying sea bag, filled with all my life's possessions, still rested lightly on my shoulder as I continued vigorously hiking toward the *Paris* outskirts. A pleasant smile beamed across my face, however, which steadied and satisfied my longest walk yet. As I progressed, however, wider streets began opening up into more industrial areas. Then, almost suddenly, I was in wide-open country. Eventually, I was met with some desirable traffic for good hitchhiking prospects on a decent highway heading north.

I was now leaving *Paris* to begin the *first* travel leg of my journey. I knew that I planned on returning before long. It was roughly arranged in my somewhat casual travel plans: *Head north from Paris 'til wherever and whenever; then, return to Paris again before heading south to wherever and whenever; then east to wherever; finally, return to Paris on time, and for one last visit, before my flight back home.* Obviously vague and general strategies.

For right then, however, I couldn't help pondering over my whole previous and precious, apartment-buildings serenading episode. With all its absolutely charming and welcoming women, I had been so surprised, impressed, delighted, and touched by all their unprompted kindnesses and generosity. As I prepared for my departure from the *City of Love* and its caring citizens, I couldn't help but reflect and cheer, "What a friendly city, and long live French women!" *Quelle ville sympathique et longue vie aux Francaises!* Vive' *Paris!*

57

CHAPTER SIX

ROAD LESSONS

Pas d'anglais Ici! No English Here

After that fairly lengthy but entertaining walk-through *Paris*, I finally reached a decent part of the main highway out of town allowing traffic to pull over and pick me up for a ride. Immediately, I set my sea bag in front of me, turned to face upcoming traffic, and stuck out my thumb resolutely while smiling charmingly at passersby. It was just as hoped. Right away, a driver pulled over and offered me a short ride to the next town of Amiens. I had two choice directions to get to my next destination, *Calais,* and that driver's ride offered one of them.

Eagerly accepting that *first* ride, I tossed my bag onto the rear seat and off we went in his small Renault vehicle for my *first* hitching experience in Europe. The young gentleman driver was friendly, but he spoke no English. Thus, our conversation was brief and committed to mostly basic, simple French phrases for my sake. Allowing for bits of dialog struggle, however, our communication was still interesting and comfortable.

"D'ou etes-vous?" he asked. *Where are you from?*

"Pres de San Francisco," I responded fairly sure of his question. "Et vous?" *And you?*

"J'habite a *Paris.* Que faire?" He lived in *Paris* and asked what I did (for a living).

"Je suis encore etudiant. Et vous?" *I am a student,* and then I asked about him too.

"Je travaille dans une bijouterie, mais les affairs ralentissent pour l'ete. Depuis combine de temps es-tu ici?" He spoke so much so fast that I was confused until we struggled to finally make his words fairly understood. He was a jeweler but business was slow. Then he asked how long I was to be there.

"Deux mois," I answered. And he looked surprised at my *two months* answer.

"Hou la la! C'est genial. Vous devez etre riche!" *Wow! That's great! You must be rich!*

"Non, je ne le suis pas, ou je ne ferais pas de!" I laughed and held up my extended thumb while shaking my head. *No, I'm not, or I wouldn't be (hitchhiking)!*

My driver laughed loudly, "L'auto-stop! L'auto-stop!" *Hitchhiking!* And we both laughed as I stated the new word for him again in English.

Then I asked of him, "Ou habitez-vous?" *Where did he live?*

"A *Paris*, mais j'ai de la famille a Amiens" *In Paris, but (his) family lived in Amiens.*

I suppose that was enough warm-up conversation for my driver to really open-up and take-off with a lengthy soliloquy about his life, his heartbreak, his broken marriage, I understood, and he also spoke of his loving children. Then he began rattling on about his life's difficulties and wanting to leave for the *French Riviera*, and on and on. . . Obviously, he had a lot to say, and I could only put bits and pieces together. So, I just sat there listening, nodding appropriately like some diligent psychologist, and letting him vent his obvious frustrations.

It certainly passed time easily, and before long we were in Amiens. My driver then said something about a turnoff to his family's home, but he generously continued on through the small town to get me on the other side for a better hitching opportunity. I graciously thanked him and shook his hand as we said our goodbyes. It was a pretty decent *first* ride.

As I mentioned previously about the countryside views during my TWA airliner descent over France, the scenery we drove through seemed remarkably familiar with its fields of green and gold and similar pastures for dairy and farming industries. Hearty wheat and oat fields lined both sides of our roadway. Quaint older farmhouses and some dilapidated barns were scattered about countered by other modern, sophisticated farms and elaborate field machinery. Except for the mild, language barrier that existed between the driver and myself, it felt like I could have been hitching a ride from anybody else anywhere over Northern California. Typical, yet comfortable and connectable, feelings arose as I considered admirable similarities of our two cultures: Family homesteads and family issues. Same as everywhere, I supposed.

Since leaving *Paris*, only about two hours had passed when we parted in Amiens once my driver decently took me completely beyond that town. It had been quite a conversational ride, even though far more one-sided with him talking and me listening and nodding sympathetically. I sensed that he wanted, or needed, to talk almost with an urgency, so I just let him ramble on. Paying strict attention, however, I listened politely and intently for sporadic words that I might understand to perhaps somehow piece together his frustrations and anxieties. I sensed he, and people in general for that matter, want and need good listeners while they vent personal frustrations. Ignoring them, or haphazard listening would merely intensify the stressed person's anxieties. Plus, I recognized that ignoring him would likely have gotten me dropped off a lot sooner with no special treatment, like the extra mile he gave.

At the same time, though, I tried gazing ahead to enjoy the scenic countryside in between his sudden, ongoing, verbal outbursts. People sure can talk when they have a mind to do so or troubles for which to attempt unburdening themselves. Also, I noted that even with my modest, limited-French abilities, that fellow sure took a lot for granted of my own translation skills. And he never even once attempted to communicate with me in English. Nor should he, I supposed. Yet, thusly, our communication was rather restricted.

"Parlais vous Anglais?" I had even asked during our drive.

"Non, absolutment pas!" he curiously but emphatically negated.

Once again alone, I quickly assumed another hitching stance. I wasn't hungry or thirsty yet, so I needed no food outlets. I simply needed my next ride to take me further toward the coastline and eventually to *Calais*, my *first* layover. Then, suddenly another ride seemed to come out of nowhere. It was an older gentleman in a weird looking pick-up truck of some sort, but I was no one to quibble. I dropped my bag in the back and climbed right in after it.

I had simply hollered, *"Calais!"* as I jumped into the back of his truck, and the obviously friendly and understanding driver just nodded. For clarification I rapped on his rear window glass and inquired, "Calais va bien?" *Is Calais okay?*

Once again he simply nodded but loudly added, "Moi aussi." *Me too.*

The next couple of hours were pleasant enough in the back of the older Frenchman's pickup truck. I just sat back, relaxed, and enjoyed the rural area's landscape and peaceful quiet for a relaxing change. Also, I was eased by an earlier decision while walking between places in *Paris*. Having some foresight and initiative when passing by another money-exchange shop, I traded another twenty-dollar bill for more francs. My *first* twenty dollars had vanished pretty fast. I was already well beyond my daily allotted budget. I had learned that lodging, food, and entertainment can exhaust funds quickly if I were not careful.

However, I figured that I'd make up for my somewhat overindulgent, *Paris*-spending behavior by living more frugally on the road. Nevertheless, I had plenty of cash funds on me right then, so at least I wasn't going to go hungry. If weather permitted, that evening I would simply find some free coastline shelter once I had found an inexpensive dinner. After a meal, hopefully, I'd locate a nice, safe beach somewhere to camp out and save lodging fees.

Beach Front History

At that next drop-off point, my kind, elderly driver left me right on the entry outskirts of oceanfront *Calais*. With brief "Au revoirs" from both of us, and many thanks from me, I found myself staring at the extremely old, but small, quaint, and industrious sea town with its bordering coastline directly ahead. *Calais* was a nice, modest, seaside-resort town that confirmed my earlier suspicions of costliness. There were plenty of tourist shops, several obviously expensive restaurants, and wonderful, ancient, rock and mortar, historical architecture developed as pricey hotels, no doubt, along with other tourist-like businesses, including any number of souvenir shops.

Also, It was an obvious gathering point, too, for all passengers embarking and disembarking from ferries crossing the famous channel to and from England. I would have checked into that aspect more closely, but as I entered town, I soon found a restaurant and decided to splurge on food. A nice café provided a heaping bowl of clam chowder, lots of delicious French bread, more cheddar cheese, and a Coca Cola. I was satisfied. Then I trudged off to the coast's edge to seek some beachfront, sleeping arrangements, hopefully on a sandy beach somewhere that I might enjoy the gorgeous *English Channel* views.

From nearby information stands, I learned more about the closely aligned coastal neighborhoods and their vivid history. For instance, right offshore before my very eyes was where the English fleet's victorious battle had taken place in 1588 against the infamous and powerful Spanish navy. After previously becoming the first Englishman to circumnavigate the world, the courageous and gallant Sir Francis Drake had become a British household name and national hero while helping lead the English fleet's victorious clash against the world-powerful Spanish Armada. Also, I recalled learning that once returning from his round-the-world sailing venture, Queen Elizabeth I had honored Sir Drake with *Knighthood*, and gossip had it that Drake actually became the queen's own, special *night hood*. As high school students, we snickered all through class over that kind of sexy reading and lecture material.

In more modern times, however, and up the coastline to my right several kilometers north, was where the famous, historically referenced battle and retreat had taken place in the famous sea town of *Dunkirk*. In June of 1940 during WWII, that brave community's residents, alongside British, civilian-boat enthusiasts, and mariners from both sides of the channel, joined in rescue efforts and support that made amazing history. It was where and when the German Army had brought defeat to Allies Forces, thus forcing dangerous withdrawals. Yet, *Dunkirk* became a symbol of Allied Forces unity as the incredibly true story of life-saving evacuations of British and French military troops in their cause against German Nazi advancing aggression.

Also, to my left and south, beginning about an hour's drive away, was where the famous Omaha Beach and other famous beach battles had taken place on June 6, 1944, during the famous D-Day, Normandy Invasion. Considering its date, I was closely nearby for its twenty-second anniversary commemoration. Given the place and time of that unique and special event, I clearly remembered watching graphic and bloody film clips of that agonizing assault while in my high school history class. Sustaining horrible losses on both sides during that slaughterous invasion, the Allied Powers had ultimately achieved victory as their forces, suffering enormous casualties, charged over those blood-stained beach heads while attacking, and eventually defeating, the heavily fortified German Army fortifications. Additionally, for touring visitors' respect, was the nearby French honored,

170 plus acre cemetery site containing graves of over 9,000 American Allied Forces military dead who lost their lives during that horrendous, D-Day landing.

It was a powerful moment for me recognizing where I stood. So much history had occurred right there practically engulfing me from up and down the coastline. I was surrounded by the area's exciting older history and its far more recent, colorful, and numerously posted dedications of facts illustrating and describing all their gruesome details. It was a moving experience full of intense presence and distressing impressions.

Having recently studied in school about those historical events, however, then reading local memorial placards honoring the events and sacrifices, and finally just being there was still difficult trying to absorb that location's full, historical significance. It was hard trying to grasp and fully appreciate the area's incredible past historical references and contributions to those terrible times. Nevertheless, it was a thoughtful and moving experience.

Additionally, staring straight out over the ocean from all my advantageous viewpoints, I could also easily guess what I believed to be seeing. Far across the English Channel before me I could clearly make out a light, almost white, low edge visible within the distant horizon. I was certain it was the popular *White Cliffs of Dover* of England. I had read about them before and had seen pictures several times before in high school history and geography classes.

Those white cliffs were a serious temptation to see up close and personal and then go beyond to visit all of the British Isles too… Indeed, a lengthy English stay was emotionally meaningful. Yet, I was forced to make a difficult choice. I actually considered right then forsaking my European travels and instead crossing the *English Channel* right there from *Calais*, France to visit highlights and sights of Great Britain: England, Scotland, Wales, and across the Irish Straights to Northern Ireland and then Ireland, itself. Oh, what a personal connection I felt with deep ancestral history of British and Irish ties, being a Chapman-McCord descendant.

Both my parents' families, Chapmans and McCords, had strong, family-emigrant connections to the British Isles. I really wanted to visit for obvious cultural, historical, and ancestral interests. Yet, I was certain that a visit there would likely consume all my summer's limited time and constrained funds. No, I soon decided that I needed to stick to my original plan to see as much of Europe as was possible under my vague schedule with its strict, financial restraints. Besides, I had some German *kraut* and Norwegian *Viking* blood in me too that helped keep me more focused on the European mainland.

I promised myself, however, that one day I would return for another journey, and I would visit Great Britain and the Irish Isle. I even hoped to replicate someday that same unique opportunity that I had on that informative, yet challenging, day and finally make the trip to those White Cliffs of Dover by ferry from *Calais*, France. Of course, today you can drive directly to either side via an under-channel tunnel, but I had no idea back then. At that time, though, it really was a perplexing issue for me.

Refocusing on that present moment, however, I studied the immediate coastline below for campsite lodging and I became quite disappointed. It was out of the question as any safe, secure, or comfortable resting spot for a night's sleep. Rough waters, rocky shoreline, and strong winds made camping impractical, if not impossible. But walking further along a coastline path, I got lucky and found a reasonable compromise. A short way up the cliff edge walk, and set inland about one hundred meters, was an empty, wooden storage shed just setting there and used for some unknown purpose; however, *empty,* and *assessable* were the essential factors. No one appeared around the vicinity, and the small, 6X10 shed didn't look occupied, so I simply opened the wooden, rusty-bolted door, bent over, and stepped right on in...

Monster

Inside the shed were a few items lying about: A small, makeshift worktable, a broken and empty toolbox, a couple open crates used for storage of some sort, and a few empty cans left scattered around its interior. Wow! It was a tiny house which seemed perfect for my immediate needs. Safe? There didn't seem to be anybody or anything else that might come around to disturb me. Secure? Obviously, the shed had been there a long time and had weathered many storms, so it wouldn't blow away from potential, high-coastal winds. Finally, comfortable? Once I shoved all the loose items over to the far end, there was plenty of room for me to stretch out. If I closed the door, the strong ocean breezes were all but eliminated. I had a camper's delight for the night!

Everything went well, and I used my sea bag for its other intended purpose. I emptied it of all its contents and carefully stacked everything neatly in piles beside me. Then I took the sea bag and laid it out like a sleeping bag. When I was ready for sleep, I'd just crawl inside and use my blanket to cover my belongings and me up snugly. Warm, neat, relaxing...

I sat by the open door practically meditating on the ocean view's beauty, its surrounding historical impact, and all the while watching the sun finish its incredible setting over those white cliffs far away. The ground was dry and hard, and that was fine with me because I'd experienced a lot of camping before on far less comfortable surroundings. Soon, darkness quickly set in, and after that long eventful day, once I climbed inside my sea bag, pulled my blanket over me, and using some clothing as a pillow, I was soon easily and deeply sound asleep...

* * * *

But like they say, "All good thing must pass," and "Mornings come early!" In an instant, I was abruptly and rudely startled and brought out of my deep, wicked-slumbering dreams of seafarers, charging soldiers, and ear-piercing screams of attacking enemies... In fact, the attackers were swiftly closing in, and then right over the top of me...

"Mon Dieu! Il y a un corps a l'interieur!" came a shrieking cry suddenly awakening me. I imagined that I heard someone in the distance screaming about dead bodies somewhere. *My God, there's a body inside!* Practically leaping from my bedding, another cry rang out. "Eeek! C'est vivant!" *It's alive!*

My wits by then barely gathered, I quickly sat up wailing, "No, no, it's just me!" I immediately remembered where I was and offered apologies for startling them. "Je suis vraiment desole'. Je dormais." *I was so sorry and sleeping.* Then, still so scatterbrained and lost for further words, I promptly stood and began mixing my languages anxiously adding again, "Je suis vraiment desole' to have frightened you. Je pars juste. So sorry, I am leaving now."

Just as I feverishly bent over and began frantically shoving all my personal possessions into my sea bag, and crudely stuffing my ruffled blanket inside too, things just naturally had to get worse. Suddenly, a gigantic, monstrous bear, or some different type of God-forsaken, enormous, mutant-canine species, pummeled its way past the man intruder. Thrusting its massive, mammoth-sized head into my small, overnight-dwelling shed, and then wildly bursting inside, it too was obviously startled and instinctively began growling protectively. With its huge ears defensively lowered and glaring red eyes piercing directly into my own shocked, saucer-sized stare, the beast dropped down for a potential springing attack and a quick kill.

Then, as that terrifying creature started snarling with demon-like growls, it even bared its quivering and immense mouthful of ferocious fangs and began hissing menacingly at me in deep, petrifying, and evil tones. I nearly cried in horror and shock from hearing its evil, canine threat, "Grrrrrrrrrrroooouuugh! Harm my master, and I shall eat you!" At least, that's what my freakin'-out mind was translating.

I didn't scream, though. No, because I couldn't. I was absolutely frozen stiff with fright. All my blood had instantly rushed to my feet. My face and skin paled in the morning dimness. I was categorically overwhelmed by paralysis and unable to move. Alas, I discovered moments later, unfortunately, that my other bodily functions had worked just fine.

But then gradually, thank God, my once paralyzed reactions began thawing. I still had presence of mind, amen, to understand full well the bad idea of extending a friendly gesture or hand toward the potentially malicious and carnivorous creature. "Please God, I want to keep all my fingers, and hand, and arm. . ." But slowly and steadily, I regained my meager composure, and then displaying mindless courage besides my own absolutely close-lipped smile, I gently whispered, "Gentil chien. Bon garcon. Bon garcon." *Nice dog. Good boy. Good boy.*

"C'est une femelle et elle ne te fera pas de mal," the weathered and indignant old man corrected me, somewhat relieving my anxiety. *She's a girl and something about not hurting me.*

All I could think was, "Praise God, and oh good! *She* won't eat me after all. Nice bitch! Good bitch!"

Ever so carefully I began hurriedly dragging my sea bag out the small door and past the beast deliberately using my bag to separate it from easy access to my throat. Once outside, I continued with pathetic, feeble, and excessive prostrations while continuously begging for forgiveness, "Je suis vraiment desole' de t'avoir derange'. Je pars maintenant." *I'm really sorry to have disturbed you. I'm leaving NOW!*

The old man had regathered his own courage and barked out, "Oui etes vous?" *Who are you?*

By that moment, I had already turned away to rush for town and potential safety, yet I called back in vague whispers, "Je suis personne. Juste un imbecile. Juste un idiot endormi." *I am nobody. Just a fool. Just a sleeping fool.*

By then, almost on a dead run, and finally sensing safety, I couldn't help myself. I laughed aloud in stress release and let out a burst of adrenaline-laced, but relief-based, obnoxiousness, "Merci beaucoup et ne laissez pas votre monstre me manger!" *Thank you very much and please don't let your monster eat me!*

The old man and his pet gorilla just stood there next to that ominous, and once again abandoned shed. Both were still reacting as surprised as any vigilant custodians might be as their eyes followed my rapid exiting retreat. No doubt, all the while staring, they were likely just as equally confused as me.

But distance began protecting me by then. So, in a fit of relieved gratitude, I ended our agitated encounter by bellowing appreciation and thanks, "Au revoir! Au revoir! Bonne journee. Bon journee. Passez une bonne journee! Louez le Seigneur!" *Good-bye. Good day. Have a glorious day! Praise the Lord!*

Then quickly, that pleasing shed, the previous night's memory of comforting but warlike dreams, that early, frenzied-morning attack, and the shaken old man with his diabolical creature were becoming lost in a thick haze of fog which I suddenly realized surrounded me. No matter, I clearly and vividly remembered my cross-country coach's warning, "Never look back! Just keep on running!"

And that's what I did. But at that moment, I couldn't help but add my own addendum, "And faster! Run faster!"

Quickly, the coastline was gone in a muddled foggy thickness, and images of the old man and his *monster* had steadily begun vanishing along with my anxiety. My *first* night out camping on the road had ended abruptly and in a bit of a tizzy, but I was feeling safe, grounded, and grateful once again. Yet, I could not help but let the world know my appreciations...

"Au revoir et je suis vraiment desole', je suis vraiment desole'," I cried out with shrill repetitions of *goodbye and sorry.*

Walking rapidly and directly toward the fuzzy, mist-blanketed, and distant town of *Calais,* I couldn't help but think one last time about that poor old, stunned man. He had probably been just as startled as I was. I wondered if he knew I was a crude, French-speaking American, or thought

I was just a vagrant homeless person, or maybe simply crazy. Perhaps, all three. Just another crazy, homeless American wandering around, sleeping in abandoned sheds, and frightening wits out of calm, decent Frenchmen on morning walks with their faithful, loving, and killer-monster pets...

Anyway, I had escaped unharmed and without being arrested. I was relieved enough to catch my breath. Relaxing sufficiently, I finally really noticed the incredibly thick fog bank which had rolled in. No wonder our frightful meeting had been such a shocking encounter for all of us. The old man and his pet monster had probably come upon that supposedly empty shed more unwittingly than I due to the blinding, treacherous fog which had likely hidden the shed's vague shape. Then came the old guy's curious peek inside, along with his pet T-Rex, and "Voila!" an instant triple clash of cultures!

By then, however, I was emotionally exhausted, stressfully famished, and anxiously ready for some hot breakfast and strong coffee. A nice, though extremely early, and foggy morning break would do me good. Plus, I would find an opportunity to empty and neatly repack my disrupted and unkempt sea bag. Also, I can't totally recall now due to memory-anxiety blockage, but I likely had to find a restroom to clean-up and change my soiled underwear too... *Je suis vraiment desole'*.

In the rather small, resort and ferry-business community of *Calais*, I soon found a small roadside café and devoured a delicious meal of hot cereal porridge, more bread with more cheese, and some actual *cafe' americain*. Finally, I was learning to ask for what I wanted, and it helped that I had read it on their menu. Afterwards, I was quickly on my way again walking, attempting hitching, and heading for *Dunkirk*. My plan was to keep right on going past it and into Belgium.

I would try to hitchhike straight to Brussels that day which was located right in the central part of that nation. For some reason, I had a thing about visiting capital cities. I suppose it was because those were typically familiar cities I had studied in school. No matter. *Brussels* was directly on a highway that turned straight north. With any luck, one good ride might take me all the way to *Amsterdam*. *If* I were *lucky*...

With any luck! Yes, LUCK was the presumptive, hopeful, idealistic, and productive word. Following my rather long but enjoyable walk-through *Paris* past all its pleasing sights and cheerfully pleasant ladies, and then during my *first* day hitching, that previous day had gone rather smoothly. Not my second day, though. As I stood outside the north end of *Calais* waiting, with gregarious thumb thrust out for time eternal, it seemed many cars passed on by while ignoring me completely. Obviously, I was not on a decent route, I began assuming.

Perhaps, the issue of any driver's concern, I eventually suspected, was trying to take a stranger, even a foreigner and American one at that, across international borders. Thus, after periodic stretches of boredom, and while slumped there at a decent hitchhiking spot just waiting and waiting for any car to stop for me, I decided that it might just be easier if I simply walked to Belgium. So, I did...

Minor Details

Please understand that I have no intention of offering day-by-day chronicles of all my less than boring travel incidents, every rather bland tourist sight visited, each meal's menu selections, or the multitudes of hapless standstills while waiting for prospective rides to my next destinations. Let's suffice to say that I'll highlight important *incidents,* name most holidaymaker tourist visits, or identify any unusual or unique dietary items varying from my basic, ordinary diet of cheese, meat, and bread, and more cheese, bread, and meat, and well, you get the idea. Due to restrictive budget restraints, food was simply and primarily for nourishment. That's all, and not for extreme deli-delight vacationing. But I'll try to mention any special or non-traditional cuisine enjoyed.

Furthermore, because I ended up spending so much time just standing around with my outstretched thumb waiting for the next ride, a hitcher's dilemma, I shall not continue describing much about those tedious, wasted-time details. It could be obvious that I walked almost daily for several miles, or kilometers, just getting through towns, cities, and often difficult open country in order to find my next convenient hitching post. I understood my predicament, though, of finding potential lift givers, so walking a lot was an accepted component of my travels.

I never knew what kind of person might pick me up, and drivers were never sure of their safety either. One, or the other, could be dangerous. Also, it was always easier to catch rides near intersections of roads. It appeared more plausible given the circumstances. Trying to hitch rides out in the middle of nowhere by standing on the side of a rode or highway was suspicious and often awkward, if not dangerous. So, main roads and easy pull-offs for drivers was much more effective.

However, perhaps now, is a good time to offer a sneak overview and brief sketch of my entire journey while traveling all around the European continent. As a reader, you can easily follow along and keep track. With my trusty map thoroughly etched with travel indicators, I know that I certainly did (keep track). Upon summer's end, I tallied up all my varietal overnight stays using fresh memories and notations from my European travel map as references.

Therefore, it is absolutely accurate to state that out of my total seventy-four (74) day excursion during that eventful summer of '66, I easily calculated all my nightly accommodations. The facts were that I spent a grand total of forty-eight (48) days staying at reasonably decent lodgings throughout Europe, and I camped precisely twenty-six (26) days and nights sleeping mostly outdoors in a variety of rough, crude, or unusual settings, such as bare ground, beaches, or benches, etc.. Although, some sites included really enjoyable and relaxing nights, certainly merely a few, but some anyway. However, attempting to provide accurate details for those more unique or lengthy overnighters, let's agree that simply sleeping on the hard ground somewhere is well, just that: Accepting whatever was available at that time simply in order to crash somewhere free for a night, or more.

Thus, by offering that little informational inset, I may more easily explain the next five days attempting to reach *Amsterdam*. I was hoping to arrive in an expedient period and fulfill that visit with my recent San Francisco contacts. However, after leaving *Paris* the first time, and as far as the next nearly three weeks went including *Calais*, until I eventually made it back to *Paris* again, I slept outside on the ground for a total of eight (8) out of nineteen (19) days. That did not include sleeping at a train station once, or another time walking all night instead. But I'll provide more delightfully stressful details later for all those. Looking back even now, I easily recall how difficult and unpleasant some of those days were, and with none planned for despicable weather. But that entire period, although mentally and emotionally challenging, was quite significant regarding anecdotal circumstances and consequential maturation. I'll explain more later...

Frankly, traveling and hitchhiking in Northern Europe during early summer was so difficult, challenging, and stressful that it was almost enough to break me and send me clamoring back to my cheap hotel room in *Paris* for the remainder of my *Journey*. But I persisted and endured. It helped that most of those rather miserable, upcoming days were somewhat broken-up by variably pleasant stays in *Brussels* and a gratifying, yet confusing, *Amsterdam* visit. Other days mostly passed, however, while standing, walking, and sleeping in the rain or waiting for dry spells inside roadside café stops at various highway interchanges whenever remotely possible. In Northern Europe during June, warm and dry cafes were often convenient places to literally get-in-out-of-the rain, so-to-speak. I would drag myself inside and hang-my-hat for a meal and a temporary break from the season's chronic, torrential weather. But I'll get into those discomforting details a little more later on.

Back to our story, though...

Game On!

After leaving *Calais,* and having walked all the way to *Dunkirk,* I passed by a few souvenir shops that sold trinkets and historical memorabilia about those amazing *Dunkirk* evacuations. It was very impressive, and in one particular shop I could sense pride in the proprietor's willingness to share information. But he too spoke no English, and conversation with him was awkward. So, I quickly perused his shop by studying several items, many exhibits, and various trinkets, nodding approvingly often, but I left quietly and was once again on my way. Walking completely through that town and further beyond, with no one willing to stop and give a decent, clean-cut, charming, and youthful guy a lift, I realized that hitching wasn't always going to be easy. I missed my California mountain hitchhiking experiences. Vastly superior... meaning easier.

I was forced to continue the rest of my march that day all the way to the Belgium border. Needless to say, a noticeably casual and mostly unoccupied border guard was a bit surprised to see some young fellow with a huge knapsack spread over his shoulder come waltzing up to his otherwise boring duty station. The border site was pleasant enough, though. There were varietal groves of trees on either side of the French-Belgian border crossing, and wildflowers were in full bloom all about. From a distance, I could hear loud noises coming from the guard's shack, and the guard inside seemed animated and excited. He was obviously listening to a radio, or something.

Occupying the small quarters while watching for Belgium's entering traffic, the guard was surprised that he finally had something responsible to do. He had to stop listening to his sports game, or whatever, check my identification, and stamp my passport. Most other travelers entering in cars just waved and passed on through the border stop having French, Belgium, or Dutch license plates identifying their vehicles and likely nationalities. I suspected that most of them probably even knew the guard; however, I was a bit unusual, no doubt. For one thing, by suddenly appearing out of nowhere, I realized that I had broken-up his intense concentration of a radio-signal blaring out a game of some sort. All of a sudden, and all at once, I was just there, and at first, he definitely looked surprised, and maybe even a bit annoyed.

"Bonjour! Bonjour! Comment allez-vous? Comment ca va?" I called out all friendly-like to him. *Hello! Good day! How are you? How's it going?*

"Mon Dieu, qu'avons-nous ici? Qui etes vous? Que fais-tu ici? Ou allez-vous?" a surprised guard abruptly stood up and responded in French also. *My goodness, what do we have here? Who are you? What are you doing here? Where are you going?*

Very politely and broadly smiling I answered, "Voici mon passeport. Je vais an Amsterdam." I gave him *my passport* and said *I was going to Amsterdam.*

"Vous y marches?" the guard smiled curiously asking if I was planning on walking there.

I held up my hitching thumb and shrugged my shoulders. Then responding frustratingly and showing my tiredness, I reverted to English, "I hope not. No rides."

"Ah, un Americain. C'est pourquoi!" *Ah, an American. That is why!* The guard laughed pleasantly as he added in mixed French and English, "Oui, tu as l'air si dangereux! Ce sera plus facile ici. Go over there, and I will help you. Bonne chance mon jeune ami." I became very relaxed with the border guard's use of my language and grinned at his teases about my looking so dangerous because I was American. Also, his offer of help was appreciated because I was just a little uncertain as to my border-crossing circumstances. Another *first*-time incident for me.

After the guard officially stamped my passport with a flourish and a smile, he handed it back and pointed again to a vehicle, pull-off point just ahead to catch a new ride. As I was walking away, the guard suddenly asked me which country I supported in the upcoming World Cup. Apparently, what I had heard blaring on the radio was a broadcast of some preliminary game determining entry teams for the "1966 World Cup Soccer Championship." I actually had to learn all that later, because at that moment, I didn't really understand the game or its multitude of international playoffs, so I remained somewhat mute.

Nevertheless, the guard pressed me further, "Which team do you like?"

"Well, honestly," I replied, "I got kicked too hard on my shins too many times in P.E. class, so I don't care much for the game. I like baseball, personally, but if I have to choose, then I'd say, 'The Americans,' of course!"

"Hah!" the guard sneeringly mocked, "You Americans are not even in it!"

"Oh, okay," I replied to him a bit embarrassed. "Where are the games being played?"

Then the guard sounded a bit arrogant and snobbish as he pronounced, "The playoff games will be in England! It is the first time ever in an English-speaking country, and hopefully the last!"

I couldn't help myself next. Having denied myself that *White Cliffs of Dover* visit, I put up a carefree defense and responded, "Well, then, I am rooting for them! Go English!" The guard just scoffed with faked indignation. I could tell he was just teasing. I learned later that by then Belgium had also already been eliminated in the games. At least the guard and I had that humiliation in common.

Later that summer, and at the end of the World Cup Finals, however, I couldn't help but snicker to myself at that silly little, nationalistic, sports-rivalry tit-for-tat with that Belgian Border Guard. It seems that no matter who, or where-in-the-world any sports challenges and competitions exist, macho male, and even female, conflicts just seem to raise their foolish heads and come so naturally to so many fans. I loved rivalries, too, but I also understood that the ol' USA had world domination with baseball, basketball, and American football. Few other nations could even manage to put up respectable teams.

Unfortunately, America had not caught on to soccer yet, so we were, apparently, a fairly lame contesting team. Nevertheless, my snide choice for World Cup Finals winner must have left the guard begrudged because it surely humored me. In the Finals, England actually won 4-2 against West Germany! Toward the end of my travels that summer, when I heard that sports news, I laughed and cheered noncommittally!

With grins and smirks, though, of camaraderie, mutual respect, and acceptance for each other's humble place in the spectators' seats of world sports, we shared waves as I hollered out, "Merci, thank you very much," and then one last "*Go England!*" I couldn't help myself. I then walked over to the guard's recommended hitchhiking zone. Afterwards, a couple of vehicles passed on through without stopping, but shortly thereafter, a lone, luxurious French Citroen Sedan, which had stopped briefly to visit with the guard, pulled over and offered me a lift to a town named *Roeselare*. A ride going anywhere was better than standing still or walking, so I accepted and quietly offered a final wave of thanks to the Belgian Border Guard.

Looking at my map I could see that *Roeselare* was at least getting me closer to *Brussels*, so that worked for me. At the time, I did not realize that it was probably a longer route rather than staying on a major thoroughfare, like the one going to a bigger city like Brugge, and then turning east from there. I was learning, though, and sometimes highway schooling teaches the hard way. But that was life on the road. You gambled every time you got inside a new prospective ride when you were unsure of the driver. Then again, the drivers were gambling too, weren't they?

In an hour or so, though, that quiet driver dropped me off on the roadside and turned in toward his town. More waiting, more walking, and a couple more rides took me to towns further up the highway. I was beginning to feel like I was playing hopscotch, and I started getting frustrated with no decent longer rides. That day was ending, though, and I was getting hungry with no shelter in mind yet. So, I decided that it was time for another break for a meal and finding lodging for the upcoming night.

Eventually, I walked past the edge of a small community and found a market selling my favorite staples. That time I also splurged for some chocolate. Delicious, and I was told by the storekeeper that Belgium's *chocolat* was the best in the world and cheapest with him. How could I go wrong when he was so right? Good stuff!

With my thirst quenched, hunger settled, and sweet tooth satisfied, I wandered around the outskirts of that small neighborhood of *Roeselare* looking for a safe place to spend the night while enjoying the walk through its pleasant community. The mostly courteous and friendly people smiled and seemed to nod approvingly, while a few hesitated suspiciously. I wasn't exactly sure of anyone's reaction, but I always waved back, or I tipped my head in acknowledgement.

After turning back toward my intended highway route to *Brussels*, I chose a fairly secluded spot well off the main roads and in a brilliant field of daffodils and other assorted flowers surrounding a small grove of trees. The rest of the evening and night went well enough utilizing my sea bag/

sleeping bag technique. It worked fine that night with no heart-stopping interruptions. In the morning, I went back to the same store again using their bathroom to clean up. With appreciated thanks to the storekeepers, and some food purchases for the road, I was back at hitching again soon thereafter.

Within minutes, it seemed, my luck changed for the better, and I was given a ride all the way into *Brussels*. The driver's English was good, so we didn't struggle to communicate. When he learned I was going to *Amsterdam* and was interested in staying at youth hostels, he told me that he knew exactly where the one in *Brussels* was located and suggested it for a good place to visit. His idea sounded great, so I agreed and he took me straightaway there. Very decent fellow.

The *Brussels Student-Youth Hostel* was a somewhat rundown, converted hotel that really just needed a little paint to spruce it up. But no matter, it was clean, had shared rooms with two or three bunks in each, and hot running water in communal, gender-separated showers and bathrooms. The rates were extremely reasonable, about five francs per night, and Belgian francs were worth about the same currency rate ($.20) as French francs. Plus, they accepted French francs as currency, as well as Dutch guilders and German marks too.

I also discovered that they would even accept American dollars too, if necessary. Apparently, they had enough USA travelers passing through that they did not mind the inconvenience. Even then, American dollars were often useful almost anywhere. I paid in advance for the coming night, found my room, dropped off my things, and cleaned up again. Then I went back to visit with the managing attendants to seek any useful tips about places to eat and tour that were also inexpensive.

Brussels's Sprouts

The managers there at *Brussels Hostel* were kind, courteous, and extremely helpful. I learned several astonishing and enlightening things about my travels so far, as well as some really useful suggestions for cheap tourist visits and inexpensive meals. A few topics they shared turned out to be quite disarming; others were shockingly alarming. At one point, I even became so embarrassed by my naivete' that I probably turned varietal shades of rose' wine red.

Let me identify and explain a few insights that both my Belgian hostel hosts willingly, humorously, and sometimes awkwardly shared: First, they clarified some of the French rudeness, especially *Parisians*, which I had detected; on-the-other-hand, they also illuminated rather disturbing realities regarding those charmingly friendly, apartment ladies and their actual intentions; they explained about language issues; they educated me about acceptable and exchangeable currency issues; and they told me about common hitchhiking problems for that early summer-time period.

Believe me, I was grateful for my hosts considerate insight and hard road lessons, but immediately following my unintended instructions and enlightenment, I quickly thanked them and retreated for some dinner. I was famished, although the clarity I had received had given me much food-for-thought. Let me explain in more detail...

For one thing, the couple was a husband-wife team, and they both spoke fluent English, as good as my own. The reason for Belgium's multilingauility, they detailed, was that Belgium was a smaller nation bordered by three others: France, Netherlands, and Germany; and four if you count Great Britain across the English Channel. At different periods in their history Belgium had been subjugated by all the others to some degree. Its nickname, they noted, is "The Battleground of Europe." So many previous European wars and other nations' battles had been done over their uniquely located soil. Other countries chose not to destroy their own precious lands, it was noted, so instead they often warred it out over Belgians' homeland.

Therefore, the Belgium government had defensively opted to use most other nearby forms of currency within their own markets. Furthermore, they had passively picked up each bordering, respective nation's language: French, Dutch, and German. Additionally, with the British right across the Channel from the Belgians, which made for easy vacationing in each's country, the English language also came easily. At that point I recognized that Belgians, thusly, were all mostly trilingual, and many spoke at least four languages, counting English too.

It brings to mind a favorite prank joke the two told me while play-acting off one another: The husband began by narrating an anecdote: "Two Belgians, just like us, were talking one day," he stated so seriously. Then turning to face his wife, he continued, "The first one asked the other, 'What do you call people who speak four languages?'"

The wife responded, "You call them 'quad lingual, naturally.'"

"Oh, I see," replied the husband. Then he questioned again, "But what about three languages?"

The wife answered, "You call them tri-lingual, obviously."

"Wow, I get it," proclaimed the husband. Then he slyly offered, "And, therefore, two spoken languages means they are bi-lingual, right?"

"That's right! Now you've got it," smiled the wife. Then she quizzed, "And do you know what you call those who speak only one language?"

"Why, you call them French, of course!" the husband blurted out loudly, and we all laughed heartily...

Of course, since then I have heard that same mocking taunt spoken about the English too, and of us Americans especially. Thank goodness for our own explosive, Spanish-speaking, Latin-American immigration, legal or not. Finally, the USA is becoming bi-lingual... But, anyway, I got the gist of the Belgian managers' humor about the French people.

France is a proud nation whose language was once being considered as the world's international language, not English. I suppose they are all bent-out-of-shape about losing out. Even our USA forefathers were all multi-lingual. In fact, in an extremely close vote at our nation's founding it is traced that by only an extremely close losing ballot, German lost out to English as our own national tongue.

Plus, it is a fact that there are many world countries which speak French as at least one of their primary languages. Those include France, Belgium, Luxembourg, Monaco, twenty various countries in Africa, Haiti, French Guiana of South America, Quebec Province of Canada, New Orleans, Louisiana, and more. Yet, the French language only rates in a tie with Arabic for 5th and 6th places as most spoken language in the world. Of course, English is #1, with Mandarin Chinese coming in a close second, and Hindi next, followed by Spanish. Soooo, "Nous autres, nous sommes vraiment desole', mais je m'en remets, France! Ou nous ne parlerons pas francais non plus!" *We others are so sorry, but get over it, France! Or we won't speak French either!*

Regarding the rude hotel keeper in *Paris*, however, the kind, Brussels managers explained to me that he was probably burnt out and resentful of me because he wanted his own desperately needed vacation to begin. They added too that many Europeans, and especially French, leave their cities and travel south to the Spanish, French, or Italian *Rivieras* on their magnificent Mediterranean Sea for summer vacationing. It is an annual seasonal migration for many French people especially in cities like *Paris*.

I had arrived during a still typically busy time, but soon the French, and particularly *Parisians*, like many other northern European countries, except for Soviet Union controlled eastern-bloc nations, would be heading south for their extended vacations. I was told that when I returned again, *Paris* would likely seem like a ghost town.

The Belgian couple also explained to me that the discourteous, *Paris*-hotel clerk was probably upset and jealous because he wanted his own vacation too, as already suggested. . . Plus, they emphasized, the French socially choose not to speak other languages, even if they are able to do so, likely due to pride issues and superiority complexes over their European neighbors. They noted that, naturally, most countrymen appreciate foreign visitors attempting to speak their host nation's language. It's considered a courtesy of the visitor and a mild form of nationalism of the host country.

My Belgian friends also shared accordingly that indubitably, that *Parisian* clerk had clearly understood me. After all, he was employed in a world-wide service trade, hotel services, and in *Paris*, of all places, an internationally famous and popular city. Both the husband and his wife were certain the *Parisian* hotel clerk was simply ignoring me.

That was when I regrettably tried adding a comedic tone with some naïve humor, "Well, I don't understand. I've always heard that French is supposed to be the *language of love,* right? And *Paris* is the *City of Love,* isn't it?"

That was also a good segue, it seemed at first, when I regrettably reported my impressions of the curiously generous kindnesses displayed to me, a perfect stranger, by all those French women as I passed through their *Parisian*, residential-apartment neighborhood.

At first, the husband and wife seemed puzzled, and then somewhat astonished, looking at each other with utterly baffled stares before studying me more closely and noting my naive face which apparently and obviously demonstrated my pure innocence. Suddenly, clarity seemed to rapidly grasp their comprehending minds, and almost simultaneously they began laughing uproariously. After calming themselves and regaining their civility, they both explained to me nearly in unison, "That *neighborhood* you visited was not so much residential apartments and sweet kindnesses. Actually, you walked straight through *Paris's* famous *Red-Light District!* Those were *working girls! Prostitutes!*"

My knees weakened, and I nearly collapsed from embarrassment and shame at my ignorance. The word *prostitutes* was a term I sort of understood but had only heard loosely used in dirty jokes during my high school gym classes. Oftentimes, in P.E. class, I'd heard jokes from other boys during showers, such as, "One day, ol' Susie *Rotten Crotch* will become the richest *prostitute* in town!" Or another, "When you're lonely, *prostitutes* make the best friends!" I'd join in the boisterous snickering anyway, though never understanding much meaning, and I was always too self-conscious to ask questions. Didn't want to seem stupid. . . However, there in Belgium being suddenly enlightened by my humored hosts, I wished I had asked earlier.

Attempting a meager defense, I blushed out, "And to think I really thought they liked me!"

"Oh, they did, Dearie," soothed the kind wife.

"Yeah," chuckled the husband, "but they would have liked your money even more, if you'd gone up there to one of their rooms!"

They both then explained some valuable *facts-of-life* that had never been explained to me before. They also told me that had I gone up to one of those "working girls" rooms all innocent looking and just expecting to visit, any one of them would have cleaned me out of all my money once they sensed my naivete and ignorance. They warned me too that I likely would have been sent away completely broke.

Then the husband teased, "But you probably would have gotten your money's worth!" He began chuckling until his wife smirked and smacked him hard on his shoulder for his insensitivities.

I was quite embarrassed, though, still not fully understanding the gravity and near peril I had apparently faced. It was enough shame and guilt, however, for me to quietly beg my imagined girlfriend-back-home's forgiveness and promise not to make a fool of myself again. After all, I was out rompin' around the world, and my poor, lonely sweetheart was back home, all alone, and patiently awaiting my return. I mentally promised to make it all up to her after I returned.

So, those several informative and appreciated tidbits from my *Brussels*, life-education instructors were yet other *firsts* on my *Journey*, although awkwardly learned lessons, at that. As I thanked the couple and headed out the front door to investigate some of their food recommendations, I am sure I heard them both laughing raucously again behind-my-back about my gullibility and state of humiliation.

After a while, I calmed down and accepted my circumstances. "It was alright," I confessed to myself. "No harm done except for my hurt pride, and often times learning comes in all forms, and styles, and means, and costs. As long as I learn, that is what's important." Then I chuckled to myself as I considered going back to *Paris* even sooner in order to *learn* some more about carnal knowledge from those cute and insistently friendly *working girls...*

Nevertheless, once I composed myself after absorbing all that information I had been forced to process, I couldn't help but snidely relate to all my learning at that hostel without some humor. After all, new knowledge seemed to be sprouting up everywhere. Thanks to those Belgian, tutoring-mentor friends, I thought of a deserved nickname for my *Brussels Youth Hostel* visit: I called the place: *Brussels's Sprouts!*

More About Me

Now may actually be a convenient or appropriate place and time to expose and explain some other misconceptions about my worldly knowledge, or lack thereof. Let me diagnose some of my personal character for readers' better understanding and/or appreciation. At eighteen years of age, I had never had sex before. I was still a virgin who, due to dominating Catholic influences, practiced complete abstinence including any masturbation. I was even being subconsciously programmed to eventually enter a seminary and become a priest. I know the idea certainly held a romantic tune to it for me, and my mother would have died of joy.

However, I was conflicted. One contradictory issue was that I had spent all my youth dreaming of becoming an army officer one day, fighting in wars, and perhaps even dying in battle. My youthful dream was ". . . to break US Civil War hero and infamous, Indian-territory fighter George Armstrong Custer's record . . ." by becoming the youngest US Army General in American history and then dying gloriously at age twenty-nine. I actually had many dreams of that nature, and my plans for adult life were seriously focused on that theme.

My other conflict and dream, of course, was desperately wanting to marry my sweetheart so that we could have sex!... Thus far we had minimal carnal knowledge of each other, but we had both exhausted ourselves coming close a few times after much bumping and grinding. Each time, however, I managed to regain self-control, and with reassuring kisses I would tell my girlfriend that we were not ready until we could consummate our marriage. I was also concerned that I was not ready for any accidental pregnancy setting back dreams and plans for our futures together. For sure, though, I was getting anxious.

As mentioned earlier, too, I was an honest, clean-cut, American boy. Although not obsessed with our church's dogmatic practices or directives, even still I was a Confirmed Catholic. As a middle schooler, and even into earliest years of high school, I was active with church doctrine. Attending mass regularly, I took confession and communion seriously. Being absolved of sin was mentally, emotionally, and rigidly and satisfyingly enforced. I even spent two years serving as an Alter Boy assisting our local priest with weekly mass services. And catechism was mandatory, not a choice. Talk about conflicted interests.

During my later high school years, however, I eventually developed into a more-or-less *convenience Catholic,* whereby *I* expediently attended mass but minimally practiced church creed. My point is that during my youth I took Catholicism seriously and its instructions to heart. The *Ten Commandments* were a way of living, something to be honored and practiced, and learning catechism lessons practically required solemn oaths of obedience. Thus, waiting until marriage for any carnal knowledge was simply not only promoted but understood as an accepted practice. Yet, *it* was hard all the time, and I'm not just referring to Catholic discipline...

Consequently, devotion to my girlfriend, and Catholicism too, caused inner struggles which developed into sincere, yet confused, natures. As a fairly innocent but rigid belief structure, my Catholic beliefs attributed to many ignorant, uninformed, and misinformed concepts of life regarding most non-pastoral activities. Certainly, I grasped major notions like goodness, love, romance, loyalty, devotion, freedom, and security as well as developing more radical perceptions of evil, hate, unfaithfulness, deception, power, war, destruction, and death. Yet, other tangential principles such as humanism, taking roads-less-traveled, ambition, duty, honor, virtue, and struggle were value studies taught in classes but really appreciated through real-life experience and only truly grasped during one's own, personal, and circumstantial endeavors.

Still, with each of those complex, multi-layered ideas discussed and debated in formal schooling, within value-clarification studies, sex education instruction was still taboo. Learning anything about sexual aspects, or even procreation to any degree of comprehension, came from either private, intense, library-research curiosity or idle, personal and lustful experimentation. Needless to say, there and then, I grasped nothing about intimate or worldly sexual practices or identities. On the other hand, my mind was a mostly empty, yet open, book, a dry, idea-starved sponge with willing advocacy for all new, different, and worldly ideas. At least, so I thought...

Therefore, that newly learned concept, *prostitution*, although still somewhat vague in its practical entirety, continued to be uniquely mind-blowing and an emotionally embarrassing proposition. I suppose *proposition* is the suitable word too, don't you think? Plus, my sudden and freshly grasped awareness, having been indirectly associated with such *carnal* behavior during that early-morning, *Parisian* stroll, challenged my own high standards regarding faithfulness and loyalty. I may have been young, but I was deeply in love.

Fact is, I was also truly hesitant about leaving my beloved girlfriend behind. Ironically, however, she became one of my most influential supporters. She had even informed me that were conditions reversed, she'd be gone in a flash. . . That suggested to me that she wanted fruition for my exciting opportunity. She was happy for me, I believed, and even envious.

So, there you have it. Once school let out for summer, I had defected for a singular existence deserting the love-of-my-life to gallivant off on a faraway adventure embracing new worldly experiences instead of being with her. Unbeknownst to me, however, I had brought along, and carried around with daily cues, quite a bit of raw, naive baggage. Throughout my journey, though, unintentional innocence gradually eased giving way to more worldly enlightenment. However, during that earlier stage of my *world-wise* knowledge schematic, there and then, I still had much to learn about ways-of-the-world. But I would...

CHAPTER 7

....

FINDING MY WAY

Brilliant Brussels

After a lengthy walk around the local *Brussels* vicinity, I found a nice, recommended restaurant and once again splurged on a very decent meal. That time it was a delicious goulash the waitress thought I would like, and it was filling and inexpensive. I learned something else new at that mealtime too, another *first*. Heineken beer was an exceedingly popular brand brewed in Netherlands and apparently distributed internationally. I did not know much about beer, but I learned that it was only about five cents ($.05) per bottle, and I could afford gallons of it at that price. Oh, yes, and after I got past the bitterness, I liked it a lot. So, a couple for dinner and another for the road, or walk in a park, and I was rolling down easy street.

Of course, fiscal restraints and accessibility kept me close to the hostel to enjoy several nearby free attractions during my two days of site-seeing. During both day outings, I walked a great deal but also caught city busses to visit other special, free, and unique sites. Among them were the beautiful *Kanal* waterway that casually meandered through the city, the lovely flower and statue-laden parks scattered everywhere, the 500-year-old, striking-Gothic architecture of the *Grand-Place de Bruxelle* (the Grand Palace), complete with a bustling and wonderful, flower-market enterprise.

Another bus ride allowed me to see two more magnificent cathedrals: *The Brussels Cathedral* is the *Cathedral of St. Michael and St. Gudula*, a medieval Roman Catholic church dating back to the 11th century; and the other was another *Notre Dame Cathedral*. This one, the *Du Sablon, was* built in the 1300's. I also visited the amazing Gothic-construction of the *Palais de Justice*, Parliament Building and Law Courts, the most important law courts in all of Belgium, celebrating exactly one hundred years (1866) since its creation.

Finally, once I heard about it, I was compelled to see one of Brussel's favorite attractions, its 1958 World's Fair exhibit, the *Atomium*. It is a gigantic, spectacular, space-age structure of a single-atom replica, only magnified 185 million times. (I appreciated seeing it because four years previously, my trip-sponsoring Aunt Jean had taken me to see Seattle's *Space Needle* and its 1962 World's Fair). *Atomium* tourists can take elevators to the exhibit's top level and escalators between its neutron and many electron spheres as visitor chambers. Unfortunately, as much fun as it looked on the outside, I could not afford to see the internal makings. Nevertheless, my hiking, sight-seeing, snack-munching, and Heineken beer drinking was really an enjoyable two-day festival for me. Late the next evening of my stay, I returned to repack at the *Brussels's Sprouts Hostel* and make plans to complete that next leg of my trip to reach *Amsterdam*, Netherlands, only a couple of hours away at most by car.

My Belgian hosts had both been kind, supportive and helpful. Besides low-priced food recommendations, they had also told me how to get around town more quickly and cheaply by bus routes. Finally, with my departure, they informed me that hitching may still be difficult because of awkward border crossings and because all the good hitchhiking was heading south for the summer. Most northerners were still working, and the off-season offered little support.

It was explained to me that soon, and especially traveling south, so many other travelers were happily on vacation. Young and broke hitcher guys like me were commonplace, and I'd likely get around much easier. I'd have to work at it, though, until then, and I would certainly learn more about that in great detail soon thereafter. However, for right then all I could hope for was just one good ride, and I'd be there in *Amsterdam*. Piece of cake.

In the meantime, it was time to say goodbye. I would leave early the next morning and attempt to catch any commuter traffic going my way. All I wanted was a ride to the darned border that day, but a fun anecdote humoring my time and worth mentioning is about when I returned that last evening to *Brussels's Sprouts* after a long day and evening out sight-seeing.

Although my hosts looked busy registering new guests, as I passed them I decided to have some fun.

Walking by, I just smiled gleefully while strutting on through the room and deliberately interrupted their paperwork by announcing boastfully that I had actually found *Brussel's Red-light District* too. Then I laughingly declared. "But the difference was that those pretty girls paid me! Now I'm rich!" Of course, if I really knew what I was talking about, I'd have probably added that I was *exhausted* too… Perhaps, only a *freebie* of my ignorance, huh? Pun intended!

At first, my *Belgian Life-Awareness Instructors* were surprised and even a bit baffled; however, my incessant giggling made them clearly aware that I was only teasing. Thank goodness, too, because if they had quizzed me for any details, I'd really have displayed my inexperience and ignorance. We all had a good laugh, though, and it ended our connection on a positive note. At least, I figured maybe they'd remember that naïve, American boy with a humbling, self-deprecating sense of humor. And I'd remember to watch out for myself and any future, curiously interesting and attractable enticements. Or so I thought...

Hard Road to Amsterdam

Long story short, however, after departing from *Brussels*, it took me two days to get to *Amsterdam*. I walked all the way through half of *Brussels* trying to reach a main thoroughfare to Netherlands. No rides came. No offers either and not even any pleasantries between me and locals. Just standing, sitting, waiting, and waiting. Then, finally, one short lift took me near the Belgium-Netherlands border, and while dropping me off in another no man's land, I began envisioning a *Deja vous* episode.

My goal that day was *Amsterdam*. A supposed visit with my contact friends there was still expected, but simply getting out of *Brussels* and into Netherlands began seeming like a reasonable achievement. By then, I was becoming somewhat discouraged, slovenly, and lazy as I continued walking up that long, lonely highway. With my left arm extended but dragging out behind me, I faced forward, not backwards toward upcoming traffic. Occasionally, I'd even flap my hitching arm up and down wildly just trying to seek any attention. As a frustrated hitcher, I was stressing from it and hoping sympathy might soften some hard-hearted drivers encouraging them to give a poor guy a lift.

Therefore, much later on it was a little amusing when after regaining my composure, readjusting my attitude and posture, and returning to proper hitchhiking standards, that a sleek, shiny-black BMW pulled over, and a German fellow offered a lift all the way deep into Netherlands. Unfortunately, he wasn't going to *Amsterdam* but rather soon thereafter splitting off east instead. I was so grateful for a ride that it mattered none to me. Forward, just forward, that was the key.

The driver spoke a little English but minimal French, so our conversation was somewhat limited. However, I surmised that he was a traveling salesman and his route was now homeward bound to *Hamburg* and the Federal Republic of Germany (West Germany). He seemed like a pleasant enough man who enjoyed his work selling household faucets, and about an hour later, we had zipped right across the border with no posted guard questions asked, and I was finally in Netherlands.

By then, it was already late afternoon, I was hungry, and I had to decide about the next leg on into *Amsterdam*. My drop-off point was kind of nice, though. It was close to a main thoroughfare that went to *Amsterdam* and was right off a large river crossing. Also, a brief hike requiring only a kilometer, or so, brought me to a small, quaint roadside café. That was where I spotted my *first* of the famous Dutch windmills. A few were scattered about and seemed very functional, and they made for a nice backdrop to my evening meal and forthcoming night's sleep under a river overpass.

Dinner had allowed me to enjoy the pleasing and picturesque surroundings, plus try out a couple new beer brews. I mentally toasted my German driver by tasting his homeland's popular brands. One was Heinekens, and the other was Grolsch, both pale lager beers. I learned that Germany's famous Oktoberfest, ale-drinking festival only allowed entries into their *Best Beer* competitions who abided by Germany's 500-year-old rule of "No additives allowed into producing beer products, only barley, hops, yeast, and water." I also learned that some beers have a 1,000-year-old history behind them being produced from over 1,000 different German breweries offering thousands of varying brands which also included wheat and oats and other grains to perfect them. For so long, so many places, and so many beers to choose from... a guy could get intoxicated just thinking about it all.

That evening, as I settled into my riverbank undercrossing campsite for the night, I enjoyed viewing windmills in the distance and sipping some other Dutch and German-made beers for a relaxing evening. While at the diner, I had also learned a little history of the unique, windmills in

Netherlands. Many of them are still very functional, I was told, but others were internally replaced with modern machinery and maintained merely for their unique aesthetics.

Their ancient purpose was using wind power to generate pumping of the marshy lowlands and dumping excessive water back into nearby rivers. It dried up the lands so they could be used for planting. Planting of hops and barley, among other grains, I imagined, so my thirst-quenching visit and windmill backdrop turned out to be a complete success. Traffic noise was minimal, the riverside was fairly flat and dry, and the river was smooth and soothing. Those conditions, combined with my beer guzzling, left me content, and mellowed for another stay outdoors. It was okay with me, though, because I recounted my money, and I was actually close to my budget allowance. The cheap *Paris* hotel, *Brussels* hostel, and great outdoors had provided extra savings to afford my touring and all my beer bashing. I was doing alright so far.

The next morning, I first cleaned-up at the river's edge and then again at the café I had previously visited. A couple of workers there, including the chef and waitress, recognized me from the previous day. Though both were a little surprised and curious to see me again, they were pleased and heartily welcomed me. I was a smiling and grateful young stranger in their beautiful land, and they seemed to admire, respect, and appreciate my visit. I even believe they deliberately heaped-on extra-large servings for my splurging pancakes, eggs, ham, and coffee breakfast.

Later that morning, I was back on the highway with my thumb stuck out again and all smiles with happy waves. I had decided, however, to shove my large sea bag back behind me to better camouflage its size and potential inconvenience to drivers. I figured that maybe when standing upright or on my shoulder, my bag may have appeared like two hitchhikers, and thus too much. Tricks-of-the-trade, or hitchers' rules-of-the-road, I determined...

I laughed to myself recalling some *hitching* experiences up in the mountains back home. Back there during summer times, or anytime actually, several of us guys might be hitching somewhere. So, one of us, usually me, would stand out next to the road and thumb a lift while the others would hide in nearby bushes concealing our intentions. A car would stop, and then suddenly a rush from my friends came, and we'd overwhelm the driver with kindness and extra passengers.

"Oh, thanks so much for stopping, Mister (or Mam)," I'd usually begin. "Here come my friends who were just over there taking a leak (or something). But don't worry, we won't take-up much space at all. Thank you very much. We are, uh, so late for a... a party. Oh, uh, what party? It's a... a swimming party. Yeah, that's it. You are really helpful. Really appreciate it."

Then I'd yell at my buddies, "Hurry up, guys! Climb on in. We don't want to keep this nice (person) waiting..." The others would all chime in too with loud insistencies of thanks...

Whatever *tricks* I used that morning there in the Netherlands after rejoining the road, it still took so long for a favorable lift to arrive. Finally, though, my auto coach did stop, and I was breezily chauffeured into the city of *Amsterdam* completing the remainder of my hitching leg that day. Conveniently, I was taken all the way into the central part of the city too. After goodbyes were exchanged, I found an English-speaking Dutch antiques shopkeeper and showed him the address for the city apartment complex I sought.

I was told that my San Francisco friends, who were apparently spending the entire summer at their rental apartment in *Amsterdam*, were nearby, but not that close. I was already at the outer edge of Central *Amsterdam*, and my friends lived in *Central Amsterdam* too. Unfortunately, with the suggested route I needed, that meant little. *Amsterdam* is a huge city, and my map's kilometric math key determined my destination to be about three or more miles away, about five kilometers.

Piece of cake, though! I felt like I could do the remainder distance in a run if I chose. I didn't even care about figuring out *Amsterdam's* bussing system but rather just enjoy the walk and new sights instead. So, I just flipped my bag up to straddle both my shoulders, lifted my arms to hold it in place, and gleefully marched on up the boulevard. I felt unhurried and unworried. No matter what, even if my contact friends were gone, I'd think of something else, an alternative to suit my needs.

With luck, I'd have a decent place to stay for the night and, hopefully, a shower too. But I would simply have to wait and see. Who knew what was up? Maybe I'd end up on a city park bench for the night. Or, or maybe I'd accidentally stroll past another *red-light district* and some nice girls would ask me to come up and visit with them overnight so they could *make me feel at home!* I grinned feverishly but instinctively shoved my wad of money even deeper into my front jeans pocket. Also, once more I apologized to a mental image of my scowling girlfriend too, "Sorry, love-of-my-life, my tainted imagination just momentarily ran amok again."

Four's a Crowd!

Soon, though, I found myself standing there on a wide sidewalk across a street from a main avenue and staring up at the tall apartment complex I sought. My friend's apartment was fairly high up I determined, so I mentally begged for an elevator to be available. It was, and in no time I was once more standing and looking up. But that time it was at the room number above my contacts' apartment entrance door.

I had done it! It had been eight days since my arrival in *Paris*, and just as I had promised, I made my word good. The only issue was whether they were there at all and if they had any spare accommodations for me. Naturally, I was a little tired and a little hungry. No, actually I felt starved! Knock! Knock! Knock!

Three knocks, three seconds, and *whish*, the door opened widely. Suddenly, there stood, closely gathered, all *three* members of my expected San Francisco trio: Dick, Dwayne, and Ron. Immediately, their obvious shock turned into joyful surprise, and they shared in delight of my accomplishment. All seemed well. The *first* leg of my European Travel Tour had been achieved. I was excited that I had managed the *first* of two committed connections initially planned two months' earlier. There is something fulfilling, meaningful, and prideful of keeping one's word. A *promise* is a *promise*, and anything less kept requires an excuse. And like they say, "Everybody's got those. *Excuses* are a dime a dozen."

My Aunt Jean's San Francisco trio were an interesting lot. All three were Bay Area Professionals. One was a middle-school teacher, another was an engineer, and the third was a medical specialist. They all had been friends with Jean and her roommate, my unofficial other aunt, Phyllis, for quite a long time; however, I had only recently met them that I could recall.

Jean and Phyllis had many friends and often gave parties that brought them together for visits. Their friends came from all over to visit too. In fact, two other close lady friends, Tommy, and Mickey, were also roommates and lived near my high school. I had actually spent my entire senior year living with them during school weekdays. They too were both professionals and treated me with great kindness and support. At that time, I simply understood that Jean and Phyllis had many *professional* and/or artistic friends, and most of them had roommates. Professional roommates, I just figured. Odd? Unusual? Who cared? I never even thought about it much.

Anyway, I had made it to *Amsterdam* as agreed upon and promised. It had taken me nine days to do so since my *Paris* landing, but that was certainly acceptable. After all, I was essentially walking, with only occasional rides in between, it had seemed. The guys were captivated with highlights of my adventures thus far, although a bit dismissive of some tales such as my stroll through the *City of Love*; however, they especially enjoyed my *Calais* monster-dog story. Anyway, the next couple of days there in *Amsterdam,* site-seeing with my friendly San Francisco contacts, began enjoyably, then turned a bit weird, and finally ended abruptly. Before I knew it, I was back on the road again, alone and on my own once more.

However, though, giving credit where credit is due, that first evening and the next day allowed my friends to show me an enjoyable slice of *Amsterdam* that I would not have otherwise experienced. After I had showered and dressed, they took me out on the town and treated me to a delicious and filling café dinner of sauerkraut, sausages, and Coca Cola. Afterward, we spent a couple of hours just wandering around touring their neighborhood.

Amsterdam is a beautiful, impressive, and clean city with so much brilliant, Gothic architecture, hundreds of years of historical events displayed everywhere, and magnificent, ancient churches on nearly every block, it seemed. Sometime into the evening, though, we all stopped for yogurt desserts, and I suppose it became obvious to the others that I was running out of energy. After all, it had been two days on the road, and I needed some decent rest.

That is when things first became just a bit awkward, and my naïve impressions and expectations were challenged. Once returning to their apartment, right away excitations filled the room. There were more joyous salutations and Heineken beer cheers which flowed freely, and we all laughed with raucous behavior as I poured out additional details of my recent travels and explorations. Dick, Dwayne, and Ron all seemed impressed, and expressed a desire in showing me a great time there in *Amsterdam* while I remained. They even suggested that *Amsterdam* could be a wonderful city for me to remain in and visit for the entire summer, which was thoughtful, but they were already aware of my travel plans still ahead, so I politely brushed that idea aside.

It had been a long day and night by that time, and my head was beginning to swirl from drowsiness, so I was the first one to bring up sleeping conditions. I began surveilling their living quarters and finally took the verbal lead. Graciously, I queried, "I really appreciate the evening and your guys' hospitality, but what are the sleeping arrangements? I am really bushed."

Each of them paused momentarily, and then one of them, I forget which, pointed through the single bedroom door to a king-size bed and announced, "Right in there! There's room for all of us."

I was puzzled and looked even more closely to perhaps discover a hidden twin bed across the room, or even a cot. But nothing else was in the bedroom. Just that one, huge bed. I'm certain the puzzled look on my face was obvious. I was still a little confused, so I persisted.

Pointing to their long, living-room sofa, I queried further, "But which of you sleeps on the couch there? After several nights on the hard ground, even your thick, soft rug right here is appealing and would be generous."

Another of the three spoke up with emphasis while repointing to the big bed, "Oh, no, not at all. There is plenty of room for all of us in there."

In my mind, I simply could not justify why three grown men all shared one large bed with their gigantic couch going untouched. It made no sense to me whatsoever, but I was eager for sleep, so I pursued my own personal interests. "Okay, guys, if this is okay, then it's fine with me. I'll just use my own blanket, though, and sleep like a baby right here on your sofa. But if one of you changes your mind, I will gladly move to the rug and be very content."

That ended the discussion, and I quickly retrieved my blanket and easily stretched out on the couch and fell asleep shortly thereafter. In the morning, I awoke totally refreshed and noted that the guys had covered me with another blanket of their own. Very decent. Their bedroom door was closed, but soon all three were up and breakfast was prepared. That was when I expressed more appreciations and mentioned how my daily budget was really being caught-up and managed nicely, thanks to them. There was a big day planned ahead, so we all were all off and running in no time. Plus, the guys had their own car rental, a green Volkswagen Beetle, so I saw so much more than usual, even if much of it was through a car window. Just being there was incredible. I loved *Amsterdam!*

The day was filled by my three tour guides continuously pointing out all sorts of interesting details about the city and its public visitation sites. What was especially impressive to me were all the free, natural exhibits and playgrounds spread out around *Amsterdam.* We drove past several of the city's beautiful canals and its colorful marketplaces. We stopped for a brief visit at the locally popular Vondelpark, a huge water and tree-lined country-park, and then cruised over to the famous Dutch Gardens. I smiled as I began thinking that their outdoor, parklike tours were on purpose for my sake, being a country boy at heart. I appreciated their gesture, and the outdoor beauty exhibits of *Amsterdam*.

Later, we drove down by the dock yards, and it was there that I spotted the absolutely enormous Shell Oil Refinery with its numerous storage tanks and exporting-distribution center. My father had spent many times working in refineries during what are called Shutdowns, where areas or sections of a plant are closed for maintenance, repairs, and/or new construction. I was really impressed partly because I recognized the household name, Shell Oil, and because of my father's contributions to their construction operations. Little did I realize, however, that years later I would become a boilermaker construction, welder like my dad, and work indirectly for Shell Oil Company in the California Bay Area. Small world.

Continuing our tour, however, the remainder of our day was spent passing and visiting another famous and magnificent church, *Basiliek van de Heilige Nicolas*, or St. Nicolas Cathedral. I remember laughing, and calling out, "Good for you, Santa Clause!"

The cathedral was less than one hundred years old, but it had been built representative of several revival styles including the Baroque and Renaissance eras. It was particularly stunning at nightfall. I would remember to keep tally and tell my mother of all these promised church and cathedral visits. She would approve.

On yet another drive, we stopped again for a special paid visit to the *Van Gogh Museum*, Netherland's favorite son. *Amsterdam* has the largest exhibit of his paintings in the world, and I was fortunate enough to see other exhibits of Vincent Van Gogh throughout my travels. He seemed to be a popular artist everywhere I went, and I'm sure to mention other museums honoring him later once I get there.

Anne Frank & Yogurt

Another walk down the city's streets alongside another wonderful canal, and I discovered one final tourist attraction when accidentally spotting it while simply passing by and looking through store windows. It was a small, very unobtrusive door right next to a little shop with a modest sign hanging above: *Anne Frank House.* Wow! Eureka! I had read her famous diary in school, and suddenly, I had an opportunity to bring her writings to life. It was amazing. A narrow stairwell leading up to an apparent trap door that, once lifted, allowed visitors to climb up into an extremely tiny shelter.

It was the very same hiding place wherein Anne Frank and her family had remained hidden away. Anne stayed there until she was ultimately discovered, arrested, turned over to Nazi occupation authorities, sent to a Jewish concentration camp, and died there at a young age from ravages and ultimate Holocaust execution during WWII. Her book, The Diary of Anne Frank, has mesmerized readers the world over ever since, including me. It was an agonizing, yet heroic, portrayal of the difficulties sneaking around and hiding out in that tiny attic shelter from German authorities for over two years until their capture. The tiny room, a vivid museum, itself, was shocking, sorrowful, and so impactful, especially having read Anne's own life story of hiding there, Powerful.

The remainder of the evening was spent with more walking, chatting, sight-seeing, and just enjoying *Amsterdam's* beautiful streets with all their glorious shopping sights and delights. It was actually on one such street that we splurged for one last special outing. I was actually thrilled and delighted to find out that my next evening's meal was another treat from my hosts, as a goodbye gift, or a reward, I supposed. No matter, I ate my fill of Dutch meat pie, drank a grog they called cheap beer, and had more helpings of my standard breads and cheeses. It was a fun, energetic, boisterous, and filling gastrointestinal delight. We all laughed incessantly enjoying the entire meal's revelry which even then still did not conclude our exhausting evening.

After leaving their VW sheltered, we continued walking even further enjoying our late evening. The neighborhood was packed-to-the-brim with so many beautiful, centuries-old architectural structures and historical, monumental statues cornering every street. Along our unscheduled city street tour, my friendly trio showed me my *first*, specially designated smoking rooms. I know now that many of those tobacco-coffee *rooms* eventually became *Amsterdam's* famous cannabis smoking rooms and coffee shops. Back then, however, they were just gathering places for men to smoke tobacco, drink coffee, and share company.

Later, having already developed a different kind of addiction, we fed a gnawing craving for another vice: Authentic, original, and specialized yogurt. We found an overabundant and overwhelming yogurt shop where I once more heartily overindulged devouring *Amsterdam's* finest creamery-craft delight. The fellows were all really great guides and had brought about another thoroughly enjoyable day there in *Amsterdam* and another entertaining but wearying nightfall. My brief stay with Ron, Dick, and Dwayne had been far more appreciated than they likely understood and so much more comfortable than any prior nights' sleep on roadsides. However, for me it was time for bed, though. Or, rather, the couch. I was leaving early the next morning and was already welcoming another night's sleep.

Returning that night to my friends' apartment, however, began a second minor episode in my summer's mini-series of unusually awkward situations. Once inside their comfortable residence, my kind, San Francisco-*Amsterdam* friends seemed distracted. It was quite late, and I was bushed just like the night before, so I did not hesitate undressing, brushing my teeth, and seeking the couch once again. Right away, the guys all but imploringly offered to share their King-size bed with me for my sleeping comfort. Still baffled, not grasping any potential consequences, I easily deflected their offers and immediately stretched out again on the sofa... "All of us sharing that one large bed. Weird," I thought to myself.

"No, thanks, fellas," I kindly refused while thinking, "Four is definitely a crowd!"

Pulling my blankets up under my chin, I reemphasized, "This spot is heaven, Guys. You have no idea how nice this is compared to hard ground with just my sea bag and my blanket as a sleeping bag. But honestly, I'll take the rug in a flash if one of you wants this couch. I really don't want to intrude..."

There was no quibbling after that. They respected my wishes, and they also soon retired for the night. Early the next morning, once again I was up before dawn when I cleaned-up, packed for the road, and waited for my friends to arise for our goodbyes. Shortly thereafter, we all had morning coffee, cereal, and roles together, talked briefly and appreciatively about our visit. With well-wishes all around, I made way for my exit.

Then Ron surprised me with an interesting proposal. He mentioned that in about twelve days, he was traveling solo by their rental car to *Paris,* then Spain, and finally on to *Rome*, Italy before returning to *Amsterdam* at summer's end. He asked if I cared to join him two weeks later in *Paris* and travel along any part of his trip for convenience. Well, I figured that I saw through his friendly ruse immediately. Perhaps even with my aunt's support, Ron was attempting to track me. I may have appeared indignant at first, but the idea of company on the road, and Ron's travel plans generally coinciding in a favorable direction for me, was enticing.

So, the idea sounded reasonable, and I accepted. But it was clearly understood that the plan would only work if I were able to successfully reconnect with him some way. We agreed that I would attempt to locate him once I returned to *Paris*, and I would certainly try to be there on time. However, I heavily emphasized to Ron that if I was a no show, or even a day late, then he was not to wait around on me at all. It would be my responsibility to contact him, not his.

But right off, I thought of an idea for a reconnection solution. I gave him a business card I had saved as a souvenir from the *Left Bank Hotel* I'd stayed at in *Paris*. That way Ron could find the hotel and either of us could leave a message for the other. Potential problem solved. If I kept to my timeframe faithfully, then hopefully I'd have a comfortable ride south to… wherever.

Go East, Young Man!

Moments later, my bag was shouldered and I was on the street once more. That time I was smiling broadly again for the upcoming day's hike, but I felt clean and fresh, well fed, and restfully energized. The most stimulating part of my plan at that point was that I really did not have a *plan*. I had not made up my mind yet for my next destination. I told the trio that I wasn't sure where I was headed next, but that something would come up, no doubt.

Then a solution came to me right away from my European map. While walking alongside the very same canal that we all had leisurely followed the night before, I took a momentary break and spread my map out on a city park bench. Only briefly studying Northern Europe and my present whereabouts in *Amsterdam*, I immediately saw my future. Modeling Horace Greeley's famous cheer for mid-1800's American West development, I cried out, "Go East, young man, Go East!" *Berlin* was calling!

With my next quick glance, it became abundantly clear. First, to *Hamburg*, West Germany, or Bundesrepublik Deutschland (Federal Republic of Germany), I would go! And then on to *West Berlin*! Well, it was *East Berlin* that fascinated me the most. One special layover that I had dreamed about for my journey was traveling beyond West Germany and into the Eastern Block of Union of Soviet Socialist Republic communist countries. East Germany, or Deutsche Demokratische Republik, or German Democratic Republic (GDR) was my goal. *Berlin*, or rather *East Berlin*, was its capitol, and it was a must-see city, I felt.

East Germany, with its *East Berlin* capitol, was an official communist state. I had read so much challenging material about that nation, and city, and the Soviet Union in school. With America's intense, anti-communist fervor and present conflict in South Vietnam against the North Vietnam Communist Vietcong nation, sponsored and supported by the Soviet Union's Communist ally, China, I dare say that I had a rather youthful, romanticized view of communist politics. It was Mao Zedong's and Marxist teachings about *power to the people*, and all that, I suppose. My youthful fantasies went wild with imagination: *Down with bourgeoisie capitalist pigs and up with working-class proletariat. Glory to honorable labor over wealthy ruling classes.*

It was just the kind of passion a young boy might feel coming from a struggling family, and industrious, union-member, laboring father. It was also a contradictory conflict when mixed with my youthful, personal designs of one day becoming a US military officer. Somehow, I wished to someday join a struggle that might correlate both and change the world to a better place. Oh, I was certainly a *God Bless America* patriot, and all that. I simply wanted to make it better by being more representative of working classes. At that time, therefore, East Germany and *East Berlin* promised the best and closest means to better observe, learn, and understand communist dogma by doing direct, immediate, and personal research for my dilemma.

After all, I had been fascinated in school with Russian history, including its dynamic and dramatic, 1917, world-changing revolution into its present Union of Soviet Socialist Republics. Add all that to Soviet Marxist-Communist ideals and the USSR's vital role in WWII defeating Hitler's evil Nazi regime, which resulted in Germany's postwar split-up, and *Berlin* thus became my second choice, communist-run city to visit, right after Moscow, itself, some day. It was, therefore, a potentially exciting place of interest for me, if I could pull it off. I'd see. Oh, boy, would I.

CHAPTER 8

RAIN ON MY PARADE

Petrichor

I still had time before Paris, nearly two weeks,, and I wanted to go north to complete my European circle. I looked forward to seeing another part of my family's heritage by visiting Scandinavia, if possible. True, I anxiously wanted to travel through East Germany to visit *Berlin*, and especially communist *East Berlin*, but I then decided that I would do that visit on the rebound from travels further north before my eventual return to *Paris*, in order to meet up with Ron again.

So, I decided right there and then to hitchhike to *Hamburg*, West Germany first and then turn sharply north and make a call on *Copenhagen*, Denmark! After that, "Hello, Sweden and Norway!" It would just depend upon dollars and sense. Enough *dollars* to keep traveling further north and enough common *sense* to accomplish it and still get back to *Paris* on time to meet Ron, . . . or not. I'd find out. Obviously, I had a lot more planned to see and do before returning to *Paris*.

Thus, the next leg of my so-called adventure began right there as I was leaving *Amsterdam*. I was ready for anything. I was used to walking, that was certain. After all, I had tripped-the-light-fantastic all about *Paris*. I had walked clear out of that city too. I had tried hitching out of *Calais* but ended up marching clear up to the Belgium border. I had walked a massive amount in *Brussels* and practically hiked clear out of that country on foot too. I had even strolled with friends continuously throughout *Amsterdam*, and I wasn't done walking yet. Not by a long shot.

For one thing, it seemed drivers just didn't care, like, or trust giving rides to hitchhikers within city limits. My sea bag may have appeared obtrusive or too bulky too. Plus, it wasn't wartime in Europe, I wasn't in uniform, and so it must have been obvious that I was no sailor. Anyway, I quickly adjusted my mindset to *go-east-young-man* strictly on foot, at least until out of town. So, I marched on toward the city outskirts with my left thumb extended yet dragging behind me to provide the impression of a hitcher, while I steadfastly trudged up the main street leading out of *Amsterdam* toward West Germany.

I had already walked out of France and practically walked out of Belgium. By then I began sensing that I was about to walk out of Netherlands too unless my luck changed soon. Needless to say, it did not, and not until much later, hours and hours later, and kilometers and kilometers further. However, let's also just say that eventually my luck did begin changing. . . True, but wrong. It got worse. Big, cumulus thunder clouds began rolling in overhead, and the air started taking on that very distinct, dry smell in the air, and calm tension. In fact, they call it, "The calm before the storm." They also called the unique smell, "Petrichor," and it was a true sign of rain coming.

Yet, I wanted nothing to do with that potential rainy-day misery, but there was little I could do except keep-on-keepin'-on. So, I simply lumbered on further up that main boulevard looking for some access point to seek temporary shelter. Occasionally, I stopped, turned, stared down oncoming traffic with wistful, begging eyes, but there was little sympathy, it seemed. Eventually, I began feeling and watching large raindrops splattering about me, so I quickly made a detour off the main road and found an abandoned business facility of some sort.

I spotted a dilapidated overhanging, probably once used as a carport covering or something, but it was large and dry underneath. For the storm, and what turned out to be the remainder of that day and night too, it became my own, personal king-of-the-road residence. I set up my bag's belongings dead centered underneath the overhang shelter and spread out my sea bag and blanket for a bed on the concrete slab beneath to wait out the storm. And wait and wait is what I did.

Actually, before the guzzler really started coming down, I sneakily cased the empty building looking for any easy entry access. *Nobody else seemed to be using it, so why shouldn't I*, was my rationalization. But there was none, and I was not going to break any windows just to get inside. I wasn't desperate, but I did want to stay dry. Being and staying dry developed a whole new significant meaning for me from then on. Okay, it was a rough, and then wet, restart for my hitchhiking campaign, but at least that early summer rain was a warm one. And for the remainder of that day, and well into that night, I did stay dry even as the late June storm poured its crying heart out to me.

Early the next dry morning, I was up and at it again and back facing traffic with a smile. Finally, I caught my first decent ride that took me to the town of *Bremen*, West Germany. Once again, while in a car there was no trouble crossing a new border, so we just kept on cruising along and making good time. Little talk, just acknowledgement from us both, and soon I was let off near the outskirts of *Bremen*. The previous rain had given way to only threatening clouds, but it was clear enough to walk, and I did just that after having breakfast and cleaning-up at a small diner. Fortunately, I had French francs to use as trade for Deutsche marks, so pricing and calculations were fairly simple. The German currency, marks, were worth about twenty-five cents ($.25) American, so it was easy for me to trade; five francs for four marks, both equivalents to one American dollar.

But that also became the "adjustment" part of my *road story* too where I began taking shortcuts... *Shortcuts* in every which manner. I took *shortcuts* through towns walking straight on through to continue my walk's advance. I took *shortcuts* through open fields, if I noted closer paths to my next needed road to wherever, and that next time was to *Hamburg*.

Some small towns where and when I was left afoot often meant unusual courses zigzagging through them in order to continue on to my next destination. Many towns had one-way streets which conflicted with my own wanted direction, so I often walked against traffic to shorten the distances. I also took *shortcuts* through interesting looking towns and cities by bypassing and skipping their potential tourist attractions altogether. And there and then in West Germany it was looking more like I needed another shortcut too, one that could somehow bypass those awful looking clouds above.

The reason was because I had already received an initial weather report warning. The previous day's surprise rainfall had also brought with it a notorious message: "Northern Europe's 'Rainy Summer Season' was beginning." And I had received no prior telltale warnings. No one had advised me of such. The weather's *natural* signs simply came as a taunt that previous day, and then they stuck around to torment me for the longest time.

Rains came and went, sometimes for minutes, and other times for hours. Sometimes they came and stayed all day, other times all night, and occasionally it rained all day and all night. The simple fact was that the next eleven days were filled with on-off downpours often leaving me stranded and simply stuck out in frequently drenching, skin-soaked wetness.

My stubborn goal was still to visit my family's partial heritage of Scandinavian countries, so I maintained a desperate focus, as planned, on *Copenhagen*, Denmark via *Hamburg*, West Germany. It rained and rained and rained, and I walked and walked and walked. Finally, right there on a major street passing through some small town, with rain pouring off my doused outstretched thumb, a decent break arrived...

Hamburger Joe

If it hadn't been for rain, my spirits would have been much better. Standing under occasional roadside building alcoves merely provided temporary and minimal protection from those huge, black, on-and-off soakers pouring buckets of soulless, spirit dampeners over me. But, finally, my luck did change, and a *Hamburg*arian citizen resident of his beloved *Hamburg* rescued me. Finally, I would see that city that very evening, after all, while listening to my driver's enthusiastic, German-only tour guidance. Yet, I was happy to be anywhere in a car, even if it only meant *out of the rain*.

Once in a while, it was really fun to get rides from people whose zeal is truly catching. In order to *catch* it, though, one must be mentally preoccupied with a need to *catch* something, even anything. Occasionally it required having an open mind, or one might really miss the unusual. And sometimes, like that very upcoming ride, it might even be the *unforgettable* experience. For myself, at that particular moment, I was ready to catch *anything* to avoid more rain. And finally, such a fellow stopped for me, and I certainly did *catch* a wildly entertaining change.

Right off, I recognized that my new driver marched to the beat of a different drum. Actually, I thought he was from the *Dark Ages,* about ten years previously, the 1950's. He drove a souped-up, rear-end elevated, metallic, green Volkswagen Bug with super-oversized, racing tires and loud, rumbling-like exhaust pipes. His ride had all sorts of interior, multi-colored lights glowing, and when he stopped his car for me to get in, and he then honked his horn, it blasted away blaring a crazy, funny, "Aaahhhooogaaa! Aaahhhooogaaa!"

It was hilarious! Brilliant! And I loved it immediately. Then the driver quickly reached over, flipped the passenger door wide open with a bang, and just hollered, "Reinkommen! Steig schnell ein!"

Initially, I misunderstood him. I figured he had said, "Rain is coming! Hurry up and get in, stupid!" But I was only partially right. It turned out to be more like, "Come in! Get in quick!"

Either way, I did not need any explanations or encouragement. After lifting his passenger seat forward, I tossed my sloppy-wet sea bag onto his wildly decorated, covered back-seat, apologized profusely at my discouraging wetness, reset the passenger seat, and practically leaped inside to join him.

Right off, he started laughing and shouting, "Hey, ich heiBe "Gustav." Komm rein und raus aus dem Regan"

I had no idea what more he said, but it was welcoming and sounded something like, "I am Gustav, and get in out of the rain!"

But that *Hamburg* driver's character was so funny, charmingly disarming, and curiously interesting that I simply had to laugh, enjoy his persona, and just go-along-for-the-ride. He was a hilarious and amusing kickback example from a B-rated, James Dean-era movie, and I was totally captivated and infatuated with his voice, mannerisms, and charisma. He wore a black leather jacket over a pure white T-shirt, with an assortment of dangling chains around his skinny neck. He had on denim jeans, maybe not Levi's, but they looked crisp and clean for hygienic effect. His clod-hopper boots bottomed off his pure white socks and were a terrific balance for his slicked-back, jet-black, duck-tail hairstyle.

And honestly, I swore I noted a hint of rouge and lip-coloring highlighting his pale, facial exterior and more than an overkill hint of smelly aftershave. Besides all that the guy's funny facial silhouette wore plastic, black-framed sunglasses offsetting sharp edges of his nose and chin. Wild! Crazy! Silly! Fun! Anyone would get a big kick out of this Wildman and just enjoy taking it all in.

Truly, I laughed to myself thinking about how James Dean would have been jealous! However, it didn't just stop there with his circus-dressed characterization, or his genuinely wild car, or even his silly, loud, horn sounding off like detonation warnings. No, and go figure! To top off the whole, ridiculously explosive vision for my inexperienced views of European young life and interests, this guy was blasting away on his car stereo with loud, powerful, and ongoing repertoires of Bach and Beethoven symphony audiotapes. "Who was this guy, and where did he come from? Mars? These crazy Germans!" I thought chuckling heavily inside. Maybe, I thought, since the war, they weren't sure who they were anymore, so they tried to be everyone everywhere. I didn't know for sure, but it was definitely entertaining.

Upon closer inspection of Gustav, though, while he happily and haphazardly zipped speedily through his favorite little burg, *Hamburg,* I recognized other idiosyncrasies about him that really did cast quite a unique characterization. For one thing, Gustav really did look like he had just stepped off a Hollywood set for some sort of weird James Dean bio. Deliberately clashing with his hairstyle, giant boots, denims, and leather jacket, Gustav was also just reeking of pungent aftershave and costume jewelry. Thick, silver chains hung around his scrawny neck, silver ornaments of some strange creatures, sea serpents, I guessed, dangled from his ears, and chains also sagged from his wrists. Plus, there were silver bobs and buttons and military-like ribbons decorating his jacket pockets, lapels, and shoulders like wartime badges of bravery.

Furthermore, every finger digit, including his thumbs, were also adorned by various sizes, shapes, and colorful styles of wood, metal, and plastic rings. No doubt about it, ol' Gustav was an original. There was no one else like him in the world, I was certain. Probably because no one else wanted to be! But he was a real card, and he was a crazy, silly joy to be around. Besides, it was raining again, and Gustav was definitely more fun than being soaked by miserable rainfalls...

His eccentricities hadn't mattered either. I had been alone long enough in that outside, miserable-wet world already that I really needed some honest companionship, and this fellow promised just that. Right away, I was instantly converted to his likeable lifestyle, averted from a wretched alternative, and reverted to a pleasing time offering hope, promise, and a really good time. I simply laughed right along with ol,' fun-loving Gustav and joined in while discovering an entertaining ride experience until its ultimate conclusion.

Furthermore, almost immediately, it seemed, he needed to stop for a hamburger, and Gustav emphasized his hunger by shoving fingers into his mouth repeatedly as though he were trying to train me, his pet chimp, to understand and mimic back in return. But, I did understand, laughed heartily, and joyfully agreed. Gustav quickly located his favorite dive and abruptly whipped his VW straight into a parking spot coming to a screeching, sliding stop. He did the choosing and ordering and retrieved fairly decent hamburgers for both of us at the self-service, buffet-like joint.

It was another *first* for me, though, as "Hamburger Joe," I decided to call him, prepared a meal for me, apparently, to both save time and demonstrate his gastronomic knowledge and skills. Our hamburger sandwiches consisted of sausage and sauerkraut in a bun with lots of German mustard! And it wasn't bad . . . Either that, or I was ridiculously hungry. No matter, *Hamburger Joe* craved his, and he pleasingly let me know it, too. "Das ist gutes Zeug!" he laughed and bellowed loudly. And it was *good stuff*, I had to admit. In fact, the whole, otherwise nasty, but entertaining evening with its tasty, culinary delights, was pretty special...

After our meal, I got *Hamburger Joe's* personally guided tour, and that was hilariously amusing too. I understood truly little of *Joe's* enthusiastic descriptions of places that he showed me, yet his enthusiasm was infective, like an emotional contagion, and we both laughed profusely throughout his animated, but unfathomable, descriptions of everything. How big was *Hamburg*? Joe's hands stretched wide apart while releasing the steering wheel from his grip as he demonstrated its enormous size. How beautiful were the women? Joe whistled loudly while waving his hands together madly demonstrating a woman's hourglass figure to emphasize his candid points, "Oh mein Gott, Tolle!" *"Oh, my God, Amazing!"* Yet, I also learned so much by piecing together all the street ads right along with his amusingly vocalized antics.

For another thing, *Hamburger Joe* smoked like a chimney. He was a chain-smoker who seemed uncomfortable without a cigarette dangling between his right-hand, middle and ring finger, or better yet, hanging from his underbite lip. I recognized filtered cigarettes, so I immediately had a self-serving inspiration. "Hey, Gustav!" I jokingly tested, "Do you like American cigarettes? Salem's?"

He sort of understood. There really is a lot of commonalities between English and German languages. Nevertheless, I reached back, dug around through my damp sea bag, and retrieved a carton of my Salem cigarettes. Hurriedly ripping the box apart, I lifted a pack and practically shoved it in Gustav's face offering, "You like? You want? I will sell cheap!"

I wasn't sure what all he said, but it was obvious. "No way!" he just laughed, "I like my own, und da Germs make da bes cigarettes, und cheaper, und dey are made right here in *Hamburg!*" His direct refusal was obvious and pointed.

So much for that sales pitch, I thought. Well, maybe the next sucker, er, American cigarettes lover, I thought, would finally take them off my hands. I was tired and frustrated just trying to keep them dry inside my sloppy and rain-soaked sea bag...

Anyway, *Hamburg,* turned out to be just like *Amsterdam,* a big, harbor city. It was huge and so widespread and beautifully mixed with ancient architecture alongside modern steel and glass skyscrapers. It's 750-year-old history made it the third largest port in all the world behind London and New York City. But just so that you understand, however, my *Hamburg* tour took place through the rain splattered windows of a Volkswagen Bug vehicle. *Hamburger Joe* spoke little English, and my German was "so gut wie nichts," or *next to nothing.* But *Joe* was so excited pointing out several highlights he believed I should appreciate that he went out-of-his-way to buzz up a few side streets just to show-off his own favorite stomping grounds.

It was late-afternoon, but I could still tell much from the wet, rain-splattered, stone pavements of *Hamburg's* medieval streets. They all sliced directly through interesting blends of ancient and medieval buildings crowded together with newer, modern architectural structures suggesting some areas were vital, active centers of tourism and activity. Laughing excitedly as he pointed out colorful sights and specific buildings to me as we passed by, I became aware that Gustav was trying to explain where he had previously been *active* with past girlfriends, or lovers, or *prostitutes* in his past.

Definitely, he was a happy-go-lucky chap with his hard, crude, sticky, German language making-no-bones about his previous, youthful, local rendezvous. I understood most of his robust, sexually suggestive animations, but I could only fake my laughter, occasionally nod my faked understanding, and pay him respectable homage and attention. No matter what happened, I was not interested in being dropped-off suddenly and having to walk out of that region in the rain regardless of my lack of understanding for so much of Gustav's obviously colorful language.

As my VW Bug Tour Guide gregariously continued with impressions of his fascinating city, Gustav eventually specifically drove us through a unique area which he seemed expressly proud to reveal. After only a couple blocks, it was obvious to me that we had entered into *Hamburg's* own, red-hot, thrills-abounding, world-famous, Red-Light District, whatever that meant. That zone was no *Parisian*, apartment-like neighborhood, I'll have to admit. It was too obviously obvious!

Even I understood by then where we were. Unmistakable night-clubs, or strip-clubs, or party-clubs were jammed side-by-side one, after another, and all with their own, uniquely glorifying billboards, street signs, and still unlit, but obvious marquees, advertising the night's coming attractions: "Madchen! Madchen! Madchen!" Or "Liebe, Lust, Sex, Spaß!" Or "Und noch mehr Spaß!" *Girls! Girls! Girls! Love, Lust, Sex, Fun! And more fun!*

And none of those local businesses even attempted hiding, camouflaging, or hinting of their deviant industry. And though my imagination was struggling trying to work overtime grasping the entirety of that district's erotic commerce, the whole, exotic-tour experience ended as a huge flop It came suddenly to a soggy let-down, or rather a disappointing wet-down. I was definitely being escorted through *Hamburg's* showcased "Ladies-of-the Evening" zone. I grasped the emphatic illustrations of my guide's demonstrative tour, but normal, male-hormone effects, excited by any momentary erogenous thrills, were just washed away by the coming evening's completely depressing rain downpour.

What a time for Heaven's skies to piss all over my otherwise stimulating field trip. In my unusually curious disappointment, however, I imagined that perhaps, in some peculiar, watered-down way, I was being rescued. My typically, sexually stimulated mind was like an open, desperately blank book begging for words and pictures, or experiences, to fill-in its pages. Instead, I got torrential downpours soaking my visions' paper-thin sheets into sloppy, indiscernible, and discardable trash.

All I could do was bow to God's wishes and let the good times roll on past. Perhaps, it was His way of protecting me from any potential, self-destructive tendencies if I were left alone any further with Gustav to gawk and gander aimlessly through those streets searching for carnal enlightenment. Only God knew what I may have found. . . Later on, and thoroughly discouraged, I simply whimpered, "Well, I never *found* nothin'!"

My initial hesitations regarding traveling further north, however, began surfacing just as Gustav finally pulled over at *Hamburg's* outer limits, and I exited my VW host's Bug, shook Gustav's hand, waved, and offered my simplest, "Danke und tschuss." *Thank you and goodbye.* Fortunately for both of us, the rain had temporarily subsided. Gustav could easily have left me marooned on a street corner with only hand signals pointing out my next directions. On-the-other-hand, I still gratefully and gracefully held my head up while I temporarily and proudly marched on through that momentary relief from much more soon returning heavy rains...

So Sad

Ever heard of SAD, or *Seasonal-affective-disorder?*. . . They say that the syndrome is most commonly seen in regions like Seattle, Washington, and Scandinavian countries (my present destination). In those places, I have read, it rains so often that the drenching climate patterns lead to widespread depressed moods due to all the miserable, bleak, dark, and gloomy weather. Let's also not forget that there is sound statistical evidence showing that more suicides occur in the State of Alaska than anywhere else, and that is a commonly known region located in the storming dark for half a year. And who knows how many sad Canadians take their own misguided, forsaken, and rain drenched lives each winter?

Is anyone keeping track? Could it be the cold, damp weather, or just the isolation? And yet, many people appreciate rain, however, suggesting all those romantic song lyrics like "Just listen to the rain" and "Raindrops keep falling from my eyes" have been written as testimonials to painfully forlorn rainy days and nights' powerful melancholic mood swings.

But, honestly, coming from Northern California, I certainly have a keen affinity for rain, and heavy rain, at that. It keeps our forests and brushlands dampened to lessen fire risks and aid with forest fire extinguishing and control. At higher elevations is snow, and both united together, melted snow and rains, fill up our lakes and reservoirs for water reserves, entertainment, and irrigation. And who doesn't enjoy those cozy, relaxing *plip plops* of "raindrops falling on (our) heads?" Nevertheless, rain wasn't supposed to happen in summertime. At least not in California, nor supposedly back there and then in Denmark, which at the time was my only basic, frame-of-reference. Summers are supposed to be sunny, bright, and cheery, not dim, dark, and gloomy.

Yet, there I was smack in the middle of 1966 desiring and struggling to go further north and deeper into my family's plush heritage of green and lush Scandinavian landscapes, at a time when monsoon weather conditions were ever threatening everywhere. Those several following days were shocking circumstances for me having received no advisory warnings nor absolutely any considerate planning. What should have I done?...

I quickly acquiesced to God, and Mother Nature too, declaring, "I shall enjoy it! Love it! Embrace it! It's all part of my glorious adventure. Daniel, just go with it and take it to heart. Mush! Mush on! Push on further. *The sun will come out tomorrow*!"

Well, I did, but nice weather didn't. . . From the point of my previous, *Hamburg-Red-Light-District*-fan, driver's drop-off point on *Hamburg's* northern city outskirts, the weather had remained calm but ominous with an obvious stench of *petrichor* filling the air. To me that nauseating smell of rain's intimidating calm and damp dryness was disturbingly threatening. *A calm before the storm*, it was.

Shortly, though, another sympathetic driver gave me a brief lift right past his own stop and clear on to Denmark's border, where he then apologetically dropped me off, turned around, and returned back to his own hometown. It was nice of him, though, and at least there was still no rain at that moment, I noted. However, as I got my passport stamped again, also came the guard's firm, English greeting, and adverse warning: "Hallo Du. You better find shelter, or you going to get very wet!"

Those words were both wise advice and a prophetic alarm. From the guard's station, I continued trudging up that two-lane, Danish highway toward *Copenhagen* when those lousy, dark, and angry clouds finally burst open and began heaving another soaking deluge upon me like rudely tossed blasts from buckets of water. Only it was actually more like standing underneath a river waterfall. The rain wouldn't stop, just continued with unrelenting force, and I couldn't help but stare up into the brooding sky noting that its deepest, darkest, and most ominous rain cloud in the entire heavens seemed to be directly over my head... Go figure.

Furthermore, after several hours had passed without mercy, or merely an iota of rain stoppage or lessening, or even any sympathetic passing vehicles, I began detecting an unstable psychosis developing within my frustrated mind. With each drenching moment, I became increasingly convinced that the nasty, overhead fire hose squirting down from directly above was seemingly not only pumping water openly on me alone in haste, but I felt like it also had a specific agenda in mind. It *seemed* to be traveling slowly and steadily northward, deliberately maintaining its own speed synchronized to my walking pace while pausing its forward movement to specifically adjust itself and coincide with my advances. If I stopped, it halted. When I moved, it began moving forward again… Frustrating… Annoying… Irritating… Exasperating…

When my miserable, rotten, and wretched cloud finally blew on past, and rains finally paused for a brief period, the night had finally passed. I hoisted my bag back over my shoulder again and began desperately racing from my immediate, temporary night's shelter found under trees somewhere alongside that highway and resumed my pace heading up the highway. More cars passed, but still no one stopped. Who wanted to ruin their cars because of that stupid, obviously American kid "… who was too dumb to even come in out of the rain in the first place? He should have starved to death at the airport!" Hours more passed by, and only my sloppy footprints on Denmark's muddy roadside remained, with even those eventually being washed away by morning's returning and persistent rainfall.

In my mind, I actually swore I could hear humored driver's voices laughing and shouting as they sped on past, "Soaking fool, you're not getting in my nice, dry, warm, and comfortable car. Besides, you're too stupid to come in out of the rain!"

I then actually began hearing my dad's grunting, scoffing, and taunting voice from the back orifices of my mind's listening post, "See, I told you so. Maybe not *lost at the airport, or starving,* but still *too dumb to get out of the rain!*"

"All of you, stop with all that 'stupid and dumb' bullshit!" I screamed aloud to the heavens above. "You're not helping!" "Enough is enough! Dad, I get the point!"

When the rains started up again, I'd run to get under the closest trees for minimal, temporary refuge. As soon as another weather break came, I'd jump back on the road and look beseechingly at all upcoming traffic. I even began trying all sorts of obscure, untested, and unproven *hitching* tactics attempting to gain attention, empathy, and sympathy: I waved my arms with an outstretched, hitchhiking thumb flagging cars as they passed by; I even began jumping up-and-down and twirling round-and-round for drivers' amusement and entertainment struggling to seek their compassion. But all I ever received was disparate apathy. There was no sympathy, nobody stopping or even slowing down, and no rides. I was going nowhere except by foot…

Much later on, I began hearing even more imagined, vehement voices from passing drivers' insensitive and cursory thoughts, "Oh, no. You are a crazy, soaking-wet person with a giant, sloppy-wet bag, and you ain't getting' in my nice, clean, dry car... no way, no how, and to nowhere..."

And then, naturally, as night began arriving, with its ominous darkness camouflaging my surroundings, it really started raining, and raining, and raining . . . Unstoppable, uncaring, and punishing, it was either God having an angry fit demanding more prayers and penance for my past infantile sins, or Mother Nature having a delightful, comic-relief scene from her latest, untimely, and disgusting stage play, Tears of Laughter! Unfortunately, I was to find out that *Mother N's* act wasn't just a *scene*; it was a three-act crisis performance and merely a dress-rehearsal for coming attractions.

Oh, did I forget to mention that this part of my dubious journey was also my *first*, real test of *manly metal*? Didn't I mention earlier that I would eventually spend so many days and nights resting and sleeping on the ground and on sloppily, inconceivably soaked ground, at that? Well, maybe I didn't emphasize that unnerving point enough, but I should have. Those days there, deep inside Denmark, were becoming critically clear to me that something had to give. Or else, someone, like me, was going to break.

And eventually something or someone did give... Was that rain I felt falling off my chin, or was I actually crying? Unfortunately, it was not Denmark's miserable weather that time; it was me. But it wasn't boohooing tears. No, it was mad, pissed-off frustration. How dare nature rain on my parade! I'd had just about enough.

And yet, I persisted with my ineffective hitching hopes, and still nobody came to my rescue. For another day and another night, I walked in and out of the rain occasionally seeking sanctuary under the thickest of roadside trees. There were all sorts of broad-leafed retreats to choose from: Birches and Maple trees, especially. They were all found along the tree-decorated highway and were beautiful, abundantly plentiful, and somewhat protective, fortunately, for when downpours became climactic. When it became even darker after the sun's setting, and still having dragged myself much further up the highway, eventually I gave in for nightfall.

Eventually, I trudged over to a nearby grove of trees and made a raised bed of leaves under a thick, leafy tree as a bed for the night. When possible, I even sought out long, dried-up, broken branches to hastily lean up against a tree's trunk and made a queasy, make-shift lean-to for additional protection from the rain's unsympathetic punishment. Then I heartily covered those branches with all the tree leaves I could muster-up as natural rain cover.

Next, I overdressed with as much of my excess clothing attire as I could manage to help cushion me and then covered my other personal items with leaves.

Finally, I protected both my belongings and my second-use sea bag with my dampened blanket for additional coverage from the relentless storm. Having by then already laid my bag out once again as a sleeping bag, I climbed deeply inside, crunched-up my cramped legs, and leaned for the night against the trunk of that specially selected Birch tree. As I sat there through the constantly dripping, rainy night, I glared indignantly at all the upcoming traffic while mimicking scolding, irritable words of displeasure at their hitchhiker insensitivities...

Rain, Rain, Go Away!

Alright, that's enough of this wallowing in self-pity. But *wallowing* sure is the right word, alright. You get the point, though. My *journey's* adventurous theme anthems had dramatically changed during that brief course from *Paris* to Denmark. Whereas my initial, fun-loving hymn which brought me to Europe in the first place was that exciting, patriotic-WWII ditty by George Cohen, "Over There, Over There!" it casually had maneuvered itself into Andy William's romantic, soft hit, "A Summer Place" about peaceful solace found during summer rains. However, that melodic chorale did not last long and was soon thereafter rudely and abruptly displaced by another core, symbolic, straightforward, gut wrenching, and imploring appeal, "Rain, rain, go away, and never come back another day... Just stay away forever and ever!"

Imagine that monotonous tune screamed out boldly over and over again repetitiously for hours on end. With a continuous barrage of sarcastic, boisterously made-up, and nearly hysterical lyrics, my downed spirit steadily declined even more which added even more to my slowly drowning mood... But don't get too hard on me. Even then, I did not quit.

Occasionally, I even sat under trees waiting for breaks in the clouds, and then I would make mad haste dashes up to the road waiting and seeking another potential ride to save me from potential death by drowning, or even from myself. I was actually beginning to visualize the following day's local, newspaper headlines: "Stupid American Youth Caught in Rain Drowns in Roadside Mud Puddles!"

To make matters worse, my mind began hallucinating as I even envisioned my own father's reaction: "I knew it! Too dumb to..."

"STOP! Enough! Leave me alone!" I screamed at myself trying to regain my troubled composure.

Then, I would race for another grove of trees during spontaneous deluges seeking more shelter and trying to rescue my suffocating mind. Occasionally, however, sympathetic short lifts would come that took me brief distances, usually up to the next highway turnoff or to a nearby town's café or gas station where I was able to enter and at least keep dry for a while. If it rained, I'd just sit, drink coffee, and wait it out until I could quickly get going again once the rain temporarily eased for another five seconds, or maybe six. Or so it seemed.

My misery was compounded by yet another night out, forsaken along the roadside, sheltering under some scarce spruce trees, or seeking refuge in another grove further down the road with still more wet sleep, and all my stuff getting soaked from carelessness. I was getting so frustrated that I hardly seemed to care anymore. I kept asking myself, "Daniel, where are you going, and why?" Or "Why are you going, and where?" And the ultimate, crisis question, "Why aren't you leaving, and when?" That last challenge began formulating greater and more serious tension as each additional, miserable, rain-soaked hour passed.

That next morning unsurprisingly brought with it an ultimate kick-in-the-proverbial butt. Of course, I was stinking-filthy, sloppy wet. I clearly understood that no sane driver in their right mind would ever even let me ride in the back of their empty, pick-up truck. Or, so, I rationalized. Then, out of the gray, dim atmosphere, a curiously odd sight began manifesting itself in the distance. As I trudged on further up the highway seeking nothing in particular to serve or support my future anymore except a closer rear-view memory of my previous night's near-drowning debacle, I saw something... It was a strange, gleaming radiance far away to my right. And then, suddenly, that image struck me like a conceptual thunderbolt.

I couldn't believe what I was seeing. I looked hard at that vaguely peculiar vision while studying and challenging it with compromised eyesight. Finally, I stood carefully under a rain-protective tree and pulled out my trusty, damp map to check for references. "My goodness!" I realized. "It had to be!"

There, far ahead in the vague, rain-clouded distance, and across some huge, magnificent bridge, was most certainly my goal. Eureka! It was my

Holy Grail, my Holy Land! It was none other than that amazing, shiny city across a bay. It was OZ, and I was certain it was *Copenhagen,* Denmark. . . It was there, right there before me, and I had made it! And that was when I really broke down...

Danish Turnabout

I actually recall slowly beginning to shudder with relief, then full-scale shaking as I broke free from anguish's bondage and shed a few tears of joy and gratitude casting away anxiety's trauma. With little help but my own two feet to dispatch lengthy distances for me, I had made it far enough to fulfill a wish: "Get to *Copenhagen!*"

And that is exactly what I made myself believe. "I *had* done it!" I had conquered Denmark with all its nasty, drenching, and Puritanical, God-forsaken elements.

And that was also when I really challenged myself: "Who actually *needs* to see up close that shiny, but disgustingly muddled city, anyway? Not I, anymore. Perhaps, next time," I conceded.

And that is also where and when I made my next dramatic, or traumatic, move. I *quit*! Right there and then, I waved a kiss goodbye to *Copenhagen,* faintly whispered some empty promise about ". . . seeing (you) on the rebound, . . ." did a spontaneous *turnabout,* and started walking right straight back toward Germany. I had done it, so I was done. Done in. No more. And no regrets.

I did not care to go north any further. No more, no way. I had been through enough. Scandinavia in the future? Perhaps, when I had more dollars than (sense). By then, all I could fantasize, however, were blue skies overhead and scorching weather toasting me on clean, dry, burning, *Mediterranean Sea beaches.* I ever so desperately wanted and needed to go south right there and then, just like all those city vacationers I had heard about. No wonder everyone else got to heck out of Northern Europe's pitiful, early-summer flood zones.

Regardless, it still wasn't really any dramatic transitional decision. The vile, angry storm covering did not suddenly break apart allowing for a miraculous, Christening sun to at last come beaming through. Heaven's, no! Hell's thick, blackened, and incensed sky covering would not allow God to shed His glorious light, thereby spreading abundant joy, and peace, and harmony to all! Hell no! Rain continued pouring over the top of me like a perpetual fountain gagging, choking, and soaking me for the next day and a half as I walked, and waited, and walked some more, and waited some more.

It wasn't until another day and a half, and late into that God-forsaken, drenching afternoon, that I finally reached on foot a previous stop I had visited a couple days earlier. I was sloppy wet, soaked to the bone, and all my belongings sounded like they were sloshing around in a dousing pool of water inside the heavy bottom of my then frustratingly hefty, canvas sea bag. Many concurrent clashing thoughts began racing and colliding within my mind.

I challenged myself to leave right then and return home to the loving arms of my forlornly missed sweetheart. I recalled the previous summer when she and I had frolicked so gaily on the lakeshores near my home. In fact, those thoughts substantiated my considerations to bail out of that maelstrom completely and go directly south to *Rome* and the *Italian Riviera*. In time, however, I recalled Ron's offer to meet up with him again in *Paris* and then travel along with him for a decent ride and his company. And that was the relaxing reminder needed, however, to refresh my present goals and appease my frustrations.

At that café-store-gas station, I cleaned-up as best I could, squeezed my sloppy-wet, bagged garments free of excess water, and bought a cheap meal. That time it was a large bowl of potato soup, with Danish rolls, and cheese, of course. For a change, I had a nice, hot cup of tea and several refills to sip on just to promote feeling sorry for my miserably defeated self. And then, right there, while killing time by just gloomily staring out at the dreary, dark-gray sky and rain-soaked landscape through the café's large plate glass windows, two, odd-ball manifestations occurred: One was mental, and the other visual... Let me explain about both...

Salem Witchcraft

As mentioned several times already, at that time I was feeling all gloom and doom. Oh, yes, I finally felt a little better about heading south for the *French Riviera,* eventually, with its promise of excitably hot, exuberant times ahead. Yes, well, that would happen right after a few wanted diversions *first,* of course, like *Berlin* and *Paris*, again. But right then while sitting in that dry café somewhere there inside Denmark, and basically on my way back to Germany, some mental operational attitude cracked inside me, and I became overcome by an extreme idea. At least, it was *extreme* for me. I had been water-logged for over five straight days already, and naturally, much of my belongings had become soaked too. But I suddenly began thinking about those still dry, not water-soaked, blasted cartons of Salem cigarettes.

For one thing, my wet sea bag had gotten much heavier carrying them around all the time. It became worse too as the bag got wetter, with water eventually even seeping inside and mixing with all my stuff. That included the cigarette cartons too. The cartons' thick, outside-wrapper paper was close to becoming saturated; however, the individual cigarette packs had all remained dry thanks to their crisp, tightly sealed packaging. With that factor recognized and appreciated, I then created my *business-backfire* plan, or bankruptcy idea, or *make-myself-feel-better-by-lessening-my-load* strategy.

Ol' *Hamburg*er *Joe* Gustav had also played a significant role with my decision-making plan. I had been shocked to find out that he did not want to buy any of my Salem cigarettes, at all. For one thing, they would have been too much for him to afford. And secondly, he liked his German cigarettes better, anyway. I had actually checked around inside those cafés and gas-station stops and found his comments to be true. Germany, Denmark, and likely every other *American cigarette* hating country in Europe all had their own, preferred native brands.

What I had believed to be real was *only in the movies!* And Europe's packs of cigarettes cost about one fourth as much as I would have needed to charge for my non-rain soaked and saved Salems, even with zero profit for me. Plus, I had already been lugging those hefty cigarette cartons around for two weeks, and then I realized that it had been for nothing. I'd never sell any of them to hopeful "Salem" cravers anywhere. Those damnable things were just dead weight for me.

Next, I rationalized three additional supportive points: First, if I dispensed of that extra *dead-weight*, my load would thus lighten respectively making things easier for me; plus, I would not have to worry anymore about keeping them dry, once they were gone.

Second, I had been so stressed out from Mother Nature's chronic drenchers that maybe smoking a Salem cigarette now and then would calm my frazzled nerves. At least that is what TV and magazine ads and the *movies* all postulated. Plus, so many adults, including Jean, my construction-worker dad, my older Navy brother, my *Amsterdam* connection trio, and then even Gustav all smoked too. How could they all be wrong? Perhaps, I needed to find out if smoking was actually relaxing on my own.

Next, I had another powerful memory flashback of reasoning. I easily recalled summer days during my elementary school years living with Aunt Jean and working for her during summers. I had already concluded that Jean partially lived a rather vicarious and imaginary existence through the characters' lives of her own favorite author, Samuel Clemens, or rather, Mark Twain. She loved stories about Tom Sawyer and Huckleberry Finn's experiences and lives on the 'ol Mississippi River. In fact, that region is also where she and my own mother grew up, and Jean loved reminiscing about spelunking, or cave searching, along the Mississippi riverbanks. As a successful author, herself, she even wrote many tales about life within the Mississippi Valley.

Oddly, I believe she may have even desired transferring her *vicariousness* onto me in some strange way. Fact is, as a young youth, ages six to fourteen, Jean used to take me on many adventures to Mexico, and Canada, and all points in between. She even allowed me at young ages to explore all over those Berkeley and Oakland hills with no supervision. Furthermore, and this was a real catcher, Jean never paid me money during summers while working for her. No, instead she paid me with inclusion on her own fun expeditions and with cigarettes. I was overjoyed to earn them both.

In my own mind, living in those Berkeley, California hills, helping to dig construction holes for projects, and carrying materials while she and her roommate, Phyllis, built incredible, residential homes overlooking San Francisco Bay, I was in hog heaven. In my own mind I was similar to Tom or Huck, and I loved it. So, I rationalized that since Salem's were also Jean's chosen brand too, she would also approve of my smoking them. . . Are you enjoying my mental stretch so far? Are you catching my drift? (Pun intended). All the smoke and all...

Finally, and this next argument was probably the weakest, but I was stretching anyway: I simply rationalized that smoking would also warm-up my insides during those cool, wet northern breezes and chilly nights, especially while it was raining.

So, there was my defense and I had made my case: Lighten my load; relax and mellow out; become an adventurous adult; and warm myself up during rainy and chilly times.

My business acumen had gone *bankrupt*, however. Besides, I also sold myself on the *smoke-'em-if-you-got-'em* idea, right after that brief interlude of irrational contemplation. So, I went straight up to the café' register and took several free books of matches off their countertop… "See," I noted to myself defensively, "Europeans all smoke too!"

Fetching a pack of cigarettes from my damp bag, and then really trying to protect the remainder packs by wrapping them all up even better, I opened my first pack of Salem's, walked outside momentarily, lit one up, inhaled, and coughed my guts out… Oh, no, re-smoking did not come easy. I had forgotten a little bit about the dizzying sensations, and my lungs had probably repaired themselves enough by then, since my youthful youth, to be re-tormented again.

But, like they say, practice makes perfect. And let me close this feeble anecdote by adding that I did *practice*. I practiced a lot, and I rapidly tore through all twenty of those packs throughout that summer's remainder, right up until I was also buying cheap, nickel ($.05)-a-pack European cigarettes and ultimately becoming just another pathetic, twenty-year smoker. Bad business… Bad habit… *Salem Witchcraft*, it was…

Happy Cows!

Now let me share a little about my *visual manifestation*. A short time later that same day and after a slight break in a downpour, I got up, said thanks and goodbye to the café/gas station/mini-market proprietors, and headed out again down the highway a bit further. Still tired from earlier walking, still getting splashed-upon from exhausting rains and a few passing, rude, insensitive, could-be, should-be, but weren't hitchhiker friendly drivers, I greedily sought out my new chain of smoky friends for company and humor.

In short order, I had earnestly and comfortably become hooked and preoccupied with my newfound, cigarette-smoking habit while steady streams of Salems dangled *Gustavishly* from my lips. Without rain to wash away my smoke exhaling effects, or extinguish my cigarettes completely, I impressed myself by how quickly I had redeveloped, and then improved upon, my childhood smoke-blowing skills. Little rings, big rings, then little rings being puffed out and shot through larger, expanding rings. I was a natural, and it a wonderful, time-killing mood manager. I might be walking in the rain, but at least I was cool, just like James Dean or *Hamburge*r Joe.

Eventually, no thanks to the rainy heavens above and while backtracking my earlier route, I eventually reached yet another previously visited, roadside business. It was still open and seemed welcoming for my return. I remembered it as a nice, pleasant restaurant/bakery just right for relaxing once more inside and resting a bit while I *got in out of the rain, Stupid*! Of course, the storm had thickened and rains were really pouring down as I shook myself off of excess drainage at the shop's entranceway. So, it was a huge relief stepping inside the establishment's dry, warm, and comfortable environment simply just to get out of Denmark's intolerable weather again. In fact, it was the very same waitress from a few days earlier that assisted me again.

"Hallo weider. Willkommen zuruck. Wie war Kopenhagen?" Something about *Hello and welcome and how was Copenhagen?*

I didn't even try to hide my zero Danish or German skills, but I first attempted using a little French to impress the pretty server. "Je n'y suis jamias arrive.' Mais je l'ai vu au loin et c'etait magnifique!" *I never made it there. Too much rain. But I saw it in the distance, and it looked beautiful!*

The confused waitress just sort of stared at me for a moment apparently not comprehending my French either, or intent. Then I remembered her English was probably much better than my French. So, I repeated my words in English, and she quickly smiled. I realized that those Danes were all likely multi-lingual with Danish, German, and apparent adequacies with English, but they all refrained from speaking French too. Comeuppance, I imagined. So, we babbled a bit in easy, simple English phrases, and then I broke out another Salem cigarette to show-off my adultness. I was certain she was impressed with the way I let my cigarette cling to my lower lip while speaking at the same time. What a stud, I was... James D. and Gustav would have been proud...

I ordered coffee and some authentic Danish rolls, and then after a brief time, a delicious, Pastrami sandwich and more potato soup. I had avoided several overnight lodging fees due to my free, outdoor, and complementary waterbed sleeping quarters, so I could easily afford another major daily meal. My budget restraints were somewhat under control. Afterwards, satisfied by the food, I just slumped back in my cushiony table seat and relaxed while burning and sucking-in another taste-killing, chain-smoked cigarette to mollify my mood...

And right there was when my next manifestation occurred. And right then was when something very weird happened...

I was just sitting there, placated, enjoying the rain-soaked, green fields and tree grove landscape across the highway. It was then that I actually witnessed the darndest sight. It occurred right there across the road and well up inside the tall, wet grassy field beyond. I tell you I was stunned...

Across that highway, in the adjoining pasture's panorama, I could see an entire herd of cows all romping around, stomping, and slopping about in those muddy fields. They acted like joyful pigs sloshing about carelessly in their muddied pig sties. Some were actually prancing about, I swear, and it looked like they were all actually dancing in gay frivolity. And all during that very same, continuing, and awful downpour that had just then driven me inside for shelter. It was as though those cows had never seen, felt, or experienced rain before in their lives, and they had all simultaneously become vigorously alive in it for their first times. They were loving the rain and having a wild, crazy party in it, to boot!

That was when some sensation, a cranial, enlightening crack maybe, sparked inside my calloused, drenched heart and brain and started a fire of awareness. I stared harder for clarity, shouted, "Look!" to no one in particular, and then I began chuckling. Quickly, chuckles became outright laughter and ultimately turned into uncontrollable belly laughs so hard I almost choked-up my lunch. I was so astounded and amused at those *dumb beasts'* obvious delight of that pouring rain that my previously water-logged mind was instantly dried-up and made clearer with a new life-lesson's reasoning: *Every situation has another side, and it all depends on how, or which side, we choose to look at things...*

I suddenly and clearly understood and appreciated right there and then that human reactions to anything happening in our lives are dependent upon our attitudes. If that miserable waterloo of rain could udderly (pun intended) force those otherwise dreary dairy cows to jump-for-joy, then why couldn't I be happy about it too? "For crying-out-loud, it *is only rain*, after all," I suddenly grasped. And I can *only* get wet... Well, really, really wet from it, but so what?

Rain happens. It keeps Denmark lush and green. It keeps Denmark's cows happy too, so they can make world-famous, delicious, creamy milk, cheese, butter products, and potato soup, and Danish sweet rolls, and sweet cream for my coffee. Plus, on-the-side they teach lost souls about *joys-of-life*. My literal vision became eminently clear to me: *Everything believed to be good, or bad, is completely dependent upon how we simply look at it, or which flip side we choose to view; all things have grander purposes.* There is no right or wrong, good, or bad, happy, or sad, smart, or stupid, or whatever. It depends upon how we look at things. *Positive attitudes bring positive change. . .*

Abruptly, my attitude began instantly changing to the better, to the *positive.* I metamorphosed into an optimistic being with upbeat feelings. I happily began smiling profusely once more, like my true, inner-natural self. Finally, after several days on end of torturous, rainy punishment, I started feeling completely comfortable again with my newly dried and warm thoughts. I became soothingly relaxed and once again at peace with myself...

Wouldn't you know it, that was also precisely when the sun finally came out too... No, not *literally.* There were no crazed, Catholic priests performing miracles across the way in that muddy, sloppy pasture and praying for blessed, rainless light while waving and blowing incense from their outstretched arms over that silly, happy herd of cows. No, not at all. Besides, I was in strict, Martin Luther Protestant country. No Catholics allowed. But figuratively, yes. The *sun* began shining once again, and even brighter, inside my heart...

Prior to those moments, I had been woefully sitting there alone at my table, wallowing in self-pity, feeling so despondent, overloaded with SADness *(seasonally-affected-disorder),* and ever so tired and frustrated from being constantly wet and simply unable to become dry. I felt little hope of ever amending my cruel dampness. And then suddenly my *happy cow enlightenment* really began helping me make constructive, positive mental adjustments.

I started focusing on appreciating life's positives. For one thing, I had to recognize, appreciate, and gratefully concede, an important fact. For one thing, no matter what, I was actually physically and emotionally right there and then in Denmark, for crying-out-loud! That, in itself was pretty cool! "Be happy about it," I demanded!

"Folks around these parts live all the time in this wretched weather, and they don't seem woefully in despair." Then I began chuckling again, "Alright, maybe they never tan, but at least they can rust!" My sense of humor was back. "Ha! Ha!" I laughed aloud. I felt like a reckless Frankenstein monster when first recognizing his rebirth, "I'm alive! I'm alive! Yay, for me!"

Okay, I was feeling better already. A little humor always helps. I thought for a moment trying to gain some more humorous-mental momentum, "That's right!" I amused myself further, "Why, Noah had forty straight days of this crappy weather, and did he complain? Hell no! He was too busy shoveling shit off his arc!"

Furthermore, I was now pointed in the right direction, and that, in itself, had to be a good thing. My goodness, look where I was going now. I was headed south for hot temperatures, sandy beaches, and tons of tanned and bikini-clad bodies, ideally, and sun-filled seascapes. My future was beginning to seem bright. With all those positive images floating about in my mind's eye and disrupting my previous negativity with actual cheerfulness, I began noting a shadow, or ray-of-light glowing over my still dampened but revitalizing frame of mind...

Suddenly, something was going on. I was startled looking back over my shoulder and then up to see a man's shape. Out-of-the-clear-blue, or rather, deepest, darkest, and rainiest of gray skies, a tall, well-kept man in a tailored suit and tie, with silver hair and rim-nosed glasses was standing right over me for the longest moment, it seemed. He stood there looking down at my obviously untidy beingness. Perhaps, he was there merely studying my wretchedness while searching for sympathetic and remorseful words of pity to somehow ease my soggy, tortured pain. That, or I could hear his agitated voice echoing from my deep, inner-memory's bowels of a recent, broken-record track, "What's the matter, boy? Were you too dumb to come in out of the rain?"

But after only a brief moment, though, the gentleman began speaking in reasonably clear and kindly, German-accented English. "Good afternoon, young man," he gently inquired. "You certainly look very tired and wet. But you seem happy, no? Are you for sure walking to wherever you are destined?"

I politely smiled, but quickly slipped back into my defensive, self-pity mode, and forlornly replied, "Yes, Sir, it seems that way, but not because I want to, or like it. Nobody gives us wet hitchers a ride. I can't see as how I blame them, though, but it sure isn't any fun for me."

However, that gentleman turned out to be the *sunlight* I sought and had even begged to find. He became my temperate salvation. True, unfortunately, my hopefully pathetic, *Aboriginal Walkabout* had turned into a somewhat miserably failed, *Danish Turnabout*. Yet, once I appreciated the point of having survived my *trial-by-fire*, or rather, *water-board torture test*, my sudden, emotionally succinct, and positive-behavior changeover had brought with it new ambitions, a renewed focus, and a true change of heart and mind.

I cheerfully bellowed aloud in my private mind, "Things aren't so bad. Actually, all considered, in fact, I'm doing great! Yeah, sure, I've had my fill, and I am still up-to-my-kazoo with this ridiculous, apocalyptic rain shower. But, hey, rain is good... at times, sometimes, for a little while, at least... And my God, Just look at those freakin'-out *happy cows!*"

And then, that decent, professional-looking fellow just stunned me by offering a ride all the way back to *Hamburg*, Germany. Positive thinking, I told myself. *Think right, be right!* After sincere apologies for my restaurant table bench's wet-stained seating and waves to the pretty waitress, the two of us were running toward his vehicle in the ongoing downpour. That professor-type chap even went as far as sensibly troubling himself putting dry towels down over his Volvo station wagon's front-passenger seat for me so as to soak up excessive moisture from my still wet clothes.

Then with my sopping sea bag once tossed in the back of his spacious wagon, quickly we were off to Paradise, as far as I was concerned. Far ahead, I could even see an end to the brooding cumulus clouding overhead. That was when I looked back and strained for one last glimpse at that fun-loving cow herd. I smiled broadly and nodded. They were still dancing... All was well in the world.

The Dane even knew where the Hamburg Youth Hostel was located and took me there straightaway so that I, and my belongings, could get cleaned-up and made dry and whole again. My pleased spirits spectacularly skyrocketed. Finally, after over three full days of torrential rain and flooded-out emotional duress, my stressful tensions had begun relaxing and dissipating as though rainbows had come out, pushed any remaining frustration aside, and began glowing everywhere instead.

Bright colors had flowed from that food shop surrounding and colorizing those flooded fields and blotted out the dim, dismal grays of the storm's heart. My spirit became content *once* more, and I felt redeemed and joyful. In fact, I wanted to joyously holler out and empty my lungs with my *European Journey's* brand-new anthem lyrics borrowed from the hit musical <u>Annie</u>, "The sun'll come out tomorrow; bet your bottom dollar that tomorrow there'll be sun! Tomorrow! Tomorrow! There's always tomorrow! Tomorrow's another day!"

CHAPTER 9

CONFLICTED COMMUNICATIONS

Hamburger Hilton!

When a *hitcher* gets a decent ride, time flies and miles, or kilometers, churn past beneath. In no time at all, we were back across the West Germany border. West German guards stamped my passport once again, and my kind, professor-driver host was leading me to the nearest youth hostel for the night. And I was correct. Mr. Professor was a teacher who taught at one of the local secondary schools but was recently released for the ensuing summer months. He had been out visiting friends and shopping in Copenhagen.

He did agree that his *shopping had been noticeably light due to the heavy rains.* I laughed and joked that my own bag, however, had been getting very *heavy* due to the outrageously heavy downpours. We laughed and shared things about ourselves that helped pass time in no time. It seems when you have somewhere to go and entertaining means to get there, time and distance are inconsequential; both just happen and pass inadvertly.

The rains had dissipated somewhat as my driver began approaching the outskirts of *Hamburg*. I spotted much of the same scenery as I'd noted several days earlier while passing through heading for Denmark. I even recognized the exact same, drop-off point for me by *Hamburger Joe* Gustav and then the precise direction he had come when driving past his beloved and glamourous, Red-Light District. Not that I had paid much attention, of course...

It was interesting to me too, how the many towns, cities, and countryside throughout Northern Europe, so far, had been outlined: Specifically bordered towns and cities with carefully placed boundaries; and lands in between them were all wide-open pastures, crop fields, wooded areas, and sporadic farms with occasional scattered country cottages.

It became obvious to me by that time that Northern Europe consisted of nations with large urban centers and then nothing but landscape views for miles and miles, or rather, kilometers and kilometers, in between. Apparently, rural folks were the wealthy farmer landowners who *owned land*, and lots of it, almost all of it, in fact. In towns and cities, though, it was rich urbanites who owned all the real estate: Houses, businesses, warehouses, factories, storage facilities, docks, ships, skyscrapers, and anything else constructed.

In any case, observers got two distinct views: Either urban, business-residential visions, or rural, wide-open fields. And no matter where I traveled, both appeared adjacent, cohesively united, and with each supporting the other. Yet, all demanded finite borders defining their limits but still seemed to gracefully manage their enormous industrial-commercial-agricultural complex. One was either country folk or citified. There seemed no suburbia in-between, and the concept may have seemed curt to the eyes but it was easy enough to recognize and accept.

In no time at all, however, we had arrived in *Hamburg*. The hostel where Mr. Professor so kindly dropped me off in front was conveniently located well off the urban center, close to the shipping port area, and near a train station. That was going to be handy because I would be using trains very soon. After checking into one of *Hamburg's* several hostels, another converted hotel, I asked the front desk clerk in English for directions to places of interest and cheap food in town. His response was nothing like in *Brussels* but a little better than my *Paris* hotel experience.

Once again, there seemed minimal effort or time spent trying to communicate with me. The clerk just pointed to a stand holding various brochures of *Hamburg* highlights along with a couple of ads for some local smorgasbord restaurants. Unfairly, I blamed his unprofessional discourtesy on his television set that he was obviously glued to watching, *World Cup Preliminaries* games still playing.

Using finger and hand gestures, however, I attempted to get some useful information such as directions to the train station and which of the *All You Can Eat* smorgies the clerk liked best. That worked better, and finally we communicated. I just smiled a lot and focused on understanding his own brand of hand signals when clarifying something along with his limited English. I appreciated any of his efforts, though, and reminded myself that I, on-the-other-hand, spoke not a word of German. Shame on me… Also, finally, my Salems came in handy again. Apparently, cigarettes had a way of making peace and forging camaraderie among people, or smokers, at least. Once I offered the clerk a cigarette, he became all too kind. He wanted to be helpful and spoke his speedy German at a hundred *kilometers an hour* rambling on with suggestions. I had little clue from his words, but his pointing and illustrative hands helped me construe much of his meaning.

"Gehe hier hin." and "Sieh dir dasan." and "Issihre." And finally, "Nehmen Sie dort den Zug." *Go here. See this. Eat there. Catch the train over there.*

As his crude, hacking words flew incoherently from his mouth past me, his flamboyant hands, nevertheless, pointed out the rest of the way. Between several shared cigarettes, I learned what I needed to know.

After recalling my earlier *Hamburg* friend, Gustav, I decided to humorously honor him by nicknaming that *Hamburg* Hostel the *Hamburg*er Hilton. The name was a natural also because the hostel, itself, had a small, fix-it-yourself kitchen inside adjacent to a larger, communal eating area. For less than one mark, I made a decent meal of sauerkraut and a beef wedge with mustard on a bun. Imagine: For about fifty cents, I got two delicious hamburgers and a Coca Cola. Good to eat, good for me, good for my budget, and good-to-go. A buck and a half a day for three meals of food, and a buck a night for lodging. I was keeping well ahead of my stringent, financial plan.

When you are hungry, though, everything tastes great, and that meal did wonders for me. In fact, I made, and bought extras, for my city touring, as well as plans to take more along with me on my upcoming train ride. Also, there were a few other travelers there in the communal dining area who were taking advantage of the reasonable food prices too. One particular couple, a fellow and his girlfriend, was from Sweden, and their English was excellent. I spent my *first* dry night in several days relaxing, talking travel with my new hostel friends, sharing Salem's, and smoking with them, laughing, and enjoying our night's visit.

The Swedish couple were on their way south to Sicily, eventually, and they too were also trying to get away from those monotonous seasonal rains. Fortunately for them, they possessed a car. After an amusing evening, and following several shared Salem cigarettes, they even offered to bring me along with them; however, I politely but gratefully turned them down. For one thing, I sort of saw myself as a third wheel, a three's-a-crowd issue. But, I sort of got the sense, however, that the girlfriend was really hot for the idea. I suppose the thought did my ego some good, but in my mind I apologized to my own girlfriend, and I begged my Swedish friends' understanding.

I had a date with destiny, *Berlin*, I explained, and after that I needed to make hasty tracks back to *Paris* in time to meet-up with my *Amsterdam* contact, Ron, once again. Yet, in the course of one evening's relaxing visit, my *Hamburg*er *Hilton* friends had quickly become welcome diversions to my recent, previously sloppy, and wet past. We all laughed the night through, and especially we all chuckled at my *Hamburg*er *Hilton* nickname. It was a full evening of thoroughly enjoying each's company.

Saint Michael's Church

That previous late afternoon, though, I had decided that during my second visit of *Hamburg*, I would limit myself to only two massive attractions: The first was *Hamburg's* famous Lutheran House of Worship, *St. Michael's Church*; and the other would be the huge, *Hamburg Hauptbahnhof Main Railway Station*. Of course, regarding the church, I was fairly certain that most of Germany was Protestant. Also, I plainly understood from explanations in my history classes that Lutheran faith followers of Martin Luther, the fellow who sternly broke from the Catholic Church in 1521 so that he could get married and have sex (that's what I mostly believed back then), were very prevalent throughout the city.

I chose *St. Michael's Church* to visit, however, for several reasons: First, because of my dad who, as a non-practicing, past Lutheran, might indirectly appreciate the odd courtesy; second, I was trying to keep a promise to my mother to soak up all the cathedral and church influence I might; third, because my younger, kid brother, Kerry, who's Christian name was also Michael, and we loved to tease him about slaying dragons; and last, but most important to me, was because of St. Michael, himself.

In Catholic circles, St. Michael is the Patron Saint of Justice, Healer of the Sick, and Guardian of the Church, or Christianity. Art often depicts St. Michael with sword in hand and a banner and is often shown vanquishing a dragon-like Satan back to the underworld. Both he and St. Christopher,

Patron Saint of all Travelers, were my kind of saints. They fit in with my *Dudley-Do-Right* image, I suppose.

The next morning, though, I said, "Bon voyage et bon chance" to my Swedish friends as they excitedly drove off toward their glorious Riviera somewhere. Immediately, I had another minor loneliness attack. I really would have loved to have brought my girlfriend along for company and to enjoy our trip together. We might have even hooked up with some friends like my Swedish couple and traveled with them, I considered. Then I remembered the rainy walks through Netherlands, Germany, and Denmark. Bad idea. I figured that for sure I'd have become chivalrous and given up my sea bag to her and slept myself, instead, on the miserable wet ground in the disgusting rain. That would have been a *Dudley* thing to do. No thanks.

Nevertheless, I was a little envious of my departing friends. The tall, pretty blond girl had a great sense of humor and laughed at everything, and especially with me. Her more conservative boyfriend was funny too, but he was the consummate planner and organizer and kept them on track. They would have been terrific to travel with, though. However, I had my own schedule to stick to, and without any rain scheduled, I waved goodbye and headed out on my own *Hamburg* excursion.

From the port zone, I could easily spot *St. Michael's Church* in the distance, so that was to be my first tourist site visit. Plus, churches are usually free to see, so I could enjoy the city walk, visit the church itself, and then easily hike to my next destination, the *Hamburg Train Center*. Without rain threatening to ruin my plans or day, and with my sea bag safely tucked away in my hostel room, I was happy to crisscross that *burg* and enjoy every minute of it. *Hamburg* was definitely an industrial giant. Plants, warehouses, factories, and businesses flourished everywhere. Plus, both the seaport and the rail lines intersected nearby for maximum efficiency. *Hamburg*, the City of Commerce, could receive any international imports, and it could deliver any exports to anywhere from its industrial megalopolis empire.

Once I arrived at *St. Michael's Church*, though, I learned that it is one of five Lutheran churches in *Hamburg*. But *St. Michael's Church* was supposedly the largest by far. There was no denying how impressive it was, and it held three hundred years of history behind it. Its present Baroque style architecture was rebuilt once after catching fire in 1906, and then again after its massive bombing destruction in 1944-1945 during Allied air attacks against Hitler's Nazi Germany. *St. Michael's Church* shape follows a common style of an enormous, Latin cross utilizing a substantial amount of red brick and a towering gray spire.

Inside, it is mostly designed utilizing stunning white marble with a magnificent staircase and an enormous white marble pulpit. Another highlight was the church's underneath crypt with thousands of coffins apparently stacked and buried on top of each other by fours. Lots of history in that crypt too, but it was mostly being used for church services. So, I avoided viewing that part of my visitation because it didn't sound anywhere near as ghoulish as the *Paris Catacombs*.

But, I had fulfilled a motherly promise and reverent duty with my visit. I had entered the church, knelt down, and offered a commensurate prayer for my family. Then, I left quickly and headed for the train station, still a decent walk from there.

Hamburg Hauptbahnhof

A nice walk can help time and distance to pass quickly too; however, from the port zone it was still a serious trek to the train station. It was there that I wished to seek information for the next morning's passage regarding a train ticket to *West Berlin* in East Germany. I knew nothing of what to expect, so everything was a wonder for me. I'd never been to a train station before, and I certainly had never ridden on a train in my past. So much was to be expected and learned. As it turned out, my initial observations complimented my expectations too. The *Hamburg Train Station* was huge.

Countless numbers of railroad tracks trailed into and out from the immense *Hamburg Hauptbahnhof Central Station*. A continuous stream of trains seemed to be entering and departing the station from and to all European destinations everywhere. I read on an English information poster that hundreds of thousands of train passengers utilized that train station on a daily basis. Once inside, I recognized clearly that I was truly within a virtual city unto itself. I was merely a fleck in a vast inner-city of bustling patron users.

The station itself looked like a gigantic fortress built in a newer, neo-Renaissance style. Yet, it seemed to manage, control, or hold masses of passengers coming and going with relative ease. I read on English-worded history posters that the *Hauptbahnhof* was designed at the beginning of the century to replace many other smaller stations scattered about *Hamburg*.

The *Hauptbahnhof,* was apparently the second largest train station in Europe, next to the biggest and busiest one in *Paris.* Unfortunately, or fortunately for Hitler's opposition, the *Hamburg Central Train Station* had suffered severe damage by Allied bombings in 1941. Then again in a 1943 bombing raid, one of the majestic clock towers was destroyed completely. Nevertheless, it was still certainly impressive, and I remember worrying during my *first* visit that the station was so immense, "How could I ever manage to find my place for a train ride to *Berlin*?" My dad's own sardonic voice seemed to echo deep inside the labyrinth of my brain, "You'll probably get lost at the train station and starve to death!"

However, a lengthy walk through the train station allowed me to constantly seek answers to my endless questions: "Wie? Wo? Wann?" *How? Where? When?,* Eventually, though, I learned what I needed and went back to the hostel. After another enjoyable evening at the *Hamburger Hilton* devouring more hamburgers, drinking more Coke's, smoking more Salem's, and visiting other new acquaintances from all over, I again noted a similar pattern. Almost all of them too were heading south the next morning for warmer weather. Several were even utilizing Eurail Pass tickets to make their ways.

Making a point to my fellow guests, I amiably joked with them, "This time of year, all you guys just want to avoid drowning in this rainy, northern part of Europe." Smiling with comprehension, my student acquaintances all nodded agreeably, though, and my tease seemed evidently true.

"After terribly long and brutal winters," they all confessed, "and then immediately following springtime thaws, which is when the summer rains begin, we all want to leave for Mediterranean sunshine." Also, they added that school studies were over too, so it was a time to celebrate. Made a lot of sense to me. I began dreaming myself of that *Riviera* sunbelt.

The difference between them and me, however, was a car or train ride versus my thumb. With decent luck and scheduling, they would arrive at their chosen Riviera destinations easily by that next nightfall. For me and my thumb and feet, however, it might take days. Oh, how I wished I could have at least afforded a Eurail Pass. All the train rides you ever wanted or needed for one relatively inexpensive summer fee. It had been designed for active students to encourage and extend their travel desires, destinations for learning, and help promote and develop their understanding, appreciation, and blending of national and cultural variances.

It sounded wonderful too, but at $150, it was vastly out of my price range. Occasionally, I began feeling a little disgruntled and especially while marching in the rain; however, I had long since accepted my fiscal limitations and related responsibilities with their restrictive conditions. As a result, I was comfortable with my own ways and means. After all, I was hitchhiking! Who wouldn't want that unique, worldly experience and adventure? Only those without a car ride or a train pass, I supposed...

Whatever! Besides, the next morning I was headed for *Hamburg's* train station in order to catch my own train, after all. My goal of traveling by coach into the communist nation of East Germany, then on to *West Berlin*, and hopefully even into *East Berlin* was happening. Oh, I was thrilled and excited at my upcoming future. Silly me...

Having struggled the day before with language barriers, and often less than helpful assistance from train station agents, fortunately, I had spent enough time watching and learning during my overwhelming visit at *Hauptbahnhof* to grasp an understanding of my required challenges necessary the following day. Checking out of *Hamburger Hilton* early, I arrived with plenty of time to catch a late morning, direct express train, with only one minor stopover to *West Berlin*. I had needed to provide passport identification and receive a visa clearance for the East German passage to *West Berlin*. Only a one-way ticket was purchased after explaining that I was somewhat uncertain but would be leaving *West Berlin* in a day or two and probably returning by train to *Frankfurt*, West Germany, which was closer for my eventual return to *Paris*.

Similar to my previous day's visit, all went well until I once again began entering the station, itself. It seemed like mob rule with thousands of Arrival/Departure Platform Gates available for/from dozens of destinations. I felt like I was virtually a single fish in an ocean of bodies basically trying to swim upstream against traffic. Congestion was not the word for it. *Massive exoduses* seemed more like it.

I swore I saw dozens of Moses likenesses trying to lead their enormous flocks to and from appropriate platform gates. Like before, a constantly steady stream of trains pulled in while others suddenly jolted, whistles blew, conductors yelled, "Alle einsteigen!" "*All aboard!*" And continual voices boomed over the station's loudspeaker system advising every one of the next trains arriving, or next departure. It seemed outrageous for even local Germans to grasp those constant barrages of instructions and directions. For me, it was ludicrous.

All I could do was smile a lot, keep asking the same question in English, then repeat in French because my German was zilch, and then continue to stick my ticket in a burdened attendant's face begging in English and French, *"Where do I go, please?"* "Ou dois-je alles, s'il vous plait?"

Sadly, I had become a lazy language student especially with those fluent, English-speaking guests with whom to talk at the *Hamburger Hostel*. I never practiced or hardly learned any German phrases at all. My skill level was null, nichts, kaputte! *zero, nothing, broken!* Apparently, most Germans and I had a mutual understanding and agreement: We both refused to communicate clearly with each other.

In my travels, I was always so impressed, yet frustrated, by various European continental travelers or Belgians who would often chide, "Yes, the first four or five languages were the most difficult to learn. But after that, it got much easier!" I was often embarrassed, but with an extremely modest application of French occasionally, and because so many did speak English, I got away with adequate communications. Plus, I continued my usually successful practice of smiling a great deal to help disarm more difficult, communicative partners. Of course, cigarettes helped too. Good ol' Salem *witchcraft* to better cast chatty spells.

However, eventually I found my Gate 44 with my Platform to *Berlin*, and I stood patiently waiting until further instructions bellowed from the speakers and a conductor for my train hollered, "Alle einsteigen!" *All aboard!*

Fortunately, I also had my extra hamburgers along to tide me over and help kill time by eating until my train's departure. Those burgers kept my stomach occupied while lots of cigarettes subjugated my lungs too. I probably smoked more than any of those polluting train stacks. . . Oddly, there were only a few others waiting along with me, and the scarce number that did show up for the *Berlin* train kept sparsely spreading themselves out along my Platform's staging area. It seemed that they were deliberately distancing themselves from each other, like any or all of us were infected by some deadly contagion. Peculiar...

Railroad Blues

Once boarded and inside my chosen train carriage, nearer the gate but closer to the train's rear end caboose, I was still surprised to note that only one other passenger occupied that same particular railway car with me. I had noticed that the scarce smattering of passengers going to *Berlin* that morning on that direct run seemed few and spread out. Nevertheless, I stashed my bag on a wide and hard, wooden-slat seat and sat down next to the window for an excellent view. With a yell, a whistle, and a jolt, quickly we were on our way to East Germany and, ultimately, *West Berlin.*

I had read and studied a little about WWII German history and what I was literally getting into, but it was still important for me to refresh my memory: After WWII ended with our Allied Powers victory over Hitler's Germany, the Cold War had begun. From the Potsdam Conference of 1945, all the main Allied forces divided Germany into four occupational zones. Where the British, French, and Americans snatched three of the Western German *zones* and combined them into one large nation, the Soviet Union grabbed the remaining eastern chunk for themselves as a judicious addition along with Poland and other bordering, Soviet-satellite states for reorganization into their vast, Eastern European realm of influence.

Thus, the Western Germany zones, with their Capitol of Bonn, eventually became the Federal Republic of Germany (FRG) and commonly known as West Germany. East Germany, on the eastern portion next to Soviet controlled Poland, was a smaller, Marxist-Leninist socialist republic called the German Democratic Republic (GDR). Its Capitol remained in *Berlin,* where the West Germany Allies argued again with their Soviet, East-Germany ally until it was resolved that *Berlin* also would be split in two halves: *East Berlin,* for East Germany under effectively Communist Soviet rule; and *West Berlin,* occupied by Western Allied forces.

Shortly after our train left *Hamburg*, West Germany, about an hour or so underway, the East Germany border crossing became very evident. No sooner had my car, near the end of the whole train, crossed past heavy barbed wire border fortifications with armed guards posted, did the train begin slowing to an eventual stop at some small, obscure train station. What became fascinating was the fact that from the barbed-wire border of East Germany, all along both sides of the railroad tracks and stationed about everyone hundred meters, or so, were heavily armed, German Democratic Republic soldiers guarding the rail lines going to *Berlin*. The guard soldiers were all at strict attention and observing our passing train. Apparently, they were watching for anyone trying to jump onto the train heading for West Berlin, for some reason, and thus sneak aboard.

Regardless, that *Berlin* Express, direct-run train did come to a jolting, temporary stop with its loud, air brakes screaming a hissing release. Our interruption was at some hole-in-the-wall station just inside the East German Border. Out my window, and much further ahead, I could depict some activity taking place at the train station's, small-staging platform. There seemed to be several, armed-military soldiers climbing aboard. Moments later, the train again jolted forward, and we were off and running once more.

I returned to my quiet and curious studies of the evenly spaced, train track guards, and I even attempted counting them but quickly and easily lost count when another sudden interruption occurred. Without warning, our train car's door abruptly slid open, and in marched two uniformed officers of the East German military. The two of us passengers in my car were each immediately approached by one of the military personnel. Mine looked very stern, almost angry, with a no-nonsense air about him.

"Reisepass und Ausweis!" the officer commanded.

That was roughly what he briefly demanded, and I did not understand his intentions at first. I just smiled and said ever so politely, "I am American and going to *West Berlin* to visit."

Then for no good reason, the soldier became instantly irritated and nearly shouted at me, "Reisepass jetzt!"

Immediately, I stopped smiling because happiness did not seem like a reasonable selling point to that fellow. But my brain did click correctly, and I recognized a part of his phraseology, the *pass* portion. "Oh, my goodness!" I exclaimed aloud to myself. "*Yes*, ja, *one moment*, einen Moment." I had heard that said before in the Central Station and memorized it, thank goodness.

Stalling further might have gotten me a smack on the head I quickly considered, so I reached inside my front jean's pocket and retrieved my passport. Handing it over to the gruff officer, however, I decided not to play meek and afraid of his bullying. Thus, I stood calm and stared straight back into his own angry eyes such that he could more easily identify me from my passport picture.

He continued mumbling some more harsh-sounding, German mumbo jumbo which I had no clue as to what he was saying. I partly thought he was talking to himself, or else he was making snide remarks to his cohort. Regardless, it sounded like he was asking me more questions, so I just chose a few responses to placate myself and hopefully him too.

"I am going to *West Berlin* to see that city. I have heard wonderful things about it, and I am excited to visit there. I might even try to see *East Berlin* too, if I want, but I am an American student traveling and trying to see as much as I can while I have a chance."

I had a feeling that he had no clue of what I was saying either, so I thought that saddling him with a barrage of unintelligible verbiage might calm him down or exasperate him. I was partially correct. He stared at me momentarily and then spoke briskly, "Genug!"

It was pure angry German, and I immediately got his point. "Enough!" he had yelled, and then the real joke was on me. He stuck my passport in his pocket, turned abruptly on his heels, and marched past his partner collecting him too as the duo started leaving our train car toward the more forward ones.

Instantly, I went into verbose action. "Just a minute, Officer. I need my passport back. I'm not doing anything wrong, so I should get it back. What are you going to do with it? When will I get it back?"

I assumed he still understood little or nothing of what I was saying, but my anxiety ridden intentions were obvious. He knew what he was doing, though. However, I then made the mistake of standing up in order to perhaps meet the soldier halfway up the aisle to recover my passport more easily. Bad move. I did not fully understand his spontaneously vile German, but I was certain of his forceful instructions, "Sit back down, and shut up!"

So, I did what I supposed I was told to do and sat down again quietly fuming and continuing to watch all the 100-meter spaced guards on either side of the train tracks all the way to *West Berlin*. Additionally, I did note that the entire remaining outer landscape was filled with practically flat nothingness. Just open, barren land, untilled, unconstructed, and a seemingly wasteful use of potential farmland. After a while, however, bored by the continuing still-life views, and with no further interaction with that offensive officer, I did become overly anxious about my passport being taken from me. "How un-American, is that?" I pondered.

When our train finally began slowing down for our *West Berlin* destination, and I still had not received my passport, I could wait no more. The impatience of youth, I imagine. So, I grabbed my sea bag and began making my way toward the front of the train. I did not know what to expect, but I planned to find that unfriendly German Army Lieutenant and get my passport back on my terms, right away. It was coincidence, though, because just as the train rapidly decelerated and came to a complete jolting stop, I spotted that same officer up ahead chatting with a couple of others. I walked straight up to him, and rudely interrupting I spoke in defiant English, "You have my passport, and I want it back."

He was probably rather annoyed at my disruption, and he just stared vilely back at me for a few moments. Then while smirking, he reached into his pocket, withdrew my passport, and almost reluctantly handed it back to me. At the same time, he spoke to me in blunt, heavily German-accented English, "Now get off the train, spoiled American!" At least that was what I perceived.

And I did just that without any further reaction. I wasn't going to give him any more satisfaction that I was upset, nor an opportunity to become engaged in legal, political, or military issues. For me, I had triumphed. I was finally there in *West Berlin*, and I was both relieved and elated. Sadly, however, I did consider that that military officer, unfortunately, was likely the truly unhappy one. He had displayed pitiful manners mistreating me. Due to his government's strict compliance regulations, or not, his rude actions should have been managed in friendlier decent terms. I was not his enemy. Or was I?

Yet, I still had even more consequences to learn about during that surprisingly unfriendly and hostile environment of East Germany and *East Berlin...*

Checkpoint Charlie

Once departing the train station in *West Berlin*, I got easy directions to the nearest local youth hostel and walked promptly there and checked in. It was relatively close due to the rail system being its main source of clientele. Apparently, there was minimal traffic going to and from *West Berlin* through East Germany, and it was a testy and troublesome event. Aircraft was somewhat restricted due to East German airspace. Trains were obviously much easier to control by East German military with so many 100-meter guards and train car inspectors watching everything and everyone.

Anyway, the *West Berlin Youth Hostel* was another converted, business-residence structure that easily adapted to modifications accommodating many visitors. I learned that several tenants actually stayed there for longer periods due to summer schooling or extended commitments in *West Berlin*. Surprisingly, there were quite a few guests already living at that hostel due to its low rates and availability. Quickly and efficiently, I was placed in a shared room with two others who were already out for the day. I only planned to stay one or perhaps two nights and then catch another returning train for *Frankfurt*, West Germany. That arrangement would put me considerably closer toward *Paris* for the same rail fare. Obviously, there was no hitching through East Germany.

Because it was still only mid-afternoon with plenty of daylight ahead, however, I decided to take my long planned, exciting adventure that I had wanted. Right there and then I chose to visit *East Berlin*. The hostel's staff was very amiable, and their English was vastly superior to my German, which didn't say much, but I understood their general directions and unusual instructions. They were sending me to *East Berlin's* most common entry-point, a place called *Checkpoint Charlie*, and it was the main entrance for visiting that communist half of the city. After stashing my sea bag under my cot and getting minimal assurances from the on-duty staff of its safety, I headed for the historic street of Friedrichstrasse, the main avenue approaching the East-West border entry point of *Checkpoint Charlie.*

My immediate observations were simple, basic, and obvious. *West Berlin* was like any other city in the world so far, to me. I was in the central, downtown area of the hustling bustling business center. Crowds of people were out enjoying the afternoon by walking about the city streets while shoppers were window gawking with armfuls of packages. Others were a riding about on their bicycles, scooters, or motorcycles while cars ripped around the busy streets. Many street people simply lounged comfortably as they relaxed under mid-day sun umbrellas for shade or sat at sidewalk tables in front of the numerous cafes, coffee shops, and first-class restaurants lining all the avenues. Every illustrious scene seemed wonderfully industrious, entertaining, relaxing, elegant, and ever-so-busy. Very impressive.

I learned also that there were, in fact, a couple other *East Berlin* entry points, Alpha and Bravo, which allowed outsiders an entrance; however, only *Checkpoint Charlie* allowed dignitaries, government officials, and foreigners through its gate. It was interesting too that no West German citizens were ever allowed to pass through to *East Berlin* for business, pleasure, or visits. Additionally, it was curious and sort of sad, I learned, that no regular *East Berli*ners nor *West Berliners* were allowed to cross over to either side.

That arrangement was rather drastic too: West Berliners attempting to cross would be soundly rebuked and rebuffed; East Germans, or *Berliners,* attempting to cross would be shot on sight. It was complicated and dangerous. Plus, there was a serious, tall wall separating both sides.

And I mean a huge, high, thick, massive, concrete wall with specially placed towers along its perimeter and controlled by vigilantly watching armed guards with rifles and machine guns readied and constantly prepared. People called it the *Berlin Wall,* and East German Guards watched diligently from its towers and wall topping for sneaking, *East Berliner* offenders who sought freedom and asylum in *West Berlin*, the British, French, and American side. Easy viewing, however, allowed there before me in the near distance the infamous, actual-entry point of *Checkpoint Charlie* on the *West Berlin* side of that ominous wall.

There was only a small, prefabricated guard shack, apparently, serving as soldier's quarters protecting the West's side of the wall, along with some rather worthless sandbags scattered and stacked about. A couple American soldiers stood by as occupational forces of the tiny, but formidable, American's wooden guardhouse. The *American,* guard-shack center had been set up to both intimidate the East German, Soviet-powered military and to serve as insurance that all Western Forces government, military, or civilian personnel would receive safe passage entering and leaving *East Berlin* through *Checkpoint Charlie.*

As I passed by our American guards on duty at their tiny shack for the West's entrance point to *East Berlin,* I greeted the semi-casual soldiers with respect and honor. Giving them an obvious civilian, but effective, salute, I commented, "Hello, Sirs. What curious jobs you have. There's only a couple of you guarding that whole, giant wall. Thank you for doing your duty. I want to join the army one day too." Then pointing, " Is everything okay over there?"

A reply surprised me but provided sufficient warning, "Hey, kid, yeah, but just be careful, and don't do anything stupid. They *are* watching you."

I wanted to entertain myself with more conversation and potential information, but his warning suggested that I ought to get my *experience and adventure* over with in a hurry, post haste. So, I walked past a large and rather ominously placed poster stating in English, Russian, and French: "You are Leaving the American Sector." I entered into the apparent, forbidding, or challengeable zone of *East Berlin*. Once past the small cubicle, guard house of the West German, American soldiers' protected side, I walked through the wall tunnel and entered the East German side of *East Berlin.*

I was immediately met inside their large guard post by stern guards who demanded my identification and passport for clearance. I provided everything they asked for, kept on smiling like a regular dufus, or Dudley-Do-Right. Then a singled-out East German Guard, who oversaw my entry, really shook me up. Strapped around my neck, I was carrying my Brownie Box Camera that I had been using for all my touristy photos throughout my travels to date. After providing all my identification, including passport, for official stamping, the guard demanded that I hand him over my Brownie camera. I assumed it was for basic examination just in case I was considered a dangerous spy, or someone attempting to smuggle something into *East Berlin* like Top Secret spy information. Of course, I did as I was told; I did not want an international incident occurring over my faithful camera.

Once the camera was in the guard's possession, however, he immediately opened the back of the camera exposing all the negative film. That not being enough, the guard then proceeded to pull out the entire roll of film inside my camera, with a week's worth of previously taken pictures for my own personal photo mementos, and then he viciously ripped out all the stream of film negatives from the roll thereby exposing and destroying every picture previously and preciously taken, plus any potential new ones. I was shocked and flabbergasted. Why had he done that? I wanted to vehemently complain and register my serious accusations against the guard, but I remembered the American soldier's warning: "Don't do anything stupid."

So, I quickly registered in my mind, "Okay, Stupid, you are a young, miniscule foreigner in *East Berlin* now, and you have a silly, camera-film grievance against East Germany's Border Guards for Erich Honecker, General Secretary of the Socialist Unity Party of Germany, or for Leonid Breshnev, himself, General Secretary of the entire Union of Soviet Socialist Republics (USSR). Let them hear your roar! Or not. . ."

Better yet, write them all a nasty gram later on. . . Alright, I was pissed-off, to be sure, but all I could do without *doing something stupid* was accept the extremely uncalled-for action of that *nasty* guard and continue on with my primary goal of visiting *East Berlin*. However, just in case the guard had missed finding another role of hidden film on my person somewhere during his full-body pat-down, he kept possession of my camera telling me in obscure German and hand signals that I didn't need it and could pick it up on my return. Dirty looks were exchanged, along with shaking heads, while both of us likely screamed silently what we thought of each other.

I walked cautiously through the remainder of the *East Berlin Border Control* there at *Checkpoint Charlie* and continued on with my personal mission: To observe and note, but no longer photograph, variances between *East* and *West Berlin*, or East and West Germany. After my long walk from the hostel to *Checkpoint Charlie*, and after having taken a nice break for some late lunch, I was entering *East Berlin* in the later afternoon, yet not checking closely with my watch for the exact time.

Once formally inside the huge wall separating *East Berlin*, my immediate reaction was again surprise and disappointment. Far across the traffic interchange of what should otherwise be busy cross streets, and hanging high up boldly in a huge pictorial, was a gigantic poster draping down at least eight stories of a twenty-story high rise commercial building of none other than Leonid Breshnev, the USSR Party Secretary. "Wow!" I thought. "Talk about Big Brother shit! There he (was), Leader of the Party, in all his glory, or infamy!" For the life of me, I could not comprehend our own USA President, Lyndon Baines Johnson, doing something like that. I imagined that in only moments, even his supporters would have ripped it down, pissed all over it, and then burned it in public. Now that's the *American* way!

But there I was finally in *East Berlin*, not to make judgements, but to observe and compare. So, my *East Berlin* expedition continued. After another quick observation, I noticed that the entire visible region for a complete 360 degrees was all painted or constructed in plain, drab, and boring gray colors. Everything matched and was color coordinated, gray to dark gray. I had to give the GDR credit for that, but the tiresome monotony was extreme.

Their apparent statement seemed to cry out, "We the people of our Democratic Republic are all conformists and unimpressed or unfazed by your Westerners' bright colors and frivolity. Over here we remain *equally* tiresome and dull." Of course, Communism is atheistic in practice, so you could not even exclaim, "In the eyes of our Lord!" But the entire city seemed very dreary and completely filled with uninteresting light shades of melancholy everywhere.

I continued on down the main boulevard while noticing a scant number of vehicles on the major thoroughfares of that supposedly important city in the world. "Whatever why?," I thought in untimely fashion, and then I found an interesting pawn shop as I passed by in which to peruse. I slipped inside and nodded politely to the proprietor who looked at me curiously and then instantly began fidgeting around his countertops tidying up and arranging various items on display. I was in no rush, so I continued with my aimless meandering while looking for some special souvenir to purchase and take back with me.

After a noticeably short while, five minutes maybe, it was obvious that the store owner was becoming extremely nervous and stressed. He even walked deliberately over to his entrance/exit door and with exaggerated motion, flipped his door sign from "Offnen" to "Geschlossen," *Open* to *Closed*, obviously for my attention. I got his point; he wanted me to leave. So, I did, bowing courteously to him with a polite "Danke" as I closed the door behind me. I had recognized the manager's nervousness, but nothing had registered until I looked at my wristwatch. It was exactly 5:01 P.M., and I was obviously one minute late in allowing the poor man to close up his shop by a mandatory closing time.

Then, with peripheral vision, I looked all about *East Berlin* and realized that the entire city was already closed down. There was obviously a 5:00 P.M. curfew for everyone and everything. The streets were empty, the stores all closed, and no one was even walking home after work or play. *East Berlin* was effectively asleep to any further outdoor activity. I felt embarrassed that even the proprietor of the pawn shop I had just visited may have likely been sweating it out upstairs from his business below for fear of having violated the curfew by one minute, thanks to me. It seemed an especially touchy matter that I may be the one being watched.

I was surprised, ignorantly confused, and curiously dumbfounded. I even walked further up the boulevard and turned the corner at the next major intersection. Nothing. Nobody. Just an empty, gray city lay before me. A would-be cosmopolitan center of what should be extreme commercialism and commerce had been laid to rest for the night by exactly 5:00 P.M. on a summer's late afternoon, with no exceptions. Bewildered as I was, I took my odd sensations with me and casually returned to *Checkpoint Charlie* watching for any unique changes about me. There was nothing except the East German Guards awaiting my leisurely approach. I considered that perhaps I had even overrun their own schedules, but I quickly concluded that they were probably working around the clock anyway.

Once inside that large, *East Berlin* Guard Quarters, I once again showed the same guard as before my passport identification. He studied it for the longest time, it felt, and then proceeded to pat me down once again, that time likely for any subterfuge I may have been attempting. Once completed, the guard gave me a brisk pointing motion to exit the building to *West Berlin*, and that was when came my single, proud moment of rebellion.

I looked the guard squarely in the eye and proclaimed, "No! I want my camera first! May I have it back, please?"

I am sure the guard was a little surprised. Perhaps, he had momentarily forgotten about taking the camera from me an hour earlier, but I doubted it. There had been no one else besides me coming or going, I was fairly certain.

Everybody was off the streets by the curfew. Everyone that was, except me. But I was not about to give up my trusty Brownie to that jackal. Maybe he even thought that he could intimidate me into just leaving it behind . . . with him. Hardly!

The guard stared blankly at me for a moment likely trying to challenge my fortitude or figure me out, I suppose. However, I then repeated similar words, "I would like my camera back, please." I then overemphasized my aggravation by using both my hands while stooped over exaggerating a mimicked taking of photographs like a game of charades.

There was actually a temporary, minor stand-off, and I even contemplated a WWIII blowup starting over my confiscated camera. But the guard broke first, thank goodness, and with a shrug of his shoulders and a snort of disapproval, he carelessly reached into a cubicle, retrieved my filmless camera, and seemingly reluctantly handed it back to me. For twice in one day, I again gave an East German Military Guard no satisfaction either. Taking hold of my property, I turned as abruptly as the train guard officer had, and with my head held high, I swiftly walked out of their guard quarters passing through the wall and East-side authority of *Checkpoint Charlie*.

Quickly, I was back on the obvious *free side,* and I was glad to be back in *West Berlin*. Yet, I felt disappointed and somewhat cheated. Although I had no souvenirs, and certainly no photos to bring home of my *communism* encounter, I had a mindful of stark realities as memories. My ultimate disappointments had led to extreme disenchantment, and I had forever changed my wannabe pro-communism attitude to one of prideful and righteous God Bless America...

East-West Divergence

The walk back to the *West Berlin Youth Hostel* was extraordinary. It wasn't because my particular return trek down the important, major avenue of Friedrichstrasse was unusual or spectacular. On the contrary, it was special because of its normalcy. Only minutes before, I had been randomly walking down wide streets meant for a great many hustling and bustling vehicles doing their daily business while cavorting about the city. But there had been only a vague shadow of any existence. *East Berlin* was a ghost town, a phantom city.

But then, in only a matter of a couple blocks distance and minutes off a clock, everything seemed as it should be once more. Cars were busily speeding down many colorfully arranged boulevards. Brightly adorned storefronts, colorful business advertisements, lively shops, cafes, an abundance of international restaurant cuisine, and all sorts of other active enterprises were in full swing and wide-open to their eager public. Music, live and otherwise, was drifting outdoors from many nightclubs and restaurants that I inadvertently passed. Noisy bars and sports clubs were blaring television screenings or radio broadcasts of still more obvious, preliminary-playoff games from World Cup Football (Soccer) '66. The measured differences from merely blocks and minutes away were astounding.

I suppose that it wasn't so much the enormous visual and acoustical reversals I had so quickly experienced. Rather, it was disappointment that was so remarkably noticeable. Oh, I loved the action and noise levels of *West Berlin*. It was a major international city, and it was acting just like it should. I personally knew from visits to San Francisco and from the entire East Bay Area of California, from San Jose to Vallejo, what industrious and busy cities should look like. I had driven through Los Angeles, San Diego, and even Tijuana, Baja California, Mexico venturing through their crowded, hectic, and multi-cultural metropolises.

As a youngster I had even traveled with my family, while Dad searched for work, that allowed us all to see, Chicago, Cleveland, Boston, New York City, Philadelphia, Washington D.C., and eventually even Houston, among many other large, energetic cities. In all of them, we had experienced thrills and chills of downtown, municipal lifestyles. While growing up, Jean had taken me along on some of her own unique excursions visiting Ensenada and much of Baja California, Mexico, Oregon, Seattle, Washington, and all over the Bay Area for a variety of cultural events in all those cities.

For actual, big, city-life living, I had already previously lived in Chicopee Falls, outside of Boston, Massachusetts, and in Pasadena, Texas, San Jose, California, throughout most East Bay Area cities, and even Reno, Nevada with my parents, all again following Dad for his jobsites. Furthermore, to date on my Summer '66 trip thus far, I had already walked through and observed large sectors of those wild, vibrant streets of *Paris, Brussels, Amsterdam, Hamburg,* and even several other smaller metropolitan areas too. The point was, I knew cities, and *West Berlin* was a living, thriving, and boisterous example of cosmopolitan life.

Sadly, and disappointingly, however, *East Berlin* had been a serious letdown, a major model of the exact opposite of what I had expected to see.

My previous, limited, and superficial readings of Russia's great Marxist revolution had filled my hard-core, union-supporting belief structure. My mind had been tantalized with ample literal and liberal ammunition by which to pour my curious and frustrated mind and heart out against. Finally, I was there to see an example for myself.

There in East Germany and *East Berlin*, the evils of shameful, capitalistic managements from centuries of decadent, bourgeoisie ruling-class royalties, and wealthy, self-indulgent, and corrupt aristocracies had supposedly been toppled. Allegedly, they had brought about a new world order of a united workers' proletariat whereby working classes finally ruled. For a struggling, young boy from a diligent, union member father, who provided basics for his family by chasing all over the country looking for basic, meager, minimal-paying, construction-labor employment, the uprising proletariat sounded romantic and exciting to me.

Unfortunately, and devastatingly, the *East Berlin* visit, and the entire experience traveling through East Germany, had been nothing like I had imagined. The initial East German soldier train guard had been hostile to me. To *me*! Little ol' me, who a day earlier would have happily gathered up a Pro-East German flag and waved it proudly about honoring all working folks everywhere, had been rudely and crudely pushed aside and dealt with harshly as a quasi-enemy-of-the-state.

Next had come the abject warnings from the American soldiers at *Checkpoint Charlie* "... to behave and watch out for myself" while visiting *the other side*. Then, the nasty *East Berlin*, *Checkpoint Charlie* Guard, who had taken my camera, deliberately ruined all my film, and only barely returned the camera to me. It all had suggested a hostility and vile temperament toward me, a would have been staunch and hearty, wannabe supporter. But, no more...

Berlin Blues

Once inside *East Berlin*, there had come a seriously cautious, visual shake-up from telltale signs of a bleak, gray city under serious scrutiny by *Big Brother*. After which, I noted additionally that during and following my brief, uneasy store visit, with its anxiety-ridden shopkeeper, an entire city had shut down for the day on a just beginning official summer mid-afternoon at 5:00 P.M.. Finally, it was the remainder of my ever-so-quiet walk about *East Berlin* while noting its almost ghostly phenomena that really stunned me. My misguided, previously enrapturing, literal impressions of *East Berlin*, East Germany, the entire Soviet Union, and communism, itself, in general, went all to hell.

It just didn't seem right. How could it be? I never imagined. . . Something was terribly wrong. And then, of course, the last straw was my closing grievance with the same border guard who really seemed to feel an actual contempt for me, and my Americanism, and maybe even the rest of the world. I wasn't judging him. He didn't know me. Why was he judging me filled with so much disdain and animosity? All I knew was that I was glad to be back in the *West*. I was no longer sure what *East Berlin*ers, or East Germans, or the whole Soviet Union side had going for them, but I was absolutely sure that I liked our Western side better.

Once I returned to the hostel, and especially after I went back to my room, I reflected on my afternoon's visit to the *other side* and decided right then to end my disappointing *Berlin* visit. After a light dinner and some brief conversations, I depressingly retired for the night. I did not even want to go out on the town and carousing with all the other happy, partying Americans, West Berliners, or others. I had felt too much remorse and sadness from my disappointing experiences.

Even trying to enjoy *West Berlin* would be awkward. How could I possibly go romping around one happy half of a city, kicking-up-a-storm, and laughing-my-foolhardy-head-off knowing full well that just beyond, over there, and just past that oddly placed, huge barricade, was the other *saddened half* probably living in quiet, curfewed depression and envy all while I partied? There was a tall, wide, and long barrier dividing my heart and blocking my cheerfulness. I could not imagine anymore that people living under communist rule on the other side of that ominous, sinister wall were happy and contented.

It was difficult for me rationalizing our *West's* viewpoint: It was *them versus us*. How could one side of a city be happy knowing full well that so many others were suffering on the other side of the very same city? I went to bed regretful that night. I never spoke to anyone at the hostel about my feelings and observations either. The staff employees and long-term residents, no doubt over time, enforcement, and desensitization had likely become calloused and casual about their existing separation and differences between those two sides of their very same city. Very odd. Very sad.

Early the next morning, after cleaning-up, repacking, and saying a few goodbyes over an obtainable continental breakfast of rolls, fruit, cheese, and coffee, I returned to the train station to purchase that evening's available direct route train ticket to *Frankfurt*, West Germany. On one side of a border, everything shut down at 5:00 P.M. precisely by curfews in order for crowd control. On the other side, it was twenty-four-hour celebrations, it seemed. Emphasizing my point of inner depression just then, right outside the train station and all along the congested streets, *West Berlin* was alive with activity and industriousness. What an amazing difference I had encountered in merely two days. It had been an up/down, up/down visitation of literal, visual, and behavioral extremisms from happy to sad to happy over and over again from one radically different government's conceptual elements to the other.

Also, at the time I was sure that even speaking about the matter to others there in *West Berlin*, I would become even more disturbed and disillusioned. I was afraid that they might simply respond, "Oh, yeah, we get that all the time. That's just life here in *Berlin*. It's them against us. Just get over it."

I didn't tell anyone either, that I had privately nicknamed that *West Berlin Youth Hostel*: The *Berlin Blues*.

CHAPTER 10

··

FINDING MY WAY

Frankfurt am Main

I didn't completely ignore where I was. I had several hours until my train departure from *West Berlin*, so I decided to make the most of it. I checked in my sea bag for safe-keeping, and I did go back out onto the wild, fun-loving, exciting, typical, big-city streets and wander around aimlessly enjoying what I imagined how any free city ought to behave. And it was enjoyable.

Somehow, *West Berliners* had managed to exclude issues of the *East Side* from parameters of their Western mindset. They seemed all involved with newest fashions, and music, and latest fads were most popular from *Paris*, London, New York City, and Los Angeles. The joyous ambiance coming from their crowded cafes and noisy bars suggested moods and focus on what was exciting or happening in the free, Western World.

It was pleasant to experience. I actually began feeling a little better than I had been earlier. I even sensed a kind of *bravo-for-our-side* attitude. I walked past a street side café advertising a very reasonable menu and had a nice, tasty meal of German Pot Roast with potatoes and carrots and sloshed it all down with a favorite, local beer. From inside the café came wild, boisterous chatter and laughter from fans following another World Cup Soccer game. "Good for them," I thought. "Good for them!"

There in *West Berlin* was also my *first* unmistakable experience listening to groups of men, mostly German men I imagined, locking arms, and singing all sorts of tunes celebrating all kinds of themes. Some songs seemed nationalistic in nature. Others sounded like tributes to women, past heroes, and especially to their favorite soccer teams. Their music was loud, rejoiceful, and honestly amusing, but sincerely refreshing. Grown men were clanging huge mugs of beer against each other's, locking arms, and joining together in honorary accolades to their special subjects. For the life of me, I could not imagine such a thing ever occurring in the States... unless it was in an Irish bar, but everyone knows they're all crazy about that kind of stuff, anyway! Great fun.

My train to *Frankfurt* left right on time, and naturally, similar conditions resulted as when I had traveled to *West Berlin*. That time, however, East German guards, who had previously checked my passport, seemed less concerned about my presence. Once they had determined that my identification was reasonable and acceptable, they returned my passport to me and left me alone. After passing into East Germany, the train guards did their passenger reviews and then disappeared. The train did stop as before at a small incidental station just before we left East Germany to reenter West Germany, but it caused little commotion and was just a formality allowing the East German military guards to exit the train.

Nevertheless, similar train track guards were stationed all along the route watching for anyone, I presumed, trying to run up and jump onto the train. I imagined that once in a while, those guards may have actually become busy chasing someone. However, the idea seemed preposterous in reality. My mind envisioned Hollywood fiction scenes of cars or horses transporting escaping runaways trying to get past hostile guards and then leaping onto fast-moving night trains to the West and freedom. "Fat chance," I cringed, "but good luck!"

Other weird observations, both going to *Berlin* and then returning to *Frankfurt,* regarded different uses of all open lands within West Germany and East Germany. There seemed like so much industry and farming happening inside West Germany. Real advantage was being taken for all its countryside and farmland. Modern equipment was deployed all over various distinct farming properties to the point that maximizing lands' uses seemed vital.

In East Germany, however, there was so much stagnation and waste. Obvious farming was going on, but it looked haphazard and undisciplined.

There appeared to be so much empty and unused land too. Even necessary and valuable farm equipment could be seen laying around rusting, out-of-date, broken down, or simply discarded and left unattended. The differences were startling and, once again, disappointing...

Upon arrival, the *Frankfurt Train Station* was as busy as anyone might imagine. Just like *Hamburg*, only nowhere near the same capacity or clientele, trains were still pulling in and leaving on a steady, regular basis. The station was also busy managing many folks planning for departures or waiting for arrivals. I was happy for its impressions of success and for the excited eagerness of its throngs of users.

I even chose to take advantage of my train station situation, sort of, and benefit myself. Being nightfall already by the time my train arrived, I decided to save a couple of dollars, or eight to ten German marks, and spend it on more expensive depot food instead. Rather than leave the station, find a hostel's whereabouts, and then hoof it to wherever, likely arriving even much later, I chose rather to stay right there in the train station for that night.

So, I found a slower and more vacated part of the train depot and located an empty depot bench to stretch out upon for the night. I figured that lots of people did that already while waiting for a train, or because of delays, or whatever. That way I could continue my people observations, save a couple bucks, and store my bag directly underneath me for security.

After a meager train station food purchase, I was set for the night. Noise or not, I was comfortable and managed that upcoming night relatively well. The next morning, I quickly made plans for the day: I would locate the *Frankfurt Youth Hostel* and check-in for the upcoming night; then I would safely leave my sea bag; next, I would get thoroughly cleaned-up and wash my dirty laundry; then, I would find something filling to eat; and finally, I would tour the exciting and pretty city of *Frankfurt* as best I might, giving myself the remainder of the day to do so. Following all that, the next morning I would be off for my return route to *Paris*.

Most of my plans went even better than I might have asked. I did find the *Frankfurt Youth Hostel*, and it was very relaxing. It was further away than I had hoped, but eventually, I located the building. It had been some sort of small school, or office building before, and what were once classrooms, or large office spaces, had been converted into dormitories with four beds each, plus amenities to make very comfortably shared quarters. The bathrooms had been separated by gender and were modified to include showers, which was nice; however, I teased myself that I was quite amiable to gender-sharing showers, after all.

There were still a few youth travelers and some older adults inside, but those already up for the day were already making plans for their own day's adventures. The manager-on-duty was pleasant, and she spoke very decent English. I learned a few highlights of *Frankfurt* from her as she proudly and delightedly shared her city's history. Then I spent the remainder of that day walking about the central part of *Frankfurt* and enjoying its ambience.

One might easily refer to *Frankfurt* as the *Fair City*. It is home to a multitude of international fairs attracting millions of visitors annually for a variety of interests including car shows, book shows, cooking festivals, art exhibits, music celebrations, and many others. *Frankfurt* is a beautiful mixture of modern architecture blending nicely with ancient medieval remnants of Celtic and Germanic settlements 1,900 years old. Also, obvious ancient-Roman remains can be found too from the 1st and 2nd centuries. Just like *Paris*, *Frankfurt* has a beautiful river running through it called the Main River. The world famous, *Frankfurt am Main* (Frankfurt on the Main River), is the city's dominant, two-century old building that eventually became a powerful stock exchange center rivalling New York City, Tokyo, and London.

The downtown central area was a splendid example of typical Germanic architecture with Hansel and Gretel, cookie-house-themed homes and structures with tall, slanted roofs and brick-and-tile roofing and sidings. Colorful pinks, blues, light rosy reds, and grays filled all the open, city squares with delightful aesthetics and charm to match all the vibrant flower beds highlighting the city's many, dynamic, historically minded statues. It was a beautiful, open city by then, but *Frankfurt* had come a long way.

Like its previous cohorts and Nazi sympathizer cities during WWII, *Hamburg* and *Berlin*, *Frankfurt* still had leftover damages from the horrific bombings and Allied Forces' attacks it had suffered so immensely as the Allies drove Hitler's German Army back into *Berlin*, and ultimately for complete, unconditional surrender. In twenty years' time, however, those cities, and certainly *Frankfurt*, had truly progressed. They had all shown strength, courage, willingness to cooperate, and a sincere, apologetic-rebuilding focus to match Western Allied Powers' financial support in helping provide destroyed German cities' rebuilding efforts and virtual rebirths.

That was why our own *Rhein-Main USA Air Base* was there: To support, oversee reconstruction, and protect Allied Powers interests in *Frankfurt*, all of West Germany, and *West Berlin too*. If necessary, also, all of Western Europe would be protected from pressures exhibited by Soviet Union expansionist desires. *Frankfurt* was definitely a survivor city hell bent on thriving once again after its nearly terminal destruction from WWII.

I spent a delightful day walking, sightseeing, and enjoying the friendly people, some hurrying while others relaxed, and passing by many businesses, busy shops, cafes, sports bars, and elegant restaurants within the <u>Main River's</u> central zone. I laughed as I walked past several beer bars also with their group arm-clinging, singalongs cheering up the day. And I filled myself with sights, German hotdogs (frankfurters) heaped with spicy mustard, and downed with two of my recently discovered and new favorite beers, Becks, and Heineken's, each for about five cents ($.05) a bottle. I was cheerfully, and probably intoxicatingly, thrilled. And top all that off with some authentic, German apple strudel dessert, followed by Salem cigarettes, I was in a comfortable space, a *Frankfurter* kind of mind.

And briefly considering my nickname game for previously visited hostels, an easy one for the *Frankfurt Youth Hostel* became *Hot Dog Hilton*, or my favorite moniker, *Frankfurter Inn*. After my day's explorations and once back, I suppose I wasn't surprised that so many of the other guests had already departed. I did get directions, however, for my route out of town and the best way to Luxembourg and eventually *Paris*. Studying my map, I actually thought I was much closer than I really was. How wrong! Sometimes, *closeness* is not always gauged by distance.

Rhein-Main US Air Base

While preparing to leave *Frankfurter Inn* the next morning, plans began fairly nicely. After another continental breakfast, I met a couple who helped me out right away. I got a ride from them all the way out of the city to the southernmost outskirts of town since they were leaving the hostel the same time as me. However, they needed to turn off right after that in another direction, so we parted company at an interchange.

From there, I began walking and hitching again but with no immediate luck. A few cars were speeding on by, yet no one would stop for me. A couple of hours later, I noticed that I was walking past the entranceway to a USA military base. Several vehicles were turning up that entry point and hurriedly heading onto the base. Once I got closer, I spotted a large sign identifying it, and I could see guard posts at the base's gate just up ahead its entranceway. I also recognized the base's name from an earlier conversation with the hostel manager.

I had learned about the particular United States military installation nearby called, the *Rhein-Main US Air Base*. Then, suddenly, it was right there before me. To be honest, at that time, I was still a little embarrassed over my rejection by Air Force Academy recruiting officials. Nonetheless, the idea of joining the military someday was still viable to me. Thus, the thought of actually visiting one of our very own military bases in Europe and greeting our brethren-at-arms appealed to me. Once again, a snap decision had to be made, so I made one. I took a sharp left turn, walked across the highway, and entered the base.

The guards at the gate were cautiously surprised, but upon showing them my ID and telling them my story, they were delighted. Of course, to be safe, they frisked me first, and checked my sea bag, but then they ushered me right onto the base. They even kept my bag stored inside their guard booth to ease my trouble, and they gave me specific directions to the mess hall, a cafeteria place where all the airmen ate. They said that I would get a friendly meal there. I suppose I looked like I could use a good meal. I admit that I got excited at the prospect too.

In no time, I found the huge mess hall, even though only big letters and numbers on the building identified it for me, and then a small plaque labeling the entrance door. Once I stepped inside, I immediately smelled delicious aromas floating throughout the giant eating area. Also, the room was noisy and bustling, and everyone seemed in good spirits. However, slowly as I attempted to gain my bearings and figure out my next step, I began noticing the room developing a hush over it. One-by-one, heads, and then eyes, turned toward me as I gained nearly everyone's interest or curiosity. After all, a seemingly lost civilian youth had just entered their sacred eating grounds. Who would dare? At first, I was a little nervous at all the attention.

Then, abruptly, a voice boomed out, "Hey, that's the kid who was out there hitchhiking on the highway!" Next, that same loud voice rapidly walked over to me and introduced himself, "Hey, young fella, I'm Tech Sergeant Tony Walters, and I saw you out there, but I didn't know you were coming on base, or I'd have given you a lift for sure."

"I wasn't at the time," I quickly and honestly responded, "but then I thought that I'd drop in, visit, and say hello to any of you. You all are a long way from home and for a long time too. So, I figured I could be a friendly face from back home."

"You mean you came all the way in here just to say, 'Howdy doody?'" the sergeant teased.

"Well, yes, and no," I sheepishly responded, "I did want to say hello to all you from all of us back home, and especially my hometown of Brownsville, California. But the guards at the entry gate said that I could also maybe get something to eat here too, maybe, if it was possible. If it wasn't going to be any trouble, that is..."

"Hell, yes, it's possible," Tech Sergeant Walters laughed. "You are going to get to stuff yourself silly, young fella. C'mon, let me show you where. . ." He then proudly began boasting aloud, "Hey, Airmen, this young fella. from California, and he came all the way here just to say hello and eat with us. Give him a *Rhein-Main* welcome!"

Winding past all the cheers, and hellos, and pats-on-the-back, and more teasing, I just smiled, and smiled some more, and laughed, and followed Tech Sgt. *Tony* all the way down to the lunch counter. He knew every civilian food server there and grinned while telling them to load me up with *groceries*. And, oh, did I recognize just how well those airmen ate. I had hardly ever seen so much food all at once in my entire life. It was as though they had their own private, enormous smorgasbord for their every meal, it seemed. Chicken, ham, burgers, mashed potatoes and gravy, biscuits, all sorts of vegetables, fruits, pies, cakes, and ice cream were served up with all you wanted. I could hardly believe my eyes and nose. I was in hog heaven, and I shook my head in awe because I noted that it was only lunchtime.

I thought to myself, "America, be proud. We are feeding our overseas troops very well. Don't worry for them. No one is ever starving!"

And then the *piece de résistance* came. My new, best friend in the whole wide world, Tech Sergeant Tony, showed me the beverages: All kinds of sodas, coffee, tea, milk, and my knee trembling favorite, chocolate milk. And I could have all I wanted, Tech Sgt. Tony said... And I did.

Of course, many of those airmen had plenty of questions for me about myself and back home in the states. They wanted details as to why I was really there. They queried regarding news of life in the states and asked about anything and everything else practically. I politely answered each question that I could in between shoveling heaps of all that great food into my mouth, and chewing, and embarrassingly swallowing almost desperately.

Fortunately, Tech Sgt. Tony finally interrupted telling the others to slow down and "Let the poor starving kid eat something first." They did for a while, but soon more gathered around for a question-answer period right after I pushed my food tray aside. Tony sort of guarded over me, I felt, and he pulled weight around there because the others listened to him respectfully.

It only took a short while before the airmen all wanted to know about my own travels thus far. They asked about all the women I had met and what I thought about them. Very perceptively, I avoided any comments about my "Parisian *Ladies-of-the-Evening* experiences, but those horny airmen gravitated to that subject almost immediately anyway.

In short order, I became surprised and somewhat embarrassed by some of their questions and remarks. Several wanted to know all about my sexual relationships since I had arrived. I am sure that I disappointed most of them when I confessed of my faithfulness to my girlfriend back home. That just led a few to expound in awkward details about their own experiences, instead, while stationed at *Rhein-Main US Air Base.*

"Hey, what do you think of all these German girls you've met?" one of the fellows piped up.

"Uh, I think they are all very nice," was my simple response.

"Well, what do you think of all their hairy air pits and legs, huh? Disgusting, ain't it?" another piped up loudly.

"Well, uh, um, I, uh, didn't really notice, to tell you the truth," was all I could muster up.

"Didn't notice?" an airman practically shouted while grinning, "Why, every time I go to town for a good time, I've got to give my date a shave just so I can manage f-----g her!"

Of course, that got the younger airmen crowd roaring with laughter, and I suppose I joined right on in faking along with their frivolity... *along* with my blushed, embarrassed awkwardness. Yet, I was ever so glad they did not pursue any further questioning for details of my own exploits. I was uncomfortable providing any specifics at all. Plus, I honestly had nothing to add either, except for maybe misconstruing *propositions* for *pleasantries* or kindness, but that would remain private.

That afternoon in the airmen's mess hall, however, was a great delight, though, and I was sorry to see the crowd slowly disperse with handshakes, waves, appreciations, and goodbyes as they all filtered out to their afternoon's respective duty stations. Tech Sgt. Tony was one of the last to leave, and he was the most grateful of all for my appearance that day... I even took down his name and address and promised to write to him once I got back home. We talked about meeting up again back in the states.

I was happy to have met him and all those other brethren-at-arms. I felt their joy visiting a civilian American, one who had showed appreciation for them, and I sensed their sad homesickness. No wonder entertainers like Bob Hope were so popular. Of course, the kind of *hope* ol' Bob always brought along with him that they really craved were all the pretty American, female dancers and singers. They might have been soldiers, but they were horny men first.

Plus, I did learn a little more history and perspective of the *Rhein-Main US Air Base* there near *Frankfurt am Main*, West Germany. Originally, the Germans designed the base to be one of their most important air terminals in Europe. In 1909, Count von Zeppelin used *Rhein-Main Air Base* as the landing site for his famous German dirigibles, including his ill-fated <u>Hindenburg</u> that crashed and burned in New Jersey in 1937. In 1936, however, the base had split its use between commercialism and use for dirigibles. Later in 1940, the huge hangers were demolished, and the base became an important part of German military operations as a Luftwaffe fighter plane base and experimental jet aircraft station.

After the Axis Power's and Hitler Germany's defeat by the Allied Powers, Germany was, of course, divided, and *Rhein-Main Air Base* became part of the US Air Force operations. For years it began serving for a mixture of commercial flights and military services. Then, during the chaotic and ongoing disputes caused by the Cold War, *Rhein-Main US Air Base* was used as a valuable site for airlifting cargo and necessary goods to *West Berlin* in order to counter Soviet controlled land access routes and supplies blockages through East Germany. After times cooled, the base continued as a troop and transport services provider and maintained that important stature throughout the Cold War.

In 1955, with other bases opening elsewhere, such as in France, *Rhein-Main US Air Base* was designated as a passenger and tactical cargo hub. In 1959, the US Military turned over the northern half of the base to German authorities for civilian commercial use. The other half remained with the

USAFE (Europe) as the principal port for U.S. Forces in West Germany. Even in 1966, the year I visited the base, *Rhein-Main USAFE* Base became even more valuable and important when the air bases in France were all closed and turned over to the French government. Historically, it remained as a strategic and valuable site for American military interests until its ultimate closing and turnover to Germany in 1999. Today it serves as yet another passenger terminal for *Frankfurt* Airport facilities.

I left *Rhein-Mein U.S. Air Base* that afternoon filled with fascinating background information, memories of wonderful camaraderie with the airmen, and an absolutely stuffed belly. On top of all that, one of the fine airmen I had talked with during lunchtime was getting off his shift soon thereafter. He happily provided me a ride off the base, stopping to retrieve my sea bag, and then taking me all the way to my next turn-off point heading for *Luxembourg* and then on to *Paris*, France.

At that particular time, I was in great patriotic spirits, crammed with nutrition, and filled with such positive vibes. My positivity seemed to be effective too. In no time at all, I caught a ride that took me all the way to the capitol of Luxembourg, *Luxembourg City*. My kind driver ushered me right out of West Germany and straight into Luxembourg with only a respectable wave to the posted, but otherwise *World Cup* enthusiasts, border guards. At that stage, I was well relaxed because I was actually ahead of schedule for my *Paris* return. Unfortunately, not for long...

Luxembourg Stroll

Giving credit where due, the drive from *Frankfurt* through West Germany and well into Luxembourg was spectacularly beautiful. The ride through both nations' plush forests and incredibly productive farmlands made me both homesick and envious of their ample greenery. Each was uniquely beautiful in native cultural scope and in natural gifts. We crossed over the other half of *Rhein-Main US Air Base's* namesake, the <u>Rhein River</u>, and it was incredibly large and magnificent as another important shipping and commercial waterway, and for private and personal enterprises. Soon thereafter, my driver and I crossed the <u>Moselle River</u> too, which served as a natural border for West Germany and my next visited country, Luxembourg. Those were the kinds of lifts a hitcher relished. They made travels seem uninhibited, interesting, relaxing, and fulfilling.

Although quite small for an independent nation, Luxembourg was incredibly beautiful and filled with history. Nestled between West Germany, France, and Belgium, it had close connections with all three border nations. but primarily West Germany, I learned. Luxemburg is a democratic monarchy with a parliamentary system, sort of like Belgium, Netherlands, and Denmark, I supposed. As with so many of those countries I had visited so far, their long histories with royalty still held on to help shape their worldly relationships. But with parliaments, the people all had voices, so each's form of democracy seemed to work well for them. Yet, Luxembourg's natural beauty was what really made such a difference. It was actually pleasant having to hike clear through Luxembourg's capitol city and well beyond even *its* boundaries.

Complaining where due, however, *Luxembourg City* also became another *first*. I have identified other cities where I had walked through large portions of them while departing their premises. Well, *Luxembourg City* became the *first* city where I traversed the entire city limits. Having been dropped off at its eastern entrance, I walked all the way down its one, major boulevard and after a bit of zigzagging, I strolled completely through its beautiful surroundings until I finally reached its far opposite western edge.

Fortunately, there was much to see as I ambled through the tiny country's large capitol. Unfortunately, I began feeling concerned about being late for my *Paris* contact with Ron. Therefore, I only stopped at a couple places in order to use bathroom facilities or buy some food, visited no tourist stops except what was visible from the main road, and then I simply kept on trekkin' while following road signs pointing toward *Paris*. "At least," I thought, "I am getting closer."

Luxembourg City, however, was a beautifully landscaped area. The center core was the primary business district, and it seemed to spread out from there concentrically in all directions, as best I could surmise from my zigzag course through the city. I had already learned to ask all the questions I needed to help find my way around. Since hitchhiking was completely minimal within almost any city's limits, I chose to follow provided directions to get me straight to where I needed to go.

In no time, I had crossed the Alzette River, which lazily curved through the city. Although not a major thoroughfare, the Alzette River was nonetheless beautiful for viewing and supportive of minor enterprises and local water enthusiasts. *Luxemburg City* definitely had its special, business-core center, too, and lesser commercial industries and urban residences developed outward from there. So many cities that I had passed through were often like stepping back in time to the fifteenth, sixteenth, and seventeenth centuries. Regularly maintained structures were hundreds of years old and gave such unique character to their architecture. *Luxembourg City* was definitely one such unique place. Its fresh, clean oldness was very appealing. My cross-city stroll actually became a visual highlight, and by shortcutting right through the business center, I saved a couple of kilometers of walking.

Nevertheless, it was another long hike that day through the city to its far western end. By that time, it was getting late evening, so I needed to find shelter again for the night. Passing through the beautiful city, I had stopped to eat, relax, and buy some for-the-road groceries from a quaint shop to satisfy my needs. I even drank a Belgian beer and lightened my load some more by smoking more Salem cigarettes, which had already become a steadfast habit. As the town's outer residences thinned out on my mainly western route toward France and *Paris*, eventually I entered into beautiful, woods-like settings similar to the Grengewald Forest I had been taken through traveling toward *Luxembourg City.*

However, it was to be another night on the ground, but that time it was clean, dry, and amazingly comfortable. I found a nice spot off a main road I would use for the next morning's hitchhiking endeavors. That night's stop was in a forest-like grove of trees and near a running brook, or creek, that likely fed into the Alzette River. It was a very pretty spot for a campsite, but of course I never used campfires for fear of getting spotted and causing some unknown issues to arise, like starting a forest fire and burning down Luxembourg.

I could imagine the next day's headlines: "Suspected Destitute Californian Burns Luxembourg to Ashes." And its byline: "Nothing Left Except Charred Campfire Remains and Empty Pack of Salem Cigarettes." Then, finally the cover story highlights: "Suspect Believed to Have Been Too Dumb to Come In Out of Dark and Assumed to Have Hightailed to French Riviera. All Europe on Lookout."

Nope, no campfires. It would be *Silent Camping*, I called it. Just me and nature. My site was nice, though, especially with its calming sounds of running water from the nearby brook. Plus, my overnight location was well hidden from view of any unlikely surprise visitors such as hikers, police, dogs. Big dogs too, monsters...

Self-Defense

The next morning, I cleaned up at the creek's edge, reorganized my belongings, and clambered back onto the western direction course I was using. After a while, I began realizing that the roadway I had taken was not a busy route at all. Apparently, most traffic was using another major route out of *Luxembourg City* heading directly south, which also eventually led into France but was instead a primary route to Southern France Riviera vicinities. Paraphrasing Robert Frost's wonderful poem, I was obviously ". . . on the road less taken, and it did make all the difference."

For one *difference*, hardly anyone else seemed to be choosing that same *road less taken* while also passing into France, and so I had to walk, instead. For another bigger *difference*, I learned something about myself: *I was too stubborn to quit* again and turn back to take another probably quicker route. No, I *stayed the course*, as they say, and committed myself to that lonely road. Besides only an occasional and random passing car, it was just me all alone with my thoughts. At least I felt good, and the walking was pleasant enough. Unfortunately, eventually I began suspecting those few scarce passing cars likely had nervous drivers who, while deliberately passing me by, must have been too leery of a lone hitcher late in the day and on an isolated forest road because of its obvious remoteness.

"Oh, well," I thought to myself, "I've been down this road before," metaphorically speaking, naturally. It was another time for me to think positively.

So, I started considering *flip sides* of that new predicament, and right away, I considered some upbeat approaches. One helpful defense was that I was grateful that while shopping at that small market in *Luxembourg City* the day before, I had at least purchased some extra food rations for on-the-road conditions. It was not any deliberately considered action, but rather I simply bought a few additional items to carry along as snacks. Fortunately, those *snacks* ended up becoming breakfast, lunch, and then also another dinner late that night. If those snacks weren't completely filling, at least they kept away hunger's gnawing edge.

Of course, thank goodness, there were those Salem cigarettes too. Yeah, that was a positive, I thought back then. They were especially useful in at least filling-up my lungs with satisfying, narcotic, nicotine-addictive fumes. Plus, they also helped curb my appetite and even filled my tedious time while blowing smoke. And that quiet, rural-countrylike road gave me plenty of opportunity to practice my smoke rings. I'd open my lips wide and exhale with a *phuff, and out would grow a b*ig ring. Then puff, puff, puff, and I'd send several smaller rings shooting right through the large outer ring with deadly accuracy.

That afternoon, I'll tell you, I became the *Buffalo Bill of Bullseye Cigarette, Smoke-Ring Shootin.'* With World Cup Championship Soccer games going on everywhere, it was easy imagining myself being introduced up on stage with other world class winners as I gratefully bowed ever-so-royally while accepting my own special trophy as the affirmed World Champion of *tremendous, smoke-ring blowing skill. Dexterity, focus, talent?* That was me! What else could I say? Puff, puff, puff...

Then, for a triumphant stage return to my adoring fans, I would entertain them all with timeless personal poetry created during hapless moments of dullness and boredom:

> *"What doust I say?*
> *Cars stayeth away!*
> *I cannot attractith awareness.*
>
> *If I stoodith on my head,*
> *Or tried to playith dead,*
> *Perhaps, they would slowith to witness.*
>
> *And be that the time...ith*
> *I'd startith to climb*
> *And leapith in their cars like gymnasts!"*
>
> *The shock wouldith stun 'em,*
> *But my manners compel...ith 'em*
> *To deliverith me with utmost quickness...ith."*

I considered that writing poetry must be precisely what brilliantly bored people do when they have too much time on their idle hands. They make up limericks and rhymes. That afternoon, I even imagined that the greatest poetry of all *great* times had actually come from "greatly" bored people who had "nothing else *great* to do but sit around thinking up *great* rhymes to fill their "greatly" empty lives. "Shakespeare," I cracked, "eatith thy heart out. I mustith be even more *greatly* boredith than thouith ... wereith!"

Yet, by smoking more cigarettes, blowing more championship quality rings, and making up idle, Shakespearian-quality rhymes, time and I marched on. With no cars hardly ever going by, and if so, never even stopping to give-a-poor-guy- a-hand, or a decent ride, the day still managed to pass, but slowly. And then eventually early evening came, the sun dropped behind distant vineyards and hills, and with still no luck, and still no rides, I casually began searching the local premises for another sparkling brook. I figured that I was going to need one more night's campout to rest and prepare for the long walk the following day. My calculations told me that I had at least another day, or even two, in which to reach *Paris,* still make my connection with Ron on time, and then make plans for traveling south together. I was still okay.

Oh, how I remember that particular evening so clearly even now. It was a cloudy late duskiness, following a beautiful reds, oranges, and pinks sunset, but darkness was clearly approaching rapidly. I had nearly resolved myself for another night's camping out and had been offering up lots of prayers for a productive hitching day to follow. *Standing on my head* or *playing dead* even became serious considerations. But I still had an easy couple of days to work with. Paris was roughly only about a hundred miles away, or one hundred fifty kilometers. Heck, I could walk that in my sleep easy, as long as I sleep-walked too.

I had answered President Kennedy's 1963, *Fifty-mile Walk Challenge.* It was part of his "Make America Fit" campaign. Fact is, I had been the only finisher from my group. True, after starting with a huge grouping early in the morning, I had completed the hike by crossing the finish-line in the dark, all by myself, and with no fanfare. Afterward, I had simply caught a bus home and soaked my feet before going to sleep. But I had done it, and I knew I could walk great distances. JFK had made us all prove it to ourselves. Plus, most recently, I'd had a few long treks already, especially in rainy Denmark, suggesting so. It was amazing to me, however, how great leaders like JFK could truly inspire. We Americans sure had loved our President.

Kennedy's "Ask not what your country can do for you but what you can do for your country," and "Go to the moon in ten years," were stunning and exciting challenges. Dr. ML King's 1963, "I Have a Dream," speech had also shaken our nation with hope and promise. Then, later came the extraordinary *1964 Civil Rights Legislation* and *Voter's Rights Act of 1965,* both signed by President Johnson, which had become even further evidence of making our United States of America more united and closer to a *More Perfect Union*. Those were great, inspirational times. So, how could a silly little troublesome skip and hop to *Paris* seem like a huge undertaking for me? In my mind, I was already there. All I needed the next day was one good ride...

As dusk began closing out, any sparse cars had already turned on their headlights which seemed deniably glaring to my outstretched thumb, eyes, and mind. As each car passed, I began waving them off with contempt. "I don't need your lift; I can walk just fine," I lied to myself.

Then, as I was about to call it quits for that day's failed efforts at ride-catching, suddenly my *night in shiny armor*, arrived. It was a silver-colored French Peugeot, and a ride to success had finally stopped. Apparently, though, it was an afterthought, because the driver had zoomed on by but then had braked, stopped, and reversed gears to drive back to me.

At first, I could not believe its stoppage was for me. I figured something else had probably happened. Perhaps, he had run over something, or he had missed his hidden turn-off somewhere nearby. I looked around studying the vicinity for any obscure turns but saw none. My goodness, no. The driver steered his Peugeot 404 straight back to where I stood and flipped open his passenger door for me. I was so surprised and elated, that I took no time in tossing my bag onto his back seat and quickly jumped inside just in case he changed his mind.

Excitedly, I burst out with basic French, "Bonsoir. Comment allez-vous. Ou allez-vous?" *Good evening. How are you? Where are you going?*

"Je vais a paris," the driver smiled.

He was going to *Paris*. "Great," I thought, "Finally, a home run!"

Then the driver continued, "Ravi de vous rencontrer. Je m'appelle Carl et j'ai e'te' surpris de vous voir sur cette route secondaire." *Nice to meet you. I am Carl, and I am surprised to see you on this back road.*

I gratefully answered while smiling back at him, "Pas aussi surprise que moi de vous voir vous arreter," *Not as surprised as I was to see you stop* Then I followed, "Merci beaucoup, Carl. Je m'appelle Daniel et j'etais sur le point d'arreter, de camper et d'aller dormir. Je vais aussi a paris." *Thank you very much, Carl. I am Daniel, and I was about to quit, and camp, and go to sleep. I am also going to Paris.*

Apparently, my driver host was French, and after lead-off introductions, however, our conversation became minimal. I supposed that it was probably because of my poor accent, or weak pronunciation, or poor language skills.

Or it was just because he was French, *and no English was allowed*. It was fine with me, though, because I did not wish to work so hard analyzing his French comments or questions and then struggle responding in order to communicate. Besides, it had been a long warm day, and I was tired from all my lengthy walking.

It became a quiet drive for some time, and I mostly focused on the sun setting directly in front of us to the west. As dusk closed upon us, and night steadily consumed all daylight, I allowed my eyes to close and my mind to wander aimlessly in eased relief...

Suddenly, I felt a strong grip on my left knee with a sort of massaging technique following. I bolted upright and instantly brushed hard at Carl's robust grasp of my knee and fervently declared, "Qu'est-ce que vous voulez?" *Take your hand away. What do you want?*

Carl released his grip, and in the car's dim shadows, I thought that I saw him smirking as he muttered something like, "Que lest le probleme? Tu n'aimes pas ca? *What's the matter? Don't you like that?*

I simply thought it was strange for him trying to get my attention by grabbing and rubbing my leg like that. His queries were baffling too. *Don't I like that?* Of course not. Weird! With no follow-up questions from Carl, though, I shifted back around, leaned against my side's door frame, and settled in again for some more restful slumber.

Later that night, and after darkness had fully settled in, I was once again startled to full consciousness by Carl's powerful grip on my knee. That time he had moved his hand further up my leg to my upper thigh and was tightly rubbing and massaging that area. Again and even more forcefully I shoved his hand away from my leg by prying his fingers loose and vigorously pushing his hand and arm to the side.

Instantly coinciding with my physical rebuke of Carl, I also boldly stated, "Arrete ca! Ne me touche pas comme ca. Qu'est-ce que vous voulez?" *Stop that! Don't touch me like that! What do you want?*

After that very odd interaction, Carl seemed to focus on driving his car while keeping both his hands firmly placed upon the steering wheel. I watched him out the corner of my eye feeling strangely concerned over his erratic, even bizarre, behavior. Eventually, we passed through another big city, Reims, but it was fairly dark and mostly closed down. Carl did not stop, and I did not ask him to do so. I had my snacks from earlier, so I ate some and still offered to share candy and cigarettes with Carl. He had been mostly silent, however, and refused both. After a while, though, I relaxed once more allowing my mind to drift off thinking about plans for the next day. I considered it possible, if Ron were early, that I might already have a message at the *Left Bank Hotel* from him stating as much.

It made me smile thinking about how nice it was going to be heading south for the warm, sunny weather to those *Riviera* beaches and all those French bikinis. I was attached to my girl back home, for sure, but I could look, I chuckled to myself. That's what eyes were for, to enjoy all the beauty of the world. Oh, yeah, I was grinning up a storm, alright... In the meantime, I also understood that wherever Carl dropped me off in *Paris*, I'd have to get to my selected hotel on the *Left Bank*. I might have another long walk ahead of me at that time.

Soon, however, my wandering thoughts were brought back to the present moment. Nature called, and I asked my driver politely, "Carl, voudriez-vous arreter bientot? Je dois aller aux toilettes." *Would you pull over soon? I need to go to the bathroom.*

Shortly thereafter, a wide, turn-off point came, and Carl wheeled his Peugeot off the roadway and came to a stop. I thanked him and got out to hurriedly answer *nature's call.* When I had finished, I stretched for a moment and leaned back against Carl's car because I had seen him walking around to probably take a leak too...

Instantly, however, everything became a blur, and I was stunned at what was happening. . . Carl all but leaped upon my upright frame, and with one of his hands trying to wrap me close to him while shoving my back harder against his car, Carl's other hand was reaching, groping, and rubbing against my genitalia area. I had no grasp what was happening except that of being physically attacked. Instantly, survival instincts kicked in and I reacted in self-defense.

I had both my knees available and my left arm free, so I immediately used them. With all my strength, I swung my left fist and caught Carl straight onto the right side of his head just in front of his ear. At the same time, I forcefully raised my right knee upward and hard. Both movements definitely jarred him forcing the release of his other arm that enclosed me while causing him to bend over forward and back up slightly. Yet, Carl still continued with his misconstrued groping or fondling of my genitalia area, and even continued struggling more as he further attempted shoving his hand down inside my jeans.

Once my right hand was clear, though, I shoved Carl backwards with all my might. That push made him completely release me and drop back a small step. Quickly then, with both hands freed up, I shoved Carl hard forcing him to stagger backward even further. Finally, striking him wildly with my flailing right leg, I warned that I would kick him again if he tried coming closer. He didn't.

I still did not understand why or what he was trying to do, but I did not like or appreciate any of it at all. Why was he grabbing me like that, I truly pondered? It did not make any sense to me. I was not a small person either. At over six-foot one, and perhaps a scrawny 170 pounds, I was tall and lean for my age, but I could hold my own. So many fights with my older, scrappier brother during our younger years had taught me well enough.

Carl, on the other hand, was a larger man and about ten years older too. However, he may have been surprised at my defensive tactics. I wasn't sure, but by that time he continued backing away just as I began simultaneously releasing a torrent of French exclamations somehow surfacing from forgotten memory banks as I surged with confused anger.

Keeping my distance while furiously waving my arms around and pointing at him, I began yelling at Carl angrily and formidably, "Qu'est-ce que tu fais? Quel est ton probleme? Pourquoi? Gardez vos putains de mains pour vous. Touche-moi a nouveau comme ca, et je vais vous vaincre!" *What are you doing? What's the matter with you? Why? Keep your Goddamn hands to yourself. Touch me again like that, and I'll beat the crud out of you!*

The more I spoke the more I shouted, and the louder I became the angrier I got. I worked myself up into a frantic frenzy of shock, dismay, hurt, and fury. Yet, because of Carl's obvious submissive withdrawal I began easing up with my forceful and vile verbal attack by telling him to leave right away. Pointing up the highway, in fact, I ordered him to leave.

Still practically shouting at him, though, I continued bellowing in my poorly, but overly excited, French, "En fait, sortez d'ici avant que je ne devienne vraiment fou! Quel est ton probleme? Juste aller! Va en enfer loin de moi! Allez maintenant! Batte-le! Sors d'ici!" *In fact, get out of here before I really get mad! What's the matter with you? Just go! Get to hell away from me! Go now! Beat it! Get out of here!*

By my last commands, I was practically screaming at Carl still for unknown, but hysterical, reasons. I couldn't fathom why an initially friendly guy had attacked me like that, even grabbed at my genitals, and forced me backward and hard against his car as though he was attacking me. It made no sense seeming ridiculous and violently inexplicable to me. Grasping my knee earlier inside his car, and being warned against it, was seriously improper of him. Forcefully and viciously attacking me while outside, however, as he groped at my genitalia, was bizarre, confusing, and absolutely unacceptable.

All I wanted was to get away from him. Fortunately, I remembered my sea bag still inside Carl's car. As he hurried around his Peugeot, I swiftly opened his rear passenger door, reached in, grabbed hold of my bag, and forcefully jerked it free from his car. Quickly, though, Carl climbed back inside, started up the engine, slammed his shifter into gear, and sped off in a crazy rush,

As Carl raced off, I angrily flipped him the *universal bird* sign yelling, "Buzz off, vous rampez!" *Buzz off, creep!*

After that encounter, I felt both relief and confusion at the same time. I had sent Carl away in a hurry. I had vanquished the wrongdoer, but I was still completely bewildered. "What in the world just happened?" I asked myself. And why? What made a full-grown man like that attack an innocent hitchhiker like me. It would have been bad enough were I a female, but I was a guy! "What was up with him, for cryin' out loud?" I puzzled. The whole entire incident seemed very strange to me.

Anyway, I was so flustered that my earlier plan, before that incident with Carl, of settling down and sleeping off the night, no longer appealed to me. I still had so much adrenaline pumping through my veins, I could do nothing else but keep on walking up that road in the near darkness. "Thank goodness," I breathed heavily, "At least I had presence of mind enough to snag my bag before Carl hurried off."

That would have been the joke of all times . . . and on me too! So, off I went hiking down the road again, *tripping the dark fantastic*, with my bag hoisted back up over my shoulder, and chain-smoking Salem cigarettes. I had plenty to think about and questions remained in my mind to resolve. I didn't even feel like being in any hurry for my next ride. Hopefully, when and if it did arrive, it would not be such an unusual ride on that *less taken road* I had unfortunately chosen.

French Connections

As it turned out, I did keep on trekkin' . . . all through that night and well into the next morning. At the time, I couldn't be sure of distances, but I gauged my walking speed to be about two miles per hour when carrying my on-shoulder sea bag. With around eight hours that I walked straight through that night, I produced an easy sixteen miles, or so, or well over twenty-five kilometers, over my "road less taken." Thinking aloud, singing, making up rhymes, continuously shifting my bag from one shoulder to the other, smoking Salem's, blowing smoke rings, and of course, walking, walking, and more walking was my night's entertainment. Fortunately, the crescent moon overhead shed some light through the cloudy skies. It was enough, though, to make out forested woods, plentiful pastures, and more vineyards surrounding infrequent but cozy looking farmhouses. The walk was okay, though, and time passed.

Later into the next morning, however, my luck changed again, this time for better. Well after a beautiful sunrise over tall, green-forested trees, my thumb, which always came out for upcoming traffic, finally worked. A large, blue Citroen, driven by another single male, pulled over for me. Of course, I still felt a little hesitant, but this older person looked kind, and he offered me a ride also all the way into *Paris*. I accepted, tossed my bag in the back, and climbed inside.

My luck had indeed changed and definitely to my relief. This driver not only took me the rest of the way into *Paris* but asked if I would like to rest and visit his family, a wife and two children. At *first*, I was suspicious and perhaps overly cautious, but I just figured that if I actually got all the way into *Paris*, and something bad did happen, I could just walk away and easily find my hotel again. My previous three days in *Paris* had taught me quite a bit about its layout. So, I went along for the ride.

My driver was fairly quiet, but he seemed amiable enough. We didn't talk much, yet I learned a few things about him. He was a traveling salesperson who had to visit nearby cities in France, Luxemburg, Germany, and Belgium. He explained to me, as best I could understand, that his daily travels usually allowed him to come home each day, but sometimes he needed to stay overnight and then return early the following day. That had been his situation that time with me. He was returning home after an early morning departure from *Luxembourg City* having already visited several sites in Belgium the previous day. He sold all sorts of jewelry, he said, and he chuckled telling me how his wife really loved his job because of all the perks from his business. I understood his wife, gift-giving concept, and we both laughed about it together. Nice fellow.

Just outside of *Paris*, I learned something new and fun about *Parisians*, or the French, or Europeans, in general. As I watched scenery develop into more commercial enterprises by noting an increasing array of large billboard advertisements alongside the highway, I saw something that amused me quite a bit. Just barely off the highway on our right side, and directly beside a giant poster touting something for sale, a car had pulled over. A man was standing there in full daylight and total view's proximity to all passersby, and he was taking a leak so nonchalantly and innocently. I had to laugh at his lack of humility.

"If you gotta go, you gotta go!" I thought to myself.

How darn refreshing it was to see. It wasn't just the Frenchman taking a leak but the concept itself that was unique. Needing to go to the bathroom was very natural, quite normal, in fact. Of course, then I considered that perhaps that *pee-free* guy had been a German who was merely pissing all over France! I laughed to myself. Nevertheless, I was impressed that the guy had no shame or embarrassment at all.

But then I also had to admit that *nature's call* activities were a guy's thing. I doubted whether many *Parisian* women, or French ladies, or even European females did the same thing. We guys have it easy. Nevertheless, that view had been another *first* for me, and I determined to keep my eyes open while traveling about to assess my theory. "Look out ladies," I joked, "because I'll be watching."

Finally, and well into the *City of Paris*, we arrived at my driver's home. His name was Mr. Lonchaire, and his home was upstairs in a condo-like structure. He invited me in and spoke to his very friendly, pretty, and nice wife. His two kids were young, but they were quite curious, it seemed, about their father's guest. Almost immediately, I was teasing them and speaking easy, childish words to them, and we all got along very well. His wife had prepared a wonderful breakfast, and they invited me to sit and join in with them. After a day and night of crackers and candy, their full meal of sausages, eggs, and pancakes, and coffee really did the trick.

Afterward, following a little more visiting and simple conversation, the biggest and best surprise of all came. Mr. Lonchaire spoke to his wife, and shortly thereafter, she gave me extra food for my travels. Then came another incredible, inexplicable kindness. Mr. Lonchaire offered to give me a ride all the way through *Paris* clear to my own hotel destination. He told me that it was no bother because he had to check into his work anyway, his whole family was joining him for an afternoon in town, and my hotel was on his way. I was so appreciative of all their kindnesses that "Merci beaucoup" simply felt insufficient. Fine family.

What that short drive meant for me, however, is still difficult and perplexing to understand. As we drove through *Paris's* busy, heavily trafficked, and crazy, driver-beware streets, me in the rear seat in between the two youngsters, we got in a car accident. Out of nowhere, another auto came racing through an intersection and bashed into the front driver's fender of Mr. Lonchaire's car. I never even saw the other car coming. But then again, I wasn't watching for it either. I was distracted and occupied while teasing the children, and we merely felt a hard slamming jolt from the crash. Thank goodness that was all. Go figure.

Just like I had previously observed myself, though, upon my initial arrival and walking tour through those wild streets of *Paris*, now I had *personal* experience to boot. And what happened as a result? The two drivers, Mr. Lonchaire, and the other guilty driver, both got out of their cars calmly, quietly and met beside Mr. Lonchaire's somewhat mashed-up Citroen. The other driver's car, some cheap, older Renault, or something, was banged up too on the passenger's front side.

Regardless, the two men just stood there momentarily discussing the situation peacefully and without terse words or anger. Together, they pulled hard on Mr. Lonchaire's car fender and freed it from pressing against the left front tire. Then they exchanged information with each other and calmly parted like friends do. Mr. Lonchaire advised us that all was well, and that the matter would be resolved through each's insurance company. No one was hurt, fortunately, and both cars were still drivable. But I was surely stunned, surprised, and afterwards quite curiously impressed.

Those nice people had shown me such decent hospitality, and it had even ended up costing them misfortune. Yet, they were unfazed by the circumstances. It was wonderful meeting friendly people on the road. I was always so pleased from compassion and charity exhibited because I felt certain that my own parents would have shown the same generosity. The Lonchaires could have easily been neighbors of mine back home, or even relatives or friends, except for language issues. But it had clearly shown to me that human kindness was surely universal.

Also, that special time with the Lonchaire family had all but dismissed any stress from the previous ride with Carl. I was in great spirits again, and I had finally returned to *Paris*, after three weeks, and once more to my favorite, cheap hotel again. Furthermore, there was no message left for me with the *Left Bank Hotel* manager-on-duty, a young woman that time, so that meant that I had actually arrived before Ron. I was ahead of him and, therefore, I was doing simply great.

So, I checked in, left a message for Ron, for when he did show up, and went up to my new room. Similar layout that time, but it was on a higher level and with a slightly nicer view. Also, I learned that the previous clerk was finally away ... on vacation, himself. He had made it south after all. Good for him, and for me too, because the young woman downstairs was much friendlier and prettier. I was content, relaxed, happily tired, and definitely ready for a nice, long nap...

Wouldn't you know it? Later that very afternoon, Ron did show up too. He was told by the clerk that I might be sleeping, so he didn't bother to contact me. Instead, he left a message in the lobby stating suggested plans for the next day: "How about a train ride to visit a French Castle tomorrow? Pick you up at eight A.M. Then we can discuss going south." It was evening time when I finally retrieved his message and things were looking particularly good. We had connected after all.

Le chateau de Versailles

Early the next morning, I was ready for Ron's arrival at eight o'clock. I had gotten up, cleaned-up, dressed, and had even already eaten a simple breakfast just in case he had too. Mine was my good old standard: Coffee, rolls, cheese, some salami, and fruit. I was refreshed, hunger satisfied, and visiting with the morning hotel clerk when Ron drove up and honked from outside. I recognized his green VW just outside by the curb and quickly made my way out to join him.

After handshakes and greetings, Ron told me about the day's adventure. He wanted us to catch a *Paris* tourist train which took passengers on round-trip excursions to *le chateau de Versailles.* In the states, we know it as The Palace of Versailles. I was excited and thought it would be nice to finally share sights with Ron again, as we had in *Amsterdam.*

On the way to the train depot, Ron complemented me on my punctuality, and we exchanged highlights of our past two weeks. I talked mostly about all the rain and my disappointment with *Berlin.* Ron had mostly just hung out with his roommates and had taken in more *Amsterdam* sights and relaxation. The key point I grasped from Ron's quick dissertation was that he had left *Amsterdam* early the previous morning and had dropped by my hotel as soon as he had arrived.

Oh, what a difference a car made. It had taken me five days to hitchhike to *Amsterdam*, and he had casually motored on into *Paris* from there in one easy day's drive. I just shook my head in envy and laughed to myself, "Well, at least I was seeing Europe up close and personal and getting lots of exercise too. Can't do that through a car window." Then I remembered that hitchers are always begging for car rides too... Something to consider.

Once again, that whole day's adventure was Ron's treat. He said it was a reward for my having done so well so far. "Done so well," I sheepishly grinned to myself and negated telling him about all the rain I had faced going north.

No matter, I was grateful, and that day's experience was absolutely splendid. *Le chateau de Versailles* is about twelve miles southwest of *Paris* by train, or about twenty kilometers. It was a wonderful ride through *Paris* and the uniquely treated routing to France's hugely popular tourist site. The beautiful train ride, itself, was worth the ticket price. It was quite an upgrade from my train rides to and from *Berlin*. There were comfortable cushioned seats, exquisite, interior-wall woodwork with decorative lighting, and windows providing a first-class journey.

Originally, the *Palace of Versailles* was merely a hunting lodge and small chateau, including a surrounding moat, built by King Louis XIII in the early 1600's. He had come there often with his father, King Henry IV, because both loved hunting. Later, King Louis XIV decided to live there, and the chateau was transformed into the French Royal Palace in the 1680's. Once the grounds and palace were deemed large enough, the king moved his entire royal court there, and the French government was ruled from that site. At that time, decadent King Louis XIV and Louis XV had initially even used pure silver to construct the palace furniture; however, that was eventually all mostly melted down to help finance costs of their war efforts.

Later, King Louis XV installed a fantastic opera house on the grounds, and ongoing remodeling continued with each new ruler. The palace remained an especially important historical site throughout the centuries too. The opera house had been built and used for the wedding of the Dauphin, the eldest son of the king, to Marie Antoinette in 1770. Several other historically momentous events also took place at the *Palace of Versailles* too, such as "The Peace of Paris" in 1783, the "Proclamation of the German Empire" in 1871, and World War I was ended with the "Treaty of Versailles" at the palace in 1920.

During the French Revolution, which began in 1789, King Louis XVI and family were removed and sent back to Paris. The palace was then stripped of its royal contents with the ouster of the royal government and establishment of the revolutionary administration. However, over the years many essential items were eventually restored and returned. The magnificent grounds include the ceremonial Hall of Mirrors, the beautifully jeweled opera house, royal apartments, and also several intimate royal residences.

Future rulers, including Napoleon and Louis XVIII considered reutilizing the palace as a governing site, but it was always denied due to such extensive renovation and maintenance costs. However, the *Palace of Versailles* is significant to USA history because that is the site where in 1783, the United Kingdom formally recognized the independence of the United States of America. The palace is now a historical monument for its amazing history and fantastic, glorious palace construction of rock and marble and walls covered with magnificent artwork of statues and paintings by the greatest artists of the time. Additionally, its lovely grounds parks, fountains, canals, unique flower beds, and tree groves staged the parklike setting in majestic form.

It was a splendid day visiting the incredibly suggestive decadent lifestyle of King Louis's families. Being true blooded American, it was difficult to accept royal living of those degrees, yet anyone would have to be impressed by its stately and regal style. It was wonderful to visit and actually reminded me of one of our own amazing museum grounds for a quasi-regal character, William Randolph Hearst, of newspaper mogul fame. In fact, it was another site my aunt jean took me to visit of that ridiculously extravagant and magnificent Hearst Castle near San Simeon, California. The two sites, Palace of Versailles, and Hearst's Castle, both have in common that they were turned over to each's state government essentially because their property taxes and maintenance care were too expensive. Also, both eventually became tourist museums to help offset their costs.

Our day's event completed, Ron and I made plans for our trip going south. We decided that he'd pick me up again the next morning, and we would head straight south through the *Pyrenees Mountains* and into bordering Spain. We'd do a little cave exploring there just inside Spain near *San Sebastian* and then let our daytrip get us all the way to *Madrid*. I was flabbergasted conceiving of traveling that far including sightseeing in merely one day. Oh, how I appreciated Ron... and his vehicle. I loved VW Bugs from that day forward...

CHAPTER 11

OLD AND NEW DISCOVERIES

Denostia-San Sebastian

True to his word, Ron was at my *Left Bank Hotel* early the next morning. True to my own, I was outside awaiting his arrival. Both of us already fed, we were ready for a long day's drive south. Leaving *Paris* was both wonderful and melancholy. The southern part of the city was as beautiful and interesting as all I had already seen and as historical and charming too with ancient architecture shared side-by-side with very modern buildings. Just as before, when leaving the primary residential and commercial parts of *Paris*, our surroundings were immediately transposed into farming and agricultural livelihoods. Right away we were entering another wine producing region too.

French wines are international favorites, and it was obvious to us both that the growers took their wine producing craft very seriously. So many vineyards existed everywhere for miles, or kilometers and kilometers. I knew truly little about wine making, but Ron was somewhat knowledgeable, so he shared some information about our observations.

Without realizing, Ron informed me, I had already traveled through France's famous Champagne region while entering from Luxembourg. I learned that only wines from that region alone could be called *Champagne*. It was an explicit copyright infringement if done so, and illegal. Other similar vineyard regions could call their wines *Sparkling*, for instance, like

Brut as an example, but never Champagne. I learned much later that it was similar to *Tequila* could only be called by that name if it were from the Mexican State of Jalisco, and nowhere else, with a couple of minor border-town exceptions. Similar rules.

What we traveled through that morning and afternoon were primarily Bordeaux and Burgundy Regions and more sparkling wine vineyards (similar to *Champagnes*) from the Loire Region, and Cognac country. I'd hoped for plenty of wine-tasting stops to evaluate the validity of superior French wine-making claims, but Ron was hell-bent on making *Madrid* that day, so I didn't ask, and we never stopped. Besides, I'd never drunk anything to compare with French wines, so they would all have been the-best-I'd-ever-tried, just like the previous bottle I'd had in *Paris* upon my initial arrival. That stuff was cheap and not bad to my tastes, but what did I know? Only that I liked it!

Regardless, the magnificently manicured vineyards surrounding our travels were very impressive to view. Also, each vineyard had its own unique, chateau-like winery scattered about with very exotic names that I could barely pronounce, let alone recognize, Yet all were majestic in nature. It was obvious: The French sure love their grapes...

Our next uniquely beautiful sights came as we began climbing up the French-Spain bordering Pyrenees Mountains. That fabulous range separated the Iberian Peninsula of Spain and Portugal from the rest of Europe. Some mountain peaks rose to 11,000 feet, or 3,400 meters. Being a mountain boy, myself, I deeply appreciated all the beauty of those sharp, rocky peaks, green spread valleys, and thickly forested mountainsides. Although summertime, I could easily imagine all the great skiing that would be available for the public in winters. Ski resorts had over 430 kilometers, 270 miles of stretching Pyrenees Mountains to use for ski lifts and cross-country ski enthusiasts too. Summers, naturally, offer thousands of miles of trails for outdoor enthusiasts.

I genuinely enjoyed France and Spain's wonderful forests and mountains. Of course, I would be remiss to forget the tiny, hidden Principality of Andorra nestled high and away, and deep inside the eastern portion of the Pyrenees. If only I had time and money to pay it a nice visit. After Luxembourg, I guess I had developed an affinity for stopovers in Europe's tiny countries. Next time...

Soon, thereafter, and early that afternoon, we slipped right on down into official Spain, got our passports stamped, and made a direct right turn west to the amazing community of *Donostia-San Sebastian*. There is some wonderful, even if mythical, history about *San Sebastian's* namesake, St. Sebastian: He was born about 256 A.D. and spent his adult life spreading Christianity and performing many miracles. He was also a Christian officer in the Roman Army. Unfortunately, that fact was determined by other Roman military officers and he was arrested there in *Donostia* as such. From orders by the Roman Emperor Diocletian during his *Persecution of Christians* Era, Sebastian was ordered to be executed. As a Christian martyr, he was tied to a post or tree, shot several times with arrows, and then left hanging in a tree to die sending a signal to all other Christians for their own would-be transgressions and fate.

However, legend has it that Sebastian actually survived the arrows and hanging thanks to rumored healings by Rome's own St. Irene. Later on, unfortunately, he was discovered once again by other Roman authorities, and Sebastian was rearrested and then clubbed to death, surely becoming a martyr and Saint after his death in 288 A.D.. The community now of *San Sebastian* claims that St. Sebastian is buried on their hallowed grounds, but most Catholics accept that his remains are in the Roman Catacombs in Rome.

I was in particular awe that likely two of three required miracles performed by a Catholic to gain sainthood must have come from St. Sebastian's simply surviving those arrows and then his hanging in the first place. His other miracle, if only indirectly, was St. Irene's own survival in Rome from the crucifying emperor for a long enough period to save Sebastian. Tough guy and girl. St. Sebastian is known for curing the ill and he is considered a Saint for Plagues. He is also considered a soldier's saint because of St. Sebastian's own military servitude. Anyway, Ron and I visited his attempted execution site and then supposed burial grounds. As a Catholic, myself, I was impressed at least enough to remember and talk about it.

Anyway, the primary and most celebrated status of the 150,000 population of *San Sebastian*, however, were the many Cro-Magnon caves near its proximity. The numerous surrounding caves harbor incredible cave dweller drawings from as far back as 40,800 years. "Wow! That's older than dirt!" I quipped laughingly to Ron.

Anyway, I had never even planned on such a tourist visit and saw it all thanks to Ron. It was breathtaking. Yet, just like those French Louvre Museum guards carelessness with the <u>Mona Lisa</u>, the San Sebastian Spanish caretakers allowed us to get up so close to their prehistoric, cave-wall illustrations that we could practically touch the drawings. I was spellbound.

They appeared childish, or amateurish in nature, as crude animal sketches. Nevertheless, they were spectacular for humanity's sake. Several drawings have been dated as over 40,000 years old and were obviously simple but full-bodied designs of various animals living at the time, like cattle, and such. Evidently, cave dwellers, and cavewomen, liked their steaks just like us.

I remember wondering if they enjoyed their meat rare, or well done. They had already discovered fire nearly a million years before that. In my mind, I imagined socially advanced cave dwellers demanding, "I want mine medium-rare, please." Then as an afterthought they'd demand, "Cook 'till it says, 'Moo.' Grunt, grunt (laugh, laugh)!" But regardless, meat eaters or whatever, those cavepeople must have loved and appreciated their art and artists too.

In itself, *San Sebastian,* with its nearby caves and cave dweller drawings, could have been an entire summer's exploration, but we visited them both in merely a few hours' time. No matter, I was impressed, spiritually dignified, and emotionally overwhelmed all during that same brief visitation period. Yet, we were soon off for our next adventure in *Madrid.* So, south we went in order to arrive there still during daylight. Thank goodness for long summer days.

Museo Prada de Madrid

A few hours later, but with late evening's twilight still brightening our day, we entered the fabulous capitol city of *Madrid*, Spain. Ron had an impressive tourist guide of hotel listings for all of Europe, and it even identified a couple *Madrid* hostel addresses for me. He had already booked himself an exclusive reservation at one of Madrid's nicer hotels, but he decently provided me transportation directly to my own hostel residency. We made plans to hook-up together again the next morning, so we could make a day of touring *Madrid* and visiting its world famous, *Prada Museum.*

The *Madrid Youth Hostel* that we chose was both spectacularly laid back and comfortably ingenious. For one thing, though, it was busy. Everyone was passing through while heading further south to vacation near any of the multitudes of *Mediterranean Sea Riviera Beaches*. There in

Madrid, though, I imagined many people looking forward to enjoying the sun and sands of Spain's own world-famous *Riviera* shores. I still had time to spare, though, before visiting those special and popular destinations, so I focused on *Madrid*. Once again, Ron, my temporary tourist guide, would show me the way.

The next morning, and right on time again, Ron was there to pick me up and allow me to share the day's highlights with him. I had really enjoyed the *Madrid Youth Hostel* that previous night. It had been noisy, busy, and crowded, but I still managed to complete the proverbial *sh_t, shower, and shave*, and laundry basics. Everyone there was friendly and seemed well organized preparing for quickly passing on through to the *Spanish Riviera*.

Upon Ron's arrival I began to figure out a rationale for his punctuality: He was a middle-school teacher and was controlled by time slots. If he were ever tardy, students would be out-of-control. So, when traveling with Ron, I prepared promptly and was always ready before he was. Naturally, him being the judicious teacher, I did not have to wait long for Ron either.

We agreed making a *straight course* to Spain's exquisite offering to the world of museums, *le Museum del Prada*. Soon thereafter, I understood and agreed, "(Oh, my goodness), what a fantastic decision."

I could not be certain at the time, but *le Museum del Prada* became my absolutely favorite visited museum of all in Europe, and that included some serious challengers like *le musee du Louvre* in Paris, and eventually, the *Sistine Chapel*, itself, in Rome. I was visually overwhelmed by *le Prada's* marvelous exhibits.

Formally referred to as *Museo Nacional del Prada*, it was the main *Spanish National Art Museum* and was located in *Central Madrid*. It is still considered one of Europe's finest collections of European art with collections as far back as prehistoric periods, and especially the 1100's to more recent, modern times of the 20th century. I also found out that it was one of the world's favorite tourist visitations and considered one of the greatest art museums in the world. It is even deemed to be the largest collected exhibit of fine, Italian masters in the world, outside of Italy.

Le Prada's collection consisted of over 8,000 drawings, 7,600 paintings, 4,800 prints, and over 1,000 sculptures. Plus, I was told, it had many works on loan to other museum exhibits internationally. It was absolutely stunning to me because through its art and sculpture exhibits and historical displays, I was able to envision a long history of European growth and development that was totally mesmerizing. In one moment, I was viewing pre-Judeo-Christian artforms, and the next I was again studying replicas of *San Sebastian* cave drawings from 40,000 years before even that.

Then I looked upon 500-year-old knights' armor exhibits while humming "Dreaming the Impossible Dream" by Frank Sinatra from 1965, a song about a fictitious Spanish hero, Don Quixote, *The Man of La Mancha*. It was enough to get my classical blood boiling. Finally, I was fortunately able to view the wonderful, Italian Masters' exhibits from the likes of Leonardo da Vinci, Michelangelo, Botticelli, and others.

It was an absolutely impressive and fulfilling day. Both of us completely exhausted and artfully satisfied, Ron returned me to my *hostel,* which I had self-amusingly nicknamed *le Madrith Youth Hothtel* because of Spain's Castilian Spanish, lisp-like pronunciations. That night, I was to sleep well. "What could possibly get nearly as good as the *Prada Museum*?" I dreamily asked myself. "Patience, young man," I was to learn. "Just wait until Italy!" At the time, however, I could not have imagined...

Valencia Epiphany

Punctual Ron picked me up the next morning once again right on schedule. Of course, kudos to me too; I was also on time. We were not hurrying at all, so we took our time cruising through *Madrid* checking out all the many hundreds of years old, if not thousands, structures, monuments, statues, and architecture some dating back to Roman Empire times. Living among ancient artifacts became quite common, I recognized, for most Europeans.

So much history surrounded me everywhere I traveled. I wondered if locals appreciated all the incredible antiquities amongst them, or whether they just took them all for granted. *Madrid's* amazing relics, so close by and near enough to visit any time, must have made their history classes more interesting. Students on their ways home after school could easily swing by local parks and visit statues, monuments, and shrines dedicated to someone or something from ages earlier that they may have even studied that very day in classes. Very cool.

Yet, Madrid was as modern as any other city might be. The boulevards were wide, clean, and picturesque, and the stores and businesses, geared toward affluent and upper-middle classes, were crowded with advertisements, shoppers, and gawkers. Cafes lined the sidewalks serving and entertaining breakfast crowds, and early drinkers, I supposed. The World Cup Pre-Finals Playoffs were still obviously in full swing, and I could tell from avid cheering that Spain was still in the running.

I had already even laughed and cheered earlier to learn that England was still very much alive for the *FIFA Finals Tournament*. I laughed not because I understood anymore about soccer, in general, or its championship playoffs. Rather, it was because my chosen team, England, was still going strong, and it was recalling with a smile the sake of my Belgian Guard acquaintance. I enjoyed that our connection was merely a competitive macho kind of thing that mostly only guys or competitors really understood or appreciated.

But Madrid was absolutely a beautiful, vibrant, active, and similarly hectic city. I might have been in any city of Europe. Yet, like so many other cities I had visited, once the tall, central, bustling-business skyscrapers and buildings ended, and then commercial and residential districts eased away, suburban zones soon thereafter came to abrupt ends.

Almost immediately upon leaving busy, ancient-modern *Madrid*, we entered back into vineyard country and agricultural farmlands. We were heading in a southeast direction on a main highway, and our destination that morning was the large seaport community of *Valencia*, only a couple of hours away. I was excited because I imagined that soon I would be swimming in the *Mediterranean Sea*.

With *Valencia* not far ahead, I eagerly chatted with Ron about the imagined, beautiful blue *Mediterranean Sea* awaiting us ahead that I had heard and read so much about with its stunning *Riviera* beaches. The thrill for me was that soon I might be romping around those famous, exotic beaches alongside multitudes of "Itsy Bitsy Teenie Weenie Yellow Polka Dot Bikini(s)," and splashing about with them all in Spain's world-famous waters. I could hardly wait...

And then the unexpected happened, . . . and I ended up having plenty time to romp and splash about all I wanted even sooner than anything I had expected. It was because shortly after my pleasant, beachside daydreaming moments, there followed a brief, one-sided conversation by me and then an abrupt parting of goodbyes. With barely a few, neutrally exchanged words, Ron dropped me off right there in *Valencia*, directly on its beachfront and then quickly disappeared rushing on up the coastal highway without me. We had parted, it seemed, ever so immediately following a terse, quickly agreed-upon arrangement for another get together two weeks later in *Pisa*, Italy.

"Oh, uh, well, okay, then. See you soon, Ron," was my awkwardly unforeseen reaction...

That sudden separation with Ron had come about probably because of my, one-way, hitchhiking experience expose I had honestly, yet naively, provided him. Ron dropped me off not long after I had privately and personally undergone a shockingly deep, confusing, and challenging awareness of life's unique but varying and precarious ocean of ideas. In one moment, I was laughing, playing, and splashing around in generous, calm, and relaxing waters of ideas and background sharing. In the next, I was overwhelmed by an unexpected tsunami of thoughts crashing down upon me with its torrential flood of new truths. After a few, honestly innocent and brief comments to Ron, and even fewer yet significant observations, an incredible outpouring of mental and emotional issues all but drowned me into silence.

I quickly became aware of new, unique, and distinct aspects of life which had always been kept secret from me before. It was that, or I had simply been overly protected and sheltered. Or, I had just been naively ignorant of life's varying existences. In any case, I suddenly faced new and shocking perceptions of life's many *oceans* of differing thoughts and behaviors. I had *accidentally* opened my mind to a flood of ideas and schisms which poured over my prior, innocent, and protective barriers. I was soon left to quickly scramble for higher ground to seek on my own a clearer awareness of life's truer totalities.

Let me explain further: It was during that beautiful, Southern-Spanish drive toward Valencia that I was soon to have life's secretive walls come crashing down upon me as I was made to grapple with important human truths. I use the term "walls" because of what I was compelled to deal with during that otherwise quiet morning car ride with Ron. My words, and then quick observations, were followed by extremely shocking revelations. They were concepts which instantly and emphatically began tearing down privately guarded blockades of understandings that had otherwise maintained my previously ignorant, naïve, and innocent and immature knowledge of life with *all* its dimensions.

All my life I had lived, or had been kept, in some sort of secret, Catholicized, hush-hush zone. Perhaps similar to the decades later revolting military practice of "Don't ask-Don't tell," for me during that summer of1966 it had been more like "Don't consider-Don't explain." It was like *East Berliners*, I later analogized, where I had previously also been kept effectively hidden away and barred from silent truths. *Truths* of life in all their struggling qualities and unique characteristics, I should add. And like *East-Berlin* citizen-prisoners, I had been concealed, shielded, or merely kept from exposure to outside, honest realities.

And then suddenly I had broken through *Checkpoint Charlie*, a passageway to candor and enlightenment. With an intimacy of words, keen observation, and an *epiphany* of human understanding, unexpectedly I became more aware. And it was a shocking awareness of a whole new world of awkward honesty and more complicated realities that, regardless, compelled living truths to show their *true* faces before me...

What specifically happened actually occurred while Ron and I were simply and casually chitchatting away during our sunny morning drive to *Valencia*. I was both completely relaxed, daydreaming (about bikinis) and enjoying the comfortable, warm, and outside environment with my window rolled down as I lay stretched back lazily and my arm hanging outside in the bright, warm sunlight. Whilst nonchalantly nattering away, and with lack of any further substantive conversational topics, I inadvertently chose to provide Ron intense and intimate details with basic descriptions of that nasty, hitching incident of my travels and exploits after leaving him in *Amsterdam*... Here's what somehow casually and innocently transpired:

Nonchalantly, I merely mentioned in passing, "Hey, Ron, I never told you about what happened to me after passing through Luxembourg. Wow, it was the craziest experience I've ever had."

I noted Ron's interest as he nodded curiously and invited further comment, "Oh, yeah?"

So, excitedly I continued, "Oh, you bet! You see, it was late, and I was riding in this guy's car, his name was Carl, and I starting dozing-off when all of a sudden, he reached over and grabbed my knee. Well, I pushed his hand away hard. But later, he did the same thing, and that time it was higher-up, like on my thigh. Man, I shoved his arm away even harder and told him again to stop."

I noted that there was little or no curious response yet from Ron, but I was already upbeat and immersed in my simple report. So, I continued even more enthusiastically, "Then later, Ron, when we had stopped so I could take a leak, would you believe it, that sucker leaped on me, forced me back against his car, and started grabbing my privates and rubbing them. . . Well, I just punched that dude right in the head, and then I shoved him away hard on his chest. Then I even tried to kick him in the balls too. The way he reacted I think I may even have. Ha! Ha!

"And then I started screaming and cussing at him in French too, 'Va en enfer loin de moi!' (*Get to hell away from me!*) And, boy, did he run for it! Gee, you should have seen him move. He raced out of there like a bat-out-of-hell! I mean, I barely got my sea bag out of his car in time, I'll tell you! Ha! Ha!"

During those last moments of my excitable verbal depiction, I had undoubtedly become loud and animated. I was even grinning over the subsequent vague comedy potential of that entire recounted incident. And my brief outpouring of personal intimacy led me naturally to look over seeking Ron's supportive reaction. Was he amused, shocked, or even angered?

But there was nothing... I noted from Ron's stillness that absolutely no communicative response whatsoever was evident. Other than his blank facial expression seemingly impervious to my details, he merely appeared more pale than usual while his hands continued tightly gripping the steering wheel. Ron was emotionless as he simply stared straight ahead unexpectedly silent to my remarks thus far.

Noticing no immediate or notable response from Ron, and wishing yet to gain some, I innocently but naively determined to try even harder. I continued, "Yeah, Ron, I'll tell you, I coldcocked that sucker, alright. Grabbing my privates like that? Boy, I popped that weirdo good and sent him on his way. That's for sure!"

I was still grinning as I stared again at Ron seeking some inkling of a favorable reaction. Was he worried and stressed over my reprehensible hitchhiking endeavors now? Was he anxious or fearful for my future? Was he angry at Carl or amused and elated over my story's results? Did he think my reactions to Carl instead demonstrated a violent and vile overreaction? No. Nothing. I got nothing. Ron just continued staring straight ahead while steering his vehicle stiffly.

Thus began a long series of self-doubt questioning in my mind. Was I a poor storyteller? Had Carl's actions disgusted Ron. Had my reactions to Carl disappointed him? All I considered was that in-the-end it was actually a pretty unusual, if not humorous, encounter to share with someone. I had been attacked by another guy and had effectively chased him away. Good for me, huh? You might think so, and I hadn't even mentioned having to walk all night for the next fifteen miles or so either. But my story really did deserve a reaction, I felt. Something, at least...

And then reality's deluge began gushing over my innocent, naïve, and ignorant but gentle sea's view of life. Floodgates began being smashed open during a tidal wave flooding over my innocence. My mind became a hurricane of questions seeking answers. One answer progressively upheaving yet another question, and that query dislodging yet another questionable response. Steadily, my contemplation onrush brought on by that surge of emotional distress and bewilderment, proffered an ultimately new understanding, an *epiphany.*

I began questioning everything in my mind, "Why isn't that a funny story?... Why doesn't Ron react to it?... Does he disapprove of how I treated Carl?... Shouldn't he be mad at Carl for his actions toward me?... I'm fairly sure his roommates, Dick, and Dwayne, would have been... They all lived together, ... and they probably thought alike,... and they all... shared... the... same... bed... and wanted me to sleep with them in their bed too!..."

My mind began tail-spinning as I progressed with my analysis, "Oh, my God, does that mean that they are all just like Carl?... How could that be?... Why, Aunt Jean and Phyllis introduced me to them... They wouldn't invite me to see guys like that, would they?... Or encourage me to visit the same guys again in *Amsterdam*, would they?... And Jean and Phyllis are their friends, sure,... and just like them, they are roommates too!... What?!! Jean and Phyllis live together, and so are they the same as Ron, Dick, Dwayne, and Carl, but women?... Oh, my goodness!"

By then, my brain was cracking in all directions at light speeds. Like Ron, I suddenly also became quiet and very still, staring straight ahead like him out my window as I continued with my overwhelming contemplations picking-up where I left off.

"But Jean and Phyllis have so many other wonderful friends too," I mentally defended. "Friends like Tommie and Mickey (whom I had just spent my past whole last school year living with at their house near my high school). They were extraordinarily kind to me, and Tommie even had a wild, crazy daughter older than me... How could that be?

"And yet, Tommie and Mickey were roommates too, and just like Jean and Phyllis, they slept together... and acted and dressed sort of differently,.. even more manly. Wow! What is this?" I continued asking myself. "What about all Jean and Phyllis's other swell friends: Other authors, artists, lawyers, doctors, teachers, businesspeople?... Why, most of those friends are all roommates too!... Coincidences?... Oh, my God!... And all of them are Bay Area Professionals too, just like Ron... and Dick... and Dwayne. . . And they all sleep together too,.. and do they all have sex together?... Yet, they have all always been so kind and wonderful and secretive to me... How can this be?... How could I not ever have known?... This is a whole new aspect of life I never even knew existed... until now!"

I was utterly speechless, and momentarily unwilling for any constructive and, no doubt, extremely awkward conversation. Besides, Ron was still white as a bedsheet and still totally focused on the road ahead. Time passed, an hour or more, and I kept on thinking of new aspects and parallels to my new advanced awareness of life. To boot, I was yet completely unaware of any terminology related to that behavior or lifestyles, such as *same-sex attraction*. That understanding did not come until sometime later in its formalities for me. However, right then, Ron and I just quietly continued our drive and even silently passed through the beautiful city of *Valencia* and then reaching its gorgeous beachfront on the *Spanish Riviera* and the spectacular *Mediterranean Sea*.

That was when I finally broke-the-ice again and offered, "Hey, Ron, this looks like a wonderful place for me to visit. How about dropping me off here, and I'll meet you again in Italy?"

"Yes, alright," Ron quickly responded, "Two weeks from today, at noon, at the *Tower of Pisa*. See you then..."

He pulled over at a beachfront parking lot allowing me enough time to grab my bag, climb out, roll-up the window, and close his car door behind me. And then, unnervingly, just like Carl's spectacular departure had been, Ron was also gone in a flash. I was left there waving at his vanishing act. Speechless. I noted that I was once more alone again after four days having traveled and visited with my friend, Ron.

But I wasn't really alone. I had a mindful of intensely conflicting thoughts and concepts to grapple with and some meaningful understanding to come to grips with. Oh, I'd swim and walk the beaches, alright, and even stare wistfully at many cute bikini clad girls, but I also had plenty of diverging thoughts swimming around inside my brain to deal with and think about...

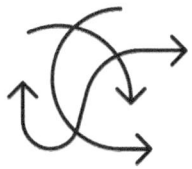

CHAPTER 12

RIVIERA RULES

Blood Money

As it turned out, I actually ended up walking along the beachfront highway the same direction as Ron while paralleling the seaside streets of lovely *Valencia* beside the beautiful Mediterranean Sea. Eventually, I stopped at a café for a meal because I had definitely developed an appetite by then. I suppose I needed food and a beverage to help digest all the multiple degrees of thought that I had recently been forced to absorb. The menu included everything new to me, but I chose some really good and inexpensive items: Cold Gazpacho soup and some tortillas. My Aunt Jean had made that type of soup before, and I recognized it. The café's tortillas were advertised as world favorites, and the cerveza was cheap too. So, I indulged and finished off my meal with Salem cigarettes ... to help destroy any delicious aftertastes.

That café lunch was also where I started talking to another English-speaking tourist hitchhiker, like me, but one who was fairly savvy with the *Valencia* area. He was from Switzerland and had been in the local area for a while and was soon returning home. His vacation time was over. The curious thing about him was that he was fairly broke too, again similar to me, and we easily got on the subject of saving money or stretching it out as much as possible. I didn't give him many personal details, but I did leave him with the impression that I was destitute.

Maybe he felt sorry for me because that was when he told me of a really interesting idea. He said that the local *Valencia General Hospital* was paying around $5 (US Dollars), or 250 Spanish Pesetas, for a single, blood-donor offer. That sounded like a lot of money to me, and easy money too. But I had never given blood before, and that would be another *first* for me. "How hard could it be, though?" I asked myself. "Somebody just sticks a needle in your arm and sucks out the blood they want, and then they hand you five bucks. Easy. Peasy." My Swiss acquaintance gave me simple directions and location to the hospital's donor center, and then he was off on his own way.

With money on my mind, I followed his route instructions and easily located the *Valencia General Hospital,* not too far from where I'd started. Of course, kilometers to me were like city blocks to others by then. Anyway, I found the entrance location, and with only English and a little French speech, I made known my intentions. The male attendant understood right away what I wanted, and after assuring me of the payment details, 250 pesetas, he directed me to the precise blood donor's area.

I was seen very soon thereafter by a young orderly who took me into a room, allowed me to set my sea bag in a corner, seated me, and immediately began prepping me for the blood-donor procedure. I was very cordial and smiled a lot; it was my habit to do so, anyway. The orderly was friendly too, but we both were a little uneasy probably because of our language barrier.

I understood, however, when I was asked which arm to use for the procedure. I chose my left because I had earlier realized that during all that prior, silent, thought-provoking time while riding in Ron's car heading to *Valencia,* my right arm had been dangling out the VW car window. It became really sunburned and was in no shape to have a needle shoved into it too. Thus, the orderly cleaned my left, inside-elbow joint area. He then tightened a restrictive band around my upper arm to build up blood pressure, I guessed. Next, he had me make a fist, and then he began searching for an appropriate vein into which to insert his large, ominous looking needle.

The orderly stabbed me once and nothing happened. I did let out a slight yelp but continued smiling. "It is worth the pain for five dollars," I grinned. He rubbed my veins' area and poked me again with another needle. Grunting a little, still nothing came of it, but I just continued smiling... The blood-drawer looked at me slightly confused and prepared another needle.

The third insertion hurt more than I liked, but still nothing exited except blood from the stab wound itself. I let out a significant whimper that time but merely shook my head at the poor, confused, and novice phlebotomist. He began looking at me anxiously, and I took it as an opportunity for *inserting* a little humor into the situation myself.

I shook my head adamantly at the orderly, pouted sadly, and woefully announced, "Sorry, I have no blood, but can I have the money still?"

He said nothing, but I was certain he understood my words. He inserted yet another needle, and that time he was momentarily minimally successful, but then blood stopped flowing. The blood-receiving tube had barely risen in contents, though. I continued shaking my head and vehemently pronouncing, "I am so sorry, but I just have no blood! But please, I need pesetas!"

The orderly seemed to have lost his cool by that time, and he left the room. Finally, he returned with his supervisor of some sort, maybe even a doctor. Another stab, another minimal reaction, and then both appeared frustrated. Finally, on a sixth attempt, the needle struck gold, or blood, and a slight outpouring began. The orderly released the tourniquet band and had me unclench my fist. Blood eked out slowly, pathetically slowly, but still I didn't know any better and was only glad it had finally worked. I even overexaggerated my excitement pretending surprise at having discovered that I actually did have blood after all. The orderly just stared at me acting quite bewildered, or annoyed.

After an interminable period, however, the blood container being used finally reached its appropriate full level, about ten gallons worth I felt, and the orderly removed everything. He then put a large gauze swab with several band aids over the entire area where their needle jabs had occurred. Finally, he gave me a slip of paper and directed me to the payment center window for services rendered. I quickly received my 250 pesetas, and while grinning up a real satisfaction storm over my ultimate success, I hoisted my sea bag upon my shoulder again, pranced right on outside the blood donor building, and waltzed satisfyingly on down the road back to *Valencia's* beach highway.

Ever since that café lunch and conversation with my sympathetic and helpful Swiss acquaintance, I had been totally focusing on the *money-for-blood* scheme. My prior mind-bending discoveries about Ron and his roommates, all three of them my friends, Aunt Jean and Phyllis, their other friends, many of which were also my friends too, and what it all meant had taken a temporary back seat to my more recent and more urgent matter of earning money. That entire revelation had temporarily become only minorly relevant. With the money pursuit's ending, I was just relieved and happy to find the blood donor activity over with after becoming a successful event. I was about five dollars richer than I had been only a couple of hours earlier. I was happy and satisfied.

Yet, that was when I began considering an alternate truth: That conniving orderly and his boss were both having the laugh of their day for having punished and tortured someone, a foreigner at that, and perhaps especially an American, for being so desperate as to give them his rich blood for their measly pesetas. Effectively, I had earned merely eighty cents, or forty pesetas, per poke. Ouch! That hurt...

Barcelona Night Life

Valencia, though a beautiful port city in its own right, was unfortunately harboring some dramatic, if not frustrating, reflections for me. Thus, due to my somewhat depressed mood, rather than stick around touring more of that colorful seaside community, I elected forsaking it and moving on ahead down the road just a little further. I'd take along with me all my newly confused thoughts and some meager, newly gained money. My map showed the well-known city of *Barcelona* merely one decent ride ahead, so I walked on, sea bag hoisted and thumb stuck out again, and tested local traffic.

The bright sunlight, pleasurable, sea-front breeze, amiable vacationing folks, and a bit of good luck got me a decent ride right away. I was soon picked up by a nice Spanish couple who were just out cruising the coastline to visit family. I learned that they were going to another seaport town near *Barcelona,* and I figured from there it would be a leisurely walk the rest of the way into town. So much for *figuring...*

During my brief ride, time passed quickly, and with no English understood and no Spanish spoken by me except, "Muchas gracias," it kept our conversation to a minimum. It was pleasant, however, just listening to that young couple gab away at whatever it was they discussed. They seemed happy, and their banter was filled with laughter and expressiveness. My mind, on the other hand, was crammed with frustrated thoughts of my ignorance and naivete. I wondered and questioned why my parents had never shared any facts, details, or truth about Aunt Jean, my mother's sister, for crying-out-loud.

"What is supposed to be so secret about Jean and Phyllis and their relationship, or any others'," I pondered. "Was there shame, or embarrassment, or just chosen secrecy involved?" Hey, perhaps my parents didn't even know either, I considered. "Maybe I am the *first* one to discover the real truth of their unusual relationship."

I imagined the shock and surprise once I spilled the proverbial beans: "Mom, Dad, I have important news to tell you. Aunt Jean and Phyllis actually love each other, sleep in bed together, and may even have consensual sex."

"What is that you say?" Mom would cry out. "It just can't be! How? Why? When?"

"Well, I'll tell you, Dear," my dad would prophetically announce, "For a long time now, I've had suspicions."

"Suspicions of what?" I contemplated. It was just too much unknown thought to deal with. So, to ease my gratuitous anxiety, I then simply and joyfully tossed the whole subject aside with the next sea breeze.

I only had *suspicions* now, myself, and I did not even understand what all it meant anyway. All I could immediately examine and relate to was that the whole matter had seemed serious enough for Ron to *desert me quicker than a vampire at daybreak.* Anyway, I had a lot to learn regarding any significance of the whole matter in the future...

For right then, however, I needed to figure out dinner and then find my next place to spend the night. The day was ending, and night fall was closing in rapidly. My onetime idea of sleeping on the beach might come to fruition after all.

After kind words of departure were shared with my Spanish lift-givers, I hiked further up the coastal highway toward *Barcelona*. The main highway had split off in the direction needed by the couple. So I chose to stick to a lesser driven, seaside roadway in order to enjoy the *Mediterranean* views. Not taking any chances, though, I stopped at a roadside tourist storefront and purchased some travel food items with my newly earned pesetas. I bought some corn muffins, dried beef jerky, an orange, some candy, and a bottle of soda pop. It was typical road food again but simply fine with me. Besides, *Salems' witchcraft* always took the edge off my hunger pangs.

On the road again, as I walked along, I began giving eyesight to any respectable place on the beach that might make a night's camp. Unfortunately, the beaches along that section had given way to rougher grounds and pebble-like, rockier surfaces. But continuing up a little further,

I happened to look inland across the coastal road, and I noticed a harvested hay field with big haystacks methodically arranged for a million acres, it seemed. That gave me yet another great idea for a decent night's layover. I'd make a soft straw bed on the backside of a haystack out-of-sight of any advancing traffic, or farmers, or dogs...

And that's just what I did for that night. I cut myself a nice bed right on the rear side of a nearby haystack and spread all my belongings neatly down beside me, as necessary. With my faithful sea bag reconverted into a hay mattress cover, and my blanket to cover me, I had dinner under that starry moonlit night. With the ocean's metronomic surf breaking on the beach in the distance, it was almost musical and really very pleasant. Sleep came to me very relaxingly and naturally. Of course, I must note that I was incredibly careful when smoking my Salem's too; I did not wish to burn to death during my hay stacked sleep or torch Spain's Riviera countryside either.

The next morning was a little rougher because I had made no plans for breakfast, coffee, or getting cleaned-up. So I did what I could by repacking and setting-up again on the highway to *Barcelona*. Soon, however, I had a decent ride all the way into the fabulous city of *Barcelona*. Once there, I was certain that I would like to stay for a while and check out all the wonderful city sights. Right away, I found a reasonable café, got cleaned-up, and had a breakfast of scrambled eggs with ham and tortillas, including coffee Americano. A Salem afterwards, and I was in a mellow mood.

The city lay spread out fashionably, and there were a lot of old, Spanish relics and buildings mixed with upgraded, *Spanish Riviera* beachfront buildings. The crowds were all there to enjoy the sun and fun on the beaches. The *Mediterranean Sea* was as blue as the sky and clean and sparkling with foamy white surf breaking offshore. Crowds were already there marking off their private suntanning spots with blankets, towels, and beach lounge recliners. The many resorts had their own specially marked sites for their private guests, but anyone could walk between them and get to the beachfront, if they chose.

I was ready for some fun in the sun and body surfing, so I found a deserted area and made a spot for myself with my blanket. Then I had my *first* dip in the *Mediterranean Sea*, and it was fantastic. The water was honest-to-goodness mild to warm, and it was very refreshing. It wasn't like the Northern California cold ocean waters I had tried. The Mediterranean Sea body surfing and swimming was fun, the water wonderful, and I relaxed the rest of the afternoon splashing and sunning on that glorious pebble beach. That is also where I got the next idea for my upcoming night's lodging: All the resort beaches had lounge chairs meticulously lining their seafronts. Any was simply perfect for me!

After finding a small seaside café and having some tasty dinner of ham and vegetable stew, and a beer or two, I hiked back down to the seashore and just meandered up the coastline awhile. The beautiful *City of Barcelona* lay off in the distance just behind the many resorts covering much of the shoreline. As it became darker, eventually I found an ideal place to spend the night.

One large resort had built a tall retaining wall to help level its grounds from the seashore. However, the grounds crew had left several lounge chairs spread out and unguarded at the foot of their retaining wall for their guests to enjoy a beach view and a day's sunlight. One particular lounge chair was ideal for me to enjoy the night's quiet and became another *first.* Calm sea breezes with sea waves breaking and lapping upon the shore added tranquil aesthetics to my resting spot. I'd had to admit that my previous night's *haystack bed* had been another nice *first,* but that comfortable lounge chair by the seashore simply beat all.

I wished only that I could afford room service, "Camarero, una cerveza, por favor. No, hazlo dos, gracias!" No, make it two, thanks! It was a nice night.

At sunrise the next morning, I was up and gone before maintenance personnel or *camareros* (*waiters*) may have alerted authorities. I mean, I had done nothing really wrong except not pay for the privilege of using their lounge chair all night, but I could forgive myself for that.   "I   was merely checking out the facility for a future paying visit," I defended myself.

Being early, though, I found a nice, inexpensive café inward from the *Barcelona* resorts and was able to clean myself somewhat and then have a nice breakfast of eggs, or huevos, and bread with jam along with coffee. It was just what I needed for a brief walking tour of that fabulous city.

Of course, like so many other cities visited, I was usually only able to see what I could find by happenchance while wandering through a city's streets. *Barcelona* was no exception, but I did manage to find some interesting sights to visit and take a few snapshots with my camera. *Barcelona* was typical of my other visited cities regarding photos and small trinkets purchased.

Fact is, for that whole journey so far, I have mentioned little about my photography or souvenir shopping. I should have revealed that I took only specific pictures of special sights to help conserve expensive films. I also purchased only very inexpensive, small, and lightweight items to carry along and take home as souvenirs and gifts. Plus, when possible, I bought cheap postcards to professionally show off some visited sights. The plan worked fairly well, and I kept everything orderly, clean, and wrapped-up inside my sea bag.

Throughout my brief hike through *Barcelona*, I used a trick I had learned originally in *Paris*. Whenever I found something interesting to view, I'd wait and listen for some English-speaking tour in the area to approach that particular site. Even if it was French, I was okay to stand close enough to get a free info guide on the history or meaning of the attraction. However, I didn't follow the same group all around to hear about everything else too. That would have been cheapskate…ish, but I did wait for the next attraction's English tour to come around. Clever…

On my own private tour, however, I did get to see things like ancient, spectacular-Spanish buildings with their gigantic spires and fabulous Gothic architecture. I visited the glorious *Barcelona Cathedral* for my mother's sake, and I read of, and listened to passing tour groups about, incredible histories of *Roman ruins* in the city, the *Spanish Inquisition*, and *Spain's Civil War*.

It was a nice, borrowed morning and afternoon visit of eavesdropped tours, but soon thereafter, I was feeling anxious to get on the road again to find some place for a lengthier stay. My *Barcelona* visit had turned out to include two separate days visiting whatever was possible to find and see. My nighttime escapades had resorted to finding decent sleepover conditions. Fine with me. Play all day; sleep all night. Yet, I longed for a lengthy opportunity and time to enjoy the sun and surf and take in all the views, especially *all* those skimpy bikinis romping around those sexy beaches. . .

Leaving the *Barcelona* area, I chose to stay right on the main beachfront highway that stayed right close to the sea. There were many small towns to pass through on the way with other hitchhikers lined up awaiting their turns. I quickly learned the "Etiquette of Hitching:" *Where and when you found other hitcher's, you must walk past them all and take your rightful place at the furthest end of the line down the road toward your destination.*

If you didn't, others would definitely let you know about it while pointedly directing you to the line's end. Of course, once in a while, I'd get a car that stopped just past me, so then I'd hurry, jump in, and wave joyously to the others, "Bye! Sorry, but they like me! It's my good luck! See ya!"

Other times, I'd stop and chat with other hitchers and try to get a *lay-of- the-land*. There outside *Barcelona* was where I stopped and visited with one traveler who told me about a place that turned out to be my most laid back, most memorable, and most emotional stopover destination so far. It was an incredibly unique and inexpensive hostel about an hour and a half ahead by car and located just barely inland from the beach.

The hitcher who told me about it was already staying there, himself, and he instructed me of what land sign to watch for and then take that turn-off to find it. It was in a small community on the *Costa Brava (Wild Coast)*, and on the furthest edge of the *Spanish Riviera* near France, he mentioned. "The hostel," he added, "is a converted castle." That was all it took for me. I could hardly wait to find it...

Castle Hostel

My directions were perfect. Two easy rides, the second, continuing all the way along the Spanish coastline toward France, dropped me right off at the castle hostel's turnoff-point doorstep near the seaside community of *Palamos*. From the main highway a couple blocks from the seashore I walked up the quaint roadway toward the hostel and passed a number of small, family-run, but particularly useful businesses for locals and tourists alike.

On either side of the road, which was made of quite impressive inlayed brick, were little markets for groceries, a couple of loud, busy bars, and small souvenir shops selling everything from postcards and film to tiny bull replicas of Pamplona, a nearby, internationally famous community for its insanely crazy, city streets bull runs. Those became my stops for outside edibles, beer, film, and toy souvenirs for home. Walking up the street, I noted that, so far, everything I'd need was right there.

Then came another *first.* As I approached one of the several small markets alongside the roadway, I watched as a small boy child, around ten years of age, come out of a store carrying a large bottle of wine. Curious of the scene, I noted two things: One was that the bottle was already opened and half empty; my other observation was that the ten-year-old was actually staggering up the street going to wherever. He was drunk as hell, and nobody around on the street said or did anything. The child just wobbled away on his unattended own.

Anyway, soon thereafter came my big pleasing surprise. I found the *Costa Brava Hostel,* and it really was an actual castle. Just to the left, and off the roadside with a short path leading to its entrance, were large glass, double doors entering the facility. Above and behind that entranceway loomed the large, granite-rock castle, itself.

It was complete with round corner towers, including wartime arrow slits converted into windows, tall curtain walls, and the main castle building, or keep, which held entry to a large, inner-garden yard called the bailey. The strongest portion of the fortification of a castle is the keep, or place to go in case of an attack or siege. That was the communal area. At first, I could not tell what was located above floors of the keep. It was an honest-to-goodness castle, though, and I instantly became excited. I was so happy I even mentally prepared to accept having to sleep in the dungeon, if necessary, or allowed. Cool!

I was to learn that long ago, in the castle's heyday, the grounds had actually all been twisted around. The onetime moat was gone, I was told, and the main entrance used to be on the far, opposite side. No matter to me. I was about to enter my second castle, Hearst's Castle being my first, but in this one I would be staying for a while, I hoped.

Entering through the large glass doors, I came into a huge community room, like an ancient, converted banquet hall of some sort but filled with card tables and chairs, a pool table, a ping pong table, and assorted chairs and couches for comfortable seating. On the far end of the big communal area was also an obvious eating area too with tables for many guests to sit and eat prepared foods from the adjacent, transformed-castle kitchen.

"Oh, this is going to be hard to beat," I thought. "What more could I possibly want?"

Inside, on a far wall, I saw an open door with a sign above that read, "Oficina." *Office*. I made my way to that spot just as some helpful hostel guests pointed me in the same direction. I walked over and entered the office room. An elder woman staff person was busy calculating and marking pages on a logbook, and she looked up as I stepped inside.

"Puedo ayudarte?" and then, "Can I help you?" the excellent, English-speaking worker asked.

"Hello, my name is Daniel, and I would be honored if I could stay in this wonderful hostel, please."

"Oh, is that right? Well, my name is Angelina, and I am the manager. We would also be honored to have you stay here, as long as your night's rent is paid on time and in advance." She then smiled and checked me out even closer. "Where are you from? United States?"

"I am California, in fact," I responded surprised. "How did you guess?"

"Because of your Americanized English, and the English are never *honored* to stay anywhere except at home. Ha! Ha! Welcome, and sit down. We'll discuss payments and rules."

Angelina turned out to be very courteous, but serious, and helpful. I was comfortable around her immediately. My immediate joyful reaction was the cheap pricing for guest fees to stay: Fifty pesetas per night, and twenty-five pesetas per meal, or only fifty pesetas for all three meals. That meant only about two dollars a day for room and board. Right away, I figured that I had a place to live for life. Who could turn that down? Of course, in order to eat there, which required a voucher, you had to be an overnight guest too. That kept the locals and riff raff from sneaking in for cheap meals.

The *Costa Brava Hostel* rules were similar to others, but with more offerings: Pay rent on time; no liquor on site; no loud noises after 10:00 P.M. when the Oficina closed; no violence ever allowed; guests and visitors only allowed in communal areas; clean-up all food messes you make; pay for all meals ahead of time by purchasing meal chits for standard, specific mealtimes given; and finally, doors get locked at midnight with no entries after that. It also stated that any overnight guests arriving after 10:00 P.M., but before midnight, and who stayed overnight sleeping in the Community Room owed for that night also. No exceptions. Guards were on duty 24/7. Overall, very fair rules, I believed.

Right away, I paid for the next three nights and days in full, and I also purchased vouchers for that night's dinner and next day's three meals because I planned to just lay around, rest, think, and soak up the environment. I might go out, I figured, but I'd be back in time for all meals. I found out that guest rooms were gender divided and all located in part of the primary castle building on site. Guests were not allowed to wander around the remaining castle grounds exploring without permission, and usually only on guided tours. I hoped to do that in time, but I was anxious to dump my sea bag in my room and relieve myself of its bulky weight. I'd been carrying that hulking thing around already for a month, and I needed a nice break from its responsibility.

Before leaving for my room, however, I had to mention to the manager, and ask about, the young child I had seen earlier drinking wine. The manager did not flinch, nor even seem surprised at all. In fact, she had a fairly clear explanation for the incident. Casually, she simply clarified,

"Here, and in much of Spain, the faucet water is unclean for drinking. One would become sick from it. Therefore, most families serve wine with their meals to all, including children. The child you saw was starting his dinner meal a little earlier than usual..." Understood.

"May I bring you something before your meal arrives, Sir?" the waiter might ask...

"Yes, thank you," I might respond. "Wine, please, plenty of it, and no water!"

My assigned room was midway down the *Men's Hallway* right off the communal/dining room and facing the outside street level. I imagined that, historically, all the available Guest Rooms there in *Costa Brava Castle Hostel* had been used for castle staff in its prime. What a lot of employees the place had needed. Plus, I was told that there were two persons per room, but each room could be converted into space for three, or four, if needed. Easily, I found my numbered room and knocked to be polite...

Love Guru

"Enter at yer own risk!" someone inside bellowed.

I opened the door and peeked in to find a red headed, and lightly red-bearded, fellow sitting upon one of the twin beds inside. The other bed was opposite him in the small rock and concrete room which also included a four-drawer dresser separating both beds and underneath a curtained, outside-viewing window. Each twin bed had another bunk style, fold-down, lift-up bed for additional guests, if required, but they could be used in the meantime to store one's belongings above.

At least that is what I surmised quickly when checking the room's layout. Then I gave the redhead my attention by greeting him. "Hello, I'm Daniel from California, and I'll take the risk (of entering). It's nice to meet you, Roommate."

Big Red gave me a quick once over, and then he grinned like I've never seen before. His huge full mouth with pearly white teeth immediately made me feel welcome. *Red* was a younger looking, mid-twenties fellow of medium build, and around five foot nine or ten inches in height. He had longer, bushier hair tied back in a ponytail, and a low cut, red beard covering his full face. He also had very fair skin with a light dabbling of freckles. I'd say he was interesting and even dashing to look at. Overall, *Big Red* was a handsome enough fellow and appeared very friendly.

194

"Well, alright?" he curiously welcomed me. "Come right on in and toss yer stuff up above there, Mate. It's decent to make yer acquaintance, California! Me name's Phillip, but ye can call me anything' ye like. Just don't call me *too-late-for dinner!*"

I laughed and did just what he told me. Then I sat down on my new bunk facing him to chat and visit a bit if he felt up to it. I offered him a Salem, and he accepted it graciously, "Bloody brilliant! A menthol too! "Outfu—in' standin'!"

I noticed that he had been looking at a Girlie Magazine, so my immediate impression was that he would not bother me. I relaxed. As it turned out, I would learn quite a bit from *Phillip* in a rather brief time. I'd hear about the castle's highlights, and he'd tell me about girls who passed through as guests, and sex, and love, and. . . And my goodness, when he got on those subjects, it was hard to shut him up.

Yet, Phillip was cheerful, friendly, and struck me as a trustworthy roomy. Actually, he even reminded me of ol' *Gustav Hamburger Joe.* They both had similar outgoing personalities and obviously both liked women. But unlike Joe, Phillip was dressed far more casually with only a faded white T-shirt, blue jeans, and tennis shoes. Phillip's big advantage for me, however, was his clear but pleasant English speech whose accent definitely sounded very Irish. I'd find out soon enough.

It was later afternoon, and Phillip asked me to join him in the eating area for dinner later on. I agreed, and then he filled me in on a bit of his own past. . . Phillip was a barber, he told me, from London. Every summer he took the month of July off and traveled south to the *Riviera* for fun in the sun. He laughed jokingly that because of all the chronic fog in London he'd had to drive a thousand kilometers just to get sunburned.

Phillip teased some more when he said, "Ninety percent of the time, Brits, and Londoners alike, hope for and *anticipate sunshine.* Unfortunately, they never get it. The other ten percent of the time, they are *disappointed!*"

Yet, Phillip did love his city; however, because he was pure Irish, he just did not like most Brits. He even said that he'd deliberately screw-up a Brit's haircut and then refuse to refund their fee or threaten to beat 'em if they didn't pay and leave. Phillip just laughed saying that it was to send word out that Brits were not welcome with him, only the Irish. Word did get out too, he chuckled, because his schedule was always filled with similar thinking Irish lads. Plus, any Brit newcomers that did drop by his shop had usually already learned to avoid Phillip's chair like the plague. Regardless, he always earned and enjoyed his vacations.

Phillip admitted, however, that of all the many *Riviera* places he had visited, he preferred the *Spanish Riviera* the most because it was least expensive and lots of ladies liked it there too. He then went on, and on, and on, describing all the beauties he had already seen or been with. Somewhat of a braggart, he was, but Phillip was lively, descriptive, interesting, and entertaining.

Deep into our conversations that first evening came a point when I felt comfortable enough talking to him about my *outside-Luxembourg hitchhiking experience with Carl* and then about my friend Ron's strange non-reaction near *Valencia*. Finally, I also mentioned my confused feelings about Aunt Jean and Phyllis and all the others too. Phillip seemed like a man-of-the-world, so I appreciated his opinion and advice. He was a good listener too, silent and nodding appropriately, which was an excellent quality for a barber; however, he loved to talk too.

I also realized from listening to Phillip that he was a decent person too. He heard me out and then explained issues in his mind's thinking simply and conclusively. With clarifying words, he stated, "Mate, ye jus' got picked-up by a gay feller, a guy tha' likes men an' boys, an' not women. They're all over, Danny-boy, but ye merely need to be more observant, more careful, and choose yer rides better. It's fair to ask even before ye get into a car. If necessary, talk about yerself only likin' girls an' not the other way. Those blokes are all usually cool, but ye got riddled by an aggressive one. Not nice."

I had mostly agonized while figuring out much of that stuff already, but I was still unclear about Ron, his roommates, and Jean, and all her friends. So, I asked Phillip about all that too. "Why did Ron keep so quiet, Phillip, and then leave me so suddenly?" I began asking seriously.

"Mate," he replied, "no doubt ye embarrassed Jupiter out of him. He's likely a cool bloke, calm, and gentleman type, but ye might have just shocked him silly. He didn't know what to say, or how to say it, so he just chose to leave the scene."

That thought was awful to consider for me. I didn't want Ron to feel that way about me. We were friends. Then I followed up asking Phillip about Aunt Jean and the others. His response was solemn and understandable to me. Yet, I could only pensively remain quiet after he explained.

"Ye see, Daniel," Phillip began, "gays are not popular in most places. Their lifestyles, and assumed sexual behavior, are unacceptable by conservative leaders and most religious groups. Back in my hometown, London, if the bobbies (police) find out someone is gay, they'll put 'em in jail, and the bloke can get hard labor in prison. I've heard it's not much better in the States either. But that's why ye never heard anything about yer aunt or her friends. It's because gay people all keep quiet about themselves so as not to cause suspicions or problems. They keep their lifestyles private and personal, and they maintain privacy and secrecy from everybody else outside their inner circles of friends."

Phillip's explanation was clear enough for me to understand and all I needed to know for then. My aunt and Phyllis, their friends like Ron, Dick, Dwayne, Tommie, Mickey, and all the others, were the *nice and friendly types* of gay people. Carl's types, on-the-other-hand, were the aggressive, even rough, and violent ones. Got it. I never knew or never guessed anything about my aunt or her lifestyle before because she and Phyllis chose to keep it private, and personal, or even secret from me. It was none of my business anyway, and that way I wouldn't judge them any less, or tell others about them either. Fair enough, and I understood sufficiently enough that the subject could be comfortably closed for the time being...

I appreciated Phillip's candor and honesty. He had a straightforward way of explaining complex issues. Of course, he had his moments of comedy and joviality too. Phillip was an Irish-Englishman, he put it. Or, as he laughed to say, "(He) was an Irish lad stuck in England, but fortunately in London."

He was obviously a very jovial barber with his own set ideas. Phillip loved London, though, and worked very successfully, he said, in an uptown barber salon. He worked five days a week, with Sundays and Mondays off, and he got a month's vacation plus holidays off too. He had already been there at *Costa Brava Hostel* for two weeks soakin' up the sun and seekin' out the ladies...

Phillip had his opinions too, however, and plenty of them. I supposed that it worked well for him with his barbering to interest or humor his clients. Phillip's opinions, mixed along with his hard-Irish brogue accent, made me always try listening more closely in order to understand his points or catch the punch lines to his jokes. When he talked about women, though, it was really amusing because he would often grin that enormous smile of his and also shake his fingers suggesting how his lady friends were always "hot stuff!"

Phillip also enjoyed advising and instructing me about how to charm girls too. But he was emphatic while warning me about bad ones versus *good ones,* or *worthwhile ones.* He stated that the good ones were the girls or women who also did small things to keep a man's attraction. He meant little courtesies like offering refreshments, or giving simple touches, or asking questions about you, or unlocking your driver's car door after being seated on their side by you. He sounded like an expert, so I was very attentive. I appreciated his advice especially because my own girlfriend back home was already like that.

Obviously, from self-depictions of my own life, Phillip could tell that I was quite naïve and also an inexperienced virgin, at that. He felt a male obligation to prepare me for my *first* sexual encounter by filling my head with all sorts of visual imagery. He explained how to hug, and kiss, and then use one hand to help start undressing a woman while the other hand massaged and rubbed and touched her gently all over. He described vividly his own favorite love-sex positions in bed, or wherever he managed to get a girl interested, like on a beach towel, or a couch, or even a back seat of a car, or wherever. They were all good places for him, he laughed, and he depicted pure pleasure describing them all.

No doubt, I was beet red at his vividly defined *Kamasutra Rules* for sexual pleasure. Enough so that I planned to buy such a pictorial book back home, once I could afford it. Phillip liked to brag, though, about how he had a few moves of his own not even mentioned in the *sex treatise*, but I didn't ask for more details by then. I was already a bit overwhelmed and embarrassed with his *sex*plicit informational details. His particulars sure managed to get me excited, however, and all his literary demonstrations just made me miss my girlfriend terribly. I sure was sorry that we hadn't practiced a few special moves of our own. All we ever did was the basic, bump-and-grind stuff, and we were great at that, but it was usually more frustrating than not for us both, I felt.

Listening to Phillip, though, I did a lot of cigarettes smoking to ease those horny moods. Fact is, it was right there at *Costa Brava Hostel* where I finally ran out of my Salem's. So, I had to switch and buy whatever else I could find that was cheap and available. Naturally, Phillip helped me there too and suggested various brands that were typically available everywhere. He was a regular guru, I admit. And thanks to Phillip's stories, advice, and visual portrayals of sensual pleasures, plus seeing all the cute girls that did pass through that hostel's portals for various periods of time, I thought up *Costa Brava Hostel's* permanent nickname. I called it, the *Horny Hostel...*

Dudley Do Right

Talking and sharing with Phillip was nice, but I sensed after a while that I was just a little too young for his own, desired, hanging-on friendship. I never wished to be anybody's *tag along* friend. Besides, he was too busy hunting down older ladies more to his likings. And in bars in the main part of town Phillip had no problems finding companionship. I would just laugh at his outrageous stories, but we mostly just spent time together when we were both in our room together and sometimes for meals. Also, he was a little too old for me too.

Honestly, I did want to learn some things about life all on my own, and not be advised or warned about everything dangerous or unsavory beforehand. It took some of the adventure away, or opportunity to make mistakes all on my own, and then learn from them. I was quite learned from prior mistakes already: Mistaken ladies, monster dogs, poor routes, stubbornness, Berlin, touchy rides, blood money, and who knew what else. I was completely capable of making my own new mistakes, and learning from them, hopefully, all by myself too.

The *Horny Hostel, however,* became a temporary permanent hangout for me. Everything I needed was there: Shelter, food, beverages, seaside, town sights, and companionship. Oh, I was fully aware that I still had much to see and do involving expected museum visits, and famous places, and people yet to see, but I had the best thing of all right there and then, *time.* I wasn't expected to search for Ron again for almost two weeks yet, and, by golly, I was supposed to be on vacation too, wasn't I?

So, it was laidback time for me, and I just wasted my days swimming, sunning on the stony beaches, wandering the village streets, and practicing basic Spanish: "Buenos dias, amigo (or amiga). ?Como estas? ?Una cerveza, por favor?" *Good day, friend. How are you? Can I have a beer, please?*

It was a very relaxed, kick-back time for me, and I took full advantage of it. After over a week, I was already sort of the old-man-on-the block, so-to-speak, and newcomers even came to me to ask questions. I was always very polite, courteous, and as helpful as I might be. I was popular enough, and others even looked for me to join during mealtimes and occasional outings too.

There were others around much of the time, so I usually had new friends to talk with, play ping pong, shoot some pool, or go to the beach in groups or just with another. I was seldom alone unless I chose to be.

Phillip and I remained friends too until eventually even he had to move on. He had a motorcycle, though. It was a beautiful brand new1966 Triumph Bonneville.

Phillip had purchased it just for that summer's vacation, and there was no doubt that he was riding in style. It was a 650 cc on/off road sportster, and Phillip said that the vibration made him stop and stay at various locations until his body calmed. His next cruise was up to Switzerland and Lake Geneva to "Get some *lake time,*" he snickered. Of course, we exchanged addresses, and I promised to come to London one day and get a haircut from him. He wished me luck with ladies and best wishes for on the road. A nice *bloke* and a pleasant goodbye...

Unfortunately, *pleasantness* could not last. After I had been at the hostel well over a full week, two completely opposite extreme incidents occurred merely a day apart. On one day, the most beautiful girl I had ever seen in my life appeared at *Horny Hostel,* er, the *Costa Brava Castle Hostel,* I mean. Then, on the next day, two wise guy, punk-rich Americans showed up late that afternoon...

I could go on and on discussing that next several days, but I won't. I'll skip over most activities by mentioning a few highlights and then get down to the nitty gritty parts: Those parts about my falling desperately in love... again, in spite of my true love back home; then about a serious act of violent behavior on my part; and finally, heartbreak. Oh, that *Horny Hostel* was an exciting place to be alright, full of topsy-turvy feelings, and I got plenty of emotional kicks from it...

First, let me explain about the *first,* completely unprepared for . . . second *love of my life:* One afternoon, while I was just flopped out on a full couch in the *Communal Center* relaxing and enjoying a do-nothing day, an absolutely stunning young lady showed up and checked right in as though she already knew the layout of the hostel and understood its program. Throughout her partial, three-day visit, I could hardly take my eyes off her. At first, I thought she was a Spanish Princess. Then I found out by asking around that her name was Monique. She became instead, I believed, a French Goddess from Lyons, France.

Talk about smitten... Almost immediately, I considered forgetting to return home altogether and moving to Lyons forever, in its place. But I was already spoken for, and thus, all I could do was look. And gosh, did I do a lot of looking. I tried not to be conspicuous about it, but there were plenty of moments when, from clear across the entire communal center, I was sure that she caught me watching her...

I figured that Monique was used to all the attention, though. She probably always received a lot of consideration, and there at *Costa Brava Castle Hostel* was likely no exception. I watched in envy and jealousy as all the other guys at our *Horny Hostel* immediately began begging for her attentions. Her suppliant beaus list included young and older male guests alike and working staff too, all trying to gain her favor and attention. I even observed some other female guests and onsite women workers interrupting her interests for private time. That made me curious. "Hmm?" I wondered, "Is it possible for someone to *like* both guys and girls too?"

Constantly she was interrupted by so many would be suitors. One person would begin talking with her for a while, then abruptly he would leave seemingly rudely dejected. Quickly, that meeting was followed by yet another admirer wielding his own charms at Monique until her ultimate rejections sent him crawling away too. These kamikaze, greet-and-crash episodes seemed endless with everyone waiting for a knight-in-shining-armor to appear and win over the demanding princess. And during all that time, I could nothing but watch her youthful, wholesome, exuberant, and glowing, gorgeous self from a far distance... and fantasize:

Yes, we joyfully met and both laughed and played together while holding hands and frolicking in the sun... We went swimming,... nude, she insisted,... and we stayed up late each night snuggling together, fondling one another while watching stars, flooded in sensual moonlight, lovingly undressing each other, and confessing our deepest love and secrets...

Of course, I never *fantasized* mentioning my girlfriend back home, whatever her name was. Temporarily, but hopefully for a lifetime, I was altogether mesmerized, taken, and absorbed into a make-believe world of love's fantastic illusions. Oh, yes, the fantasies were such that many times, because of my fatal attraction, I completely forgot about love's loyalties back home. My girlfriend would have been heartbroken, no doubt. At that moment, however, I could hardly remember, or care.

No matter, I couldn't help myself. I was helpless. Monique was absolutely stunning the next morning in her matching beach and lounging outfits that always were elegant, stylish, and oh-so-sexy. She had long, silky black hair with curled bangs. She was tall, but not too tall, and her lean body was immaculately tanned, shapely, and athletic. Her lipstick and nails were always complementary in deep reds, and her smiles, laughter, and hand movements were sexy enough to die for.

Oh, I was captivated, alright, just like all the other *blokes* in that *Horny Hostel*. Greedily, I was even grateful that Phillip had already departed. "Too bad for him," I thought. "I don't want to compete with him, though, for her affections especially since I am far too shy to make any sort of moves on my own toward her." How could I? I was already spoken for... What would Phillip say and do?

Monique's first full day there at the hostel came and went. I watched her from a distance, and a couple times I was sure she saw me watching her too. Embarrassed, I pretended to be merely glancing all about the large communal center with no particular focus on her. She knew I was lying. She knew I was interested. I saw her glimpsing my way and smiling. Oh, I was so nervous...

The next late afternoon, however, the very opposite sort of factor happened. Two young, twentyish-looking guys checked into the *Castle Hostel* and immediately began boasting about their charms, wealth, and upbringing. They were rich guys from the States somewhere, but I didn't really care. Their types were unwelcomed with me no matter where they came from. It was definitely a *proletariat versus upper bourgeoisie,* ruling-class thing. At first, I didn't mind their arrogance so much; some guys are just in love with themselves. They just sounded impudent, rude, and ridiculous to me.

However, those two chumps proceeded fouling the air with their nasty-mouthed antics continuing throughout all that afternoon, dinnertime, well into evening, and even after nightfall. Then came their fatal mistake with me. They weren't satisfied talking so boldly and boastfully about themselves or even each other. No, instead, they also started putting others down.

With me, it was one thing bragging while attempting to make themselves seem more important. That was just foolhardy and contemptable. It was another whole matter entirely, though, to put others down in order to stand on top of their humiliated victims in order to feel taller or bigger. That was altogether vicious and mean spirited, and I could never stand for it.

At first, they began picking on different, innocent guests at our hostel as targets for their insults and putdowns. The poor hostel sufferers may not have even understood those fools' meanness. I ignored them because their jokes were merely words, and those other victims needed to stand up for themselves. Then, the two jerks began making fun of our *Castle Hostel* and its amenities as unbefitting their high falutin,'aristocratic tastes. Again, I just steamed with irritation while trying to ignore them; we *others* enjoyed the place regardless of their ignorance, and those fools would soon be leaving, hopefully. "Good riddance," I thought.

But finally, came the last proverbial straw, and I could take no more from either of them. Separately, and both together, the two clowning buffoons began making fun of local people, the community patrons and citizens of *Palamos*, the Spanish people, in general, and then all of Spain, in its entirety. Within that whole, hostel-center audience, those two fools were the only ones laughing and carrying on. Each was trying to outdo the other's ignorant and viciously cruel comments. Just hearing their insulting remarks about the common gentry, jokes about lower-class poorness of the town's residents, and laughs about the overall squalor of Spain, made it difficult to avoid. Their disgusting humor and cruel laughter became too much for me to deal with.

Right there in the hostel's communal center, the two fools had taken over its pool table for their self-indulgent speech podium. I casually walked over to both of them and looking first at one, and then the other, I stated very calmly and clearly, "Hey, why don't both of you knock off the foul-mouthed, nasty comments about everything. No one here wants to hear your nasty opinions and nonsense."

"Buzz off, Nitwit," one of the two said while chalking up his pool stick. "It's a free country, and we can stay and say, *as long as we pay*, anything we like." The other jerk just laughed at his buddy's rhyme while mocking me irreverently.

What came next was merely spontaneous. With flash reactions on my part, instantly I leaped at the second snickering clown, grabbed him by his shirt front, spun him around, and threw him flailing hard backwards and crashing and collapsing into a set of fold-up metal chairs against the far wall. I then quickly jumped at the other surprised fool still holding his cue stick, and in one swift motion lifted him up on his toes, spun him around, and slammed him down stiffly upon the pool table. His mouth wide agape and his frightened eyes bulging he dropped the pool stick to the floor from his fumbling fingertips and just stared at me frightened as a chihuahua during fireworks. Then I gave him and his ignorant crony the sternest lecture they'd both ever had, since maybe their prep school days, by bigger and tougher bullies.

Standing hunched over between his spread-eagled legs, with my left arm stretched across that suddenly quieted loudmouth's chest and pinning him to the pool table, I leaned over even further, and pointing my right finger straight into his face, up close like a gun, I gave him warning.

Nearly growling with clear contempt, I fumed, "I don't care what you say, or what you think aloud when you are back home with your revolting, spineless friends. Here, however, and around me, you had better watch your step and your language...

"When you are in a foreign country," I angrily continued my criticism, "just like this beautiful nation, you are honored guests, and just like honorary ambassadors, you represent the best of the United States of America. You should remember that you symbolize what America stands for. You are here on behalf of our country, and you better try to impress folks over here with your good manners and deeds..."

At that point, I stuck my face up close to his with our noses almost touching, and I continued growling a serious warning, "If you don't, and I hear about it, and I can find you again, I shall pick up whatever club I can find, and I am going to beat you both into such bloody shit stumps that you'll both be shipped home on a hospital plane. Do you understand me?"

I was calmly but angrily huffing and puffing by then, adrenaline flowing like crazy. The fool on the table just submissively stared at me and faintly nodded. I released him, roughly shoving him away from me, and then I swiftly turned and glared straight at the other. Right away he began nodding his head profusely.

I sensed that the idiot sprawled on the floor amongst the spilled chairs was the weaker one and subordinate to the other, hot-shot loudmouth lying bent backwards on the pool table. In any case, they both quickly stood up, gathered their wits, made some remarks about going out to get a drink, and swiftly made their way out the building.

Once they both had vanished, stress started attacking me. Quickly, I began attempting to refocus by placing the spilled chairs back in place and straightening up the pool table cue sticks again. I needed to do something positive and distracting. Meanwhile, all but shaking myself, I tried relaxed breathing to calm down...

And that was when I casually turned around, and right there standing beside me was none other than Monique with her sexy, stunning smile. I was startled at first probably turning ten shades redder than her luscious lipstick, but I managed to slightly return her inviting smile. Then I apologized.

"I am so sorry about all that," I begged. "Those guys just ticked me off, and I got really mad at them."

Then I remembered that Monique was French, so I tried making up for my rudeness. "Je suis desole'. Ils m'ont rendu fou. Veuillez pardonner mon comportement." *I am sorry. They made me mad. Please forgive my behavior.*

Gently, Monique took my hand and spoke in clearest English, yet with an exotic, sensual, and erotic French accent, "It is fine. Come with me."

Like a helpless kitten, my hand in hers, I followed Monique across the communal center floor way. She guided us straight out the front entrance door where she suddenly stopped. Then as we both stood there closely tied to each other under the front porch lamplight and an incredibly romantic moon, sparks began to fly. I sensed a piece of heaven...

Monique turned to face me directly as she closed in tightly next to me, her body against mine. My heart began pounding and my face heated as she suggestively looked slightly up and into my startled eyes. I could only stand there, all but paralyzed, my tongue hanging out, and likely dragging on the floor below, while I continued gawking at her incredibly beautiful and smiling face.

"Those two were very rude," she softly spoke, "and you were very brave, Monsieur." And with those simple words, Monique raised up and kissed me fervently on my lips.

Naturally, my knees weakened and I melted right there under the intense lights while in her outstretched arms. She practically had to scoop me up off the porch, remold me again into human form, and hold me upright so that I could react again. Her kiss, however so enthusiastic, gave me courage and unbridled passions of my own.

I gathered my strength, looked straight into her eyes, and blurted out, "Oh, my God, you are so beautiful!" I then grabbed her shoulders, and gently pulled her closer to me. Bending my head ever so slightly to the side, I excitedly kissed her hard, heavily, and passionately on her lips...

Monique was ever so receptive and such an amazing teacher. And as an avid student, in the moments that followed, I learned all there was to know about *French kissing*. Her tongue went deeply into my mouth sweeping its roof and bottom before practically plunging far into my throat recesses and teasing my tonsils with her erotic tongue whips. Immediately, I reciprocated and attempted copying her style. I was a good student too, and I could tell that she enjoyed me because our tongues lashed together in almost frantic mouth dancing.

We were still under bright lights and in public, but I could barely contain myself. With one hand on Monique's back holding her steadily and firmly close to me, my other hand began frantic exploration of her large and pointed breasts, slender waist, and gorgeously firm and rounded buttocks. After a moment, I switched arm positions and let my other hand get its fill of her wonderful body. At the same time, I periodically took a moment to gaze into Monique's inviting eyes and then eagerly, firmly, but gently, covered her mouth with mine again and continued tongue licking and kissing her with sincere, uncontrolled desire.

That was when Monique abruptly broke away, took my hand, and excitedly said, "Come with me."

Again, already deeply in her spell, I did exactly as she requested; I could do nothing else. Monique practically pulled me by hand back through the community center toward the ladies' dormitory hallway. I could see the center's other guests, especially the guys, watching us enviously as we practically raced through the large room. Covetous eyes were bulging in awe, respect, and envy of my advanced stages with Monique. They could all but wonder, drool, and imagine...

Heartbreak

I was being swiftly guided down the Ladies Hallway to what I quickly imagined was Paradise created. Monique hurried like there was no time to spare. We arrived at her room, and she quickly thrust open the door, entered, and still holding my hand, pulled me hard inside with her, and then closed the door promptly behind us. I had come along ever so willingly, but there was no doubt that Monique was in charge and directing this flirtation. I was still somewhat in a state of shocking delight, expecting more, but uncertain as to what or where anything may go.

Monique sat down on her twin bed and extended her hand inviting me to join her there. I did, and still holding hands, she smiled, and we both looked longingly into each other's eyes. We kissed lightly and then began talking briefly about incidental topics regarding life, and interests, and hopes, and love. She told me about her dreams to finish college and then work in a famous art gallery like *le Musee du Louvre* in Paris. And then playing upon my own lustful fantasies of her, Monique told me how sweet I was, and what a gentleman I had been, not to crowd her like all the others. She admitted that she was drawn to me unlike all the other male guests at the hostel. If her beauty had not been enough, I was completely engulfed, entrapped, and spellbound by her sensuous words too.

No matter, Monique knew exactly what she was doing, however. For myself? I was speechless and allowing her to lead all the way. I was nervous as all getup, and yet I became a very willing subject, prospect, or even lover, if God saw my way clear. Then in quick graceful moves, Monique pulled me over to lie down beside her. She then stretched out her legs upon her bed, reached over, and wrapping her arms around me, drew me completely over and on top of her fully extended and invitingly prone body. Monique really started kissing then. Her mouth was all over my face and neck while her arms rubbed and massaged my back and buttocks fervently.

That was not, however, how Phillip had explained things... Oh, my girlfriend back home and I had gotten into some pretty serious action before. But I was always mostly leading the way, right up until I would foolishly call everything off. Just before taking our clothes off, I'd suddenly stop, climb up and away from our frolicking temptation, and with both of us exhausted and frustrated, I'd pause to redirect our uncontrolled intentions by suggesting we rejoin our friends or family.

Yet, that time with Monique was completely different. For one thing, I had utterly forgotten about my girlfriend back home. For another, Phillip's sexual dissertation had always proposed and assumed me as the one in charge. I appreciated his notes because of previous experiences with my girlfriend. But that did not work at all there with Monique. She was absolutely in charge and definitely steering our oversexed buggy drive. I was just along for the ride, so to speak...

In a cat's meow, our passions rose to explosive tones. Our hands flailed all over each other as we both began unbuttoning, untying, unzipping, and pulling, ripping, and tearing whatever was in the way, or needed removal. In between buttons undone or cloth removed, we kissed passionately encouraging the next step. We were desperately trying to get where we both wanted, naked and in each other's craving arms.

I was so excited and energized I could barely contain myself. This was it! Right then, I was finally almost there! Monique would be the one! She, the Queen Mother Goddess of all beauty and sensuality would be my *first!* I was finally going to become a heroic man-among-men, grow into that Don Juan, he-man specimen, and do it all with the most beautiful creature on Earth. Monique, just show me the way!...

Suddenly, the dorm room door burst open, and in walked Monique's unexpected roommate. In any other situation on Earth, one might expect courtesy to claim its just rights. Any other reasonable person in the world would excuse themselves and discreetly back out of a room applying accepted apologies so that anxious lovers inside could continue partaking within their eruptive needs to fulfill explosive destinies. The key words there were *reasonable person*. Those were not to be associated with Monique's *roomie*, however.

Initially, Monique and I barely gave the girl intruder due attention; we were both quite vigorously occupied. But she just stood there, hands on her hips, staring indignantly, and waited to gain our attention. Momentarily, I glanced back at Monique's intrusive roommate, gave her pleading and forlorn looks, and waited myself, hopefully, for appreciative understanding. No such allowance was offered.

Instead, the roomie stared rudely at Monique and then menacingly at me. With a slightly contemptuous tone in her rather acceptable, but angry English voice, she demanded of me, "What are you doing in here? No boys are allowed in this wing. You better leave before I call the night guard."

I gulped anxiously while awaiting Monique's stepping up and taking control of the situation. I expected her to defiantly order her roommate to go drink a soda pop and stay gone for another twenty minutes to a lifetime, or so. But no luck there, either. Monique was obviously subordinate and subdued by her overbearing, control-freak roommate with *House Rules* on her side.

So, I did the courageous thing, and took all the blame. "I am so sorry, Miss," I gushed, "It is all my fault. I begged Monique to let me follow her here and be alone for a while. I apologize about breaking the rules. Please forgive Monique; I am to blame."

With one last intensely enthusiastic kiss, and then staring deeply into Monique's sexy and brilliantly blue eyes, I told her goodnight and that I would visit her in the morning.

With that awkward moment passed, I climbed out of Monique's bed, turned my back on the roommate, and put myself back together, clothes wise. Turning quickly, and with a wave and blown kiss to Monique, I then begrudgingly whisked past the roomie, stepped through the still open door, and raced like hell down the Ladies' Hallway and back into the communal center. Once there, I found the coffee machine, poured a cup, and finally lit and smoked my, what should have been, post-sex cigarette. It did help hit the spot, though... whatever or wherever that was!

Regardless, I relaxed and had time to reflect on the previous brief time smiling at my accomplishments with Monique. Sex wise, it was further and more frantically passionate than anything ever before with my girlfriend back home. And it was such even though we were so rudely interrupted and disparaged by Monique's jealous roommate. But all was well as I recalled my favorite song lyrics: "Tomorrow, tomorrow, there's always tomorrow... Tomorrow's another day!"

I went to sleep that night thinking and then dreaming about Monique. *Tomorrow* we would be together permanently. I had also produced another fantastic plan. I would simply ask her to go hitchhiking with me to Italy for as long as she had time. I would even hitch us rides for her eventual return to Lyons, and then I could check out her home conditions. It would be great. Girls always got the first and best rides anyway. Cars would pass up guys and then screech to a stop right beside a girl, or girls, hitching midline, or even at a line's end. Guys with girls even had better chances at rides too.

I would have Monique stick her thumb out while I hid. When a car slammed on their brakes stopping to pick-up her lovely body, I would jump out from behind some bush and come running over with apologies for being busy with nature. Besides, Monique was so attractive that no driver sap would ever refuse her a lift. It was a perfect idea. I decided to catch up to her in the morning at breakfast and tell her all about my plan . . . or rather, our plan. After that night of wanderlust, Monique was surely an angel on my shoulder. . .

Early the next morning, I was up and cleaned-up bright and shiny as a new copper penny. I raced down the hallway to the communal center-cafeteria and searched achingly for Monique. She was not there yet, it appeared. I smiled to myself bragging internally that after the previous night, the poor girl needed some extra sleep to make up for the emotional drain I had forced upon her. I just stood there beaming and waiting. . . Then my eyes focused out the open Entrance Doors of the facility and looked beyond. . .

There outside, and just below the entry steps to the *Horny Hostel*, was a brand new, bright red, MGB sports car. Seated in the front seats were those two, ego-bruised, American rich guys, laughingly joking and staring at a road map. They were oblivious to my stares, and just as well it was so. Because right there, sitting sideways and outstretched on the back seat of that juicy, red-hot rod was none other than the new, love-of-my-life, Monique...

My mouth dropped open, and I could only stand there frozen, helpless, while staring at her wistful beauty. In only a moment's time, she caught sight of my gaze. At first glance, Monique suggested the slightest hint of embarrassment; however, she then merely tipped her stylish sunglasses down her nose a trifle to show off her glimmering blue eyes. Next, while tilting her head slightly to the side, raising her drawn and outstretched palms up, Monique offered a bent smile and just shrugged her shoulders. It was to say, "Oh, I am so sorry, my love. It was really nice with you last night. But these boys have lots of money, and just what else is a girl to do?"

In another moment, the MGB's gears were ground into place, and in a leap and a bound, that car, with my love inside, jumped forward and raced on down the narrow street. I was never to see Monique again, or those clowns either, but my memory has never forgotten her, or them either, for that matter.

I had a couple more days of remorse to lay around the *Costa Brava Hostel*. In rejection's pose, I wandered the town's streets all alone, drank beers by myself, smoked cheap, ghastly Spanish cigarettes endlessly, and tried slowly to collect and regain my tarnished and very dimmed wits. I also considered various future apologies to my wonderful, faithful girlfriend back home for my inexcusable transgression, should I ever mention them again to anyone. And finally, I even drafted a poem recalling my unrequited love and shame..

Charade

That first glimpse pierced my naive soul while stealing heart's endeavors.
Surrendered I, right from the start, though I had met her never...
Seeing her there that summer's eve' sharing a night in Spain,
My heart was churned by love's sweet pull teasing me with its pang.

Seduction so conspicuous, temptation all around,
Gave thought for some romantic whirl sensing love I had found.
Sensuous curves implying sex with lustful looks that showed
Her Mediterranean eyes took my heart as she glowed.

Burgundy lips and pearly teeth, feigned smirks to please lost souls,
Could vanquish men with melting ease to purgatory's tolls.
Silken black hair, allurement's sin taunting with its delight
Left me content with Satan's pits for one embrace that night.

And her attraction for me too was evident from smiles
Past others praying they were meant as signals for their wiles.
And how the beaus did flaunt their means enticing her with charm
In hopes some rune might conjure up dreams of her in their arms.

But their advances won no place, so keen her sense of mind.
Her challenge was my innocence, this sorceress defined.
Throughout a day as she contrived craved spells to drift on by,
While craftily plying her gift, I could not sense the lies.

And conspiring a vixen's scheme to steal my prime away,
My thoughts were such: "The only crime would be were there delay!"
Then steadily, her guise secured with magic all in place
To lure with a paramour's call, my heart quickened its pace.

Her temptress smile, seduction's gaze, had determined my course;
Fates only option was to bring me closer to the source.
And weaving through the crowded room, I paused but once… to stare;
Her radiant beauty altered enchantment into dares.

Besotted by her countenance, false courage begged for fame,
'Twas love's intoxicating mask that pardoned me of blame.
With false bravado's anxious quest, answers I sought to learn.
But truth be known, 'twas more than not, of carnal facts I yearned.

Yet, giving in to me that soon presented less she knew,
So, teasingly, she let me guess of all I wished to view.
Then testing my nerves she whispered of a night's lovely plan.
A smile at me- and the end of my innocence began.

She spoke of seeking art and love, and how we two were blessed,
And how sweet men (like me) were few to want her, she confessed.
And drinking each fermented word, my head commenced to spin.
All thoughts awash I was so swayed, "Conquest was by night's end."

At last, the moment of triumph came as I begged a kiss.
If it were wrong, then let me sin; I could not stand to miss.
Succumbed by her lips' dominance, gratification's show,
She took me to her private room that only we should know.

Of others she feigned not to care; her mind seemed mine alone.
With talk of travel, art, and love we shared dreams of our own.
And fantasies did we contrive with pleasures sought to share,
But less was I to realize, of truth I should beware.

Our night's sojourn so gently spent- a naive lad's escape-
Gave morning's hope to catch my love and embark on our fates.
Yet, when the dawn brought on its chance to seek her sweet embrace,
My disillusioned heart did find truth's miserable face.

Our night's intrigue was falsely meant; she could not share my trials.
Those other men, though less intense, gladly paid for her styles.
So, saddened by her curt parting, my heart broken in two,
I watched my sweet dreams cast away their soured rendezvous.

And swooning over sacred love, I realized how stale
Some shallow souls could really be; hearts truly were for sale.
Thus, passions spent, and lessons earned, that summer's escapade,
The price, though high, was cheap, I learned: **Love is but a charade!**

CHAPTER 13:

....

LIVING TOO LARGE

Mistaken Identities

After two days of tortured self-pity and collecting all my remaining pride, I gathered up my cleanly freshened belongings, reloaded them, hoisted my sea bag once again upon my shoulder, and said goodbye to *Castle Hostel's* Manager, and a few other select staff and remaining guests. Given the circumstances, I appreciated the vast majority of extremely relaxing and comforting times I had enjoyed at *Horny Hostel*. Sure, I had lost my temper and control with a couple of deserving, foul-mouthed, and embarrassing slugs. Plus, of course, I had allowed my innermost feelings to dreadfully *shatter and ache* due to my innocent gullibility, and my heartstrings were sensitively damaged by Monique's *charade*. She had given a truly Academy Award Winning performance.

Yet, I was steadily becoming more comfortable with myself again. Indeed, I knew that I would eventually get over those harmful and hurtful feelings. Violence was not in my natural character; nor was I willing, I hoped, to chance baring my heart again by laying it upon my receptive sleeves. With my moderately blemished conscience, however, I had to agree and accept that I had actually escaped both quality, life-learning episodes mostly unscathed.

Afterwards, I became more aware of potential sources of my violent behavior. Stress could build fairly rapidly, and I would need to be careful.

Also, I came to better terms with my heart and mindful of influential characteristics affecting it. I never wished to pursue either anomaly again. Yet, in my mind, I rationalized that I needed to be prepared. One never knew, did one?

Soon, I was back on the seaside route toward France once again. Once there, I immediately recognized that I had been too slow with goodbyes. I was once more the last man on the hitching totem pole, which meant I was *sent to the end-of-the-line.* As I passed several guys and girls hitchhikers, saying hello or goodbye to several, I smiled inside at my earlier premise of a hitching scheme: "Monique," I merrily laughed, yet disdainfully, "you don't know what you're missing. You actually chose a gorgeous, hot-rod ride with two, celebrity, richly-dufus clowns when you could be spending time together with intense, lover-boy me... at the end of this incredibly long line of other anxious hitchers? Too bad; so sad. Your loss, but mostly mine. That's fine... I'm alright now, and at least I still have my loving woman back home... waiting eagerly... while she anxiously anticipates my return..."

Surprisingly, the hitchers' line shrunk fairly rapidly. Others joined our hitchers' line after me, but before long, it was my turn. My next ride was with some surfer dudes who were heading as far up the coastline as it took to find *fresh waves,* whatever that meant. I supposed that the waves nearby were so small and bad that good ones were crazier further down the road, whatever that *meant.* For me, though, and for another hitcher the Spanish Surfers had previously already picked up, it meant a ride clear to our next stop, only hours away, *Nice,* France.

Once in Europe, and after studying my map, I cleverly sniggered that one day it would be nice to see *Nice.* So, I simply planned to stop there and see what might happen. I did not know of any hostels, nor did I need them. The beaches were free, and if I shoved the darn nuisance pebbles aside enough, hopefully, I could manage to uncover enough sand, or a soft spot, for my bag mattress. All was well with me.

As it turned out, the other hitcher in the car with the surfers also decided to bail out in *Nice* too. At least he temporarily chose to join my endeavors for the time being. I think, also, that the two surfers were just a bit salt-water-taffy-brained intense for him too. For what I saw, or had seen before, or knew anything about, their waves so far had been merely acceptable for kiddie surfing and body splashing. They were nothing like those fifteen-footer Mavericks just south of San Francisco I had shivered with thrills seeing before. Downright scary, those were. And the surfers there were insane.

So, we both bailed out wishing our surf riders, "Bonne chance," with waves. My new mate's name was Harold, or Harry for short, and he was from Naples, Italy. But he spoke very reasonable conversational English, so we had no problems communicating as long as our words were confined to simple phrases. The only Italian I knew was waving my arms around wildly to emphasize some point, and Harry laughed at my joke.

Harry was working his way back home, eventually, but not until he had ventured a bit further into Northern Italy before circling back and heading for Naples. He had already visited a small part of Spain, and France, so he wasn't in any hurry. Thus, we agreed to hang out together and find some reasonable shelter around town. We'd even split costs for a hotel room somewhere, if necessary.

I explained to Harry that I would eventually be traveling in Italy too, first to *Pisa* and then at least as far south as *Rome*, which was a mandatory stopover for me. Some of my favorite history studies had been those of Roman Civilization, its Empire, and of the Caesars. *Rome* was a *must-see* place for me, absolutely. Anyway, after a bit, we agreed to find a mutually acceptable hotel for the night, but first we'd find a nice bar in *Nice* to have a nice time. Okay, I won't play that silly homograph game anymore. But, nevertheless, we agreed to similar expectations...

Over the past ten or more days, I had saved quite a bit of money with my frugal-living conditions. My recent lodgings had been very inexpensive, and I had saved a lot of money on food costs too. Therefore, I felt like I had room to splurge. I could afford spending more just enjoying myself, not that I needed to *cry in-my-beer* anymore, either. So, with hotel expenses resolved no matter the cost, Harry and I agreed to find a fun nightclub to visit first, my *first* time. We would indulge ourselves in some delicious party food and cocktail-type drinks, like gin and tonics, Singapore Slings, or whatever, just something fun and special.

Harry was only carrying a small, lightweight satchel, like a really large man purse. He was a light traveler, obviously, and I envied his luggage factor. In all honesty, over that summer my sea bag had steadily become heavier, bulkier, and more cumbersome, it seemed. Therefore, I tried harder to find a fun place wherein to eat, drink, and drop my bag. Soon we came upon one.

It was already late afternoon, and I spotted a nightclub that already had its neon sign blazing showing off martinis, food, and dancing. It was getting terribly busy even by then with a steady stream of vacationing/ patrons arriving. We went inside and, fortunately, were quickly guided to our own table. For the time being, Harry and I both forgot about mixed drinks and, instead, started off with BBQ ribs, fries, and cold beer. Afterwards, I even ordered more beers for us both. We were enjoying ourselves and really starting to relax.

In a while, we were politely requested to move to the bar because our table was needed for other diners. So, we amiably did so and were delighted to find that our next round of drinks were on-the-house. I had been listening to other drinkers and heard someone else order just what I wanted: A *Banana Daiquiri*. Then Harry ordered a *Roman Candle* which looked good too. Next orders, we switched drinks to sample each other's choice, and kept em' coming.

We continued just sitting there enjoying ourselves, sipping our martinis, or whatever they were, and watching the crowds pour in. Soon, the place was really hopping with standing-room-only. In fact, there were so many people that many just started dancing for lack of anything else to do. They all just gyrated to juke box music of mostly American or British favorites. It was a nice time in the Nice town that night... Sorry, I was getting drunk.

Then, some fellow wandered over and said hello to us. I greeted him, quickly finding out that he spoke English, French, Italian, and a little German too, because he mentioned so when inquiring where we two came from. "Wow!" I laughed, "Hey, Harry, this guy's got four tongues in his mouth!"

I started laughing hysterically, nearly falling off my barstool, at my own frivolous humor, and then Harry and the new fellow joined right on in. However, they were mostly laughing at me, I acknowledged later on. Harry also spoke Italian, French, and some English too. I was the weak, barely bi-lingual speaker. What seemed funny to me was commonplace for them? No doubt for that whole International House of Languages too. I should have been embarrassed, but I wasn't. I was busy getting blitzed!

Anyway, joining with our joviality, the new guy introduced himself as Raul and offered to buy us both another round. "Bring 'em on!" I hooted. "The more the merrier!"

Our next free drinks arrived, and soon Harry and I found ourselves doing ever so well laughing up a storm enjoying ourselves. Our new friend

Raul kept ordering more free drinks for us, and I started trying variations of *Tequila Sunrises*. After those, I forgot what else I drank. All of them were cold, sweet, refreshing, and intoxicating.

Harry kept right on slugging down his own choices too. Laughingly, he announced that he was already an Italian wino, so he could drink anything and not get drunk. "Good for you," I screamed joyously, "but I'll just stick to liquor!" and then I almost fell off my barstool again. Oh, criminy, I was on a roll... Dreadful.

More free drinks followed, and soon another fellow came over to the bar to joined. Raul introduced him as his friend, Pepe, and they both suggested we all get a table as soon as one became available. "Table schmable," I laughed uncontrollably, "This bar stool is fine for me, but if you're buyin,' I'll sit wherever you want!"

Fact is, however, both Harry and I offered reciprocating and buying the next rounds, but our new acquaintances would have nothing to do with that. Drinks kept coming, and time kept getting later. We did learn that Raul was a local dentist, and Pepe was an electrical engineer. Both of them were professionals who were out partying late on a weeknight. "Whoopie for you," I laughed, but drunk or not, eventually I told Harry that we needed to find a hotel room for the night. We still had a way to go in the morning for our next, agreed-upon destination: *Monte Carlo*, Monaco.

That was when our new drinking friends both surprised us, and one of them spoke up, "What, you don't have rooms for the night? Why don't you both stay at our place for the night? We have to get up early and go to work and you can leave from there. In fact, we can even give you a ride to the main highway in the morning. Come on. Save your money."

Saving money hit a reasonable frugal nerve, even in my liquor saturated state, so I checked haphazardly with Harry, and he accepted. Actually, though, at the time I think I could have suggested Harry jump off a cliff and he would have obliged. He was pretty far gone by then, and I wasn't *far* behind him either. But it was *fate fatale* in my state of mind, so I teased earnestly, "Sure, show us the way, but I hope it's not far to walk. My bag is kind of heavy."

"No problem," our new hosts assured us explaining a short ride to their condo in their car. So, Harry and I grabbed our respective bags and practically crawled outside while bumping into each other several times before eventually falling inside Raul's car. Pepe followed behind us, and our host driver zipped around town until finally parking at a *nice* condominium complex. As it turned out, those two were roommates also, and they shared a small flat with a kitchen, two baths, a medium-sized living room, and no bedrooms, just a double bed and a fold-out couch.

"Hey, fellas," I slobbered, but still somewhat aware of my surroundings, "we don't want to take over your sleeping arrangements," I only spoke in English. "We can leave, or at least sleep on the floor." I couldn't exactly remember what or where, but that scenario was sounding a little familiar to me.

"No. No. No. Absolument pas," said Raul as he pulled out the sleeper sofa for us and arranged some blankets. "Both Pepe and I must leave early for our work, but we are fine over there on that bed," he said pointing. "Rest well. Goodnight."

The lights went out, and Harry was already sound asleep before his head even hit his pillow. I also was ready for a good night's sleep too. My head was really spinning... Yet, a light sleeper anyway, I was still somewhat uneasy.

Later that night, or early morning, it was still pitch black when I suddenly became startled awake... Hands were under my covers massaging my leg vigorously and kneading their way up toward my privates. "Oh, my God, not again!" I thought. In an instant's reaction time, I bolted upright into a sitting position, drew back both my legs inward, and then reflexively struck out upwards, fast, hard, and decisively toward a darkened, target area... Surprisingly, I caught the subject square on his chest area as I kicked with all my might.

In the darkness, I heard a mighty crashing as all hell seemed to break loose. A moment later, my eyes adjusted to the dimness, thanks partly to a nightlight glowing from the then newly opened room adjacent to the living room. It was obvious that I had struck a decisive blow. I could tell that, inadvertently, my swift kick had sent one of the roommates, a sexual predator or not, falling backward right through a paper-thin wall separating a bathroom from that apartment's main room; the same room where we had all previously been sleeping soundly.

In the clearing dimness, I recognized Raul, our original acquaintance from the nightclub, our generous drinks' donor, and finally Harry's and my overnight host. He was lying completely sprawled out inside that other bathroom's bathtub. The entire, separation wall for that second bathroom had been destroyed, and an enormous hole was evident from Raul's having crashed through and landing squarely in the bathtub.

Trying to remain as calm as possible and avoid freaking out, I quickly leaped up from my prone stance, reached into my pants' pocket, and retrieved my sharp, three-inch blade, pocketknife, which I always carried with me, and swiftly opened it. Then while sitting firmly upright on the foldout couch's edge there beside the large hole in the wall, I ordered Raul to get out of the tub, go back to his bed, and return to sleep. I then warned him that if I felt any further shenanigans, I would strike out with my knife blade next time.

"I don't like that, and we're not that way." I stated firmly, if not fiercely. "Now go back over there and go back to sleep!" I commanded.

Awkwardly, and gingerly, Raul climbed back up and out of that bathtub and, after stepping through the huge wall hole, he moved back to his double bed arrangement with his roommate. All the while, Pepe merely watched intensely in wide-eyed silence. It took the three of us a long while to return to sleep too. I was so frustrated at how quickly, naively, and easily both Harry and I had lowered our guards and been effectively set-up for that unwanted interaction. And to think that Phillip had even warned me to stay alert too. Once more I hadn't.

"Why hadn't they just asked, or volunteered their interests at the time," I frustratingly challenged my mind. "We could have settled our differences right there inside that nightclub."

It would have saved them both a lot of money, potentially, all the stress, and me another anxiety attack having to deal with that unacceptable behavior again. "Why do some people act nicely toward others," I continued confronting my thoughts, "and then expect more than nice in return?" After a brief pause for further consideration, I answered myself, "It's called dating, Daniel!"

I considered that throughout history, men have so often continuously overstepped expected boundaries with their dates. Having had unfair anticipations after their often-expensive expenditures, they *often* expected too much in return. I supposed further, however, that if such dates, after an expensive and gala evening out, were willing to spend a night on their fellow's couch.

I was still conflicted, though, by other fellas being unable to differentiate me from *women dates*. I was a guy, and we had both said clearly to each other, "Good night, and sleep well." Case was closed, as far as I was concerned, and I figured, therefore, that Raul had his misery coming to him. I was also appreciative, however, that neither he nor Pepe were violent types.

The next morning, we all rose with minor hangovers. The household was silent, though, as Raul and Pepe completed their morning constitutions in the other usable bathroom. Harry groggily got up, dressed slowly, and helped me straighten up the fold-out bed back into a couch. Once prepared, he and I just headed for the front door, and I called back sincerely, "Merci de nous avoir laisse' passer la nuit." *Thank you for letting us spend the night.*

With that, Harry and I ended up on the street struggling to find our way back down to the coastal highway. Minutes later, both our hosts drove swiftly past us without stopping or even honking. Of course, I had not pressed our luck asking for that promised *morning lift* from either. Once outside, though, as we rambled down a hill toward the sea, Harry mentioned in passing, "Did you see that huge hole they had in their wall? That's going to take some serious repairs."

It was obvious that *Dead Head Harry* had slept completely through the entire ordeal during that previous night. However, I felt no need to entertain or traumatize him with any unsavory details. The whole incidental matter was better just left alone and forgotten. No harm done, sort of, and no need to raise concerns.

I simply dropped the entire issue with an honest retort, "Yeah, Harry, I did see that hole, but 'I hadn't noticed it at all when we *first* got there. Too bad."

Tuxedo Night

"Two 'hitchers' are better than one," is not necessarily a good rule to follow. However, time lost because of car drivers' skepticism regarding picking up two passengers over one is often outweighed by companionship gained from another hitcher helping pass time away. I already mentioned about benefits of another *hitcher* who is female. That theory seemed sound from continual observations, reports from other hitchhikers, including male/female teams, themselves, and plain common sense. Besides, it just seemed like more fun, although I never learned for sure for myself. Darn.

Nevertheless, Harry and I hung around modestly entertaining each other until finally a lift arrived. That driver took us along the coastline all the way to our next scheduled stop, the tiny *Principality of Monaco*, right on the coastline and surrounded by France on its other three sides. Also, it was near the Italian border. Our main attraction of interest, of course, was the world-famous *Monte Carlo Casino* in *Monaco*. Neither of us had much money to spare, but we both wanted to drop some of it on those exciting sounding gambling tables, or in any generous slot machines in *the casino*. Who knew? One of us, or both, would leave rich...

Monaco is a fun location. Size wise, the entire city-state is only about the same extent as Central Park in New York City. For hitchers, it's a dream because you can walk completely through it in an easy two hours' time or less while enjoying all its sights and scenery. It is made up of five tiny districts, and *Monte Carlo Square*, located up top on an overlooking hillside with its high-class casino, is one of them.

Naturally, with a warm, sunny, and beautiful day ahead of us after arriving, Harry and I found something to eat and then played around on the pebbly beach and wonderful sea surf for the remainder of the day. That evening, after a light dinner of fish, chips, and beer, we made plans to hike up the hill to the classy casino overlooking the entire community of Monaco and the sea below. For us, from sea level and looking back up the tall hillside above Monaco's seaside zone, *Monte Carlo Casino* looked like an extraordinary, shiny, golden palace on a hill. From our distance, it stood out strikingly with features of wealth, grandeur, and decadence. Both Harry and I could hardly wait until we saw it up close, personal, and had a chance to clean it out of all its cash.

High above the main town, it was a steep climb following the beautifully paved roadways getting there. Yet, with swimming, eating, goofing around, and finally the hillside hike, it was already getting late when we finally reached *Monte Carlo Casino Square*. As we approached, it became very obvious, too, that the casino was everything anybody had ever suggested. Already lit up for the night's gambling and entertainment activities, and with limousines, numerous Mercedes, and fancy sports cars all arriving to be valet parked, the entire scene was gaudy, fat-cat rich, and glorious to a couple of poor boy yokels from Naples, Italy and Brownsville, California...

Arriving guests were all dressed in their classiest best, and we both assumed that they all must have had plenty of money to burn. I became excited to finally get a chance to go inside and start looking around for famous personalities. Sean Connery, or rather, James Bond, was actually inside right then and having a deadly game of Baccarat with Dr. No. *Monaco's* beloved Prince Rainier was there too and holding hands with his lovely, recently new bride, the world-famous actress, and now Princess Grace Kelly. Hopefully, they were both inside shaking hands, facing adoring fans and tributaries, and awaiting Harry's and my arrival so they could get our autographs, give us a tour of their palace casino, and then offer to let us drink and play to our hearts' content, and all on-the-house, their treat. Dreamy...

We both quickly determined that we did not wish to drag our awkward bags all throughout the casino floors. After all, we would be so engaged while greeting famous celebrities, placing bets, watching our cards, pulling down arms on those colorful, noisy, and generous slot machines, and finally collecting and counting all our winnings. We would be far too busy to keep watchful eyes over our spare underwear. We needed a safe place to stash our stuff, or rather, just my sea bag and Harry's shoulder bag. They weren't much, but they were all we had.

After a brief search, we discovered a fairly safe place behind some decorative landscaping beside the casino structure. We cautiously tucked our belongings under a broad-leafed, lower bush's camouflaging coverage and then made our anxious way back to the casino entrance. Harry and I were both so excited as we prepared for our glorious entry and introductions into the thrilling night life of highest-class society and world class gambling. . .

We all but bounded up the marble steps as we both eagerly anticipated entering those beautiful, wide, brass and glass revolving doors. The entire entranceway was designed with ornate, and classy mixtures of glass and gold-colored trim and molding. It was truly a remarkable sight and a spectacular introduction to the thrilling and colorful interior. Inside, and through the slightly tinted glass entranceway, we could just barely make out all the elaborate red carpets, brilliantly lit up gambling tables, and flamboyant, multi-colored slot machines. Oh, boy!... Ooops!

Just as we took our leading steps toward the wide doorways and make our excited entries, two large, powerful looking door guards dressed in enormous and tightly-fitting, but very sophisticated looking, tuxedos both held out their arms stopping our advancement. They were not smiling at us at all but appeared even a little annoyed. Quickly, they announced their nullifying grievances.

In a brief, matter of fact, and hardline tone, one of the guards explained, "*Ce soir, c'est uniquement la soiree smoking. Vous ne pouvez pas entrer sans en porter un.*" Tonight, is Tuxedo Night Only. You may not enter without wearing one."

Of course, I could not let the poor, helpless, security guard off that easy, so I had to beg and plead language ignorance trying to attempt a different outcome. I began almost whimpering, "Oh, please, we don't understand. We just traveled so far to get here. We only want to stay a little while, and we promise not to win very much. Can't we just go over there to that quiet area? Pleeeaaase?"

Then the same guard's gruff, no-nonsense, perfect-English spoken answer ended our debate, "No, Fellas. No tux, no entry. Goodnight. Now beat it!"

Well, so much for good times in the world of glitter and gaudiness. That little riff with the guards abruptly ended Harry's and my exotic plans of *breaking-the-bank*. Just thinking of all that money, we lost out on winning was depressing. On the flip side, it was frustrating to think that those rich owners were so wealthy that they could afford to sacrifice acceptance of our hard-earned cash on their gambling tables and slots. And all over a silly *suit* rule.

Oh, the unfairness of bourgeois depravity and their self-indulgences. How dare they reject us and our good money. Heck, I couldn't afford to *rent* a tuxedo, even if I wanted to, and I didn't. They could just keep all their high-falutin ideals, and rules, and all their money too.

So, on that late evening, Harry and I left the *Monte Carlo Casino* rejected, dejected, as broke as when we arrived, tired from climbing that stupid hill to the top, and then still facing a new, but same old, issue: Where to sleep for that depressingly dark night?

Yacht Night

Right after being shamefully forced to leave *Monte Carlo Casino Square*, Harry and I retrieved our bags and wandered over to a nearby lookout-railing spot arranged for guests to view the entire Monaco coast with its shoreline village enterprises. Right down below us was the magnificent *Monaco Yacht Harbor* and the beautifully lit up city-state of *Monaco*.

I remember thinking to myself, "How charming the whole, brightly lit-up *Monte Carlo* community was. Big things really do come in small packages."

However, earlier Harry and I had been so absorbed focusing on having casino fun that we had made no plans whatsoever for our night's sleeping arrangements. That was a thoughtless mistake. Perhaps, we felt like we would win so much money gambling, we would just rent a room at the casino palace and stretch out in luxury for the night there. Unfortunately, our plans did not materialize as we'd hoped. We were temporarily facing a conundrum.

Then something fun occurred. An idea. While staring down from our hilltop perch and gazing upon the lovely community below, I absorbed all the wonder of *Monaco*. I could easily make out its breathtaking views of the Mediterranean Sea and the wonderfully exclusive *Monaco Yacht Harbor* below.

As I dreamily ogled and enjoyed the sights of all those magnificent boats and yachts docked in the harbor, I immediately centered my vision on one particularly special yacht. It was by far the largest and most glorious watercraft in the entire harbor. It appeared as though it were at least one hundred feet long from stem to stern and three levels high, not counting below deck. It was very impressive... and very empty.

"Harry!" I exclaimed loudly, "I just spotted our night's sleep over. Look! Down there! See that huge, gorgeous boat in the harbor? No one is around. Let's make it ours for the night."

"Are you serious?" asked Harry. "What if we get caught?"

"It's empty, Harry," I responded. "Nobody is watching. We can sleep and be gone before the break of dawn. C'mon, let's check it out!"

With that said, I excitedly hoisted my bag once again up onto my now rejuvenated shoulder and headed for the long walk down the hillside roadway toward the yacht harbor. Harry willingly yet warily joined right along. It took little time for us to make our way winding through the community and finding the *Monaco Yacht Harbor* entranceway. Although it was late by that time, the Entrance was still open, unguarded, and left available for passages both ways.

We easily slipped right on through the entry gate and made our ways up the walkway leading to the boats. Soon we reached the turn leading to our exclusive yacht choice for our night's slumber. That was when Harry decided to bail out on me. It was too much for him to deal with. The *trespassing* aspect went against his firm, moral character almost as much as fear of getting caught. I understood his wishes, but the thought of innocently relaxing on a beautiful boat for a night was just too compelling for me.

On a darker note, I sort of chuckled and excused my plot with an inappropriate defense, "Ah, shucks, besides, *trespassing* is sort of in our American nature."

Fortunately, however, right on the dock's walkway, at the turning point to the yacht, was an overturned rowboat just lying there unattached and unattended. That was when Harry produced his own creative idea.

"Daniel," he announced, "this is the spot for me. I am just going to climb underneath the rowboat and sleep undisturbed until morning. I'll be fine right here."

I did not want to dispute the matter, so I accepted his wishes. I even helped lift up the rowboat for Harry to climb under. Once he was entrenched, I wished him a good night and made my way to the beautiful yacht. I had already experienced many solo nights, so another one like this was not going to be any issue for me.

The rest of the night went extraordinarily well. The yacht harbor, itself, had many night lights glowing to light up its surroundings. The magnificent yacht, named <u>Enchanted</u>, was indeed empty, and no one else was aboard. I easily slipped over the dock railing, climbed up and balanced myself on the yacht's gunnel, or siding edge, and then stepped right onto the boat's decking. Quickly, I made my way to the aft deck with its visible lounge chairs.

In no time at all, I rested my sea bag beside me, stretched out on an incredibly cushioned and comfortable lounge chair, and using my blanket again as covering, I relaxed for the night. It was amazingly quiet and peaceful, and no one came around at all. If they had, I would have heard them, I figured. Plus, I would have also had a decent view of any approaching arrivals. It was sweet dreams coming for me...

However, early the next morning, and just as I had pre-considered, I did hear rumbling a way off on the approaching dock. It was loud laughter and commotion awakening me and forcing me to quickly look around and study my surroundings. Sure enough, in the distance and just entering the dock area, there was a small group of four or five people briskly and happily heading up the dock ramps eventually coming directly to the yacht I was still resting on.

In a flash, and keeping as low a profile as possible, I hopped up, grabbed my bag, stuffed my blanket inside it, slipped around the corner, and jumped back up onto the yacht slip's docking. With my bag hoisted high, I swiftly, but without running, made my way back up the dock. Just as I passed the small group, who had by then noticed my approach, I began nodding while confirming my honest thoughts to them all.

"Incredible yacht!" I began. "Marvelous boat from stem to stern! Very lovely! Very impressive! Wonderful name too! <u>Enchanted</u>, I am for sure. Very nice!" I hustled past them all with a final round of, "Good morning to you all. Have a nice day, and goodbye."

Compliments and positive words are usually very disarming to most folks, I had learned. The small group was surprised enough to give me confused looks yet with somewhat accepting approval. Everything had happened so suddenly I was fairly sure none of them had any idea what had just occurred. It was just some guy walking past who had been admiring their boat... at 6:30 A.M. .

Also, I knew that once they were aboard the yacht, they would notice nothing out of ordinary. All was well. I then quickly made my way to the rowboat with Harry likely still slumbering underneath. Knocking soundly upon it to awaken him, I hoisted the boat up once again.

Speaking out hurriedly and anxiously, though, I loudly whispered advice, "C'mon Harry. It's time to go! The owners are here."

Harry awakened with a jolt and moved faster than I ever did. In no time, we had hustled ourselves and our gear off the docks and hurried up the entrance road to the main highway. Soon thereafter, we found a nice café for our morning's coffee and meal, and right after that we were back on the highway heading out of town. Our little *Monte Carlo* night's adventure had ended, and we were merely *richer for all the experience* is all. Italy, here we came.

Pisa Ron

Not long after that, our next lift took Harry and me to our eventual parting point. Just inside the Italian border, we came to a division where Harry needed to break off and head north, as were his previously intended plans. On-the-other-hand, I remained with our car lift hosts, a French couple in a Citroen, who were traveling on to *Florence*, Italy. My own plans were also to go there eventually, but I had already arranged to meet up with Ron in *Pisa*, Italy before then. Truth is that Ron and I had crudely scheduled to meet that very day at the *Leaning Tower of Pisa* at noontime.

That is one of the difficult issues with making specific plans when one of the *plan makers* is hitchhiking. Looking back, I surmise that I should have gotten my head back on straight much sooner while at the *Horny*

Hostel. Leaving one day earlier would have given me plenty of time to meet up with Ron at the *Leaning Tower of Pisa.* By the time we arrived near *Pisa,* however, there was no chance I was going to make it by noontime to meet Ron. I would be a couple of hours late, at least.

It bothered me a great deal to not keep up my end of an agreement. I didn't want to impose on Ron at all. He had already co-hosted my wonderful visit in *Amsterdam.* He had shown me a fun time in *Paris* at the *Palace of Versailles.* He had driven me all the way to *Valencia,* including side excursions in *St. Sebastian* and *Madrid.* Finally, Ron was going out of his way once more to greet me in *Pisa* at the *Leaning Tower* to offer me yet another helpful lift to *Rome.* I definitely owed him the courtesy of punctuality.

On-the-other-hand, had I left the *Costa Brava Castle Hostel* one day earlier, then I would have missed hooking up with Harry and lost out on his friendship. Together, we would have missed our debacle overnighter in *Nice* with those two oversexed roomies due to *mistaken identities.* The very next day we would also have missed out on our getting *tossed out* of the *Monte Carlo Casino* and then even sleeping at the *Monaco Yacht Harbor.*

True, we may have missed out on winning a small fortune, or even a large one, and our destinies may have been completely different, but nevertheless we did miss out. As a result, I was late and had to figure up an alternative for missing my appointment with Ron. The only option I could produce was going straight to the *Leaning Tower,* anyway, and wait for Ron. I would wait just in case he was still there, or came again later, looking for me. What else could I do?

My French lift hosts were a nice, elderly couple from near Marseilles, France, and they were very cordial about my needs. Harry departed after we had shook hands and exchanged addresses and contact promises. Always made in good faith but not always kept earnestly, we amiably agreed to stay-in-touch. Great fellow he was.

The French couple and I jabbered back and forth a bit while Harry was with us, and I continued cheerfully yacking away with my trivialized French chatter after he left us. They told me that one of their vacation treats was going south from Marseilles, Italy and picking up young hitchhikers to help them on their journeys. Although seemingly impressed with my meager French, true to the rule, however, neither spoke any English. It was okay with me because I enjoyed my practice.

Eventually, they let me off at the turnoff toward *Pisa* and the *Leaning Tower,* and we parted on appreciative terms. I had told them not to go out of their way once we got near the city and *Tower*. I needed to do some things myself, regardless of consequences. If I were lucky, I might catch a quick easy lift all the way into town and get really close to the *Leaning Tower*.

Wouldn't you know it, just after I stuck my thumb out attempting to garnish a short lift into town, some guy on a motorcycle just up ahead of me and across the main road stopped to offer me a ride. How he planned to get both me and my large sea bag on his bike, I did not know. However, his next move showed his true intentions and aspirations. The motorcycle driver formed a closed circle with his right hand and then began pumping it rapidly to and away from his mouth. I wondered for a moment, but then I caught on quick.

At least that guy was making his ultimate objective known without a struggle between us. It was his silly hand signal suggesting that if I wanted a ride, then all I had to do was suck his "you know what." Or he was offering to suck mine if I'd let him. Then as a reward, or payment I surmised, he would also give me a lift to my next stop.

I was learning fast and actually amused. Once I caught onto his intentions, I was even somewhat appreciative of his advance warning. I just laughed whole heartedly and shook him off with a kind wave. The biker then just shrugged his shoulders and sped off.

"No play? No way!" I just laughed. Now, at least, his crudeness was deliberate relatively clear *communication*. Both parties expressed themselves, and no harm was done. If only everyone could communicate so clearly: "Would you like to have sex? What? Oh, no thank you? Okay. Have a nice day!"

Anyway, a silly laugh encounter to get me on my way. Thankfully, it was not too far to reach the *Leaning Tower* by walking, but unfortunately and obvious by that hour, I simply could not help being late. Nevertheless, I got there on foot fairly quickly, easily spotting the famous *Leaning Tower* from quite a distance away. Even still, by matter of habit, I picked up my pace and hoofed it the final distance as fast as I could. With my sea bag rhythmically bouncing on my shoulder. I think I had hoped that once I arrived and met up with Ron, he would have noticed I was out-of-breath and, therefore, had at least attempted to be on time.

Alas, I rushed up the grassy knoll over to the amazing *Leaning Tower*, and I began searching all the faces of everyone nearby in hopes of glimpsing Ron's. No such luck. I recalled telling him with added emphasis the first time that he was never to wait at all when trying to find me in *Paris*. And back then I was even early for that *first* rendezvous. Yet, in Valencia we had agreed upon meeting-up at noontime that very day for our *Pisa* connection, and I was already several hours late. I would not blame Ron if he just left me. After all, that was our unspoken deal.

No matter, I still waited and waited for Ron's potential return, but to no avail. Eventually, I did the whole tourist thing walking all around the *Leaning Tower* and photographing it. I visited the nearby *Duomo*, a terrific, medieval-architectural structure used as a museum. Originally, it was the main part of the church.

In my brief walk through the *Piazza del Duomo Square*, I learned that the *Leaning Tower of Pisa* began *leaning* early on, with its unique, dazzling construction, during the 12th century due to soft ground, and it worsened through its completion in the 14th century. While viewing the *Tower of Pisa*, I read that it was already leaning five and a half degrees, very noticeable to nearby observers on the ground.

I paid a small entry fee using French francs, and as I climbed to the bell tower at its top for viewing, the *leaning* was very obvious while going up the stairs. On the leaning portion, I was naturally forced to fall against the downside wall. I was told that the *Tower of Pisa* was originally constructed to show off the wealth and prosperity of the city of *Pisa*. I considered that the tower's *leaning* probably hadn't served its architects' reputations much positive feedback at the time. Were they the laughing stocks of *Pisa,* or even of all Italy? I know that I sure laughed… Sorry, architects.

Once returning to the surrounding grounds of the *Duomo Square,* I also stopped at a few souvenir shops, dilly dallied, and purchased a couple small mementos. Throughout all my tourist time wandering around, however, I kept a vigilant lookout for Ron's sudden appearance. After a while, I even returned to the *Leaning Tower* sitting down to continue waiting and watching.

When Ron did not show up by late evening, I began accepting my circumstances. I recognized I may need to go to Plan B. Oh, right! I didn't have one yet. However, darkness was nearly again on hand. I still needed food and another place to sleep for that night. So, I definitely had plans to make.

That evening, dinner from one convenient and inexpensive restaurants near the tower, provided me with a cheese and chicken pasta, lots of delicious bread, and more delicious wine. Any time I drank anything alcoholic, I was taking a chance because I did not really know one make from another. So, I judged wines by their color and price. I decided on another nice, cheap red selection. It was a perfect choice, and I enjoyed a genuinely nice mealtime as I proceeded with my munching, drinking, smoking, and all-the-while continuing my perusal of passersby, just in case Ron was still actually also looking for me.

Nightfall came, and I did not have a clue yet as to any nearby hostels for sleeping arrangements. *Pisa* was a large enough city, around 100,000 people, so any decent hostel could likely be even close to the *Leaning Tower*. However, once it got late, I made another modification to my unmade *plans*. I chose to stay close by in order to be back at the base of the *Leaning Tower* the very next day. I would be awaiting Ron, especially at noontime, just in case of his unexpected return. It was a chance I would take, and Ron deserved my extra effort of waiting or trying to find him.

Furthermore, I rationalized, if I did not find Ron, then I fully understood I was alone for the duration of my summer excursion. Ron would thus have no decent update report to make to anyone back home of that fact. If, of course, he was even doing such, and I strongly considered that he was. That was another time when my imagination ran rampant again:

"I'm sorry Jean, and Parents," Ron could quip, "I left Daniel in Spain and he never showed up at our next rendezvous point in Pisa. I never saw him again after that. Too bad. So sad. He was probably picked up by some aggressive gay people again. Then again, actually, I believe he can take care of himself."

That silly mind lapse also suggested, however, that Ron might hopefully actually return once more to the *Leaning Tower* again the following day, just to be sure of my absence. What was a two-week away rendezvous time, anyway? Thirteen days, or fourteen, or fifteen? Who's counting? I would see.

When it became so dark that only moonlight provided any means to find my way around, I determined my next path. Plan "C," if you will. Far off in the distance, behind the *Leaning Tower of Pisa*, was an enormous, beautiful meadow of colorful flowers. I had become noticeably aware of it during that afternoon and especially from the top of the bell tower of the *Tower of Pisa*. The blooming flowers were spectacular and deserving of due attention. By nightfall, although darkened by sundown's shadows, they also became my next proposal for another sleepover.

I believed that for anyone watching, I simply looked like somebody out for a late evening stroll in the lovely and picturesque Begonia, sunflowers, and many other colorful flowers meadow. Truth be told, that was exactly what I did. The difference was that once I found myself mostly out of sight of any further potentially curious observers, I simply stopped and dropped. Then, quickly, and judiciously, I emptied my sea bag carefully over the pretty flower garden, stretched out upon my sea bag/mattress converter, and covered myself up once more with my blanket. I was comfortably set for another beautiful night.

The brilliant, rainbow-colored flowers were all tall enough so that I was abundantly hidden from any onlookers. However, my own view of anything was fairly well obstructed too, so I could only see lights from the *Square's* rooftops and that from the *Leaning Tower*, itself, whenever I sat up. No matter. They were nice and the moon and stars were stunning. It all became a very serene and pleasant overnighter. Much later, I learned about the world-famous beauty of Italy's Tuscany Region, especially in Springtime. Summer's gorgeous Begonias and blossoming flowers all over that area were objects of delight for world travelers everywhere. And to think that I just slept through it all! Pun intended.

The next morning, and all repacked again, I was back over to the *Leaning Tower*, and just in case, I sat there calmly waiting for that early-bird riser, Ron. Later, the shops all started opening, so I ventured to another café for coffee and rolls, fruit, and cheese. Plus, I used its bathroom to get myself cleaned-up as best I could. Once I was refreshed, I went back to my post at the foot of the *Leaning Tower* and waited. And waited. And waited...

When it was well past noon, but still only by minutes, not hours, and just when I was first considering giving up, I got a great surprise... Up until noontime, I had been looking, watching, searching, studying, and seeking out any countenances that resembled Ron, but to no avail. Also, it would be a mistruth if I did not admit that I had mentally begun considering other options.

First, I could pack up and head out for *Rome* on foot by hitching from the same spot where that French couple had dropped me off the previous afternoon; second, I might go on to *Florence*, which Ron and I had only briefly spoken about while traveling in Spain (It had been another rendezvous consideration, and I thought we might just accidentally bump into each other there); third, I ought to head straight over to *Venice* and then up to Austria, skipping *Rome* completely because of wanting to see my friend who lived in *Vienna*; or fourth, I should just stay put in *Pisa* and continue waiting for Ron each day until noon at the *Leaning Tower of Pisa* until summer ended.

The last option about *waiting* forever would really serve me right, I thought... I deserved to have to wait just like I had likely made Ron wait...

But no, our arrangement was that he would not wait for me, nor I for him… The option about skipping *Rome* was out of the question too. *Rome* was a life's dream, a bucket-list, sort of thing for me. I had to go there, no question…

Florence and *Venice* visits were plausible to visit right away, too, but they threw off my entire mental map… I had planned to see them both anyway on the way back north from *Rome* as I eventually headed back toward *Paris* via *Vienna*… Thus, *Rome* won out the *options exercise*, and I was just mulling over various details when I was suddenly interrupted from my daydreaming…

"Well, there you are!" came a recognizably friendly voice. "I wasn't sure if you'd make it after no appearance yesterday, but here you are today. Well done!" said Ron.

I leaped to my feet in delighted surprise, and immediately lied, "Hi, Ron. It's great to see you. Oh, yes, I've been here for two whole days already!"

Then I grinned like a Cheshire Cat and told him the real truth of being late the day before. Actually, it had only been less than one day in real hours. Ron was not perturbed, though. In fact, he seemed impressed that I had even made the connection at all, considering everything. Later on, I contemplated that when I had not shown up the previous day, Ron may have believed I had skipped out completely on him considering our last awkward, one-way conversation in Spain. But I did not bring that subject up. No need. I was so relieved and grateful he had actually showed up to find me.

Since we had both already toured the *Leaning Tower,* and the rest of *Piazza del Duomo Square* next to it, it was Ron's suggestion that we leave *Pisa* right away and drive further on to *Florence*, one of his favorite destinations. I was very agreeable because, having studied my map closely, I knew after that, I would have my straight ride south to *Rome*. All was well.

From art studies and history class, I had also read about *Firenze*, or *Florence*, Italy. It would also be a pleasure visiting its museums, especially since Ron knew what to seek. I respected his knowledge. Plus, I really appreciated his car! Volkswagens ruled!

Going for Broke

The drive from *Pisa* to *Florence*, Italy was brilliant. Italy certainly loves its art, music, food, and colors, and our brief excursion into *Firenze* was an absolute showcase of it all. The picturesque views along the highway from splendidly colorful fields of flowers to the rustically manicured pastures of crops and hay fields were wonderful combinations. On the way there, Ron treated us to classical music and Italian Opera. It really helped set the stage for our tour of the city. The drive was brief, though, and we had barely gotten started before we were already arriving in *Florence*.

Of course, Ron's and my conversation was kept mildly related to historical sites that we would visit in *Firenze*. I deliberately refrained from bringing up our previous conversation on our way to *Valencia*, Spain, and I imagined that Ron also appreciated its absence. I did not need to embarrass him or make our drive and visit awkward, so I simply ignored the topic. I felt that if Ron wanted to discuss anything further with me, then he would bring up the subject. Furthermore, I saw no reason either in mentioning the prior incident in *Nice*, France, when Harry and I spent the difficult night with the dentist and his engineer roommate. No personal harm had been done, and no unnecessary stress was needed. Besides, I had already determined that Ron was one of the *nice,* other-type guys.

Upon approaching *Florence*, Ron had a pleasant surprise for me too. He had already booked a room at a hotel in town, and he asked if I would like to share the room with him or find a hostel somewhere. In passing, Ron also casually mentioned that his hotel room had two separate twin beds, so my minimal concern was immediately remedied. I quickly offered to split the cost with him, but Ron stated that the room was the same price with one or two persons. It was very decent of him, and I gratefully accepted.

We soon located the hotel, checked-in, and dropped off our belongings. For some reason, I did not feel it necessary to talk about my other, previous-night layovers like the ones on a haystack, a hotel beach lounge chair, a yacht, and even in that gorgeous field of Tuscany flowers. That description of *roughing it* might be news that somehow filtered to my mom, and I was afraid my seeming homeless conditions or circumstances might alarm her. Fact is, I had refrained from talking to Ron much even about all the rainy nights in Denmark and sleeping on cold, wet ground. Just more unnecessary, potentially worrisome information for back home. Oh, I'd for sure tell everybody about them all after I returned, but it wasn't needed just then. I had survived it all well enough . . . so far.

I was also grateful for the hotel sleepover because my travel funds had become drastically low. So much so, that I was beginning to worry about being able to finance my trip much further even while staying in more hostels, let alone any hotels. I'd have to see where I'd end up, financially speaking, once in *Rome* to seriously study my looming budget crisis. Although I had slept outdoors many nights so far for free, those other hostel expenses, little souvenirs, and the excessive dining, drinking, and smoking costs had rapidly depleted my budget savings. I wanted to pay my own way, but the realities of affordability were beginning to rear their ugly head.

After our quick hotel stop, we went out for lunch, and I ate very minimally, suggesting that I was still quite full of breakfast. Afterwards, Ron easily maneuvered his VW through town to a special museum for our first visit and treat. Ron asked me if I had ever heard of Michelangelo, and I responded that I had seen pictures of his famous paintings inside the *Sistine Chapel* in *Vatican City*, but not much else. He then told me that I was in for a treat.

When we approached a museum, I then offered a surprise to Ron. In appreciation for the coming night's hotel stay, I bought both our tickets into the *Academia Gallery*. It was well over my budgetary means, but I wanted to thank Ron in some small way. He was incredibly grateful, and that pleased me.

However, my true pleasure came once we entered the *Academia Gallery* museum. There at the end of a wide corridor, called *The Hall of Prisoners*, was a world renowned, seventeen-foot tall, fantastic Renaissance sculpture of *The David* by Michelangelo, done in 1501 to 1504. Additionally, along both walls in the hall were four other unfinished sculptures also by Michelangelo called the *Prisoners*. Thus, the Hallway of . . . *The David* was breathtaking, and it truly displayed Michelangelo's genius as a sculptor.

Carved from one, single, huge piece of marble, *The David* character was from the famous, Biblical verses of David preparing to do battle with the giant Goliath. A viewer could easily spot a rock in *The David's* hanging hand to be used in the sling draping over the statue's shoulder. His stare was mesmerizing too, suggesting his focus on the upcoming fight, and Michelangelo left nothing to the imagination with his nude sculpture's visually stunning appearance.

I also learned that, originally, *The David* had been exhibited outside in *Florence* for over four hundred years. But, in the 1900's, it was moved inside that museum for protection from the elements and potential human vandalism. In fact, the original sculpture had at one time displayed golden leaves adorning *The David*, but rain and weather had eroded the golden paint washing it away. That also prompted the city authorities to move the statue inside. Two other exact replicas of *The David* also exist in *Florence* in other locations, including the original site of the first sculpture's placement before being moved. Both copies, however, are in bronze but otherwise remarkably similar.

The remainder of the museum was filled with additional great works of art from the Renaissance Period of the late fifteenth through the seventeenth centuries (1490's-1700). Masterpieces from that era included textile art from the period's clothing attire, incredible paintings, and many more sculpture exhibits. If not the most famous museum in *Florence*, the *Academia Gallery* is said to receive the most visitors. I understood why after our visit.

The most famous museum in *Firenze*, however, was the *Uffizi Gallery*. That was our next stop, and Ron, appreciatively, reciprocated by paying my entry fee. It was another incredible exhibit of ancient through Renaissance Period art with more wonderful masterpiece paintings, sculpture by the period's masters, and centuries old artifacts that overwhelmed viewers with their beauty and history. Inside the *Uffizi Gallery* were housed many more magnificent statues including the world-famous marble *Venus de Milo* from the ancient Greek, Hellenistic *Period* of 300 BC to just after Christ's death AD. Such a marvelous exhibit, I knew that I had visited a great rival for those previously seen museums like the *Academia*, the *Prada*, and the *Louvre*. I didn't realize it, but I was definitely being set up for my upcoming Roman holiday.

Therein, however, lay the greatest issue before me at that time. After another light meal at dinner trying to save funds for the remainder of my journey, I finally felt the weight of unavoidable destitution facing me. I was becoming stressed that I could see no way how I had enough funds to last me for my remaining eighteen days. That was the total time left until my flight back home from *Paris*, and I still needed to cover all my remaining sleeping accommodations and meals.

Even if I refrained from purchasing any further souvenir trinkets, spent no more on non-essential goods like beer, wine, or cigarettes, visited no more pay-to-enter museums, and slept a majority of my remaining nights on the ground, I would not afford making it back to *Paris* without serious hunger issues. It was obvious to me, right there in *Florence* and while with Ron, that I needed additional funding to cover my absolutely minimal expenses.

After we finished touring *Florence,* we had a reasonable dinner of Fettuccine Alfredo, and I drank plain water. It was then that I decided to spring for help from Ron once we returned to our hotel room. I just simply and plainly explained my situation to him by explaining my feeble, remaining travel funds and clarifying my future plans. It wasn't difficult to paint a bleak picture of my circumstances and approaching financial crisis because that was what I actually already saw for myself.

I strictly budgeted the remaining days for my journey, and I produced a realistic funds figure to complete my trip and make it back to *Paris* sufficiently. I needed an additional fifty dollars American to get by. So, I simply asked Ron for a loan and was once more gratified by his generosity. Upon my explanation and request for help, Ron immediately handed over fifty dollars with hardly a blink.

I was flabbergasted and so appreciative. Ron had truly come to my rescue. I believe that in order to gain his further support I could have given descriptive details about my skimpy days sleeping outside in the elements, but I didn't bother. Nor did I need to do so. Ron was truly an understanding gentleman, and we just agreed for me to return the loan once I got situated back at home. I gave him my word that I would repay him.

The next morning was our four-hour drive from *Florence* to *Rome*. I was in a good mood and feeling incredibly grateful for Ron's additional financial assistance. A traveling companion, tour guide, transportation provider, room-and-board provisions helper, and now an additional trip financer, Ron had become essential to the success of my summer trek. I remained forever grateful to him, and after a very relaxing drive to *Rome*, and review of Ron's <u>European Hotel Travel Guide</u>, we found my next layover at the least expensive hostel available in *Rome*.

Furthermore, Ron drove me directly to that hostel's location, and it was where we formally parted company for the final time. I felt that he could send decent enough reports back home advising of my wellbeing. Unknowing of any difficulties I had ever encountered in Europe thus far, with the exception of the night driver/attacker in France, Ron might deliver only positive reports of my successes up until our separating in *Rome*. Thanks to him, I was feeling financially flush again with enough remaining funds on hand to complete my journey. Ron was departing, I believed, feeling satisfied and comfortable with my status too. As for me, I was in great spirits.

Afterall, I was finally visiting my long-yearned "City of History," *Rome*. All was well. . .

CHAPTER 14:

....

ROMAN HOLIDAY

Happy Hostel

*R*ome's *Beautiful Youth Hostel* that I selected from Ron's hotel guide was true to its name too. It was overflowing with beautiful, international youth. As a smaller, but inexpensive hostel, it was filled with ever-present laughter, raucous celebrations, small group studies, and general busyness everywhere. It offered all the necessary amenities too: Clean and secure rooms, visiting and entertaining areas, and a very reasonable, buffet-style cafeteria adjacent to a lounging area with enough table settings for all.

The hostel was very appealing and comfortable right away. I easily located the fluent, English-speaking manager, and she arranged for my stay in a medium-sized dormitory room with four twin beds strewn around in a relaxing array with two dressers for sharing. The building was another office complex or small school converted into a well-located, short-term place for budget-minded travelers, particularly students, who enjoyed sharing experiences, meals, and conversations.

After I finished checking-in and unpacking my sea bag of personal belongings into assigned dresser drawers, I went back out to the hostel's main auditorium. It was arranged to accommodate multiple groups for activities, socializing, and eating in its adjacent dining area. Immediately, I was welcomed by other guests who invited me to join their conversations and tell them about my travels to date. Once again, I learned that coming from the San Francisco Region was extremely popular, and many had questions for me hoping, themselves, to visit there one day.

Fortunately, having spent so many summers with my Aunt Jean, I had been to San Francisco often for visits with her friends, social entertainment, viewing its many museums, trips to Fleishhacker's Zoo, hiking through Golden Gate Park, the Japanese Gardens, De Young Art Exhibit, and Museum of Natural History. Also, just relaxing on the city's Pacific Ocean Beach and general tourist-type activities like Fisherman's Wharf were enviable.

Although not a travel expert by any means, I could certainly share what I did know, and the other guests were eager to hear. Of course, I pressed any other hostel guests for information regarding their own hometowns and travel experiences too. Often, listening to others and expressing interest and appreciation in them and their stories is even more important that sharing one's own anecdotes. It is easier to draw listeners into your own circle of friendship when they believe you care about them and their histories.

One of the best points about that hostel? Two words: Very cheap! It cost more than *Costa Brava Castle Hostel*, but that was understandable. I was in *Rome*, for cryin' aloud! *Rome* was an internationally popular and major city of the world, and I expected high rates. Such was not the case, though, at the *Rome Youth Hostel.*

Other *Rome* hostels were more expensive, but their unique highlights and extra-style were of no issue for me. My choice hostel was very inexpensive, really fitted my budget well, and it was very centrally located. Right away, I learned of easy and economical means to get around town by bus, and even motor scooter rentals, which I mentally registered for future reference. But I was quite pleased with the hostel's accommodations, its low-cost rates, the other joyful youth travelers, and the hostel's location near so many grandiose Roman sites that I planned to see.

The *Rome Youth Hostel* became an ideal sanctuary for me to return to daily as I skipped around the city utilizing its bus system visiting various attractions. Most evenings I would return exhausted from all the walking, hiking, and touring of *Rome's* highlights. I always made it a point, however, to return in time for the last dinner meal of the day. With only a few exceptions, I could not afford to miss the hostel's inexpensive dining. With hostel costs for room and all three meals, I was spending a meager four American dollars a day maximum.

I remember also being mollified by the ridiculous conversion rate for one American dollar to Italian lira. It was outrageous, like over a thousand lira to one dollar. I felt rich, but I handed out vast amounts of lira for each purchase. One certainty was that spending so many lire each day made me very conscious of my cost outlay. I became very frugal and began avoiding unnecessary frivolous spending such as for beer and wine. Lunch and dinner meals were always served with complimentary wine, too, as was their custom. While outside and touring, however, I gave up purchasing alcoholic beverages partly because of extra costs, but also because free beverages suited me better. Occasionally, I sprang for a soda, but freely served water or wine was more than adequate.

Nevertheless, the *Rome Youth Hostel* was perfect for me, and I utilized its amenities fully each day. I made so many new friends there, too. The place was packed with other thrift-minded travelers, and there was always someone to join visiting some site if I wanted. Yet, although I shared stories with so many, I actually had learned to appreciate seeing most sights while going solo. That way I was not caught up by others' timetables, schedules, or interests conflicting with my own. As I toured that marvelous city, I went where I liked, saw what I wanted, spent as much or little time as I wished, and made my own agenda. Besides, the other hostel guests were coming and going all the time, so I did not want to get caught up feeling obligated to accommodate others' wishes or needs. I was perfectly happy touring alone much of the time.

Back at the hostel, though, I enjoyably socialized with other guests. That was nice and always acceptable. I shared a sleeping room with three other guys. It was necessary to be hospitable and friendly. During meals, there were always other travelers that liked sharing each other's daily adventures in our conversations. The *Rome Youth Hostel* became a focal point for ideas and advice regarding visiting that city. It was a useful and happy place to talk and learn and suggest ideas with each other. For me, an easy nickname arose for that youth hostel facility in *Rome*. It quickly became: *The Happy Hostel*.

Roman Splendor

For the next week and a half, the *Happy Hostel* became a springboard for my daily adventures. Like *Paris,* there was so much to see that incorporated art with history. Statues from the Hellenistic Period well past the Renaissance Era identify so many street corners and decorate entranceways to museums throughout Rome. Although I gawked at various museums and enjoyed so many attractions from a distance to avoid entry fees, there were a few memorable tourist visits that I was happy to pay to see.

The Colosseum

No one can see *Rome* without visiting the *Roman Colosseum*. It is a massive, almost 160-foot-tall, oval structure also called the *Flavia Amphitheatre*. Built between 72-80 A.D., it is comprised of limestone, brick facia, and concrete. In its heyday, it would seat from 50,000 to 80,000 spectators for special events and entertainment such as battles between gladiators and fighting with wild animals.

It was impressive wandering through the various levels and seating aisles. I could not help but wonder if I were actually standing where various emperors of the Roman Empire had walked or sat during games presentations. The *Colosseum* was used for over four centuries by Roman rulers and public spectators until political and military struggles of the empire, along with changes in public tastes, put ends to gladiatorial combats and other entertainment during the sixth century.

Once inside the *Colosseum*, I was initially struck by the absence of the colosseum's flooring. Decay had long since caused the dirt and timber floor covering to collapse exposing a huge array of walkways and chambers beneath used at different times to harbor wild animals, slaves, and gladiators utilized during celebratory games and entertainment. It was impossible not to let one's imagination run rampant thinking about those ancient, spectacularly epic games produced there. I visited the *Roman Colosseum* twice to get my fill, but its enormity could be seen from long distances while touring the city elsewhere.

Fountain of Trevi

The spectacular *Trevi Fountain* was built between 1732 and 1762 and was dedicated to three different and popular Roman Catholic Popes who created it. It is by far the largest and most beautiful of all *Rome's* fountains standing a massive eighty-six feet tall, or twenty-six meters. The fountain, itself, is supposed to represent the Ocean Kingdom with the sea god Oceanus (Neptune) and other glorious horse statues and more suggesting abundance for all. It has a viewing area opposite it with many rows of seats placed in semi-colosseum style seating. At night, its unique lighting gives the whole scene a magnificent spectacle of human art, nature's water, and lighting science for special effects.

I also learned that throughout *Rome* there are over 2,000 fountains overall scattered about, and around fifty of them are considered monumental works of art. It was difficult to travel anywhere in *Rome* without spotting another fountain for an area's artistic aesthetics. There are more fountains in *Rome,* it is said, than in any other city in the world. Each one that I personally viewed was beautiful in its classic design and meaning.

However, two curiously interesting points regarding *Trevi Fountain* are also worth mentioning: First, it is said that should one toss a coin into *Trevi Fountain's* water pool and make a wish, "That same individual would one day return to visit *Rome* and the fountain again; the second point suggested is that many women go to visit the *Trevi Fountain* because they can likely expect some sexually, hyper-active Italian male to pinch their bottoms.

To the first point about "… *Trevi* coin tossing and returning," I am living proof of its potential validity. There and then in 1966, while visiting the *Trevi Fountain*, I certainly did toss my coin into its pool and made a wish, although only a small coin at that. Exactly forty years later to the month, however, I returned for another visit when taking my mother on a tour. Thus, that incredibly old expression is either a truism, or it's one of the best, travel-advertising gimmicks ever invented. Worked on me . . . sort of. I did return but did not get my wish.

To the second point regarding "Trevi Fountain area's butt pinching," I can personally attest to having observed that very activity take place. As I sat calmly and restfully one evening watching the fountain's flowing waters and enjoying crowd sights, I directly observed a typical, casually dressed Italian man swoop up behind an unsuspecting attractive woman and pinch heck out of her buttocks. At first, I was shocked, and then only moments later, I was overcome with laughter over the hilarity of the incident. The victim, however, or bottom-pinched woman, just shrieked mildly and then casually continued on her way as though it were not her first time. The Italian *pincher man* then simply went on about his business melding into the crowd once more as though he were merely a group actor upon a special stage performing his notably starring role... over and over.

Vatican City

A visit to *Vatican City* requires at least an afternoon's time, if not a whole day, or more. From the *Happy Hostel,* in central *Rome,* it was only a half hour walk to its entrance. Although *Vatican City* is its own city-state principality, independent from Italy, it is mostly well known for *St. Peter's Square, St. Peter's Basilica,* and its *Sistine Chapel.* Of course, St. Peter, one of Jesus's twelve disciples, is considered by Catholicism to be the church's first pope. The basilica and square are both named in his honor, and St. Peter is said to be entombed beneath the basilica, itself.

Directly in front of the huge domed *St. Peter's Basilica,* or Cathedral, is the exceptionally large plaza known as *St. Peter's Square.* Although the square, itself, is surrounded by two semi-circular structures on either side, the square also offers a very sizable entranceway and big entry to the domed basilica. In the square's center is a very tall obelisk which was originally constructed by a pharaoh of Egypt over 2,000 years ago.

The obelisk was then transported to Rome in 37 A.D. by Gaius Caligula. Well over 1,500 years later, it was disassembled, moved, and placed and resurrected in its present location. The *Vatican Obelisk* is the only remaining ancient Egyptian obelisk still standing. The cross at the obelisk's top is said today to possess within its special relics of Jesus Christ.

On each side of *St. Peter's Square* are two semi-circular colonnade structures housing Roman Catholic Church headquarters, office spaces, vast living quarters for the pope, quarters for all papal staff, museums, and private church libraries. Also, deep beneath the basilica are located the tombs of all previous Catholic Popes. What is so special, however, is the huge multitude of statues adorning the tops of the colonnades, including the basilica, itself. Crowning the facade of *St. Peter's Basilica,* for instance, are thirteen magnificent statues representing *Christ the Redeemer* in the center flanked by eleven of the twelve disciples. St. Peter is not included; however, *St. John the Baptist* stands in a place of honor on the right beside Christ. Very stunning by themselves, the colonnades flanking either side of the square are also both crowned by 140 statues, seventy on each, of all the known saints up until St. Thomas Aquinas in 1703.

The original church, located on Vatican Hill, was named a basilica by church authorities after it was pronounced to be built over the burial tomb of St. Peter. Construction of *St. Peter's Basilica* was ordered by Roman Emperor Constantine, the first Christian emperor in 319 A.D., and completed thirty years later in 349 AD. The basilica lasted 1,000 years, but deterioration caused fear of its eventual collapse, and thus, ultimate demolishment and rebuilding was designated. 120 years later, the present basilica was created from the design genius of many Renaissance art masters including Michelangelo, Raphael, Bramante, and many others.

St. Peter's Basilica is completely filled with wondrous works of art from all the ancient through Renaissance Era masters including marvelous paintings, statues, and wonderful artifacts. What was special to me too was the fact that there was absolutely no entry fee to the basilica. It was a completely free admission for the public, with only a charge for tours, or to climb to the top of the Michelangelo Dome.

The *Sistine Chapel* is one of the chapels of the apostolic palace within *Vatican City State*, and it is the official residence of the Catholic Pope. The chapel further serves as a place for special papal church services, ceremonies, and unique events. One such event is when the *Sistine Chapel* serves as seat of the church's enclave, the meeting where the College of Catholic Cardinals meet to choose a new pope. Fairly so, that part of a *Vatican City* tour does require an entry fee, but the *Sistine Chapel* is well worth the price.

Once inside, anyone's breath is surely taken away at sights of the great art masters' incredible contributions to *Sistine Chapel's* beauty and consecration. Michelangelo stands alone as the most significant of all those contributors, and his influence on modern definitions and concepts of God are very evident in all his paintings and amazing frescoes. It was interesting to learn that many of Michelangelo's rivals were humored by his receiving a commission to do the artwork. It was because, originally, Michelangelo had refused due to his belief that the project required too much work. His rivals believed that he would fail miserably at the task. However, it took Michelangelo four years to complete the task, and its incredible success solidified his placement at top of the Renaissance Era's list of great artists. For me, the *Sistine Chapel* was a glorious ending to an amazing day's visit.

Pantheon

Another special visit on another wanderlust afternoon was an excursion to see the famous *Pantheon*, or *Basilica of St. Mary*. It is considered one of the best preserved of all the ancient Roman buildings. When I visited, it was 1,900 years old, and it is still considered the oldest standing, non-reinforced, concrete domes of Roman construction of its time. Originally, the entire structure was designed as a church honoring Roman gods but was later recommissioned in the seventh century as a Catholic Church honoring St. Mary.

What stands out is the enormous cylindrical building with its large granite portico, or entrance, supported by sixteen tall granite columns, eight in the front and two sets of four in the rear. The cylinder portion is covered by its amazing giant dome. Interestingly, both the dome's height and cylinder's diameter are 142 feet. To me, the *Pantheon* was simply just one more leisurely hike in order to visit another fascinating Roman structure scattered throughout the fun city of *Rome*.

Roman Forum

Another day's wanderings took me to visit *Rome's* famous *Roman Forum*, or plaza. It is an important and huge rectangular structure surrounded by ruins of several ancient government buildings considered the center of the ancient city of *Rome*. In ancient times, the citizens referred to its marketplace area as the "Forum Magnum," or just simply the *Forum*. The forum served many different, useful, and important roles for the government and *Rome's* citizens.

For many centuries, the *Forum* served as a place for business and commercial interests. It was where important triumphal processions took place, public speeches were made, criminal trials were dealt with, and even gladiatorial matches occurred. Many believe it to be the most honored meeting place of all time in the entire world. Statues and monuments were erected in the area celebrating all the great men of *Rome*.

Once again, for me the *Forum* represented another moving experience while touring through its site because of what I imagined took place all around me throughout history. It was highly likely that where I walked, stood, or sat at many spots in the *Forum* was precisely where great rulers, Caesars, emperors, powerful Roman Senators, masterful artists, and important foreign dignitaries and tributaries had passed. They did so while doing business, shopping, or entertaining themselves with activities of their day. Throughout my travels across Europe, I often sensed highly significant vibrations at times that I was walking with ancient ghosts of mankind's giants. I suppose that is why *Rome* is still so important to me because of its fascinating, colorful, and influential history, at least for Western Civilization.

Roman Ruins

Ever heard of Roman aqueducts or Roman arches? Of course, we all have, and those concepts and practical uses have been copied throughout the world for over two thousand years. Roman arches can be dated as far back at 315 BC, when they were first utilized in construction of building projects throughout the Roman Empire.

Within *Rome*, itself, ancient arches were used to construct the *Colosseum* and for vast development of aqueducts. The Roman arch has been considered by everyone as the ancestor of modern architecture. Its design allowed Roman Empire and modern architects and developers alike to create larger buildings, longer roads, and superior aqueducts to anything previous. Furthermore, its evidence is worldwide but very noticeable throughout any travels in Italy, and especially in *Rome*.

I would have needed an entire summer's time to try and visit all the ancient, *Roman Ruins* located about the city. Ruins could be found on any walk, or tour, or visit in any direction from my *Happy Hostel*. There were famous *arches* honoring this spot or that guy all over the place throughout *Rome*. Each of them was particularly important in significance demonstrating superior Roman technology, strength, industry, and power. Like the famous saying because of Roman influence around the world, "All roads lead to *Rome*."

Of course, I'd have to say two other things about *Roman Ruins*: Romans loved to pray, and they loved to party. Due to the number of church structure remains, and then other unique, Roman ruins in various locations throughout *Rome*, it was easy to find ancient religious ruins and also remnants from several Roman circus sites in the city. Romans loved to worship their pagan gods, and then, ultimately, *Rome* became the epicenter of Christianity. At the same time, those adoring crowds revered in opportunities celebrated with festivals, games, parties, and even unique circuses still modeled today around the world.

Many *Roman Ruins* I merely spotted or found by accident while heading toward some other specific destination. It was obvious, though, that *Rome's* history was prevalent everywhere I traveled. Seeing so many ruins, and visiting a few of them, were only a couple of factors, however, that made *Rome* so endearing to me. Obvious, if not blatantly incredible, history was evident no matter where I went while touring *Rome*. Sometimes, I wondered if all those amazing historical ruins made Italians proud of their heritage. Or, if on-the-other-hand, Italians were embarrassed by them because of past glory but present slippage on stage on the world's arena. No matter because I'm not even Italian, and I felt enough pride for Italy's and Roman history to make up for it all. Wonderful stuff. . .

Motor Scootin'

This next section is the portion of my story which caused me the second most amount of personal guilt. *Catholic guilt*, I suppose. The first, of course, was my shameful back-stepping in my relationship with my girlfriend, sweetheart, lover in all my dreams, back home. I was still trying to get over that major emotional mishap. However, the second most guilt was what I decided to do for one entire day while visiting *Rome*.

As financially broke as I had felt in *Florence*, enough to ask Ron to help bail me out, once I was in *Rome*, I was feeling fairly cash friendly again. With great savings at the *Happy Hostel* for lodging and meals, and minimal costs seeing so much in *Rome* and *Vatican City*, it seemed as though I was virtually rolling in spare change. In other words, without going berserk, I believed that I could afford to spend money on one wild day of fun and carousing. And I did.

As it had turned out, on-and-off during my stay so far at *Rome's Beautiful Youth Hostel*, my *Happy Hostel*, I had met an interesting fellow from Prague, Czechoslovakia, or near there anyway. It was like me saying I was from San Francisco so others could easily form a mental map of my own home front. Even though I actually lived two hundred miles from there in Northern California mountains. Rudolf, or my new friend Rudi, also lived many miles away from Prague, but I imagined his general hometown whereabouts thinking about Prague's location.

Anyway, Rudi had a lot more money than I did to burn. He even had a Eurail Pass for all the railway systems throughout Europe, but he barely even used it except to travel to *Rome* so far, and then he would just return back home with it. "What a waste!" I thought. But then, like I said, "Rudi had money to burn!"

He also spoke excellent English. What was it with all those people? Everywhere I went, there I was speaking English with some European. Good thing, I guessed, or I'd have felt pretty lonely except in France. So anyway, one morning, after I'd been at the hostel for quite a while already while gallivanting about mostly alone around *Rome*, I visited with Rudi again during a breakfast.

Just like me, he always seemed like he was in a good mood, and that made me appreciate getting to know him better. While enjoying our Continental Breakfast together of fruit, cheese, assorted luncheon meats, various vegetables, fruit, toast, and coffee, Rudi sprung an idea on me.

"Hey, Daniel," Rudi exclaimed all excitedly, "how about we rent motor scooters and go touring all over this city on them?"

At first, I was taken aback, but then all my saved dollars thus far started burning a hole in my pocket. "Wow! Really?" I hesitantly responded. "You think we could do that, huh?"

"Of course. I have one back home, and I ride it all over the place," Rudi reacted supportively.

Fortunately, a few years earlier, our dad had bought my older brother and me a small, Italian Vespa motor scooter to play around on. Later, we even got small, Japanese dirt bikes to romp around the forest with; however, I had zero experience driving anything except a car in a big city. I did learn to drive using a Volkswagen Bug romping all over the East Bay Area and San Francisco hills, and I had actually helped drive already to Los Angeles to visit my girlfriend in other cars. So, I was at least a little comfortable making my way around a city. On a motor scooter, however, was an entirely different kind of animal.

I had already easily observed city traffic in *Rome*. Like so many other European cities, the prominent, upscale, downtown, and busy thoroughfares were all wide and nicely paved. Outside those areas was where you would find the city's quaint cobblestone and brick layered streets. However, *Rome*, just as crazy as *Paris*, it seemed, was one enormous traffic accident after another just waiting to happen. Cars were zipping by each other, honking, or not, and cutting each other off dramatically while zig zagging through busy traffic. The line about RED means STOP; GREEN means GO; and YELLOW means GO FASTER seemed like natural Italian rules-of-the-road.

And then came the scores of motor scooters whipping about town in mad dash frenzies. Those drivers truly felt like they owned the roads, and they possessed them as though they did. With their intense leaning and bending in either direction, scooter drivers zipped around other cars like they were standing still. Car drivers were constantly honking at scooter drivers' insensitivities and dangerous mobilities, but it only encouraged them to go faster to get away from any potential arguments.

Anyway, thus explained my momentary hesitancy with Rudi's suggestion. So, it took all about three seconds for me to calculate the value of my life compared to the fun I'd have, and I joyfully replied, "Sure thing! When do you want to go?"

"How about today? How about now?" Rudi began laughing.

"Gee, I don't know, Rudi," I smirked. "How about letting me finish my coffee and toast first?"

Rudy chuckled, and we had an immediate adventure for our day's horizon. Rudi was a college student, and a couple of years older than me too, but we hit it off really well. I comfortably wanted to let him take the lead, and I'd just follow along. "Hopefully, it will be in his wake, not in his wreck!" I gulped.

He had also been in *Rome* long enough, or enough times before, to know where to go and what to do. After breakfast, we walked downtown to a place Rudi knew, and in no time, we were both set up with our own scooters for some adventure. My California Driver's License and testimonial was all I needed. Rudi did all the talking, and his Italian was very passible. Amazing to me again.

He touted to the salesclerk that I was from San Francisco, so therefore, I could drive anything anywhere in the world. Rudi's nonsensical braggadocio worked because the agent was nodding his head, and soon thereafter, he gave me a set of keys. The *thereafter,* however, was *after* I paid the extra fee for insurance, of course. The overall rental was still fairly inexpensive, though, and besides, my money was burning a hole in my pocket.

After I gave my scooter a once over to check out its running condition and highlights, including buttons, and levers, and pedals. I was good to go. We both checked, and our scooter tanks were full. At eighty miles a gallon, or twenty kilometers per liter, we felt like we easily had a full day's riding ahead for us with just one tank. With Rudi in the lead, I was right out the gate behind him and onto the streets with ease. After I got a sense of the brakes, I was beginning to feel fairly comfortable with my Vespa 150 cc. In Italian, Vespa means wasp. I understood the name's meaning. Our scooters were fast and dangerous.

There was no getting around it either. Rudi was far superior in skill, dexterity, knowledge, and familiarity with his scooter and *Rome's* streets and traffic. Finally, at one intersection early on, I had to assert my demands and spoke harshly to him.

"Rudi, you need to slow down for me at least for a while," I began. "I am actually a real country boy who is used to racing around trees and bushes on my bikes back home. But trees and bushes don't move and won't crash into me! If you keep going so fast, you are going to lose me, and we are going to end up spending the day riding our bikes alone. What do you want?"

"Okay, sorry, you're right," he admitted. "I just got excited and started showing off, I guess. I'll slow down and let you keep up with me."

"Within reason, Rudi," I added. "I'm not going to zig when you zag, and I'll follow you, but if you lose me, don't make any unexpected turns. Just slow down until I catch up. Okay?"

"Sure thing," Rudi grinned. "When we get to some open areas, traffic will let up, and we can ride together easier. Just follow me."

After that, we just played hide-and-seek for a while. Rudi would inevitably get way ahead of me until I simply lost sight of him, and then I would just carefully maintain myself keeping an eye out for him. When I did find him waiting, I did not even bother to slow, or stop, or pull over for him. I just zipped on by forcing him to race and catch up to me. It made for good laughs, and we started measuring each other up even better.

One interesting observation I made, while *scootering* around *Rome,* was all the wild cats meandering the streets. In some locations, cats were everywhere. They were racing across streets, lying dead in gutters, climbing in trees, hunting in bushes, up on rooftops, and even sitting on various statues, or wandering around the many historical tourist sites we encountered along our touring. Cats simply ran amuck throughout most of *Rome* and especially in some cat haven neighborhoods.

It reminded me of what Aunt Jean had told me about *Rome.* "Cats are everywhere," she said. "They get killed on the city streets," she added, "and nobody ever even stops to help them. You'll see what I mean if you go there."

I did see, and it was bizarre. Cats were all over the place, and I deliberately slowed down on my Vespa so that I did not have to make any emergency stops or turns trying to avoid them. Little Roman cats ruled the streets. However, the major highways were a little different. Any sights of cats there were usually dead ones.

Naturally, though, on terribly busy thoroughfares it was other traffic I needed to watch out for. Speedy cars and other motor scooters were continuously flying past me like I was some sort of obstacle on their private roadway course. After a bit, I even got into the infectious, Roman-honking habit of other Italian drivers and gave anybody I felt like a "Beeep!" from my horn.

"Hey!" I'd holler, "I'm drivin' here. Be careful!" Plus, I got a big kick out of Italian sign language. They were so expressive with their finger, hand, and arm signals directed toward other drivers who had offended them.

Unlike American's driving lessons of *defensive driving skills*, over there it was, "Everyone look out for yourselves," and "Defensive drivers, get out of the way!" Also, I noted that the *California Hi* (middle finger) sign was universal!

Time flew by as fast as our little scooters, though, and soon it was lunchtime where we stopped for a nice sandwich and soda. The city had been so much fun, and I was becoming so relaxed with my scooter, we considered venturing even further. We talked about some different ideas, and I finally produced the winner.

"I've got it!" I exclaimed. "Let's go swimming in the Mediterranean Sea. It's only about fifty kilometers (thirty miles) from here. I've seen it on a map."

Rudi immediately liked the idea and got all excited about it. "Great idea," he started nodding. "I know the highway going there. Try to keep up, or I'll see you on the beach!"

"Yeah, sure. Once we get on the freeway, let's just see who can drive the fastest," I lied.

Our drive to the sea was spectacular fun. However, no matter how fast we tried to push our twin Vespas, freeway auto traffic forced us to the slow lanes as those other cars flew by us in panic paces. It reminded me of an Italian story I had heard once about driving in Italy:

> *"It was a sad day in Italy one foggy morning when two Italian drivers approached each other from opposite directions on a highway. It was so terribly murky that both drivers had to stick their heads far out their respective car door windows in order to see better. Unfortunately, while passing each other, visibility was so bad that they both became Italy's first truly Head-On Collision fatalities. . ."* So sad.

I shuddered at the thought but was glad we had a beautiful sunny day ahead for ourselves. I easily kept up with Rudi, and within an hour, we were there at a nice public beach. We parked and spent the afternoon splashing around, swimming, and sunning ourselves on nice sandy shores. Neither of us were modest, so we both just wore our underwear for bathing suits. At least mine were boxers, but Rudi's skimpy shorts showed he had no shame. It was okay, though, because I was embarrassed enough for both of us. . .

However, being from Czechoslovakia, Rudi was a real landlubber, and I had no fear of the ocean. I was definitely the better swimmer between us. But we both got to do a little body surfing in Italy's and the wonderful Mediterranean Sea's modest warm waves. The day belonged to us both. . .

Pizza What?

We had actually rented our scooters for the entire day, so we had until early evening to return them. Therefore, time was on our side, so when leaving the beachside, we agreed to find a reasonable restaurant and splurge for eating dinner out and skipping the hostel's meal that evening. It was an hour's drive back, more-or-less, so we had plenty of time to stop for supper somewhere and still return our scooters on time.

When we had reached just outside Rome's city limits, we both signaled each other after spotting a nice Italian restaurant close off the highway. It was a smaller place and looked like a Mom n' Pop establishment. We were met inside by an exceedingly kind, elderly, and welcoming waiter who spoke only Italian. After being seated, I thought of a great idea for our dinner. I asked Rudi if he had ever had pizza before. He admitted that he had not, nor did he even know what it was. I just told him not to worry; he was in for a treat.

We both ordered Coca-Colas, and then I did the ordering. "Si, signore," I began, "Una pizza. Pepperoni, per favore e grazie." I smiled, so proud of myself for using the most useful words anywhere: *please and thank you.*

However, the waiter just stood there smiling but nodding his head in a confused state while repeating the word, *"Pepperoni?"*

I said it again happily, "Si, that's right! A pepperoni and cheese pizza, per favore, e uno grosso, e grazie." *A large one, thanks.*

Still smiling, but now the waiter was decidedly perplexed when he stated, "Un grande cosa? Vuoi un grosso pezzo di peperoni?"

I didn't understand, so I looked to Rudi who was puzzled himself. He stated, "The waiter wants to know what it is you want. Do you want a big piece of peperoni, or something? Is that what a *pizza* is? A large slice of pepperoni?"

"No!" I reacted indignantly. Then I restated for the waiter's close attention, "Signore, una grande peperoni pizza, per favore." My Italian was *niente* (nothing).

The waiter still looked befuddled, and sad, and awkward while raising his palms up and shrugging his shoulders, "Pi, pi, piiiizzaa? Pizza peperoni?"

I yelled out happily, "Yes, si, that's it! Una pizza peperoni e una grande, per favore!" I was relieved at finally communicating. But not for long.

The waiter continued standing there scratching his head. "Signore, non capisco. Che cos'e la pizza?"

Now I was really frustrated. I looked to Rudi, and he was just shaking his head in bewilderment too as he interpreted, "The man says that he doesn't understand. He wants to know what *pizza* is."

"What is a pizza?" I exclaimed loudly, half laughing. "You've got to be kidding. This is Italy, for cryin'-out-loud! It's *Home of the Pizza*."

There were quick words between Rudi and the waiter. Rudi then asked me gently, "Daniel, he wants you to describe it (pizza) to him."

"Describe it?" I laughed. "I don't believe this! Okay, I will." Then I went about my way holding my hands out widely, while Rudi interpreted. "About this big," I continued, "Made of dough, bread dough, or flour, or something. Just big, and round, and flat. And about so thick," I showed him by holding my thumb and forefinger less than half an inch apart. "Then you spread tomato paste all over it and bake it hot until its done. That's it!" I finished in an exhausted crescendo.

Rudi had been talking rapidly throughout my description/explanation, and he was just as exhausted as I was when we both finished. The poor waiter was nodding, nodding, and twisting his head as though he were curiously questioning some aspects. Finally, though, he backed away stating repeatedly, "Okay, signore, e grazie, e grazie." Then he vanished into the kitchen area.

I was tired but a little shell shocked with bewilderment. I couldn't believe that an Italian did not know what a pizza was. Come to think of it, though, I had never even seen any pizza joints anywhere in all of Europe, so far. But this was Italy. Surely, they must have pizza.

Rudi and I amused ourselves chatting about the day's events, and I tried to build up his delightful surprise for his *first* pizza. In about twenty minutes, or so, our waiter returned holding a large round pan above his head. Once at our table, he pushed items aside to make room, and then he set his prized pizza creation down before us. All I could do was stare blankly. . .

It was a huge, round, one-inch thick, doughy, bread-like item with tomato sauce spread thickly all over its surface. To add insult, but it was my fault, there was no pepperoni and no cheese atop it anywhere. I had forgotten to remind our waiter again, so pepperoni and mozzarella had been excluded, or simply not even considered. The poor waiter/chef truly did not have any idea what he was doing or making. I realized right there and then that at least some Italians did not know anything about pizzas. It was obviously popular in the States, of course, and somewhere else in Italy, but it sure wasn't known there outside of *Rome*, or likely even inside.

I just started laughing and thanking the waiter anyway, "Excellente. Molto bene!" I held my hand up shoulder high forming an *"A-Okay"* sign with my thumb and finger touching, and shook it, "Molto bene! Grazie mille!" *Very good! Thank you very much!*

I was not about to embarrass the waiter over our pizza debacle. I understood that he had no idea how to make a pizza other than by my feeble directions. Yet, the kind man went far out of his way in order to please and serve us what we desired. He deserved credit and appreciation. Chuckling some more, however, I told Rudi that our *pizza* was far from reality. However, I advised him to check out American pizzas when he got home. He could become a famous, rich, pizza chef someday. "Just don't forget the *pepperoni. . . and cheese*," I laughed.

We both tried some, and because we were hungry, we gulped down portions of the bready substance. It really was difficult to stomach, though, but we did eat some. After a few bites, though, I suggested we thank the chef again and head back home. Our pizza disaster was my fault, so I paid for our meal too. Once outside, almost running to our parked scooters, I laughingly suggested to Rudi, "If we hurry, we might get back in time for dinner at the *Happy Hostel*." We raced back...

PART THREE

Travels with "Caesar"

CHAPTER 15

....

"CAT"ASTROPHIES

Saving "Caesar"

My wonderfully fun, interesting, and happy times at *Rome's Beautiful Youth,* or *"Happy" Hostel,* had end. I had learned so much about Roman and *Rome's* history. I had seen some of the greatest art in the world and visited spectacular architectural wonders. Many acquaintances from *Happy Hostel* became friends, especially Rudi, and we all exchanged names and addresses and gave duly meant promises to remain in contact with one another. Nice...

I kept an address book inside my sea bag for references once I got back home. It was held separate and bundled together along with all my many small souvenirs: Tiny animals, finger-sized dolls, replicas of architectural wonders, picture postcards, used film rolls, and small denominations of coins and currency from each country visited. They were all secured and bound together inside my sea bag. All safe and sound. . .

I had seven nights and eight days to go before my home flight from *Paris.* My plan was heading north to *Vienna* and visit with my high school's foreign-exchange student and friend, Ingrid. From there I would work my way back to *Paris* and arrive just in time for my flight home. A week was plenty, I thought, to get back in time for my TWA plane. I had overspent a bit while in *Rome,* considering all the special-exhibit entrance fees and side excursions, and I had stayed there at the *Happy Hostel* longer than anywhere else by far, except for *Horny Hostel* in *Costa Brava*, Spain. Yet, I was in adequate financial shape to still make the final return route to *Paris* without much issue. No concerns. . .

Then, an interesting event occurred the very next morning just as I was preparing to leave *Happy Hostel* and head north toward *Venice*, Italy. It was an incident that would change the entire remaining complexion of my journey. No longer would I mostly always be thinking of myself. I would have a new little friend which would dramatically reshape my thinking, planning, touring, and traveling endeavors. Fact is, I was accidentally introduced to a new travel companion.

Remember my mentioning about wild cats roaming the streets of *Rome*? Their sneaky, frivolous characters could be seen everywhere roving through neighborhoods. Occasionally, their unfortunate carcasses could also be found scattered about side streets and boulevards too, victims of vehicle accidents. Even in our community around *Happy Hostel* would those sly, devious, or nonchalant feral felines be found snooping, hunting, snoozing, or just relaxing in the sun or shade, completely oblivious of, and undisturbed by, humanity. Also, occasionally, their *littering*, dead-feline corpses would have to be removed from streets or sidewalks where their lives had expired...

My introductory *event* happened while I was cleaning up last minute rubbish and taking a bag of garbage from my *Happy Hostel* guest room outside to the alleyway garbage cans for disposal. As I dumped my rubbish into a large trash container sitting beside the hostel's exterior walls, I saw in the near distance an unusual, but obvious, loosely folded blanket laying up against the building's wall and filled with little objects. Approaching closer, I discovered a crudely strewn together blanket with a litter of infant kittens. They were all squirming around each other seeking warmth from their mother. Plus, they were so tiny they could barely even move around much within their blanket bedding placements. Truly, they were only a week old, or two at most, but enough to be wriggling around like dickens for their absent mother's shelter and food.

I was immediately concerned for their welfare. Notoriously known for dead Roman cats lying about everywhere amongst vast numbers of living feral felines, I imagined that the litter's mother may also be among those lost and gone. Right away, I brought my discovery to the attention of *Happy Hostel's* management, and the agent-on-duty informed me that those *litter* types were a commonality around *Rome,* and even a real nuisance. Little could, or would, be done about it until any remaining carcasses just needed disposal.

Typically, I was told, entire *litters* were dumped into trash cans along with any other waste until garbage, pick-up trucks arrived on certain days. I momentarily considered that the term *litter* cans for *trash* containers was invented precisely for that situation. It also seemed apparent too that the mother cat had vanished by accident, or choice, and that the newly discovered litter of kittens was eventually destined for a rubbish, *litter* dump somewhere.

I loved cats and had even cared for my very own pet in prior years. That previous kitty, a gray and white mix, named Tiger, had been brutally killed by a disturbed neighborhood youth, and the experience was dreadful. Therefore, I felt extremely sorry and worried about potential outcomes for all those little critters I had just discovered. So, right off, I tried exploring available options.

Happy Hostel management personnel were unwilling to take responsibility for any of the little, endangered-infantile kittens. Management experiences with cats in the past had not been positive, so they were forbidden to take on care for any cats in general. No other available staff were willing to assume care for those baby kittens either. Furthermore, no guests were in positions to accept any babies. "The responsibilities (are) far beyond (our) abilities, or desires," they all basically emphasized.

A couple of hours later, following my disappointing adoption efforts for the helpless litter, and with no further signs of a returning mother, I perhaps committed a mental error. Or maybe it was simply an omen. Caring about those little babies, I reached into the mad, craving group of abandoned infant kittens and touched them all attempting to reassure and comfort the group. Almost immediately, the entire brood began whining loudly and crying emphatically. It took my touch to set them all off in a frenzy of anxious bawling.

Instantly, too, one kitten in particular among the entire litter sprang into action. It alone clambered upon my finger and began pulling itself desperately up onto my hand. Its eyes were still closed shut, and it was barely coordinated, but it refused to let go, and using its strong baby claws it clung frantically onto my hand for dear life. It then proceeded to pull itself, millimeter by millimeter, climbing even further up my hand and forearm. It begged for attention, food, or life ostensibly craving its salvation.

The remaining members of the infant kitten litter continued crying and fumbling among themselves and still squirming to get more comfortable berths on their blanket bed or seeking food. But the little critter on my arm had managed a hasty getaway. That connection, or momentary bonding, led to my next mental link, or lapse, or mishap. I recalled my aunt's story about ". . .all the wild cats roaming the streets of *Rome*." I suddenly considered a decisive idea that resolved two distinct issues: *First*, a genuinely *purrfect* (pun intended) thank you gift for my aunt; and second, a sparing of life for at least one of those motherless, defenseless, and doomed kittens.

I resolved to take one of them, the one *hanging-on-for-its-dear-life* by hooking its baby claws frantically into my arm. I would attempt saving its life. Then I would bring it home to my aunt as an appreciative gesture for her support of my summer's journey. Jean loved animals, all sorts of creatures, particularly dogs, but I figured a kitten from *Rome* would be a spectacular tribute to her.

Second issue, of course, I did not think much beyond my primary concern right then of merely trying to save the kitten's life. Other conflicting details regarding a *kitten gift* had conveniently escaped my thoughts. However, those rapscallion details were not to be avoided for too long, of course. In fact, often those *details* would return to haunt me with stress. But for right then, my mind was made up. It was going with me for the remainder of my journey. . .

The little fellow had almost pure white fur, little rounded and bent ears, and with little black and gray markings on all four of its feet. Its blue eyes were fully open, but it still didn't have any teeth, which led me to believe that the litter was barely two weeks old. I wondered how long the blanket and kitten litter had lain there in that deserted alleyway without notice unless both had been dumped very recently. And where was momma cat?

My next immediate consideration for the little rascal anxiously clinging onto my arm would complete our "bonding effect." I started thinking about giving it a name. "Bright Eyes" or "Old Blue" were initial ideas. Its feet markings made "Boots" an obvious and natural choice also. However, those names seemed so commonplace and mundane, upon further thought, that they sounded boring. Then, suddenly it struck me! A unique name came to me with decisive clearness. We were in *Rome*, the city of great, noble, and triumphant past rulers. My brand new, tiny, traveling-companion kitten's name would become "Caesar" to commemorate its royal patronage, if only in spirit.

So, there we were. Little "Caesar" had by then already caused me to become a couple of hours late in my departure. So typical of royalty, I assumed. However, I actually was behind in my makeshift schedule with a long-planned hitching leg ahead of me, er us, as it were. Thus, I needed to make haste and figure out, first-and-foremost, how to keep "Caesar" alive. Thoughts of those other kittens on their litter blanket would just have to weigh heavily on the minds and hearts of *Happy Hostel's* other occupants. I had committed to Caesar and was doing far more than my share already.

Desperate Times

With a soft bed made of tissue paper in the side pocket of my light windbreaker jacket, little *Caesar* sat there stiffly crying up a storm. My worry that he was likely starving was my first reaction. As I said goodbye to my *Happy Hostel* hosts and remaining friends, I snagged a small container of cold milk and a piece of soft meat from the kitchen to offer *Caesar* for its nourishment. Then I, er, we trudged off to catch a bus to *Rome's* main highway heading north toward *Venice*, my next destination, er, our destination. *Caesar* continued its whining, and while on the bus, I attempted feeding him first the meat and then from the milk carton.

No luck at all. *Caesar* refused both offerings. I then realized that *Caesar* needed to nurse and just couldn't eat yet, or drink right from a container. I got an idea and quickly spotted a pharmacy on our way. They might know what to do, I thought. Jumping up, I begged the bus driver to stop, "Per favore, signore, stop now and a transfer, per favore."

Fortunately, the driver understood me clearly, pulled over right away, and handed me a pass to continue my, er, our travels. We ran back to the pharmacy, and I explained my needs hurriedly to the storekeeper. He knew just what to do. He sold me an eyedropper, something *purrfect* for feeding an infant kitten, we thought. Then I walked back to a bus stop, and we soon caught our next ride going all the way to the highway drop-off point.

However, there continued being no luck with *Caesar.* He still would not touch milk even from the eyedropper, and I was becoming very anxious. *Caesar* was not cooperating, and instead, he just continued howling for nutrition, I assumed. I was in a quandary with no clues as to appropriate steps necessary for that helpless little creature. I began feeling helpless too. Enough so that I nearly wanted to join *Caesar* in anguished cries of my own. What kind of rescuer was I to remove baby *Caesar* from his litter and then just let him starve to death right there in my own jacket pocket? How cruel was I? Didn't he rightfully deserve to die back there with his siblings?

From our spot on the highway, however, I noticed a pedestrian overpass which led to a nice restaurant. By that time, I figured I could at least get a cup of coffee and try to figure things out for little *Caesar*. Then was also when my very first thoughts of abandoning the little feline fellow began creeping into my contemplations. The restaurant owner, or a worker, or patrons of the place might wish to save the baby kitten and keep *Caesar* for their own. It was an idea I might pursue if necessary. *Caesar* was already a bit of a nuisance, even if only a tiny burden. But I couldn't help but consider: "What can I do? How can I help *Caesar* survive?"

After entering the restaurant, being seated, and ordering coffee and a roll, I brought screaming *Caesar* out of my pocket and set him on the table along with the eyedropper, meat, and milk container. *Caesar* immediately garnished serious attention from his squealing, and many pairs of eyes were watching me, us both. The waitress, a kindly older woman rushed over to check out the ruckus. I pointed to everything, and I'm sure my face expressed all my exasperation.

In desperation, I broke into my limited French, "S'il vous plait, ce n'est pas bon. Il ne mangera pas. Je suis desole'." *Please, it's no good. He won't eat. I am sorry.*

The kind, motherly waitress stared at the wailing kitten for a moment, next at the meat, milk, and eyedropper, and finally at me. Immediately, she shrugged her shoulders, snorted in distaste, and shook her head. What happened next was amazing, wonderful, and exciting to watch.

First, the waitress spoke in fairly decent English, knowing full well that my accented French was weak, at best. "Young man, the kitten is starving, but you must give it warm milk, like from its mother. Yes?" She then hurried to the kitchen.

In barely a minute, she returned with a small container of warmed milk. I used the eyedropper again, and *Caesar* almost swallowed the entire contraption whole, gulping down the warmed milky liquid into its toothless mouth, so desperate was he for a decent meal. I looked up at the waitress in astonishment and gratitude and kept repeating, "Grazie. Grazie. Grazie"

She then gave me explicit instructions, "You must feed this baby cat at least every two hours, or it will cry again. Capisci?" *Do you understand?*

Yes, of course I did, and I continued thanking her, but the kind, motherly waitress just shrugged off my appreciations. When I prepared to leave and pay my bill, the amazing lady just shushed me off saying, "For you, it is free. Be careful."

We both left the restaurant happy, and *Caesar* was delightfully full. Later, it was crude, but I used my cigarette matches to warm some milk directly in the eyedropper. Then I let the eyedropper cool off using my water bottle, and the process worked like magic. *Caesar* was as happy as a clam in deep water, and I laughed myself silly with delight.

Later, I found an empty can and heated up small portions of milk in it, and that worked even better. I made a mental note to get a fluid lighter when possible, so I wouldn't keep burning my fingers from the matches. We were a team, and little *Caesar* mostly just slept once his belly was full. I was anxiety freed, and once again I became focused on getting us a decent ride to *Venice*.

Our next ride was a kind couple in a beautiful Mercedes Benz. They were going quite a way further, but not all the way to *Venice*. Any ride was a good one by then. Their automobile was the finest car in which I had ever ridden. It was almost silent as it cruised up the highway at breathtaking speeds. They were a genuinely nice German couple, too, but neither spoke any English, nor I any German.

After a bit, *Caesar* became very restless, so I let him out of my pocket to squirm around on the car's beautiful leather rear seat. As soon as I did so, he began crying and whining. Both the driver and his wife were surprised, but the wife was especially astonished and delighted at what I possessed. I didn't understand their discussion, but I figured it was complementary. Here was a young man with an infant kitten attempting to rescue it, somehow.

All I could say to them was simple French, "C'est la vie ou la mort." *It is life or death.*

The couple understood and nodded in appreciation. After a while, I became a little sleepy, so I laid my head back and soon fell fast asleep. Sometime later, I felt the car coming to a stop, and I looked around sleepily to get my bearings. We were at a highway pullover just before a major turn that the couple obviously wanted. It was their turnoff point heading to wherever they were going; back home, I supposed.

I opened the rear car door, put *Caesar* back in my jacket pocket to sleep again in its bed, and I grabbed my bag gently lifting it out of the car. That was when I spotted the "accident." *Caesar* had pooped all over their shiny, leather rear seat. It was disgusting and enormous. How could so much crap come out of such a tiny creature?

Fortunately, the couple did not notice anything. Both their eyes were on us departing and with me quickly stepping forward to say goodbye through the wife's window. They wished me, us, good luck and waved as the husband floored the gas pedal, and they zoomed away. I was so embarrassed that I waited a bit for their car to come to a screeching halt, suddenly rip an angry U-turn, and return to scold us both furiously. There was no sign, but a few minutes later, I could have sworn that I heard anguished German screams from a man far ahead. I begged for another quick lift to save both *Caesar's* and my hides.

About then, I began having serious doubts again over my ridiculous plan to save that miserable kitten's life just in order to bring it all the way back to California. The entire plan began unraveling in my mind seeming completely foolhardy and impossible with which to succeed. All the *how, what, where, when, why,* and *who* questions pounded my brain for legitimate answers. I had few.

The whole scheme had begun on a whim, a skimpy, nearly false premise that I was somehow responsible enough to supposedly manage, control, handle, and deal with this obvious "*cat*"astrophe all alone. Heck, I was having a difficult enough time just trying to manage life for myself. And now with a cat? No, a kitten. . ? No, an infant, crying, screaming, and shitting little creature that would become the death of us both yet.

Cars were passing me by, and before I realized what I was doing, I found myself holding *Caesar* up high in the air with me would be right, hitching hand to approaching vehicles. I pointed directly at Caesar with my left forefinger and started shouting at all passing traffic. "Here! Right here! A kitten for you. He's free! Please, help me. I can't do this anymore. Help!"

I figured that under the circumstances, hollering English was just French, or whatever. Everyone except the French or Germans spoke it, it seemed. Although, I believed that even they could understand English too, if not also speak it, but they all just lied about it. Anyway, any passing vehicles' passengers could hardly hear or understand my own wailings. They only saw my frantic hand pointing at something mysterious in my other outstretched palm. If anything, people became alarmed at my activity thinking I was peddling drugs, or selling crap, or something. Cars mostly just sped up to get further away from me, er us, and quickly.

After a while, *Caesar* was hungry again and started squirming and wailing on his own, so I warmed up another meal for him, and he wolfed it down. Then, oh my goodness, *Caesar* started licking my fingers gratefully as if to thank me for all my attention, care, love, and loyalty. Gee did that little critter surely make me feel ashamed. *Caesar* was oblivious to my momentarily ill nature and intent, and he was, instead, only grateful, and appreciative that I was his caretaker. Indeed, I was his nurturer, his provider, his protector, and his master. Or, by then it was the other way around. I was no longer sure. . . No matter, I got a little choked up, though, and suddenly I wanted to confess my ill will and begging for *Caesar's* forgiveness.

I began professing my transgressions intimately, "*Caesar*, I'm ashamed and sorry that I tried to give you away. I accepted this mission and challenge to rescue you for my aunt. So, from-now-on, unless something tragic happens, I shall do my best to see it through." It seemed that right there and then, I decided that I owed *Caesar* his life's opportunity; I owed Jean my promised gift; and I owed and deserved any future trials and tribulations only to myself.

Following that temporary and unfortunate back-stepping, I was once again back on the right track again with little *Caesar*. From *there* on, who knew what might happen? One thing was sure, though. Whatever it was, we would go through it together. We were a team from *then* on....

Venice with "Caesar"

My thumb was out again, and before long, we had a good ride all the rest of the way into *Venice*. *Caesar* slept quietly in my pocket the entire ride. Just as we approached a good drop-off point, he awakened, and it was time for another feeding. I decided to use *Caesar* for some good, so I exposed him again inside a nearby restaurant. Naturally, I, or he, received immediate attention, and I made my feeble request for some warm milk. The waitress was more than happy to oblige. Onlookers were surprised and delighted while *Caesar* made a complete pig of himself again. I had a light dinner too and picked up a sandwich for later. Then we were off for *Venetian* sights.

I asked a dock worker for directions and explanations, and I understood from his broken English that off in the distance was a pick-up point for tourists who wished to go to certain destinations. Or they could choose a waterway tour of the beautiful *City of Venice on the Sea*, usually lasting several hours each. It was already late in the afternoon, and I wasn't sure about going anywhere in a boat after dark. So, I decided that we'd better hunker down for the night somewhere, and then we could make a whole day of it the next morning.

I had only heard a little about *Venice,* and seen a few pictures, but I was anxious to see for myself how an entire city could actually be floating on the ocean. Well, the land sites for all its various structures were supposed to be supported by large pontoons. Naturally, those air-filled floats were regularly maintained to provide strength and endurance. Even still, it was an incredibly unique concept, and I wanted to choose a complete tour for *Caesar* and myself to get a good viewing and understanding of that floating city.

On our walk over to the docks, I crossed through a meadow and small grove of trees. It was far away from usual visual contact of anyone and seemed like a decent spot to make a camp for the night. Once I located a nice resting spot, I made my bed and let *Caesar* flop around on the sea bag cover. He still couldn't move very much on his own and after giving him a little bed of his own, he mostly slept. I just enjoyed the rest of the evening and contemplated our futures.

The next morning, after *Caesar* and I both ate, I made plans for our day. Reloading my, our belongings, I hoisted my sea bag, stuffed *Caesar* back into my pocket, and walked to the boat dock. Once there, we got in line for the tour boat, and right away, *Caesar* started earning his keep. He wasn't hungry, but I held him, to protect him from someone accidentally slamming into my side. But, as soon as I held him, he began mewing, or crying loudly. I wasn't sure which, but his noise started attracting much attention. Before long, we had quite a crowd of curious observers, many of whom wished to touch or pet *Caesar.* I would not hand him over to anyone, but I held my palms open allowing anyone to reach in and touch him.

To everyone's delight, *Caesar's* howling continued and gained even more interest. It went well enough, though, and when it was my turn to pay our fare to board the tour boat, the booking agent just smiled and waved us both aboard *au gratis.* The entertainment was worth our ticket, I guessed. I grinned like crazy for the free passage, though, and thanked the agent graciously. *Caesar* was really helping to pay our way.

Our tour boat turned out to be a round trip to *St. Mark's Square*, the most celebrated attraction in the city, to many. We were told that we could stay as long as we wished and return from the same drop-off point back to our starting dock. After a nice cruise all around the open waterways of *Venice* with closer looks at some other *Venetian* highlights, like the *Grand Canal, Rialto Bridge*, and an island with beautiful, Gothic-palace buildings on it, we docked at *St. Mark's Square*.

We had all the rest of the day to wander about checking all the curiosities of the floating *Square*. There were so many inner walkways and tall, arching footbridges crossing multitudes of canals to other floating landfills. The mini-islands were jam packed with homes, businesses, churches, and hundreds, maybe even thousands, of residents, plus tourists everywhere. An extremely popular place.

Many of the small museums were free to tourists, so I took advantage of those. Some were historical, some artistic, and others were of modern textile manufacturing. It was grand, and all the time, *Caesar* mostly just slept in my pocket. He would let me know, though, when he became hungry again. Also, I had to change out his bedding often because he had no manners and pooped and peed in my pocket whenever he chose.

In the meantime, I became awestruck with wonderful visits to *St. Mark's Basilica* and the glass encased *Tomb of St. Mark*. In there, St. Mark lay encased in a large glass viewing casket, of sorts. He was one of Jesus's Disciples and author of the "Gospel of Mark," in the <u>New Testament</u> of the <u>Bible</u>. It was as meaningful as St. Peter's entombment beneath *St. Peter's Basilica* in *Vatican City*, Rome.

St. Mark's Square was really large and enclosed by specialty shops, museums, souvenir shops, restaurants, *St. Mark's Basilica*, and other religious buildings. It was fun just wandering around, snooping, studying, and stopping for a coffee, with cream to have warmed up for *Caesar* for his two-hour meal ticket. Every time I brought him out of my pocket, it was a signal for him to start screaming, and his racket would draw onlookers, and especially any children nearby. Their little ears were directly tuned in to a kitten's mewing.

That was the *first* time and place that I misled the crowds of spectators. Either that, or I simply allowed them to mislead themselves. Anyway, the children all felt sorry for *Caesar* and wanted to feed him to quiet his crying. Naturally, they believed he was crying for food, but in reality, *Caesar* usually just cried whenever I held him until he was fed, or not. But the kids brought half eaten sandwiches and leftover cookies, and luncheon meats for his appetite, and I graciously just accepted it all.

"Grazie," I'd say. "He is not too hungry just now, but I'll save it for later." After the crowds dispersed, I ate *Caesar's* free lunches. Shame on me. *Caesar* didn't mind, though, because he didn't even have any teeth yet; however, the kindly food donations were gratefully accepted anyway.

More walking and touring continued while checking out all the pontoons from a distance that held up portions of *St. Mark's Square* and all its structures, including *St. Mark's Basilica* and *St. Mark's Campanile*. *St. Mark's Campanile* is part of the Basilica and is, in fact, its bell tower. It is very recognizable from a far distance and is the tallest structure in all of *Venice*. I was reminded of our own bell tower, the *Campanile*, on the grounds of U.C. Berkeley in Berkeley, California. During summer stays with Aunt Jean, I had visited it many times, riding its elevator to the very top for splendid views of the entire Bay Area. Both towers, or campaniles, were quite similar and both special.

Late that afternoon, it was time to return to our home dock and make another plan for that night's stay. I had already predetermined that our nesting spot from the night before would work out nicely again for our coming sleeping arrangements. It was safe and secure, near the previously visited restaurant for our meals, and we could get cleaned-up there a little too. Plus, it was close to the highway for the next leg of our journey to *Vienna*, Austria.

So far, so good. It had been the *first* fully relaxing day with *Caesar* and even kind of fun overall. He remained in my pocket most of the day while we traversed the city, but *Caesar* mostly slept anyway. When he awakened, which usually came right after I picked him up, he was always hungry, so I let him sleep a lot, if possible. But when awake, *Caesar* was full of life. His eyes were big, bright, and blue, his ears were becoming sharply pointed, and he seemed full of awareness, although he still did not move around too much.

But *Caesar* had been a real trooper that day while entertaining all the gawking children and many adults too. We both had eaten plenty, *Caesar* with his warmed milk, and me from his leftover food gifts from all the children. *Caesar's* second-hand food had been delicious, and what a variety: Sandwiches, cookies, even pretzels, and whole cartons of milk. There had also been lots more walking again all over *Venice* too, but no matter. We both had enjoyed our day's excursion immensely and would both sleep the night away like contented kittens on full bellies...

Operatic Trucker

Both *Caesar* and I awakened early, cleaned-up at the restaurant, and both got warm meals. Mine was a corn porridge of some sort with rolls, fruit, and coffee. *Caesar* got his regular eye droppers of warmed milk, but I was sensing that he might be ready for some soft kitten food before long. Little teeth were slightly emerging suggesting that soon I could introduce soft substances to his diet like kitten chow, or something. He'd let me know.

Heading back up to our highway hitching spot, I decided to try a new technique with *Caesar* too. He was still feeble and uncoordinated, but I decided to try him out sitting on my shoulder. I thought the idea might work well, especially when I was standing mostly still while hitchhiking, because *Caesar* did not crawl around much and clung tightly to my clothing for his support. Once we were adjusted by the highway, and my thumb readied for extension, out came *Caesar*, and I placed him securely on my right shoulder. It worked simply fine, and like I thought, his little claws bared deeply into my light jacket. I don't know what he could see with those cute, little blue eyes, but he was taking in our surroundings.

I think he may have brought us luck too. Shortly thereafter, a large, medium-sized freight truck pulled over for us. It was unusual because the driver was on the right side, just like the English drive. It was fun too because the driver simply rolled down his own window and hollered for us to go around and climb on up. Of course, he yelled at us in Italian, but his arm-waving sign language was easily understood.

I quickly hoisted my sea bag and quickly ran around to the highway side of the truck to climb in. A big step up, and I opened the truck door to toss my bag inside. The driver shoved it to the rear section of his cab, and I swiftly climbed in and seated myself. The driver took one look at me, and his eyes bulged out. Immediately, I remembered that *Caesar* was still sitting on my shoulder, and I almost panicked from the driver's stare. I pulled him down and comforted the kitten having forgotten completely that he was still sitting upon my shoulder and not again back in my pocket. *Caesar* cried a little at the inconvenience, I guessed, but he was fine. Our shoulder setting idea had worked well enough.

The driver was speaking rapid Italian at breakneck speeds, but I caught occasional hints that he was mentioning *Caesar* and me in the same breaths. He was smiling, though, and even chuckling too, so I assumed we were accepted. Once we were off and running, I pretended to understand a little of what the driver was saying, but I didn't really. He seemed like an incredibly happy fellow, however, and time and kilometers passed easily.

Then came our Italian driver's homage to the classical arts. He obviously loved his Italian opera, and he sang along with his truck's feeble radio to any songs he knew. Before long, however, that driver abruptly turned off his radio and broke into his own rendition of some Italian opera. I had listened to a good deal of classical music at my aunt's home, including Italian operas I had assumed, but I knew little about much of it, and absolutely no lyrics.

Well, maybe with the exception of one favorite ballad: "O sole mio. . . Who's got B.O? And I don't know, just what to do...o, and I might die...o because it stinks sooo!" Actually, I could have offered that perverted quip, and our driver may not have known the English difference, but I took no chances.

Anyway, our Italian driver gave a resounding performance of his musical choice, and I listened intently and appreciatively. When he completed his selection with a high vibrato ending and raised a hand dramatically for emphasis, I started clapping and yelling, "Bravo! Bravo! Magnifico!"

He was amused at my delight and thanked me. However, that was also when he turned the tables on me. With his left hand extended toward me, our Italian operatic driver demanded that I take a turn and sing too. "You. You," he repeated. " You turn. You now."

What was I to do? I had not sung anything in years, not since eighth grade while in the school's choir. Even then, the music teacher only allowed me to remain because I was tall and rounded out the back row. On-the-other-hand, naturally, I was often quite brilliant in the shower, of course. Nevertheless, however, I tried to shy the persistent driver away, "Me?" I pleaded, "Oh, no, I can't sing. I don't know any songs."

But Maestro Truck Driver would have nothing of it. He just continued insisting, "No! You sing!"

Alright, I was on the spot, so I started thinking of what to do. In only a moment, though, I thought of one of my very favorite songs by John Gary, a popular singer of that time. My song selection was "Faraway Places," from Gary's Encore album, and his version, a special preference of my parents' and mine, seemed appropriate.

So, I just took in a deep breath, relaxed, warned *Caesar* to close his ears, and I cut loose with my own perilous rendition:

Faraway Places

Far-away places with strange sounding names
　　Far-away over the sea
Those far-away places with the strange sounding names are
　　Callin, calling me

I'm goin' to China, or maybe Siam
　　I wanna see for myself
Those far-away places I've been reading about
　　In a book that I took from a shelf

I start gettin' restless whenever I hear
　　The whistle of a train
I pray for the day I can get underway
　　And look for those castles in Spain

They call me a dreamer
　　Well, maybe I am
But I know that I'm burnin' to see
　　Those far-away places with their strange sounding names
Calling, calling meeeeeee
　　Calling, calling me

Joan Whitney & Alex Kramer (1948)

"Bravo! Bravo!" yelled my maestro, Italiano, operatic driver. He seemed entirely pleased and delighted with my high-pitched screeching. Perhaps, though, he was only glad that I finished. Anyway, my awkwardness was over, and I felt okay about my embarrassed moment after all. Never again, of course! And *Caesar* didn't mind either. He slept on my lap throughout my entire rendition, and I figured it was probably because he was so young that his hearing had not purrfected (yuk yuk) itself yet. Lucky for him.

Our pleasant ride mellowed out for the remainder of our lift. Our kind, happy driver was also going all the way to *Vienna*. We had really lucked out with that truck ride. Occasionally, I reset *Caesar* upon my shoulder for periods of time so that he could get used to the feeling sitting up high. Also, we were already up high in that truck for a good lookout of passing countryside.

The drive provided us very pleasant views past meadows, forested lands, and pastures. The towns we passed through were picturesque, clean, and very quaint and comfortable looking. We stopped at one small community store to use its restrooms and grab snacks for ourselves. It was a good time to feed *Caesar* again too, so that naturally drew attention and appreciations. Plus, I always got the remainder of *Caesar's* milk, and he was starting to drink it a little bit colder too. We even took a moment to sit at a small table set up outside our market just like the ones at many of the small cafes and restaurants arranged for coffee or tea guests. The relaxing people all looked very content, cheerful, and even greeted our driver as a recognized regular visitor.

One half of our ride that morning and into late afternoon was through the remainder of Italy. We stopped briefly at the Austrian border, and our driver exchanged words and some paperwork with the border guards. There was no issue with me, though, and we were off and running in short order. The other half of our drive was within Austria, and initially it seemed to be very much a continuation of the same Italian landscape. Then I began noticing much more forested country. It was exceptionally beautiful.

A couple of hours later *Vienna* came into view. It looked magnificent in the distance, and I began getting excited. This would be the fourth time that I was to be at a certain place at a generally promised time. However, I had given no precise assurances to my classmate, Ingrid, of just when I would show up at her house, except during summertime some time. Not much to go on. But I had an address, and that was all I needed to try and find her, hopefully. If not, oh, well, it was back to *Paris*, anyway.

Our kind truck driver pulled over inside the city limits, and he wished me a happy journey. I shook his hand, thanked him for the terrific ride, and wished him well too. With *Caesar* back on my shoulder, I lifted my bag up and jumped down from the truck. It had been a fine ending to a really decent ride.

Caesar and I were ready for another hike through this town after I found out where to go. But we were both up to it, though. Another light meal for us both, and with *Caesar* hooking his claws deeply into my jacket, T-shirt, and shoulder skin, we headed off up a boulevard seeking appropriate directions. We had completed our next leg and were finally in *Vienna*, Austria, beautiful city home of my school friend, Ingrid...

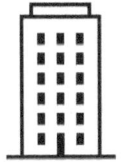

CHAPTER 16

VIENNA CONNECTION

Bad Timing

J ust like back home, while passing a gas station, I figured the attendant inside might have a city map and offer decent directions. The young man understood my needs and did pull out a city map of *Vienna* to give us help. With his aid, I determined a beginning for our hike. It looked like we were going to be crossing another famous river, the Danube, before long, with quite a walk after that. Fortunately, we still had quite a bit of daylight ahead of us. That would work to our advantage.

Did I forget to mention the Tiber River in *Rome*? I should have because my motor scootering friend, Rudi, and I must have crossed that river a dozen times while racing around *Rome*. Rivers and waterways were always very noticeable too throughout my travels in Europe. It seemed like every major city was split and separated by some magnificent river, or a city was directly next to one, or on a waterfront. My two previously visited major waterways had been in *Rome* and then *Venice*, which floats directly upon a port area of the Adriatic Sea off the Mediterranean Sea. Then came *Vienna*, cut in half by the huge, poetically, and musically famous, and beautiful Danube River.

Geographically and historically, it seemed so obvious that success of large cities often depends upon location near waterways, or even on them. Rivers and open sea accesses are vital sources and conduits for hydration, irrigation, manufacturing, fishing industry, recreation, and transportation. Even back home, so many major cities grew alongside important rivers, including my own high school hometown of Marysville, California which was right next to two intersecting rivers, itself.

One, the Yuba River, was famous for its gold panning history during the California Gold Rush of 1849, and still produces gold today. Thus "49ers" those early gold prospectors were called. Marysville, and its co-river neighbor, Yuba City, are separated by the Feather River, also another gold mining river, and one which also flows into the big, traversable Sacramento River, itself flowing clear down into the Suisun Bay and San Francisco Bay. Rivers are obviously particularly important.

Then right there cutting through the middle of big, beautiful *Vienna*, was its great and magnificent Danube River. Once we reached its edges, I could see many bridge crossings up and down the river offering a variety of means to cross over. Eventually, we came upon a wide traffic bridge with a nice walkover for pedestrians. At some points on the Danube, I could even see smaller canals breaking away from the river's main flow and used for special services. Or maybe those offshoot canals were access to expensive home developments. There were nice private boats going in and out of those canals too.

By early evening, we had walked through one major *Viennese* downtown area and had continued until coming to yet another bridge and then crossed the Danube River. Eventually, we came upon one more important business area on the north side and just had to keep on walking past it too toward our destination. Time had gone by, and it was mealtime for us both again, so I found a nice café and ordered up some soup, Coca-Cola, bread, and more warm milk for *Caesar*.

Once again, a waitress was delighted with my little friend and expressed her appreciation with extra servings of soup and bread for me. Thank you very much, *Caesar*. Plus, the milk also became free, although I drank most of it. Deeply sorry, *Caesar*. I actually considered requesting a (free) chicken dinner for *Caesar* too, but I backed away from my own giddy, but selfishly conniving and depraved, cravings.

Of course, as was the case throughout much of my travels since Denmark when I began smoking, cigarettes helped pass time, thwart my hunger pangs, and relieve occasionally frustrated nerves. While atop my shoulder, however, Caesar disapproved of all the smoke ending up in his face. I was being insensitive and inconsiderate. I had to try and remember to smoke when I could exhale away from him. Restaurants did not mind smoke-filled air, but *Caesar* drank his milk and then was content returning to his smokeless, pocket pouch haven.

I asked the waitress if she recognized the address I sought, and naturally, her English was excellent. I couldn't get over these people. I supposed that so many little countries scattered all around Europe, and all speaking different languages, just made it useful to be able to communicate. But even for English? I was always extremely impressed.

Of course, Ingrid spoke English like an American, almost. I had always liked her slight German accent. Kind of gravelly and sexy it was, as I remembered. I had been told that English and German had many similarities too, although I learned little while traveling there. I was just a spoiled American, I supposed, just like what that nasty East German soldier had called me. However, if it worked, then good for me. Danke. Danke.

There was no doubt about it, however, it was getting twilight, and we still had a way to go according to the nice waitress. She actually scribbled a crude map and highlighted the main streets I would need to find in order to get where we needed. Off we went for our hopefully last long stroll before locating Ingrid's home. If she were gone, then we would simply sleep on her front porch until morning. Nothing else to do.

Blocks passed, and more blocks after those. Kilometers passed, and more kilometers after those. Our main street turned this way, and then that way, but we simply continued just staying-the-course. Eventually, pure darkness had come upon us. It was well after nine o'clock at night, and I was beginning to feel that our timing was not very well timed if we made it at all. Second thoughts and negative vibes started filling my brain.

"What if she has moved?" I challenged myself. "What if her address turns out to be fake, after all?" I began with self-doubt.

"What if Ingrid answers the door," I asked myself, "and says with terrible shock, 'Hey, I didn't believe you. Are you crazy? Sorry, I was just kidding. Get lost!'"

Well, then, it would be back to *Plan B. Caesar* and I would still sleep on her porch and leave early the next morning. If she had us arrested, then we'd sleep in jail. "They feed people in jail, don't they?" I pondered…

It was not long afterwards, though, that even in pitch dark, I found a side street which crossed directly into Ingrid's own home street. We were almost there. Thank goodness. I felt like *Caesar* was also probably getting very tired bouncing up and down with each of my steps, so I brought him back down and replaced him inside my pocket along with clean tissue from the earlier restaurant stop. He was immediately happier and went soundly back to sleep.

Minutes, or so later, however, we stood before a large apartment complex. It was the same address I had, and I understood the additional numbers for Ingrid's address as the floor and room number of her apartment home. Wow! We had made it! Maybe. Hopefully.

The entry gate was unlocked, so in we went, and then we found the correctly numbered complex unit, and entered that entry doorway too. Next came a stairwell to the third floor, which we anxiously took, and then a long hallway past separate apartments. Just a few more steps, and we would be able to rest. Maybe. Hopefully.

However, just about then I began hearing a loud commotion. People were arguing. No, they were downright having a high-pitched screaming frenzy. It was coming from the direction I was approaching...

Once I came upon the door number I sought, there was no getting around it. A loud verbal fight was going on within that apartment supposedly belonging to Ingrid. I was in a difficult position. What should I do? Leave and come back later, like tomorrow? Leave and never return? Go inside and take my chances, or punishment? Maybe get thrown out a building's, three-story window as innocent collateral damage?

Oh, it was so late, though, and the noise was so loud. I finally decided to help stop the fight. I would simply interrupt it, and thereby, hopefully, bring about a temporary cease fire. At least the fighting might stop until I was gone again. At least maybe. Hopefully...

So, I knocked upon the front door boldly and definitively. A moment later, the door cracked open slightly, and a pair of eyes stared at me with curious bewilderment. Then the door swung wide open, and Ingrid was standing there almost shrieking with delight and hollering to her embattled parents. The ruckus did cease immediately, and Ingrid rushed to grab me and squeeze me with welcomed gratitude and appreciation. I had indeed stopped an uproarious family squabble. Yet, the father seemed the one mostly perturbed and upset. Perhaps, he had been wronged and never got his chance for reprisal. I had ruined it for him.

However, Ingrid was beside herself with shock, dismay, near disbelief, and joy. She broke into her Austrian German, and I understood nothing about what she was pouring out to her mother, except sensing her excitement. Ingrid's frustrated father did not stick around for salutations and instead left briskly into another room, presumably a bedroom, and he was absent for the remainder of the night. The mother, however, somewhat embarrassed, but having listened to Ingrid's joyous screaming, began carrying on about what an amazing, wonderful thing it was for my surprise visit.

I reminded Ingrid that I had indeed *promised* to visit her, but then I apologized for not having given advanced warning and asked if it were alright for me to be there. If not, I emphasized that I was amply prepared to leave and find another place to stay for the night... (like on their front porch)... But I was absolutely most assured that I was very welcome to stay and spend days and nights for as long as I desired.

That felt very comforting because I was beginning to show a few signs of fatigue. That was when I asked for water, and Ingrid thoughtfully asked if I was hungry. "Oh, just a little," I confessed. Then I reached into my pocket and withdrew sleepy little *Caesar*. Right on cue from being handled, he began wailing away, and just like so many others before, *Caesar* proceeded to stun and delight his new onlookers. Ingrid began squealing herself, and her mother was shocked and decidedly pleased with my little pet.

"His name is *Caesar*," I explained, "and I rescued him from sheer death in *Rome*. I'm taking him home as a gift for my aunt who sent me over here. She loves cats." I lied a little to make a positive impression.

"Oh, Daniel, it's amazing," Ingrid spoke nearly awestruck. "He is so cute. Is he hungry?"

"Oh, as a matter of fact," I stressed, "he probably is. We, I mean he hasn't eaten in a long time. He needs warm milk that I feed him through this." I showed them both the eyedropper.

Ingrid's mother turned and rushed to their kitchen and shouted some instructions to Ingrid. Right away, Ingrid asked if I'd like to get cleaned-up before eating something, and that she would make a comfortable bed for me on their living room couch, if that would be alright with me.

I couldn't help myself and joyfully conveyed, "After so many nights on the ground for us, a couch is like sleeping in heaven. Thank you so much, Ingrid."

Soon after using their bathroom, washing-up, and changing *Caesar's* pocket linen, we were both presentable for a wonderful meal. A delicious stew of meat and potatoes and cabbage was served with loads of dark bread and glasses of milk for me and warmed milk for *Caesar*. I even attempted breaking off a small piece of meat for him. Although he seemed interested, he could not yet manage it, but he gulped down vials of his beloved milk, slightly warmed. "He is actually even accepting it colder now," I proudly noted.

With our meal over, we moved to the living room, and both Ingrid and her mother had many questions about my travels thus far. I gave them several details and insights as to some interesting aspects, but I left out a few unnecessary highlights., or lowlights. I made it a point, too, to emphasize to Ingrid's mother just how popular Ingrid was at our high school.

"Ingrid was a great student, "I stressed, "and she was liked by everyone including all the other students, teachers, administrators, and even the other staff too." Ingrid blushed, and that was my intent.

Shortly after eating and following a continuous barrage of questions from both Ingrid and her mother about me personally and my trip thus far, my eyelids began drooping. Fortunately, Ingrid's mother caught sight and understanding of my obvious tiredness. She encouraged me to ready myself for bed, gave me another welcoming hug, and retired for the night. Ingrid promised that she and her mother would show me *Vienna* the next day and then followed her mother's example by hugging me goodnight too.

"Daniel," Ingrid said while shaking her head in amazement, "I never thought in a million years that you would ever visit me. Everyone always says that, but they were all just being polite and kind. You actually did, and I am so happy."

"I'm happy to be here too, Ingrid," I replied. "It was a long haul getting here, though, but I always figured that I'd make it. Remember, I promised?" With that I hugged Ingrid again suggesting, "Let's talk more tomorrow. I want you to show me everything about your wonderful city. It's so famous."

Ingrid smiled and agreed, explaining that her father would be off to work early, so I was not to worry and just to sleep as long as I needed. The way I felt, I *needed* a lot of sleep. I was already tired just from the long drive from *Venice*. Then came the exceptionally long walk-through *Vienna*. Finally, there was all the excitable visiting after having had a large and delicious meal.

I was stuffed, relaxed, content, and tired, and I would feel even much better with a nice night's sleep. *Caesar* was already soundly asleep and purring away on his makeshift bed from a towel Ingrid had provided. I looked forward to our rest and the coming day's events.

Magical Vienna

The next morning came later than I expected. It did because Ingrid's family were all so courteous allowing me and *Caesar* to sleep in late. Upon finally awakening, I was surprised to see Ingrid and her mom dressed and ready for the day with a full breakfast of Viennese sausages, biscuits, fruit, and coffee already prepared and set on the table awaiting my appearance. I apologized for oversleeping and immediately jumped into gear readying myself for the day and siting down to visit and enjoy my meal. As soon as *Caesar* came awake from my handling him, he immediately began screaming for his milk meal. Spoiled Italian.

A small container of milk run under hot water for several seconds was all it took for *Caesar* to gulp down his nourishment. Once again, he was fat and happy. However, I needed to clean his bedding towel and the tissue inside my pocket while we all went out exploring. I could not leave him alone because he still needed to eat about every two hours. *Caesar* was still not moving around much, and he would continue remaining comfortable in my pocket, or on my shoulder, I appreciated. Things would change in time, however.

Our day of *Vienna* touring began, and right away it promised to be special. It was one thing to go exploring all over *Rome* with Rudi as we saw and learned about new things together. It was another thing visiting parts of *Madrid* and *Paris* with Ron, and especially *Amsterdam* with Ron, Dwayne, and Dick. They all knew that city somewhat from longer-term visits which they gladly shared with me. Even seeing the night-life part of *Hamburg* from Gustav "Hamburger Joe" was special. However, getting to tour and visit an important city from actual, citizen inhabitants of that urban community seemed special indeed. I would learn directly from Ingrid and her mom about the most vital aspects, important places, and worthy highlights of *Vienna*, Austria.

Schonbrunn Palace

Have you ever wondered about how rich people live? How about the filthy rich? How about the filthiest, richest people in the entire world? Well, a visit to the *Schonbrunn Palace*, home of the Habsburg Dynasty, gave you fairly good insight on how royalty live, anyway. The Palace grounds' spectacular beauty, its structure's, and grounds' immense size, all its incredible furnishings, including famous artwork and sculptures, and glorious architecture was absolutely mindboggling.

Simply entering the site and hiking to the palace entrance was considerable exercise, in itself. It takes an entire team of gardeners working all year round to maintain its stunning glory. Once inside, to walk from one end of the *Schonbrunn Palace* to its other required several rest breaks. But a tourist got those desired pauses just from stopping to absorb the beauty of the palace's interior, its furnishings, world famous paintings, and amazing sculptures from multiple periods of history.

I learned that the Habsburg Dynasty had earned its name and steady growth into worldwide power, wealth, prestige, and influence since the twelfth century. The Dynasty, itself, ruled its vast empire including rule over Spain and the Holy Roman Empire from the mid-fifteenth century (about 1438 AD) until its breaking up around 1740. Its last ruler, Charles I, went into exile in 1918 during WWI, when his abdication was forced. For six hundred years, though, the Habsburgs ruled over a vast kingdom.

I could only fantasize about which rooms the various rulers and their families enjoyed the most. The numerous, incredible-banquet halls, multitudes of wonderful garden areas, and ballrooms suggested some insight. However, I could only imagine the enormous and magnificent hunting and riding grounds would have been some of my own favorite's areas. It felt as though anyone could probably get lost while wandering around inside that palace. It was obvious that the Habsburgs lived well.

Belvedere Palace

Our next stop was only to walk the free grounds of the stupendous *Lower and Upper Belvedere Palace's* grounds. Their designs were more medieval and Baroque in nature and offered incredible viewing. The gardening was designed by the same fellow who had designed the wonderful gardens of *Versailles,* outside *Paris.* Apparently, their interiors were also filled with some of the greatest artwork from the medieval period to more modern times, but we chose to just enjoy the exterior grounds for our afternoon visit.

An interesting aspect of the two palaces is that both separate palaces, eventually combined into one, were built uniquely as bedroom and home suites for different members of the ruling family. The *Lower Belvedere* was built initially as a summer residence, completed in 1716, for the champion

Prince Eugene, who had heroically defeated the invading Turkish armies, and actually lived there.

The *Upper Belvedere*, named such because it was built on higher grounds, was completed in 1724, and then the two palaces were linked by one of their spectacular garden areas. That new, combined special palace was unique because it was the home of Duke Ferdinand, heir to the Austrian throne. Franz Ferdinand lived on the grounds from 1894 until 1914 when he traveled to Sarajevo and was assassinated bringing about the start of WWI.

It was also the *Upper Belvedere* where more modern history was made. On those grounds, finally in 1955, Foreign Ministers of the greatest of the Allied Powers from WWII, France, Great Britain, the Soviet Union, the United States of America, and Austria signed the Austrian State Treaty which restored Austria's autonomy and its independence.

St. Stephen's Cathedral

From my evening chat with Ingrid and her mother, they had obviously caught drift of my respects toward my mother. Later that afternoon, they surprised me with a nice visit to yet another example of the Holy Roman Catholic Empire, the magnificent and impressive historical site of *St. Stephen's Cathedral*. It is a wondrous, Baroque monument and amazing architectural marvel standing as a special symbol of religious influence, historical value, and a highly recognizable tourist attraction for world visitors.

Having taken nearly twenty-five years to build, its construction was commenced around 1137 and completed in 1160. However, it nearly completely burned to the ground in 1258, but it was later reconstructed and then consecrated again in 1263 using only the two original and surviving towers for its rebirth. Since then, besides repairs of damages from WWII, large portions have been rebuilt along with other towers, extensions, and a variety of additional decorations over the centuries.

One of the most obvious architectural standouts of *St. Stephen's Cathedral* is its gigantic towers which can be seen from far away. The south tower alone stands a staggering 136 meters, or 446 feet, high and is a highlight of the *Vienna* skyline, visible from most parts of the city. It is said that Beethoven was first noticed as becoming deaf when he saw pigeons flying away from the north tower but could not hear its bells ringing.

Saint Stephen, the namesake of the cathedral, is considered the patron saint of stone masons for good reason. The cathedral's masonry is a true tribute to stone masons' artistic endeavors. Saint Stephen, himself, is considered to be the very first Christian martyr to die shortly after Jesus's own crucifixion. The cathedral's interior is also a tribute to all saints with so many solemn, stone-sculptured faces peering down upon observers from high above on its walls.

Other important items in the cathedral include an iconic stonework of St Mary with Jesus. It had been built originally in Hungary as a Byzantine-style Catholic shrine there but was moved by King Leopold I in 1696 to *Vienna* and *St. Stephen's Cathedral* after the icon was supposedly said to have been seen crying real tears. Furthermore, in one of the many chapels within the cathedral is where Prince Eugene, of *Lower Belvedere Palace* fame, is buried. Also, of interesting note, are the facts that both Wolfgang Amadeus Mozart's marriage and funeral occurred at *St. Stephen's Cathedral*. I suppose one can say that ol' musical Mozart was *married* and *buried* at the same place. Interesting, but curious.

Prater Amusement Park

After our late afternoon touring, we ate at a nice outdoor restaurant, and I splurged by paying for all our meals. It was a favorite casserole dish of theirs with bread, cheese, and refreshments. Fortunately, I had been very thrifty to date, so I was still doing alright budget-wise, but I had to be a little careful. No overindulgences. Once our dinner was finished, and *Caesar* got his own eyedropper fillings, though, we continued throughout the evening touring in their family car throughout *Vienna*. In their car, *Caesar* sat happily on my shoulder again.

We enjoyed all *Vienna's* beautiful scenery, active and colorful city life, its lovely Danube River, and many other fabulous architectural achievements including the *Hofburg Palace* and classic *Vienna State Opera* house. After darkness arrived, all *Vienna,* along with its impressive cultural, historical, and architectural glamour, was especially charming and glimmering when lit up for night viewing.

Then came a really delightful surprise when I was taken and introduced to their own personal, favorite-tourist attraction of all *Vienna*: The *Prater Public Amusement Park* with its iconic, giant Ferris Wheel. I had only been on one other Ferris Wheel before, when I was much younger, but it was much smaller. The *Prater Ferris Wheel* was huge and glorious, with spectacular views of all the surrounding areas.

I was glad *Caesar* was with us, too, because I needed to be extra careful regarding his presence while the three of us humans all crowded together in our Ferris Wheel seat. With *Caesar* in my pocket busy, jostling amusement park crowds could have squashed him. With him in my hands, or while gripping tightly with his little claws onto my shoulder, I enjoyed our ride immensely not worrying too much about him.

Alone at Ingrid's home, though, I felt *Caesar* may have become confused and frightened again, like in *Rome*, without his mama. However, going along for the ride, so-to-speak, we both appreciated the personal time with Ingrid and her mom. Also, little did I know at that time while riding the *Vienna Ferris Wheel* attraction, that within a year, I would actually be operating another large Ferris Wheel at a different amusement park in Santa Cruz, California while working my way through college. Perhaps it was that *Viennese* experience's influence, I later wondered?

It had been a great day visiting and catching up on times with Ingrid. She was starting college in September too, like me, and we both promised to stay in touch with each other. Back at their home again that night, I ate another great meal, and Ingrid's mom packed a meal for me to take on the road, the following morning. I had three days left to get back to *Paris* before *Caesar's* and my flight home to San Francisco. That seemed like plenty of time, considering Ron and I had driven so much further in one day, *Paris* to *Madrid*, even including an out-of-the-way tourist stop in *San Sebastian*, Spain.

I needed to leave early the next morning, though, and Ingrid's mom offered to drive *Caesar* and me to a good hitching spot on the outskirts of *Vienna*. I was grateful for Ingrid and her mother's hospitality, kindnesses, and companionship. As my co-hosts for that wonderful, classical-metropolis visit, together they made my stopover there a very memorable outing, and they presented *Vienna* in its best form as a truly beautiful and magical city.

CHAPTER 17

....

STRUGGLING BACK TO PARIS

Tainted Views

I wish that I could end this entire story with a happy conclusion. It is always uplifting, encouraging, and exciting to hear or read about somebody beating probabilities, defeating impossible prospects, and winning against all odds. That is always a nice story,... *happily ever after*, and all that. Unfortunately, such are not always the realities of life.

After leaving *Vienna,* and my dear friend, Ingrid, my best intentions were to race straight back to *Paris*, rent another cheap, favorite-sleazy room from the *Left Bank Hotel,* stay cleaned-up, and hang-out a little more in that incredibly romantic city just before catching my final flight home. Heck, I even considered strolling back through that friendly and sexy district that I had previously been so charmed by earlier and saying a fond farewell to those delightfully enticing ladies.

At least I knew that I'd have a little more experience under my belt, so to speak, that next time. Perhaps, I could even have full conversations with any of them. Plus, I didn't have much money left, so none of those beckoning ladies could get much out of me. However, "What might I get out of them," I giggled. The thought made me as giddy as an oversexed and unrehearsed teenage boy.

Like I stated before, however, "Things don't always happen like you want."

Castles and Decadence

In *Vienna* I had been given several terrific meals, compliments of Ingrid's family. Plus, Ingrid's mom sent me off with a nice lunch for on-the-road and a small container of milk for *Caesar*. I was fairly sure he would start eating soft meaty foods soon, so that was going to be a relief. Better to give him my scraps, than me sneaking away with scraps meant for him. Embarrassing, but not really. We were a team, and I used him whenever it seemed convenient.

"Oh, such a cute little kitten. Is he hungry?" an eager observer would ask.

"Gosh, *Caesar* (they all loved his name) could eat practically all the time, if I let him," I aptly replied. "But we just don't have much food. That's all," I mostly fibbed.

Ohhhhh, here, have some of this sandwich," came an offering. "Does he like cookies?"

"Believe me, everything will be gone by tomorrow," I told truthfully.

Oh, okay, now I am ashamed, but at that time I was looking out for the two of us. Any donations from anywhere were welcomed meals for us both. Yet, feeding *Caesar* was really becoming the least of our problems. Getting back to *Paris* was looming as the major obstacle in my mind.

Once again, I was heading for *Paris*, and I could not seem to get a decent ride. Also, even though summertime was receding somewhat, I was heading north again. All decent traffic and congenial picker-uppers of hitcher hikers were either going south or already there. Perhaps, it was even *Paris*, itself, that was the problem again. So many people seemed to want to get out of there for summertime. Perhaps, any other drivers were suspicious of anyone else actually trying to go there. Maybe I just didn't make sense to anybody.

So, we started walking again just for the sake of getting somewhere slowly. My map suggested that it was about 1,130 kilometers, or seven hundred miles to Paris. If I walked steadily at about three miles per hour, and slept about 6 hours a night for rest, we could get to Paris in about fourteen days only stopping to grab more food and go to the bathroom. It was still no good. Walking some was okay, but we needed a seriously good ride. I wondered if *Caesar* could play sick, and I could call for a veterinarian ambulance.

"Help, my kitten is dying to get to *Paris*," I'd exclaim. "Can you take him, er, us? I'll give you all my extra cash."

Of course, I was daydreaming again. Plus, *Caesar* and I were back to sleeping on the road again too. I figured that, in reality, I had just enough funds remaining to eat meagerly while getting us to *Paris*, sleeping at the hotel for one night, and then I, er, we would finally eat a decent meal on the TWA aircraft flying us back home. In a haphazardly perfect world, that plan sounded ostentatiously well enough. We'd make it back to *Paris* reasonably on time, and our next and final meal(s) would be on the plane going home. Sounded great on paper.

No cars stopped. No rides were offered, and we just trudged on. Soon thereafter, off in the distance, I could see a spectacular castle-like mansion, or palace-type residence, with wondrous fields of grain and orchards and vineyards surrounding its enormous, magnificent villa. The decadent homestead and surrounding landscape suggested bountiful food and relaxation for all its inhabitants.

"What would you care to have for dinner tonight, darlings?" I could almost hear its Lord-King, or Duke-Almighty, castle owner calling out to his multitude of fat, slovenly, already-stuffed guests. "Filet Mignon, or Pheasant Under Glass?" he'd request. "We have so much of either, I haven't the faintest idea what to do with it all…"

"Just invite me," I hollered out in my mind. "I'll show you just what I'd do with a lot of it. And then I'd tell you where you can stuff the rest!"

I suppose that I was just getting a bit hungry again, and thus, envious of banquet table spreads. I began fantasizing about my own mom's Thanksgiving dinners. Talk about banquets! If anyone went hungry, it was entirely their fault. However, back on task again, I was grateful for Ingrid's wonderful mom's lunch provided to us.

The food package survived until just past the drop-off point before being devoured. Less weight to carry around, I figured. But I did also feed *Caesar* his milk bottle again, and I even let him begin nibbling on some small, mashed pieces of *Vienna* sausage. Although uncertain at first, he seemed to at least enjoy the possibility, I thought.

Liechtenstein Crawl

A ride finally stopped, and we were off again. That time we were being taken all the way to *Vaduz*, Liechtenstein, one of the tiniest countries, or microstates, in the world. It shares borders with Austria and Switzerland,

and although heavily Catholic influenced, speaks German as its primary language. My drivers were staying in *Vaduz*, so it meant I needed to keep on traveling to get closer to *Paris*. *Zurich*, Switzerland became my nest destination goal.

We were definitely in wooded countryside. The entire ride through Austria took us through forest lands, farmlands, and pastures. Made me think about home a lot. Incredibly beautiful the many small towns and communities were all clean, quaint, and definitely with German architectural influences. Lots of cookie-cutter homes that made me think of <u>Hansel and Gretel</u> stories.

Also, along the way were more of those incredible, spectacular, palace-like residences surrounded by so much agricultural industry. If farming was their income, those farmhouses looked like castles and their residents probably lived like kings and queens. I did not have the money for tourist entry fees, but I imagined that they all allowed for public visitations... for a price. However, they all merely became nice for me to see from a distance.

The stop in Vaduz became our parting point, and I thanked our driver hosts for the favorable lift. With Caesar on my shoulder once again after waiting long enough to feed him, and time enough for me to grab another favorite meal of meat, bread, a piece of fruit, and a soda, we were off hiking down the road once more. At least the walk-through *Vaduz* and the rest of Liechtenstein was colorful, shaded by so many trees, and brief. Unfortunately, it also became the end-of-the-line for that day. Little traffic, and no ride offers, wasted the remainder of the day while *Caesar* and I just walked and walked. Fortunately, we both enjoyed the great outdoors, or I did anyway. Plus, we managed to walk clear out of Liechtenstein and past the border gates. I was able to have my passport stamped again with a welcoming into Switzerland.

At that point, I really began regretting not having gone out of my way to visit Andorra, the tiny principality within Spain in the Pyrenees mountains. After all, I had already walked a great deal through the *Capitol City of Luxembourg* and its tiny nation of *Luxembourg*. Then I visited *Monaco* with *Monte Carlo* and hiked through most of them. Later, I even traversed nearly the entire domain of *Vatican City* while racing around *Rome*. Thus far, my travels had touched upon many tiny lands. *Vaduz* and *Liechtenstein* were yet my latest.

To emphasize the point, I guess, we got little past the border when I stopped for the day. I wanted daylight to know where I was heading, and apparently, we were not going to have further light for further potential rides. Therefore, I found a nice forest grove of trees, and my little friend *Caesar* had a chance to move around a bit on a bed I made for him next to my own. Although we were technically in Switzerland, I decided to commemorate that night's stay with our quick walk and visit through *Liechtenstein*. After all, that tiny country was practically only a stone's throw from our night's stand. Also, it was barely a stone's throw to walk across it.

Zurich Night Train

The next day was mostly more of the same. We walked and walked. Me with my sea bag shouldered on my left side, and little *Caesar* clinging onto my right shoulder. We'd hike and hike, and then, hearing an upcoming car, I'd turn around facing traffic with my thumb out attempting to hail any potential, well-intentioned drivers. Time passed, and so did any decent luck, it seemed.

Finally, we came to a friendly market and stocked up on travel groceries for us both. *Caesar* would try eating soft meaty foods, but I wasn't sure how well he might digest them, so we continued with his eyedropper milk feedings. At least he didn't seem to mind less warmed-temperature milk. That had been a big inconvenience always having to heat-up his servings of milk.

Eventually, a brief ride took us to the east end of *Lake Zurichsee*, well inside Switzerland. Our driver and his friend were out for a day of fun on that lake. Unfortunately, as much as I wished to join them for an invited outing, I was feeling pressed to push on toward *Paris*. Spare time was rapidly decreasing, and our flight going home was literally only a couple of days away. I was truly feeling pressured with little time to spare.

Then began another excruciating walk alongside the beautiful Zurichsee lake. I shall never forget the hike because of the entire day passing as I walked the complete length of that lake alongside its shoreline drive. Any other time, and it would have been truly splendid. A very pretty and clean lake on one side of us with a virtual forest wall on the other side. It should have been very relaxing and comforting to stroll up the highway with such scenic wonders to appreciate. Unfortunately, it turned out to be about ten hours of tiresome striding with stops only to feed *Caesar* and getting a bite to eat for myself at a tourist trap along the way. At least *Caesar* did not complain. He just sat atop my shoulder bumping up and down, synchronized and coexisting with my long strides, and seemingly nonchalant about the whole endeavor.

When we finally came to the end of the lake, we actually entered the city limits of *Zurich*, Switzerland too. Another stop at a restaurant got us our next meals, the same old thing for us both, and then I had to figure out that next night's retreat. I was tired of sleeping on the ground, but the hotels in that area were likely to be too expensive. So, I needed to think of some alternative. Just as we crossed over some railroad tracks, though, I saw Zurich's train station off in the near vicinity. That gave me an idea.

I walked us to the station and found the ticket agent. Fortunately for me, he spoke very decent English. Amazing people. I learned that nearly all Swiss citizens were also quadrilingual, just like Belgians. They spoke German, French, Italian, and English for convenience.

That was also why Switzerland managed to stay neutral during most wartimes. They could easily communicate with nearly everyone. And I'd heard about all their secretive bank accounts for people and countries all over the world. Control the money, and you controlled the depositors. Furthermore, they were also world famous for guarding the Pope at the *Vatican City.* Best not let him down. Finally, I laughed to myself when I remembered that the Swiss were likewise famous for making great watches. They knew *what time it was!*

Anyway, my idea was simple. It was getting dark, so I learned that the station had an inexpensive train ride to Bern, Switzerland that would take about eight hours round trip, including its layover in Bern, before returning. The ticket was much cheaper than a hotel's price, and I could sleep on one of the train's softer bench seats all the way to Bern and then back to *Zurich* during that coming night. It sounded *purrfect*, and *Caesar* would not mind at all as long as his belly was full. With round-trip tickets in hand, we boarded our train and settled in for the night. We only had wakeups to provide tickets for my round-trip passages, and then from jolting stops arriving in Bern, and again in *Zurich* the next morning.

Upon our return to *Zurich*, we were both rested, but hungry again. Money was getting desperately short after that unplanned train ride, but we both had to eat. So, a small market provided us with milk and a couple road-trip snacks. It was getting fairly obvious that most assuredly our next real meals were likely to be on our plane flight back home to America.

We would make it, though, and I was getting reenergized with a second wind. No longer tired, and now somewhat fed, we both marched on. All we needed was one good lift...

Black Forest

Caesar and I hoofed it clear back up to the main highway entering *Zurich.* The thoroughfare was also an interchange which turned into other points going north and south. With *Caesar* on my shoulder and my thumb stuck out boldly to passing traffic, almost immediately we then got a ride that filled me with joy? An English couple, a husband and wife, traveling to *Paris,* themselves, in a two-door, British Vauxhall, stopped and offered me, us, a ride all the way there.

Our wonderful driver hosts were indeed heading to *Paris,* but with one small catch. A nice highway further ahead that they wished to travel on went north for a way and just happened to pass through Germany's world-famous *Black Forest.* Asking in pure, excellent English, of course, they wanted to know if I didn't mind going that far out of the way with them before turning west again for *Paris.* Knowing it meant that we would still arrive in *Paris* that very day, I almost fell down while scrambling over to get inside their automobile and offer my acceptance speech.

In a flash and a blink, I screamed out in my mind, "Goodbye, Zurich! Sorry I didn't see more of you. Loved the train ride, though. Hello again, Germany! Long time no sees. Can't wait to find out just how dark it gets in your famous Black Forest. Paris, I'll see you soon. Yay!"

Those were just a few of the wild, crazy thoughts rushing through my mind as I rushed around to the opposite side of the English car, helped the wife shift her seat forward so that I could hurriedly toss my sea bag onto the couple's rear seat. Then practically leaping inside to my spot, I joyously exclaimed, "Of course we'll go! I love forests, and so does *Caesar.*"

Momentarily surprised by my little, shoulder friend, the couple were immediately pleased with our company. A moment later, *Caesar* and I were on our way again to finally complete the last leg of our tenuous journey returning to *Paris.* Catching my breath and allowing our good fortune to sink in, I took note of our hosts' actual offer. Their route was basic enough. Rather quickly, we began traveling further westward to Basel, Switzerland and into the French Mountains. Then we turned north and drove up into Germany and its Rhine River terrain.

During that magnificent drive through mountainous country, and finally deep into Germany's darkest wooded areas, we were able to experience the splendid woodlands making its *Black Forest* name so famous. It was like stepping into a Grimm Brothers' fairy tale with really quaint and charming villages speckled about through really dense, evergreen forests. The *Black Forest* name comes from the very dark color of the many pine trees from that region.

Having been raised in pine tree country, myself, I really appreciated the thick, heavy foliage of that area. In fact, coupled with the picturesque and often colorful, but curious-looking villages, I kept half expecting to see Hansel and Gretel wandering into some vibrant house made of candy and cookies. Or else, I'd see a mean old wolf tracking down Little Red Riding Hood. The entire side trip was very pleasant and well worth it.

The only minor issue came when we stopped for a break at a peculiar looking restaurant fresh out of a Brothers Grimm fairy tale. I had to excuse myself from the offer of joining the couple during their lunch break. Instead, I just explained that I only needed to get some milk for *Caesar* and to freshen up in the restaurant's eerie sort of restroom. Sort of dark and sinister, it was.

Nevertheless, *Caesar* was hungry again, as usual, so after cleaning us both up, we split a container of milk. My funds left me with just enough money for one last light meal and necessary bus fare after we finally arrived in *Paris*. That was also when I decided that our best bet would be just to go directly to *Aeroport de Paris-Orly*. We could simply stay there for the upcoming night while awaiting our following, late-morning flight.

After enjoying the *Black Forest* drive, my English hosts did turn westward again, and we headed straight for *Paris*. On the way, we shared highlights of both our previous journeys. They had been to Italy and were on their way back to Great Britain. They explained that they did a similar trip fairly often, so it was nice changing their pace and offering me a ride. Apparently, I looked to them like I really needed it. *Road weary*, they called it.

Caesars and my final ride into *Paris* were somewhat uneventful after that. I even became so relaxed, with worrisome stress vanishing, that I drifted in and out of peaceful sleep. When I became aware enough to notice, I saw more vineyards and pastures along the way. We had turned west toward *Paris* once we reached the bordering city of Strasbourg and then headed straight up to Metz, once again for me, and through the famous Alsace Lorraine region.

Then it was "Hello, again, France!" as we crossed the Moselle, and next the Marne River, both second times for me. Also, from Ron I had learned and recognized that we were passing through Champagne country. Actually, a glass of Champagne would have been perfect too. I definitely felt like celebrating. Our ride was extremely comfortable too. Nice car. Everything deserved a toast.

Approaching *Paris*, energy from my excitement began building again, and it was complemented by a new realization. Our kind-hearted driver and his gracious wife decided to do something extra special for us. As a very decent favor, they went out of their way by taking us directly to *Orly Airport*. God Bless the English! I made a vow to visit Great Britain one day. Unfortunately, however, even with their kindness, it indirectly reinforced and made even more certain my prior decision. *Caesar* and I would eat lightly at the airport using my last funds, and our next really good meal would be on the airplane going home, itself, late the next morning.

I thanked our hosts with warm goodbyes. All was well... Well, as *well* as I could tell and expect, I suppose. Sometimes, however, life just cannot leave *well enough* alone. Sometimes, it just has to throw a curveball into the melee to mess everything up, and best laid *plans* can become disoriented, distorted, and even struck out by the *unexpected*. *Well, enough* is not always willing...

CHAPTER 18

DOING TIME

1966 Airlines Strike

Nevertheless, with my bright eyes and *Caesar's* bushy tail, we sauntered into the TWA Departing Flights Terminal Building feeling in great spirits. I was all grins and my mood was very chipper. Even Caesar felt excited. After all, he was possibly following in his, Puss 'n' Boots paw steps, kind of, by traveling across the ocean, just like Christopher Columbus, seeking a new land.

He had begun shifting around nervously a bit more often, and I began thinking he was ready for a little, transient-movement exercise for himself. I determined that once I checked-in my sea bag at the terminal desk for flight storage and shipping, *Caesar* and I would be freed up to wander around, grab a nice, final airport bite to eat, and relax somewhere until we could enter the deportation zone early the next morning.

Initially, while pacing through the terminal building, I was a little curious as to why all the TWA lines for flights were so short. In fact, there was hardly anybody around there. I just assumed it was because I was there quite a bit early, the day before my flight, actually. No matter, I moved quickly up to the ticketing desk and produced my passport and return flight information for the Ticket Agent.

I honestly even hoped to get special courtesy assistance because of *Caesar's* presence sitting comfortably there on my shoulder. Unfortunately, the agent was hardly in any good mood. Fact is, she seemed even rather nonchalant, bored, and condescending as she studied my documents and then patronizingly explained my new state of affairs...

"I am sorry, Sir," she began sounding like a broken record repeating itself over-and-over. "All flights have been cancelled indefinitely due to the airlines strike in the States. I am sorry, but there is nothing we can do." It was as though she were making a speech that she had given hundreds of times before.

"What do you mean 'Nothing you can do?'" I practically stammered in instant shock. "I have to go home. Here is my ticket. You have to take me home. I don't have anywhere else to go."

"Sir, as I explained," her rather cold and repetitious voice repeated, "there is nothing we can do. We are waiting ourselves for further instructions. Perhaps, we shall hear soon that flights are opening again, and we can assist you at that time. But, for now, we have no flights available going anywhere. Please just check in with us later this week. Sorry..."

"Sorry? How can you do this to me?" I cried out. "I hardly have any money left! I need to go home now."

"We are terribly sorry, Sir," she haughtily lied. "Just keep checking in with us. You understand, of course, that we have been on strike for nearly a month already, don't you?"

"A month?" I bellowed. "What do you mean a month? I was here earlier in *Paris* a month ago. Nobody said anything. What am I supposed to do now?"

"We're so sorry, Sir..." were the last insensitive words I heard before the obviously aggravated ticket agent turned and walked away. Frustrated unbelievable, I also turned away to sit down on a bench across the room and think through this new dilemma.

Caesar helped me refocus. He needed to eat again, and I too was definitely getting hungry. My snacks from *Zurich* were long gone, and hunger pangs were starting to settle in. I'd find some milk somewhere to feed *Caesar* and then try to think out a new plan. But what could I possibly think about? I had already planned things down to almost our last meal. We were supposed to eat again on the airplane, simple as that. Whatever was going to happen next?

During that summer's journey, I had already gone through quite a few, "What-am-I-going-to-do-now?" experiences. Yet, all of those encounters had typically resolved themselves just by *keepin'-on-keepin'-on*! I had simply needed only to continue on walking, and hitching, and getting on to my next destination. I always had time on my side before. Not then, however, and I was up in the air with what to do.

Time was no longer on my side. In fact, *time was up! Gone! Finished! Fini! Ober! Terminado! Finito! Caesar* and I had no other place to go. We were completely in the hands of others by then; in TWA's hands, in fact, and they had definitely dropped the ball. Dropped me!

Or, how about putting ourselves in the Almighty's hands? Maybe I could sneak into *Notre Dame Cathedral* and sleep on one of its pews. Perhaps, sympathetic priests would feel sorry for us and give me that upcoming Sunday's Collection Plate donations to exist on. Hey, I'd been an Alter Boy for two years. They owed me!… Obviously, my wracked mind's warped imagination was racing to reap havoc.

But there was nothing else I could do. I was dependent upon others by then and no longer helping myself, all by myself, and with only my own wits. So, I did what many people do when faced by a crisis such as that. *First,* I found some leftover milk on a small cafeteria table to warm up and feed *Caesar.* Then, once he was satisfied and resting again in my pocket, I found a row of airline terminal seats to lie down upon and take a nap too. I needed to sleep. Maybe when I awakened, my insane nightmare would be over…

Orly Airport Drama

I slept through that night and well into the morning. Of course, even then there was no more luck for me. Besides, I was feeling like I was in a somewhat awkward, conflicting situation. Apparently, the International Association of Machinists Union had gone on strike over a month earlier, on July 8th. That was nearly a month after I had first arrived in *Paris.* The strike had grounded all flights for six major airlines, including TWA. Unionists were striking for higher wages.

As upset as I might be, I knew about unions a little bit, and I had paid attention in history classes studying about their rise and impact on our American economy. Plus, my father was a welder and lifelong member of one of America's earliest and strongest unions, *The International Brotherhood of Boilermakers.* He was a union man and believed in supporting all of them for working classes. Naturally, like father-like son, I grew up believing in rights of honorable workers and in labor unions supporting their just causes.

Unfortunately, my dilemma there in *Paris* during that Summer of 1966 became a serious issue for me as an individual stuck in the middle. TWA had no answers for me except apologies, and as giant representatives of management's powerful ruling side against labor's struggle, I was unlikely to get any further assistance from the ticket counter workers. Another sad but true fact is that many of those meager airline workers were caught up in TWA's *strike fight* themselves. Likely, many of them had temporarily lost their jobs too because airline travel had been so drastically restricted.

Regardless, that USA/TWA labor/management issue had become very personal for me. Because of it I was pretty much stuck at that airport with no food, no ride to go home, and with no hopeful prospects. I was in dire straits. I had a tiny bit of money left, but not even enough for any small, yet expensive, airport meal. However, airport kitchens were still open and serving passengers who were still flying to other destinations with other non-striking airlines. They were less affected by the USA airline strike. I was truly in a quandary, though, as to what my options might be. A summer spent traveling throughout a distant part of the world, and suddenly, I had nowhere to go and with no means to do it, anyway.

It's embarrassing to admit that after that *first* day at the airport had passed, I was forced to roam through various cafeteria areas seeking reasonable leftovers to help feed *Caesar,* and even munch on decent scraps, myself, left by unkempt travelers. *Caesar* was actually adjusting well to drinking room temperature milk, and he was beginning to chew with his tiny teeth on mashed up meat products. It was still a difficult process for him, but he seemed to want to eat substantial foods as much as drink his milk. Fortunately, finding leftover milk cartons was not much issue. Neither was finding sympathetic and caring folks who came over to observe and pay respects.

Caesar and I hung around the Orly Departing Flights Terminal for the remainder of that day and into the night. I suppose that early on I was waiting for some miracle to arrive whereby an enlightening someone would come running over to me offering an alternative means to going home.

"Sir," I imagined an anxious employee shouting out at me, "we have found a flight for you. TWA has made a special exception just for you and your kitten because of your courage and stamina and kind faces. We *must* help you."

Something good had to happen. They just couldn't let me, us, die there. Or could they? I began imagining going home in a casket. Or I recalled warning those foolish, spoiled American brats at the *Horny Hostel* about *going home on a hospital charter, if they didn't change their ways.* Wouldn't that be a fine reversal-of-fortune and a regretful kick-in-the-proverbial-pants? I would be sent home on a hospital flight after having passed out from starvation at a TWA Airlines Terminal? But, hey, maybe that was a way to get a meal and a ticket home after all…

Naturally, a distant voice began whispering in the deepest recesses of my stress riddled mind, "I knew it! He got lost and starved to death at the airport!"

My imagination was not helping. It was not serving me with reasonable solutions for my problems. I continued returning to the TWA Departing Flights ticket counter and questioning the staff about any new changes. Of course, there were none, but one surprising new piece of information did arise. One of the agents finally noticed *Caesar*, who at that time was settled up on my shoulder again.

"What a darned cute little kitten that is," a male attendant remarked. "What are you going to do about it when you are able to fly back home… whenever that might ever be…? You know that you can't leave it here at the airport."

"Of course, I know that" I snapped. "He's going with me back to California as soon as you guys get us a plane before we starve to death."

"Well, you do have all its papers, don't you?" he retorted right back at me.

"Of course, I do!" I quipped. "He's totally legal," I added. "I got him fair and square. But what *papers* do you mean? Like an animal passport, or something?"

"Well, sort of," he smiled, feeling a sense of power and authority. "You have to have Travel Clearance Papers from an official veterinarian stating that the pet is free of sickness and has all its shots. You can't take him on the airplane without those signed and stamped papers."

"Well, sure, that's easy," I lied. "I was just going into town to get those vet papers so that we're both ready for your next flight out to San Francisco."

"Good for you," he smirked. "But I wouldn't hold my breath about that flight. Not just yet anyway."

It was getting late again at the airport. I had spent the whole day waiting for something miraculous to occur which would send us home on a next, new, and especially planned flight to San Francisco… But it was too late to do anything else about anything at all by then. All I could do was find some leftover snacks again and locate those bench seats again for that upcoming night.

In the morning, we would go into *Paris* on the bus, and we could eat there. Food was much less expensive. Maybe afterwards, I would find a kind veterinarian who might accept what small amount of money I still had left. Or maybe he or she would take an IOU, to cover expenses for *Caesar's* shots and travel documents. Hopefully, something good would happen in the *City of Love*.

I found some more remaining, leftover milk for *Caesar,* and he gulped it down right from its opened container. He was learning fast, and that helped my mood. Unfortunately, there were slim pickings for me, so I went to bed hungry that night. I planned to eat an entire loaf of delicious French bread when we got into town. We'd take the *Route 1 bus* again, and since I knew its routes fairly well, I'd get us close to downtown. A nice walk would do us both good...

"Pompeia:" Above Suspicion

In the morning, after cleaning up in an airport restroom, I pulled out my souvenir collection and gathered from it all the foreign coins currency I had collected from my travels. It wasn't much, just lowest paper denominations and small coins from each country visited. Yet, together, I almost prayed, they would amount to a useful sum. I found an airport money-exchange office, walked in, and plopped all my currency collection on his countertop.

I must say, the agent was a bit surprised at first, but then he smiled and seemed to understand. Perhaps, due to the awful airline strike circumstances, I was only one in many preceding me to do the same thing. Anyway, he kindly and diligently counted everything while keeping a sheet of notes for his calculations. Finally, he smiled and handed me over a slip of paper to sign as his receipt, and he then gave me my exchange amount in French francs. Altogether, my return was a little over forty francs, or better than eight dollars. Added to my last remaining pocket money, *Caesar* and I had enough money for some decent meals and maybe even enough for his vet's services.

The Route 1 Bus took us straight into Paris to familiar grounds for me. That was my third visit to the area, so I sort of felt like a prodigal son returning to his family of friends and memorable homestead. I knew the area, and cheaper places to eat, and with luck, I'd find a reasonable veterinarian to help us out. Vets loved animals. That's why they do what they do. Human doctors only have to know one type of body structure mostly. Veterinarians have to know hundreds of body structure types. They are truly animal humanitarians. If they couldn't give me a break, then maybe they'd give *Caesar* one.

Soon afterwards, while chomping on a French loaf with a chunk of cheese, I asked the store clerk if she knew about an inexpensive veterinarian in the area. The clerk was happy to oblige and even pointed us toward a side street leading toward her recommendation. Okay, finally *Caesar* and I were going to take care of one minor problem. Then we would deal with the others later.

We continued on up the avenue and then side street until we found the recommended vet's office door. Going inside, I kept *Caesar* on my shoulder to impress the doctor with *Caesar's* and my bonded relationship. Momentarily, a kindly, elderly man in a doctor's coat with small, thick, and round glasses took a look at us and teased.

"Etes-vous ici pour faire retirer chirurgicalement le chatgon de votre epaule ou vous du chat?" *Are you here to have the kitten surgically removed from your shoulder, or you from the cat?"*

I had to think for a moment, but then I got his humor. Laughing, I slowly responded with my carefully pronounced best French, "J'ai peur que ce soit les deuz! Mais aussi *Cesar* a besoin de ses photos et de ses papiers pour aller en Amerique avec moi. Peut-it partir?" *I am afraid it is both! But also, Caesar needs his shots and papers to go to America with me. Can he go?"*

Then the doctor shocked me with very excellent English, "Ah, a young American! I should have guessed. You Americans really enjoy taking our animals home with you. Where did you find him?"

Smiling, and relieved to continue in English, I lifted *Caesar* down from my shoulder, presented him to the doctor, and simply explained the truth, "He was abandoned in a litter while in *Rome*, and we have hitchhiked back here to *Paris* to return home. Now there are no flights, but I have to get prepared for when we can fly home."

The doctor did seem impressed as he shifted *Caesar* around in his gentle hands. *Caesar* was whining again, but he always did when being manhandled. Then the nice veterinarian proceeded to shock me. Not once, but twice.

First, he said, "Yes, I will take care of the shots and papers for you, and because of your own kindness to this creature, I shall only charge you twenty francs for the medicines and paperwork."

I was beside myself with joy. "Thank you, Doctor, so much," I grinned. "We have very little money left until we can get a flight back home"

Next, the very decent veterinarian surprised me again with his words. In a congenial, but almost teasing, manner, he quipped, "You call your kitten, *Caesar*. But you do know that it is *she*, not *he*. Your kitten is a *female*."

I was shocked, and all I could utter was, "You're kidding, right? My *Caesar* is not a *Caesar* after all? Oh, no. Now what do we do? He's, er she's got to have a proper name, and especially for her papers to go home with me."

The doctor was less concerned with that new issue and quickly went about his business giving my ex-*Ceasar* its shots and preparing its paperwork. I had to think of a good new name for my kitten. After a few puzzling minutes, though, I thought of her new name. It came from my history lessons at school reading about the life and times of Julius Caesar.

I remembered reading that Julius had been married three times. His first wife, Cornelia, had died after fifteen years into their marriage. Then, his second wife, *Pompeia*, daughter of a rival to Julius, was his wife for nearly twenty years. Then later, *Pompeia* was found in a compromising situation with a man attending her "Women Only" festival while dressed as a woman. Whether *Pompeia* was innocent or guilty, Julius was supposedly embarrassed and divorced *Pompeia*. His wife, he said, "…ought not even to be under suspicion."

Although Julius remarried again to Calpurnia, and fathered a child with Cleopatra of Egypt, and later was assassinated on the Ides of March, or March 14th, on 44BC, for his Emperor ambitions. Little more is known about *Pompeia*, but she may have remarried and lived out her life in quiet solitude.

However, the original *Pompeia,* being distrusted by her husband, Julius, and then cast aside to save his face, was meaningful to me. Trust in a marriage was especially important to me, and I felt sorry for her. Then there was the factor of *Pompeia's* secret party and her supposed, disguised male suitor which was intriguing to me. My kitten had been disguising itself as a male for over a week so far with me. Thus, it became very appropriate. I informed the kind doctor to put down the name *Pompeia* for those shot records and travel documents for my kitten. *Pompeia* became official…

Vagrancy

We left the doctor's office, and I was even more in a tizzy. Well, fine, *Caesar* had been a female all along, and so what? He, er, *she* had a nice new name now. *Pompeia* suited her well too. After all, both had been rejected at one time, and both were from *Rome*, sort of. Yet, with all her messy butt cleanings, and all my nasty pocket cleanings, plus her many disgusting bedding changes, and that poor Mercedes Benz disaster, maybe her new nickname, I considered, should be *Poopoo*…

Anyway, at least one other problem had been resolved. Now *Pompeia* could at least fly home with me. I still didn't have any home travel answers, though. However, I decided that the next day we would go back out to the airport and check on return-flight conditions. I didn't have much hope, but something would have to happen to help us. I mean there we were stranded in *Paris*, and that was no joke. I needed to think and determine some solution someway.

I knew that sleeping in a hotel, even my old favorite, *The Left Bank Hotel*, was beyond my means. Every dollar, or franc, counted. We'd have to eat again that evening, and then find some place to sleep off the night. Food was cheaper further away from the downtown area. So, after we walked a distance for dinner, we could then wander around *Paris* and at least enjoy the wonderful city lights.

Eventually, a small café provided a nice, tomato-based soup, with great French bread, and milk, of course, for *Pompeia*. She had grown so much, and she was much more active and willing to assess her limbs and crawl around a bit. I wanted to get her more meat, or even some kitty chow from a market. That became yet another goal. In the meantime, after our meals, we just walked, and I tried enjoying the coming nightfall. With *Pompeia* sitting soundly on my shoulder, we strolled down the famous *Champs-Elysees Avenue*.

I had hiked down that avenue several times already, from one far end at the *Place de la Concorde* clear to the other end, well over one mile distance, to the famous *Arc de Triomphe*. Along the way, I decided to splurge and buy a soda pop and a tiny packet of kitten food from a side street market. We were almost broke, but we were in *Paris*, I kept telling myself. One had to live… a little, didn't one?

After darkness had almost arrived, our walk had timed itself *purrfectly* to bring us to the enormous circular drive around the *Arc de Triomphe*. Side streets and avenues turned off from the center hub of the grand arc like so many spokes on a bicycle wheel. The great Archway was one of *Paris's* central attractions and drew spectators from all over the world to visit its iconic images.

It is said that Napoleon began its construction, but it took thirty years to build and was finally dedicated in 1836, after several rulers had already come and gone. Today, it is still considered one of the world's most famous commemorative monuments and stands as a unique symbol for French national identify. Covering the entire arch's surfaces were inscribed names of all France's great victories and generals during its revolution. I had just missed the extremely popular and annual military parade that previous July. It actually begins at the *Arc de Triomphe,* and its day is known as both the French National Day and Bastille Day.

The *Arc de Triomphe* is definitely a very massive monument, and its splendor drew me to it. With *Pompeia* clinging sturdily on my shoulder, I carefully crossed that busy boulevard circling the grand arch. I did not want to become some mishappened pedestrian casualty, which seemed so typical while wandering around *Parisian* streets, and especially busy ones like near the *Arc de Triomphe.* However, we made it safely to the monument, and it was a wondrous view.

Of course, the history, meaning and purpose of the *Arc de Triomphe* were significant. At night, the city lights, coupled with the arch's own artistic lightshow, were spectacular along with all the *Paris* traffic whirling around us while busily splintering off in all those many directions. It was impressive to watch. Even *Pompeia* was curious once I allowed her to wander a bit, but she stayed close by. It was her *first* intriguing search, however, and it was entertaining to watch her as she carefully checked out the unusual premises.

We had found a nice place upon which to sit that was actually the wide berth of the Arch's own foundational base. It was about four feet high and at least two feet wide while supporting the massive archway monument raised up above it. Plus, even in mid-August, the limestone and cobblestone material of the *arc's* base was cool to the touch. As the skyline really began darkening, and nightfall came upon us, all the artistic glimmering of the monument, the city, and traffic lights began mesmerizing and wooing me into a slumbering, peaceful state. With my trusty sea bag spread out lengthways and used as a pillow, and *Pompeia* laying comfortably on my chest, I too stretched out to relax and enjoy the serene night...

The next thing I remember was being prodded by a gentle hand and a kind but firm voice calling out to me. "Monsieur, monsieur, vous devez vouslever et partir," a man spoke. "Vous ne pouvez pas dormir ici. C'est contre la loi." *Sir, sir, you must get up and leave. You cannot sleep here. It is against the law."*

"Hein?" I spoke out dreamily. "Oh, je suis vraiment desole," I collected my wits and continued. "Je ne voulais pas m'endormir. Je me reposais juste. La greve des compagnies aerogenes, et je n'nai ni argent ni endroit ou aller." *Huh? Oh, I am so sorry. I didn't mean to fall asleep. I was just resting. The airline strike, and I have no money or place to go."*

The nice voice, which I now recognized to come from a *Paris* policeman stood beside me with his hand out to help me down. "Leve-toi, s'il te plait," the soothing officer requested, "et viens avec moi." *Get up, please, and come with me.*

I quickly did as I was instructed. No problems with me. I needed no more issues. Following the police constable, however, was already a little alarming. With my bag over my shoulder and *Pompeia* huddled in my hand against my chest, we followed the policeman back across the wide boulevard and straight to one of the many opposing street corners. I noticed immediately by signs on the windows and door that the corner building was a local police precinct. Apparently, I was under arrest…

Once inside the building and office space, I quickly recognized the barred jails opposite the night sergeant's desk. The officer who had brought us in quickly filled out some paperwork and then gently encouraged me to follow him. He quickly walked directly past the first heavily barred jailcell, which at that hour only had one forlorn looking occupant, some unruly drunk, I imagined. The policeman then continued on to the next, adjacent jailcell, which was completely empty at that still relatively early hour.

The officer unlocked the jail door and held it open for me to enter and find a place to sit. I did as I was told, not knowing what to expect. However, at that time, I was so perplexed and still sleepy that I decided to let the morning, itself, figure out whatever was to happen to me and *Pompeia*. I was sorely exhausted, both mentally and physically, and I just sought more peaceful escape with slumber and dreams. I tossed my bag under the long, benchlike chair inside the jail cell, stretched out once again like at the *Arc de Triomphe*, and was soon soundly asleep. But I remained fully cognizant of any potential disturbances from incoming prisoners forced to share my cell…

Suddenly, however, the very same kind officer abruptly once again awakened me. He held his fingers to his lips and whispered, "Shhh! Viens avec moi. Prenez-les et allez tranquillement. Que Dieu vous benison et soyez prudent ou vous dormez." "*Shhh! Come with me. Take these and go quietly. God Bless You and be careful where you sleep.*"

As I prudently obeyed the policeman's orders and tiptoed after him, I realized that he had already prepared coffee and croissants for me to gratefully take along with me. I also could not help but notice that my jail cell had been left completely empty of any other cellmates. I had been left alone to have the cell only to myself. On-the-other-hand, the adjacent cell was literally packed and stacked with sleeping bodies piled one on top of the other.

It had obviously been a busy night for the patrolmen and jail attendants. After I had been enclosed in my cell, the officers-on-duty had obviously gone out of their way to not disturb me with their arrests and incarcerations. I was bewildered, dumbfounded, and then entirely appreciative of the policemen's kindnesses and extended considerations. I figured that they had analyzed my own situation and determined that I was no vagabond, or criminal-type, but just another lost soul stuck in the middle of that airline crisis.

Plus, *Pompeia* must have indirectly come to our rescue again too. "Any kid taking care of a tiny kitten couldn't be all bad," they must have assumed. On my way out the police station, the assisting police officer also gave me a container of fresh milk just for *Pompei*. All I could do upon exiting was bow while thanking them graciously, "Merci. Merci beaucoup. Merci. Au revoir."

After departing the police station and heading indirectly back down the *Champs-Elysees Avenue*, I shared *Pompeia's* milk with her and made a distinct and definitively new plan for our day. I decided not to spend more money and lost time for a bus to the airport where I would likely determine no new changes for my situation. I chose instead, to take matters into my own hands. I needed to talk directly to someone who was in charge of the whole damned mess.

After all, that was already the second day of my cataclysmic condition being abandoned by Trans World Airlines in the middle of *Paris*, France with no solutions or support for my next moves. I was without much money, a few dollars at most, and with no place to stay. I had already been picked up for vagrancy, had to spend a night, although decent enough, inside a kindly jail cell, but then still released to the same predicament as before. It was not right. None of it.

TWA owed me, and bigtime. They could not just let a client of theirs, a valued customer, and a youthful minor at that, just wallow in the expensive streets of *Paris* all alone and forsaken. Oh, no they couldn't. I would see to it… That, or I'd end up getting tossed in jail again, and that next time would likely be for really disturbing the peace…

"Listen to ME, TWA!"

After a few inquiries from several smaller, local businesses there in downtown, *Paris* France, I was able to locate the actual European Headquarters of Trans World Airlines. I should have guessed. It was one of those gigantic, skyscrapers crowding the entire downtown metropolis, and it was one of the tallest buildings I had noticed many times before for its enormous height, but not its occupancy. In only a matter of minutes, I had climbed the entry steps of the TWA Central Headquarters and was standing right there outside and before its enormous, glass-doored entranceway.

With *Pompeia* held snugly within my palm and firmly against my chest once again, that time I stood motionless for a few seconds taking several deep breaths helping to hyperventilate myself into an agitated condition. Then, after roughly formulating a mental strategy, and with my sea bag hoisted onto my shoulder, I used my other arm to burst open the large glass entrance door and storm into the building screaming at the top of my lungs.

"I want my airplane ride home!" I bellowed. "I want it right now! I am penniless and starving! I have no place to sleep. I got arrested last night for vagrancy!"

True, I exaggerated a little bit for effect, but that was my purpose. I wasn't done there and then, however. I knew I had to continue with my outraged claims until someone took steps to stop me. I continued.

"Get me a plane right now!" I screamed. "I want to go home! I should have gone home three days ago, and now I am starving with no place to sleep. Take me home now!"

The entire staff of that office building immediately knew they had a mini-crisis predicament on their hands. Yet, none of them had simple answers for my questions nor resolve for any of my issues. In only a moment, though, two security guards from opposite ends of the entry lobby moved swiftly toward me with goals likely to contain and/or restrain me. In another moment, an executive-looking fellow quickly signaled another office attendant to get on a phone. There was definitely anxious activity spawned by the loudness and tension from my voice.

Swiftly, that same executive rounded the corner from behind their front reception counter and came rushing over to me while waving off the two security guards. Smiling broadly, he extended a welcoming hand to me, and as he pointed to a nearby hallway with his other arm, he politely requested that I please calm down and follow him to an elevator. He stated that he wished to take me to see someone else who might surely assist me. Or at least he was wisely managing to get me away from the lobby and public clientele area. I was not good for appearances sake or business.

I wasn't about to let up my stage act, however. I had my audience on the edges of their seats, and I was not about to let up with the tension. I picked up my sea bag, though, and holding *Pompeia* tightly, continued with my barrage of anxiety-ridden accusations demanding that something be done immediately to assist with my apocalyptic conditions. The TWA, main-floor executive kept trying to calm me down, but I kept up my tour-de-force affront on their pathetic and irresponsible treatment of dependent traveler clients.

After many upward floors, and with me continuing my huffing and puffing trying to maintain my hypertension, we came to what seemed to be the top, or next to the very top, floor. A hurried walk down a nicely decorated executive corridor, and the agent quickly opened-up wide, double doors to the "Vice-President of International Relations." The large sign on the entrance door's front read as much.

No matter, I followed the agent inside an office suite wasting no time as I continued even louder with my outraged anguish at TWA's irresponsible treatment of its abandoned travelers. I dropped my sea bag at my feet and let my new observer, and supposed VP Assistant or Secretary, have both barrels of my torrential and angry outpouring.

As the floor agent excused himself, while backing out and closing the office doors behind him, I could not help but notice the absolutely spectacular view from the top of that executive suite. Far off in the distance, I could easily see *la tour Eiffel*, and down from it, *la cathedrale Notre-Dame*. The city's expansive view was nothing short of brilliant. However, TWA's service to its dependent customers fell far shorter, and I let that Vice-President's aide know all about it.

In only a few seconds, in walked yet another executive with a rather concerned look on his face as he approached me. "This must be the boss," I told myself. "Okay, well he's going to hear directly from me now!"

"Young man, Sir," he faintly smiled, "What seems to be the problem?"

"How can you do this to your customers?" I started on him with my rampage, "We buy round-trip tickets from you in good faith and honor, and we expect to be treated with the same good faith and honor. You have stranded me far from my home in San Francisco. I have no money and no place to stay now. I even got arrested last night for vagrancy! *Vagrancy!* I was put in jail right along with thieves, and burglars, and drunks, and prostitutes! How can you do this to someone? I want to go home now!"

I never even let the poor sap have a moment to interrupt my angry address. I let him have all the anguished facts I could think of as I pronounced my grievances and postulated my worrisome conditions. True, I lied a bit about the jailtime, but he did not need to know the real truth; the truth about the *Paris* jailers and how they had actually been great. But I did mention again the part about the jail, itself, being filled with all sorts of anti-socials. Though, I wasn't sure, for sure. Maybe they were actually all kind, decent, and misunderstood individuals. However, my version made for good fodder.

Finally, after pausing to take another deep breath in order to continue with my assault on TWA's management, the VP used calming and expressive words attempting to relax me and bring me to a negotiable state. After offering me a glass of water, he asked me to sit down… "and calm down, please." He smiled oddly at my little *Pompeia,* who was likely frightened out of her little mind.

"Please, young man," he began soothingly, "I am so sorry about your predicament. If there had been anything we could have done to help you, we surely would have."

"Baloney!" I roared, "Your people just scoffed me away at the airport when I went there to catch my flight home. Your plane, my flight, was my absolute next meal, and all they could do was apologize and send me on my way. My cat and I are starving now with no place to go and no money to do it with, anyway. We got rudely thrown in jail last night for vagrancy and sleeping on the streets, for crying-out-loud! What are we supposed to do?"

"It's a terrible situation, I know," he comforted. "But I have a solution, if only a temporary one. Would you allow me to help you?"

"How?" I pretended to nearly cry. "What can you do for me? There are no flights, and I need to go home. I have college starting very soon."

"Well, young man, although it is true we have no flights just now, that may change any day soon. Would $100 cash help to satisfy your needs temporarily?"

"Oh, okay," I responded unevenly while grinning like a Cheshire cat inside at the amazing offer. That'll help, but I still need a flight home as soon as possible."

"Just keep checking-in with the TWA Ticket Counter at the airport, even daily if you can. Here is their phone number, too," he wrote down the number for me as he also opened a desk drawer and carefully began counting out $100 in small bills.

I casually took the money from him but never let him believe I was satisfied. It was one of those proletariat-bourgeoisie, or labor-management negotiations, and I would never give him the upper-hand. We separated, not as friends, but with me temporarily mollified but expecting much better treatment in the future.

"Please contact me in the future if you have any further problems, Sir," the VP lied without offering his personal business card. "We are here to help."

"Yeah? Well, this helps," I stated blandly holding up the cash and then abruptly stuffing it into my jean's pocket, "but I still need a flight. You can really help by getting me a plane home. You owe me that. I'll be at Orly again tomorrow. You can bet on it, and every day thereafter too, until I go home."

With that, I ushered myself out the VP's office and hurried down the hall to the waiting elevator. As soon as I entered its opened doors, I looked around for any cameras spying on me. Seeing none, and as soon as the doors closed, I started dancing a happy little jig singing, "*Pompeia*, tonight we're gonna celebrate! Tonight, we get a feast to stuff ourselves. Plus, we're going back to our favorite home, the *Left Bank Hotel*."

Upon leaving the TWA Headquarters office building there in *Central Paris*, and with my head held indignantly high, I was feeling a little better than when entering. My overripened anxieties had been relaxed, if not removed, for the time being. Yet, with reasonably supportive funds now in my pocket, much more than any I had previously held while budgeting for any brief portions of my entire journey thus far, I still held a degree of uncertainty in my mind. I still had no idea how long it would take before I would have my unscheduled return home to America, to California, to San Francisco, and to my dearest, hometown community of Brownsville. I still did not know just how much longer my supposedly *ended journey* would be *extended*.

Buying Time

To get that next phase started, however, during our "Waiting-Period," I kept my word to *Pompeia*, and we headed directly back to the *Left Bank Hotel*. I really needed to get cleaned up, clean up *Pompeia*, clean my jacket pocket again, and most importantly, drop-off my sea bag for temporary storage. Throughout and after the entire ordeal at *Orly Airport*, my sea bag had begrudgingly been dragged along when I had expected to have already been ridden of it. Then came all the downtown walking, the *Arc de Triomphe* "resting" error, the overnight *Paris* jailing, the stress attack (my *stress attacking* them) at the TWA Headquarters, and finally our hike back to the *Left Bank Hotel*, where I was returning once again. During all those episodes, my sea bag had become an enormous and burdensome extra weight to manage.

By that time, my sea bag, with all my personal effects and journey possessions inside, was supposed to have already been dropped off with TWA. In fact, we would have likely *already* been en route back home, at that particular time, if not arrived home already. The whole debacle was frustrating and worrisome, to say the least. Nevertheless, trying to stay positive forced me to walk straight to the hotel, check in, take care of matters, and then plan for another visit to *Orly Airport* early the next morning. Hopefully, we'd hear some positive words about a soon-to-be homecoming.

The trip to *Orly Airport* would also mean a relaxed break for *Pompeia* from me, and vice-versa. She could rest on our hotel room bed in my absence; and without responsibility for her, and for that cumbersome sea bag hanging on my shoulder, I could strut about as light as a… kitten… or *kitten less*! However, during that first night, after checking-in, we both did get cleaned up, eat dinner, rest, and enjoy the remainder of the afternoon and evening. That night we both fell soundly asleep too.

Early the next morning brought a quick solo trip to *Orly Airport* for me, where I went directly to that same TWA Ticket Counter. Once again, the officials still provided no new insight or hope for any potential resolve. "Nobody knew nothin'," like the saying goes.

"What anybody does know, or thinks, though, would probably fill volumes," I thought while grumbling and mumbling to myself. "But nobody is talking, no matter what." All I could do was "keep-on-keepin'-on" and check-in regularly with those TWA ticket counter folks.

So, I just made further plans to see them again during the upcoming days. Apparently, it was going to be like visiting an unemployment office looking for part-time work: I would seek prospects early every morning when checking-in for potential flights (jobs). Then, when and if something became available, I would run like crazy back to the hotel, get all my stuff and *Pompeia (tools)*, and race back to the airport just in time to catch that elusive airplane *(job)..., and go to work (home)*, come hell or high water.

In the meantime, after the bus ride back into *Paris*, and a brief stop at a market, it became necessary and important to purchase a couple absolutely timely and useful items... like some real kitten chow, more milk, and a bottle of wine. After all, we both deserved a little reward for having survived panic attacks far that long a time already. We may have been stranded there in *Paris,* but then *Pompeia* and I were not broke any more. We could get by for a little while longer. I just wished I could make up a better plan than just wait, and wait, and...

Climbing High

Well, one thing was for certain. At least we could enjoy ourselves to some degree. By the way, re-checking into the *Left Bank Hotel* was sort of a reunion, you might say. Ol' stick-in-the-mud (Charles was his name), Hotel Concierge, Head Clerk, and Chief Bottle Washer, was there again, and he remembered me, even if he didn't like it. Actually, to his credit, he was in a much better mood having returned from his own lengthy vacation to the *French Riviera*.

However, I took no chances in his presence, or with his attitude, so *Pompeia* remained snugly in my pocket during hotel registration. It went easily on a day-by-day arrangement, and Charles even seemed to be sympathetic to my circumstances. Although not taking any time inquiring about his glorious holiday, nor sharing any details of my own, regardless, I remained polite to him and continued hoping for his reciprocated considerations.

Anyway, when I returned from *Orly Airport* later that morning, and after feeding *Pompeia* again with her agreeable soft and meaty kitten chow and more milk, I tucked her back into my light jacket pocket until we were back out on the street. Once outside and with *Pompeia* hoisted back upon my shoulder, the two of us headed out for an afternoon of exploration and relaxation. Soon, we stopped for me to fill up on a nice lunch of salad and pasta of some sorts. I still had my bottle of wine with me, so I made plans to sip on that in a nearby park while we enjoyed all the friendly and bright city sights.

Another wonderful thing about *Paris* is that one does not have to travel far to find a nice parklike setting. Parks seemed to be nearly everywhere and were filled with elegant statues and beautiful, artistic sculptures placed appropriately on corners and within the squares, themselves. With *Pompeia* on my shoulder for her secure ride, and for sake of all those excitable youngsters and observant spectators, we were awarded plenty opportunities to share her cuteness and our past's awkward and difficult circumstances to whatever degrees and with whomever was curious.

Quickly, as soon as *Pompeia* was noticed by a child or its parent, the barrage of insensitive inquiries began. I had to continuously maintain my protective posture while being as courteous and polite as necessary under the circumstances. Our interactions, however, often went like the following:

"Oh, quel joli chaton!" most squealing began. " Ou l'avez-vous obtenu?" *Oh, what a cute kitten! Where did you get it?*

"A *Rome*," I would usually respond, "lorsque nous sommes revenus ici pour rentrer chez nous a San Francisco." *In Rome, when we returned here to return home to San Francisco but got stranded by the airline strike*"

"Ahhh, San Francisco. Comme c'est gentil! Oh quelle honte. Mon enfant peut-il le tenir?" *Ah, San Francisco. How nice! Oh, what a shame. Can my child hold it?*

"Non, je suis desole'," I would retort very composed, "mais ce ne serait pas sans danger pour le chaton." *No, I am sorry, but that would not be safe for the kitten*"

Typically, after that, all brief interactions would quickly end. Either they would depart shortly for their own continued activities, or *Pompeia* and I would continue with our walk. Soon, however, the next visual contact and expected formidable exchange would take place. It was nice, though, but I never allowed *Pompeia to* leave my own personal, direct control. Her safety was my absolute responsibility and accountability. Kids are delightful, inquisitive, and ever so loving, but they can instantly become dangerous. Especially if two or more want to play with an infant kitten at the same time:

"I want to hold it!" one controlling child might yell.

"No, me! It's my turn!" demanded another. "Give it to me now!... Let... me... have... it!"

I imagined wise King Solomon's decision for the two arguing mothers who both demanded rights to the newborn child: "I shall cut the baby in half and give you each one portion to share..."

"Aaaahhh! Oh, no!" I'd have screamed at the deviant children. "Not on my watch! This wise king is going to keep his baby all to himself, thank you very much. Beat it, Brats!"

We continued on through the nice park and eventually found a comfortable, empty bench to sit upon, relax in relative seclusion, and I had opportunity to open my bottle of wine. It was yet another nice, ruby red, cheap brand. Fortunately, I had splurged for a corkscrew because my pocket-knife would have likely been a disastrous mess. Soon, I was slurping away straight from the upended bottle, and with each swig, I toasted another of our recent moments of good fortune.

"Here's to: Getting back to *Paris*." Gulp. "Here's to: *Pompeia's* girlhood!" Guzzle, guzzle! "Here's to: The nice *Paris* Police." Swallow, swallow, swallow! "Here's to: TWA's free money!" Swig, swig, swig, swig!

I would likely have kept on boasting and toasting more events worth mentioning, like the *Left Bank Hotel* reunion, but the bottle was empty. And so was my brain, it felt, as I was getting very light-headed. So much that I figured I could probably just float to the top of a nearest, tall, statuesque-bronze sculpture of some famous French celebrity, maybe even Napoleon, himself, that decorated that *Paris* park that afternoon

Frankly, I do not recall clearly, nor remember much of what happened immediately following, nor does it matter much. But apparently, all that concerned me back then at that moment was climbing abreast that big monument, sitting upon his shoulders, and shouting out to all *Parisian* passersby about my unfortunate misfortunes and circumstances, but also offering my undying love of *Paris*, regardless. I did love them all, even if most of them refused to speak English to me.

"Thash, okay," I burped, "'cause I'll jush shpeak *Francais* to all of yous, inshtead, from way up here, an' yous won need to anshwer me in Eenglush…"

Eventually and somehow, I managed to get back down from that illustrious, and hopefully undamaged, statue with *Pompeia* probably clinging desperately, but still safely, upon my shoulder. I also survived not breaking my neck climbing down from that monumentally high view of *Paris.* And perhaps most importantly, I slipped off that sculpture without ever being seen by, or reported to, police officials, who would likely have quasi-arrested me again and forced me to sleep-it-off yet one more time in their city jail.

Later on, when soberly considering my previously foolish antics, I understood sensibly that during a second night in that *Paris* jail, I would probably not have been provided similar luxuries or favors of seclusion within my own cell. Rather, I'd have been jammed inside a cell with half of all *Paris's* other foolish riffraff of counter-productive anti-socials. Then again, *Pompeia* really was cute… No matter, we left the park area and returned to our hotel room unscathed. We knew full well, however, that we would both just need to continue wasting time, but we must do so in orderly, civil, and sober states-of-mind while waiting for something ideal to happen for the two of us…

It was a day-by-day situation, and we were to fill in our days with varying but acceptable, if not boring, activities until finally being told that our special *day* had ultimately arrived. In the meantime, we just found reasonable things to occupy ourselves: We paid daily fare for our hotel accommodations; we purchased varying, but reasonable, nutritional items from stores and restaurants that suited us both; and we spent occasional francs on whatever else came up for our needs. We were just *buying time* with TWA temporary financial credit.

Van Gogh Museum

Naturally, we both made daily trips out to Orly Airport to check on our flight conditions. Our mundane journeys with TWA staff's humdrum responses eventually stretched out to every other day, but my anxiety levels, when conversing with those TWA ticket agents, never lessened. I remained a desperate client as far as any of them were concerned. I even believed that some employees may have been directed to watch out for me by officials from TWA's, Headquarters, if not the VP, himself. It was fair to say that those Orly Airport TWA staff certainly recognized me, knew my predicament, and were usually congenial, if not helpful.

I even imagined TWA Management's watchful, studious, and concerned instructions, "Hey, keep an eye out for that young kid. He owes us money."

In between bus rides to the airport, several days were spent on long, leisurely walks along and across *la Seine*. We also strolled up the *Champs-Elysees Avenue* and made additional visits to the huge, surrounding park of *la tour Eiffel*. Also, further trips took us to look again upon the magnificence of *la cathedrale Notre-Dame* and *l'Arc de Triomphe*. Besides, splendid, and amazing architecture was everywhere any visitor turned while touring that fantastic city. Art exhibits, galleries, museums, wonderful building structures, and fancy shops lined all of *Paris's* marvelous streets.

Furthermore, an inexpensive, and almost daily treat was riding on *Paris's* extraordinary and colorful bus system. Although refraining from using its subways, or any further underground explorations, *Pompeia* and I got our aboveground fill of many streets and destinations of *Parisian* routes. It was a certainty that any routed bus would eventually end up right back where we climbed aboard. Also, the drivers were all truly kind and supportive. Even when we returned from approaching directions, usually the driver of the very spot would inform me where we climbed on in the first place. It was a cheap and entertaining way to see the city.

Perhaps, people wonder about, or are curious regarding, that peculiarly friendly zone I first visited while passing through, during my initial visit and leaving *Paris* the first time. Well, I'd be lying if I denied thoughts never crossed my mind reconsidering another visit with those *friendly, working girls*. However, even if I had substantial funds in my pocket, although they were petering out steadily (perhaps a poor choice of words, I must admit), but nevertheless, I had distanced myself from such prospects.

In a matter of days, hopefully, I would be back home and visiting with the love of my life. I no longer even remotely considered disloyal behavior or toyed with thoughts that might tarnish our relationship. I wanted a clear conscience to share with her and no betrayals to muck up our reuniting. Those previous, behavioral back-stepping's had been honest, emotionally warping, mental mistakes. After I had become overwhelmed, I still ended up remaining uncommitted, and with only a momentary mislaid deed of near unconscious lust with Monique. After all, she had literally and figuratively drained me of all reasonable sensibilities, and I had no longer been myself. Love or lust, I learned in time, can do that.

For my final days in *Paris*, however, I promised to remind myself daily just how much in love I was with my sweetheart back home. Although *Paris* was such a romantic city in so many aspects, and the *City of Love*, to boot, it would only serve to remind me how desperately in love I already was. Besides, I had *Pompeia,* a truly faithful friend, to keep me company and focused. We had many stories to share already with others, and certainly more yet to come. Of that I was unassured at the time, but it became even more evident as time progressed.

Then one special afternoon, on one of our daily strolling adventures, *Pompeia* was straddled, of course, atop my shoulder as we patrolled past many beautiful, older, wonderful buildings, homes, and edifices along any of *Paris's* incredible streets. It was by complete accident that I stopped to read a simple sign while passing by yet another interesting mansion which was practically connected to others on both its neighboring adjacent sides. After only brief moments of reading, I realized that the mansion before us was none other than a unique museum dedicated to only Vincent Van Gogh and his art.

I was immediately intrigued and interested. That innocently found *Vincent Van Gogh Museum* would be an absolute necessity to visit by anyone's art-loving standards. So, up we went past two flights of access steps to the entrance door. Once inside, we were met by a cordial lady who smilingly accepted my entry fee and then pointed the way up an immediate stairwell to the upper floors. I took the first level of steps, and then I turned to present myself to the next remaining stairs to the second floor…

Above those steps, and all aligned evenly on a viewing wall directly before me, were obvious and spectacular works of art by Van Gogh, himself. I was electrified. Then the balance of that entire floor, and the next one beyond, were all beautifully designed to show off the incredible talent of that artist from the Neo-Impressionist Period. At that time, I knew little of what that meant in artistic terminology. However, I did fully understand and appreciate that I had accidentally been given a most beautiful and opportune visit of a lifetime. To this day, Vincent Van Gogh still stands among my very favorite artists of all time. For *impressions* that last a lifetime, I duly believe "There is something to be said about 'Being There.'"

Similar to my initial viewing of Da Vinci's greatest work, *Mona Lisa*, in *la Louvre*, many other visits had left their extraordinary marks on my memory. Other unique sights had impressed me too. The Soviet Union's evil catastrophe of the *Berlin Wall* and *Checkpoint Charlie* were one example. The magnificent frescoes and ancient artifacts in the *Prada Museum* in Madrid were yet memorable also. Then there was Michelangelo's fantastic sculpture of *The David* in *Florence*, and his brilliant masterpieces on the ceiling of the *Sistine Chapel* in *Vatican* City that truly took my breath away. Finally, there, and right then once again in *Paris,* were some of Vincent Van Gogh's finest works, if only copies, for anyone to visit up close and personal. Every show was awe inspiring. My entire summer had been filled with artistic and thoughtful magic.

Orly Conniption Fits

Steadily, however, days passed and my funds diminished. I was being relatively frugal, but money simply had a curious way of vanishing. So, with mild stress beginning to rebuild due to fear of soon becoming broke again, I modified our daily game plan once more With *Pompeia* on my shoulder, we began returning more frequently to *Orly Airport* and the ticket counter of TWA. It was no lie or accident that I was honestly becoming more anxiety ridden.

Days passed into a week and then nearly two. My extra-long stay in *Paris* was becoming ridiculous to me. What was I supposed to do once my tentative funds completely ran out again? Was I expected to run amuck inside the TWA Headquarters once more? I did not have that energy still left inside. The initial tantrum incident was all anger, frustration, and stress related. That effect might not work again. After all, $100 was a lot of money.

No, I needed to be directly there at *Orly Airport* and begin demanding that TWA do something for me right there and then immediately. I literally could not keep going on the way I had been. *Pompeia* and I needed to camp there, ourselves, and right in front of that TWA ticket counter within clear view of all TWA's staff.

My nasty stares would eventually become burning glares making them all uneasy. My repetitive inquiries would eventually become tedious, demanding questioning causing everyone burn-out and tension disorders, themselves. It was a consequential matter of personal survival that had evolved rapidly into a behavior pattern illustrating and demonstrating my angst and dreadfully stressed belief: "The squeakiest wheel would get the oil."

The staff began keeping a close eye on me. When any of them noticed I was making my way toward their counter, I could tell that their previously faked busyness, due to minimal clientele, ceased, and personnel quickly scattered to use restrooms, or some errand far off. The slowest, or last staff member left standing, had to deal with my interrogations. And I was getting more unpleasant as each day progressed.

Final days arrived when I just started barking demands while deliberately working myself up into daily tizzies. I repeated over and over my growing stages of destitution. I even begged them to consider *Pompeia's* health and well-being. Later on, I often thought that had I been just a little more pleasant, perhaps some of those employees would have allowed me to stay in their homes while I waited for a miracle's transition. But I wanted no one's charity, other than little things for *Pompeia*, perhaps. TWA's funds were strictly business and did not count in my mind. They owed me that support.

It was only a matter of those last few days there that my presence was becoming a threat to their own sanctity, a real thorn in their sides, a heavier burden upon their backs, and a noose around their necks. My funds were desperately running out thanks to expensive airport food prices, and I complained about that too. Perhaps I had become the greatest nuisance among all of TWA's many stranded tragedies. Maybe the staff just determined that something had to change, if for no other reason than to finally just get rid of me.

It seemed obvious that I was not good for their positive business outlook. I certainly was no good for those employees' mental and emotional health either. After two whole long weeks had passed since my own, regular flight had been scheduled to depart, and I had been physically stranded there in *Paris* without an immediate back-up plan, none of us, not the TWA Staff nor I, were in good spirits seeing each other. It was simple: They needed me gone. And believe me, I wanted *to be gone* too. Simple.

PART FOUR

Going Home

CHAPTER 19

··

CAT'S MEOW

Shoebox Solution

I t was perhaps because of my persistent and continuously annoying check-ins at that *Orly Airport* TWA Ticket Counter that ultimately brought on a brand-new reality check for me. Under all that pressure over the airline strike, no one before had ever informed me of a serious issue that I was likely to face. *I could not board any aircraft just holding a pet in my hands or pocket even though it was fully registered and permittable.* I was informed that if authorities realized I was attempting such, they would have my pet confiscated at the gates, or I would be denied boarding. I was required to have reasonably safe shelter for my pet in order to carry it onto any aircraft.

"Oh, for crying-out-loud!" I whined. I was instantly smacked upside the head by yet another unprepared-for predicament. What could I possible do about protecting *Pompeia* while stuck at an airport? Immediately I began running through the terminal past airport shops looking for such pet-carrying devices. Soon I found several, but the luggage-type, pet-carrier prices were outrageous, and nothing I could even remotely afford.

Sure, in my emotionally stressed state-of-mind, I admit that under those circumstances, I even imagined swiping something from an airline shop and then running like hell to get away. However, that notion fell very flat and very quickly because I despised theft of any condition. That included lying too, so if questioned, I would have to tell the truth. However, under certain situations, there were always exceptions, *exceptions* for *exceptional* circumstances. I also passionately believed that embellishing the truth, or avoiding certain unnecessary particulars, like omitting some truth, was also acceptable, but only when appropriate. And I would always be the judge of that. After all, that's what acting was all about…

Then, suddenly as I raced down the long, wide airport shopping complex, I spotted a certain store, got a bright idea, and stopped to check out the possibilities. It was a shoe store, and I imagined that a nice shoe box filled appropriately with tissue lining would be an excellent shelter for a small kitten. The store clerk I visited was extremely agreeable, and in only a few minutes, I was fixed up with someone else's discarded shoe box. Instantly, it became the new temporary home for *Pompeia, hopefully,* for the remainder of our airport travels.

For that time being, our next immediate crisis was resolved. Now I could return to the TWA ticket counter and not be concerned over *Pompeia* anymore. No more worries, anyway, until the next time. And any *next time* would definitely be judged as a major, worrisome concern. But, for the time being, I was temporarily at ease and just waiting and praying for those TWA people to give us some decent news. In the meantime, at least for that coming night we could find our common bench seat again and try to sleep off some of the weariness.

Rescue

"Monsieur….. Daniel! Monsieur…. Daniel! Please… wake up and come with me!"

At the same time as I felt a prodding on my shoulders and an urgent voice softly calling my name, far off in the distance somewhere I vaguely even heard my name being spoken out lightly over the airport's loudspeaker system. "M..o..n..s..i..e..u..r D..a..n..i..e..l…, please come to TWA's ticket counter immediately… Monsieur Daniel…"

At first, my name commotion was all being rudely mixed into vivid dreams about chasing after cars, and trains, and planes. I struggled trying to push away the unwanted disturbance. But the awkward disruptions continued, and I was gradually brought roughly to consciousness.

"Huh? What's the matter?" I groggily spoke out. "Where's *Caesar,* I mean *Pompeia*?" After quickly leaning over from the bench I had been completely asleep upon, I immediately checked inside the shoe box that I had been carrying around for the past two days. Having placed it protectively underneath me, I relaxed and breathed, "Okay, good, she's right here in her home. So, huh, what's wrong? What do you want?"

"Monsieur Daniel," the male person repeated, "please come with me. We have a flight for you. You must hurry and check-in your bag. The plane is leaving soon. Please come with me."

I was still somewhat in a daze, but the words, "…a flight for you," instantly became emblazoned upon my thought processing.

I did not pause to ask any questions. I reached down and grabbed *Pompeia's* shoe box, then hoisted my sea bag up high onto my shoulder and was quickly ready for a dead run to wherever that man wanted. Staying right on the attendant's heels, I followed him straight on down past other airline counters until we arrived at one named, Air France Airlines. Apparently, they were the company rescuing me, and I was not about to question anyone or anything's *rescue* attempt.

That last interaction I had with TWA was likely the *straw-that-broke-the-camel's-back*, I figured. I had whined about being hungry and broke. I had even complained about poor *Pompeia* not having any milk unless I took it from abandoned tables. I protested the airport's expensive food prices and being unable to afford anything, thus forcing me to sneak off with others' leftover meal remains, yet again, in order to ease my hunger. Finally, I emphasized how tired I was from sleeping there at the airport night after night, instead of in a nice, comfortable hotel bed because I could not even afford a cheap one.

Obviously, the TWA counter staff had already heard every negative report I could possibly dish out to them. No doubt they must have been nearly as stressed as I, having lived through my hardships, because they had been forced to hear relentless reminders of them all. Something had to give, and maybe that previous tortuous evening being obliged to listen yet again to me complain still more was finally the proverbial *straw that broke TWA's back.* Finally, they had figured out a rescue mission for me, and I was being awakened from my relaxed slumber to "Respondez s'il vous plait!"

Staying right behind the TWA agent, I rushed up to the Air France Ticket Counter and thrust my passport before the watchful, but hurried, clerk. He took my sea bag from me, posted some tag information on it, and quickly tossed it onto the baggage conveyor belt behind him. Then, the same agent typed some more information, jotted down additional data on another sheet of paper, and handed the whole paperwork slew over to me, along with my passport.

The TWA Assistant, who had guided me thus far through the hurried registration and ticketing process, once again took over and mostly repeated himself, "Monsieur Daniel, hurry and follow me. Your flight is waiting for you."

As the assistant all but dragged me off toward the Departing Flight Gates, the Air France Ticket Agent called out hastily and unevenly, "Your bag…gage… will… fol… you… Re…mem… Chi…ca…go……."

Off we went in another whirlwind of activity. For the second official time during my entire summer's journey, I was again without my trusted sea bag. The *first* time had been when I came to Europe through TWA originally. Now, Air France had been entrusted with my luggage and life's possessions. Regarding *Pompeia*, she had been a sleeping angel so far, obviously really enjoying her shoebox home. Fortunately, that earlier evening I had fed her before lying down for a remaining night's sleep.

Nevertheless, I had *Pompeia* inside her shoebox and tucked snugly under my arm. I was completely focused while following my guide to my departure zone destination. A minute later, we were being hastily ushered through flight customs with brief instructions from my French TWA guide to boarding agents that I was holding up an entire flight. *Pompeia* remained peacefully asleep through it all.

Shoebox and all, I was then practically shoved through gaps of other dawdling travelers while being pressed on toward my own already emptied gate. Then I was all but thrust upon Air France agents at my new departing flight gate. Brief words were exchanged between them, and that was where my guide practically took his first breath since waking me. It was also where he took his leave and bid me adieu, "Good luck and bon voyage, Monsieur Daniel. It has been difficult for you, but we at TWA are all glad you are going…"

"Thank you. Thank you. You have no idea how much this means to me either. Tell everyone that I am sorry if I seemed too unpleasant, but now that I am finally going to eat again on this flight, I shall survive."

I was then rushed past their Air France Departing Gate counter and out some doors to the runway leading to an awaiting Air France aircraft. For some reason, which was also when I finally abruptly paused and focused on what was essentially happening, I became aware of my circumstances. Feeling very puzzled over my situation, I wanted to stop, rustle through my paperwork, scan its pages, and attempt settling a big question: "Where was I going?"

An airline stewardess was standing at the foot of boarding steps climbing up to the airplane's entry door, and she motioned for me to hurry and board quickly. I did, and another stewardess quickly showed me to my vacant seat. I could have cut all the drama in the air with a dull knife when noting the multitude of hardline stares coming at me in all directions from those delayed flight passengers. Apparently, they were more than slightly annoyed at my inexcusable behavior which, in their minds, had caused the flight to be temporarily hindered.

I had an aisle seat, and quickly apologized to my seat mates, "I am so sorry for any inconvenience. Only a few minutes ago, I was sound asleep…"

"Harrumph!" came an immediate response from the lady sitting beside me. "What an excuse! Why weren't you paying better attention? Sleeping! I dare say that is very immature."

"Yes, Mam," I hurtfully attempted to explain, "but a minute before that I was left stranded here by TWA at the airport for two weeks. There were no flights to go home. Finally, just now a man awakened me from my sleep and told me to hurry here for this flight. Honestly, I still don't even know what's going on."

That bit of information created some sympathetic awareness in the lady's eyes, and she slowly began acknowledging difficulties out of my control and her potential erroneous leap to conclusions. However, people can sometimes be slow to accept or admit when they are wrong. Often they need further prodding until venturing forth any appropriately due apologies. Yet, as far as any of the other airline passengers were concerned, I should just as likely have been swiftly beheaded with a French Guillotine to make up for their annoyances.

Still, that was when I gathered up enough courage to politely ask of the lady and her apparent gentleman companion, "Excuse me, but can you tell me where this flight is going?"

"What? You're kidding?" the gentleman spoke up. "You mean they didn't even tell you where you were going?"

I immediately got extremely nervous. For all I really knew, TWA had tried so desperately to get rid of me that they chose to stick me on a flight going back to *Berlin*. Or maybe it was even going to Moscow. Serve me right, I imagined. I really had no idea, though. Everything had happened so quickly. But I politely, if not meekly responded, "No, Sir. Like I said, everything went in a blur, and here I am. Maybe, they did tell me something, but I was so rushed that I didn't even hear what they said."

"Well, young man," the lady interjected, "this flight is going to Montreal, Canada and then on to Chicago, Illinois. Isn't that where you want to go?"

'Well, Mam," I explained, "TWA was supposed to send me home to San Francisco, California. If this flight gets me to America, though, I am fine with that. I can hitch hike the rest of the way back home easy."

"Hitch hike?" the amused man laughed. "You think you're going to hitch hike all the way from Chicago to San Francisco? Hah! Give me a break!"

"Well, Sir," I began indignantly, "I just spent the entire summer hitching all over Europe from *Paris* to *Denmark,* to *Barcelona,* and then *Rome,* and then returning to *Paris* through *Vienna,* and just in time for the airline strike. I think I can manage an easy little hop, skip, and jump once I'm back in the States." Then, because I was on an Air France Airliner, I became sort of braggadocio, "Besides, everyone speaks English back home, et je n'ai plus besoin de parler francais ou quoi que ce soit d'autre." …and *I don't need to speak French, or anything else, anymore.*

At that point, I opened up my flight papers and took a closer look at what had just transpired back in the terminal. For a moment I even calculated whether I should hold up everything, jump off that Canadian flight, and wait for another better one later on. Nope, too late, I rationalized. My baggage is already on its way home, so I am too…, and besides, so is *Pompeia* on her way to her new home.

Studying my flight papers more closely, though, I realized the incredible modifications TWA and Air France had made for my return flight: I was first going to Montreal, Quebec, Canada; then, after remaining on that plane, I would continue on to Chicago, Illinois; after going through USA Customs in Chicago, I would next board another Air France flight to San Diego, California; then after disembarking there, I would catch another short hopper to LA International Airport; and finally, the next day, I'd catch yet another journey ending, return flight to San Francisco.

"No wonder I had been stuck in *Paris* so long," I thought to myself. "It had taken TWA two weeks just to plan and organize those separate, return-home flights for me." It was that, or I imagined that they were finally getting even with me by ridding themselves of me once-and-for-all by sending me home on a perilous mission forcing me to try and find my way.

If I got lost forever, then they could always flatly deny wrongdoing and state, "Hey, we did our best under his horrendous circumstances. He just wasn't up to the task!"

"Oh, but I *am* up to it," I imaginatively cursed. "Just get me going," I muttered defensively, "and I'm already there! Hello, Home Sweet Home! Here I come!" Well, almost, I figured. Soon, hopefully, barring no unforeseen difficulties, that is...

Surprise Passenger

Once the airplane had lifted and we were finally air born, a huge sense of relief came over me. I was okay then. I was on my way back home. Since my new flight plans had sunk in, and I understood them, I even got a little excited. I was going to eventually be flying straight into Los Angeles. That was where my girlfriend lived. It would be easy to call another friend to pick me up at the airport there and help me with a terrific, sudden surprise visit with Sue.

After an entire summer apart, what a great way to reunite with her with a bombshell surprise stopover. I missed her very much and had so much to share with her about my summer's exploits. Of course, some incidents like those from *Costa Brava Castle Hostel*, or *Horney Hostel,* would remain anonymous. It was like still telling the truth but just omitting some unnecessary details that might simply muddle up matters. After all, I wasn't in a courtroom swearing my testimony to be "the whole truth and nothing but the truth." It wasn't necessary. No sense going there at all, for Sue's sake, or mine...

Refocused after fully underway during that flight to Montreal, I decided that it was time to give *Pompeia* some fresh air. She had been miraculous so far during the boarding, although I did have all her necessary documents available to reassure any flight personnel. Her shoe box had been nestled under the seat in front of me, as per instructions for takeoff. I gently lifter the box and set it on my lap.

My curious, seat-sharing gentleman acquaintance quickly had words with which to comment. "Gee, young fellow," he attempted a bit of self-amusement, "you mean you have carried an extra pair of shoes with you for your sore feet all over Europe too? Ha! Ha!"

I didn't bother responding to his snide remark. Instead, I let my actions do my talking. I lifted the lid, reached carefully into the shoe box, and brought *Pompeia* out to greet the airplane's world. Right on cue, and as soon as I gripped her snugly, she began wailing ferociously. "Meow! Meow! Meow! Meooooooow!" *Pompeia* let everyone know she was alive and kicking. Also, she was probably alarmed with her new circumstances and no doubt starving. I had salvaged some milk still in its carton from the previous night, and I began arranging to feed her again right there.

My seat mates were astonished. "Oh, my goodness!" they both proclaimed practically in unison. Of course, *Pompeia's* frantic cries for food brought spontaneous looks and anxious searches from all the other passengers bewildered by her sudden outburst. Then my seatmates both had sudden rushes of questions flailing away at me.

"Where did she come from?" They both took turns with their solemn but curious inquisition. "Why do you have her here with you? Did you sneak her onto this plane? Oh, the poor dear thing; she must be starving."

"She's going to eat right now," I responded politely. "She'll be fine once I feed her. I rescued her in *Rome*, and I'm taking her home as a gift to my aunt who helped send me over here in early June. I have her papers, and she's legal. Her name is *Pompeia*, which was one of Julius Caesar's wives."

Oh, if that couple beside me had been previously perturbed with my holding up their flight, and had distanced themselves from me as a result, they became downright social butterflies toward me after seeing *Pompeia*. That cute, little kitten had gone ahead and saved-my-bacon yet another time. She was definitely worth every bit of struggle and inconvenience I had ever suffered because of her. We were true partners.

Children on the flight were squealing with delight by then also. There would still be no manhandling, but eventually, once the flight allowed for movement about the aircraft, swarms of onlookers came flooding over to gander looks. "Oh, how darling!" came one callout.

"Look, it's just a baby!" cried out a shocked viewer. "How old is she?"

I briefly offered details, "She was about two to three weeks old when I found her with an abandoned litter. That was over three weeks ago, so she's just about six weeks old by now. At least that's what the veterinarian told me."

"Why, that is amazing, young man," a concerned passenger stated, "but she should still be with her mother until at least after six weeks."

"I know, Mam," I politely responded with facts, "but the litter's mother had been killed by a car in *Rome*, so the locals were just going to toss the whole lot of them into trash barrels. I took this one to try and save one of them. It was hard going at first, but here we are, and she is pretty healthy and feisty."

"Remarkable!" "Adorable!" "Amazing!" "So cute!" "Why, I've never heard of such a thing!" and other positive and supporting comments flooded the passenger compartment. Everyone seemed delightfully happy and intrigued with their secret passenger. If any fault toward me had been held before, it had completely vanished with *Pompeia's* welcomed presence. We then had an airline full of passenger friends and allies. Even the crew were shocked and delighted. No one took her from me, but I allowed most to touch and pet her, although *Pompeia* mostly busied herself by gorging on the container of milk.

Pompeia earned her next "Badge of Worthiness" when the flight meals became available. By that time, I was really hungry. I hadn't had a decent meal in several days, but all that discontent came to a colossal end when meals were served. Of course, I got my own, but the stewardesses packed on double servings of the on-flight meals for me. Double soft drinks too. Then came extra milk for me and specifically for Pompeia. "Here," the flight attendants seemed to keep repeating themselves, "have some more, and here is some extra for your kitten."

"Oh, thank you so much," I started teasing back. "She really likes roast beef and filet mignon, and Champagne too. Of course, I'll finish off any of her leftovers!" I got the laughs I wanted, and extra food kept pouring in from other passengers too. I was never sure whether they were trying to overfeed *Pompeia*, or they felt sorry or impressed with me. Either way, I got to eat more than I had at any mealtime during the entire summer, it seemed. I shredded tiny pieces of meat from the gift-package meals for *Pompeia*, and she showed off her new teeth and agility with pride. She had definitely earned her wings and ranking as a carnivore by then.

More Bad News

For the remainder of that flight to Montreal, Quebec, Canada, I attempted to answer as honestly and completely as I might the flood of questions that prevailed from appreciative and admiring passengers and crew. They wanted more details about *Pompeia's* existence in *Rome*. They asked about how I had ever managed to take care of her. They wondered about our travels together.

After responding earnestly to all with as much candor and honesty as I could, many just shook their heads in appreciation and awe. Everyone loves a good kitty cat story, or a dog adventure. So did I! I even shared my mishap with her name change from *Caesar* to *Pompeia*. That got plenty of laughs too. Of course, *omitting* some truth was beneficial too, I felt. That sympathetic group did not need to hear about our *Paris* jailing incident, for example. *That* sort of story, with less time for supportive details and facts, was inconsequential. Besides, I saved those hearty particulars for Home, Sweet Home.

When joy, happiness, full bellies, and entertainment satisfaction all around had nearly completely immersed and fully satisfied that airline cabin, leave it to my closest onlookers to spring the very next "Anxiety Trap" upon me. Things had finally quieted down. We were in high stride gliding up over a northern route, and then presumably dropping back down into Canada's airspace, when I became stunned yet again by unexpected news. My seatmates had obviously been discussing a personally concerned matter between themselves and had determined to find resolve. They simply had to know my answer, so they inquired skillfully, yet harmfully.

"So, young man," the woman smugly began their questioning, "you are going on into the United States through Chicago. Is that right?"

"Yes, I guess it seems so from my paperwork," I answered with the slightest hesitation and trepidation. "Then I'm supposed to get on another Air France flight there and fly on to San Diego."

"Well, young fella," the gentleman began again very patronizingly, "you do understand that any new animals brought into the United States from outside its borders must go through a two-week quarantine period to check them for diseases and such."

"Oh, no, it's okay," I responded quickly and defensively, feeling both suddenly anxious and perplexed. "I paid a *Paris* Veterinarian, and he gave *Pompeia* all her shots and clearances. She's okay to enter the US."

It then seemed like both of them slightly smirked with "Gotcha!" glares in their eyes. Faintly smiling, the woman said, "Unfortunately, young man, it doesn't work like that. Your cat is okay for *Paris*, and even, perhaps, for this airplane, but not for entering the USA. They will probably force you to put your kitten into a two-seek quarantine, and you will be responsible for the fees. Isn't that just awful?"

I'm not going to confess how I really wanted to respond to them. But let's just suffice to admit that I allowed their somewhat deliberate and hurtful informational sharing moments to be the end of our conversational dialog. I calmly placed my food stuffed *Pompeia* back into her shoe box, held her dearly and closely on my lap, and became mostly silent. I then pretended to lie back and sleep, so as not to be bothered anymore by my seat mates' smug condemnations. I had plenty to think about before getting off that plane in Chicago to face US Customs.

After our flight landed in Montreal, and many passengers unloaded, the remaining flight to Chicago left several empty seats available for any takers. It was my chance to make a move, and I did so. Courteously bidding adieu to my annoying travel mates, I made the lame excuse that *Pompeia* needed to stretch her legs on one of the open seats. I was happy to switch seats for any other place on that plane, thus removing myself from unabridged and unwanted stress.

It was also time for me then to really start thinking of some plan to get *Pompeia* through US Customs without having her confiscated. There was absolutely no way that I could afford paying for any two-week "Quarantine Period," if what I had been told was accurate. We both needed to get all the way back to California and at least together. I knew that I needed a solution to that puzzle. There had to be some reasonable plan that would allow me to bring *Pompeia* along with me and onto our next flight within the US.

It was obvious, however, that we would absolutely have to go through US Customs. That was the only way to get into the USA legally and then onto our next preplanned flight from Chicago to San Diego. Perhaps, I could just ask someone in Chicago for guidance and get a reasonable alternative for our dire situation. I worried during our short flight from Montreal to Chicago, which was over in a fleeting period. I held *Pompeia's* shoe box tightly to me as we disembarked at Chicago O'Hare International Airport still wondering what to do…

Crazy American

From the airport tarmac to the terminal building, and then down the long walkway and hall ramp, I leerily and casually edged along. I kept imagining why people called those places "Terminals." The name concerned me. Was this place "The End?" As I continued through US Custom's Entry Walkway, eventually all passengers from recent arrival flights were united and joined together in a huge auditorium-like room.

Each individual traveler was instructed by airport officials and overhead or standing signs for which line to enter and pass through for recognition and approval depending on their destinations. Some were foreigners entering as *Visitors;* others were non-USA citizen residents; still others were returning *American Citizens;* and then there was me sneaking in with a hidden baby kitten held firmly in a shoe box under his camouflaging arm.

Nobody had given me any suggestions as to alternative entries for bringing in a *foreigner* kitten. Honestly, I was afraid to ask either, for fear of "kitten" news quickly spreading through the giant theatre just like parade excitement. Or worse, like a "terminal" virus. I worried about all those previous flight passengers who had earlier delightfully feigned interest over *Pompeia* on the aircraft like she was their own special, uniquely adopted baby.

Then I considered how sometimes, depending on circumstances, people's viewpoints or attitudes can quickly change based on new conditions. I remembered reading about how the poor original "Pompeia" had been cast out into oblivion by her image concerned husband, Julius Ceasar, because she was "under suspicion." Then I remembered from my history class about Julius Ceasar, himself, who was later even killed by other Roman Senators who had turned against him for his outrageous ambitions.

Anxiety began spreading through my mind like a viral parade. Would my *Pompeia* become spurned again and "tossed into oblivion" once more for "suspicious circumstances" just like her namesake? Would I be arrested, and my criminal character *assassinated,* because of my smuggling activities of an illegal, potentially diseased cat into the USA? As we approached the US Customs counter, I became even more fearful, and my imagination began running wildly rampant.

"How dare you infect the feline world of America!" some policing agent might yell as he learned about my actions and collared us both.

With each of his hands grabbing the naps of both my neck and poor little *Pompeia's,* another angered Customs Agent would shout out orders as we were being dragged away, "How could you be so thoughtless, careless, and cruel! You will be thrown directly into jail right along with your sick cat."

Then, his incensed and frustrated supervisor would come rushing up, "In fact, put them both in a cell with all Chicago's other arrested prostitutes, and junkies, and thieves, and murderers! After all, he is charged with being a "potential, cat-infecting killer!"

"No! Wait!" the Customs General-in-Charge would start commanding to all as he stormed into the foray, "Send them both back to *Paris* immediately to be beheaded by their French Guillotine. Let both their heads then be stuck visibly atop tall poles and cruelly exhibited for ultimate viewing by the entire French public. In fact, place the pole directly in front of the *Arc de Triomphe* for all to recognize and ridicule!"

Then I began imagining all the cute, friendly girls from *Paris's* Red-Light District to come wandering by and seeing *Pompeia's* and my head dangling above on our sticks, would solace, "So sad, and he was such a nice boy. We never had a chance to earn his money."

Needless to say, I began hearing vague voices from my surrounding populace in that large Customs' Interrogation Quarters. "Psssst!" I could imagine frightened, American returnees quietly exclaiming to their inline neighbors. "Look! There's an illegal cat being snuck in! It might be diseased! Call the police! Customs! Supervisor! General-in-Charge, HELP! We're being affronted and attacked by a sick animal and its irresponsible cat smuggler!"

But, nervous as I could be, I just kept my mouth shut and proceeded up the line ever closer and closer to the US Customs Window Counter. I watched closely as each Customs Agent called for another citizen, or family group, to approach a window and then begin industriously checking all their passports for proper identification. The line continued shortening, and those Customs Windows got closer and closer for my turn of recognition and deliberations.

So far so good. Fortunately, no one from the *Paris*-Montreal plane we had been on was around to notice me and bring attention to my shoe box. If I had been recognized by another Air France passenger entering Chicago too, I quickly developed a harmless lie (not the truth, but not completely a mistruth, either) in which to respond to the questioning person.

"Oh, hi," the other passenger might exclaim, "you're the young guy on the plane with the kitten. How are you doing with it?"

"Oh, it is very sad," I determined to reply, "but I was told that I had to dump the cat in order to enter the US. It was heartbreaking!" Then I would quickly turn away separating myself as much as possible from that other Air France passenger just in case *Pompeia* came roaring to life in abrupt and abject indignation.

Fortunately, *Pompeia* continued sleeping like a newborn kitten, as hopefully as I could wish. Ahead of me the line steadily reduced further as *Returning Americans* took their proud places before Customs Agents at their counters, and they all obediently produced passports for themselves and any family unit members. The agents all appeared dutiful and serious. Every entering citizen had to stand silently before their respective agents as they were face checked against their passports with each's inscribed picture inside.

Then the Customs Agents next asked a series of questions of each *Returnee* regarding where they had visited and otherwise. I strained my head forward attempting to listen closely to those Customs questions, but the distances to each counter, with its protective partitions, made comprehension impossible. I was fairly certain, however, that each anxious citizen was specifically asked if they "... were by any remote possibilities attempting to smuggle in stray kittens from Europe, and especially from *Rome*?"

However, I gained some reassurances, though, from various *Returning Americans'* responses to questioning when I observed them all noticeably shaking their heads to further questioning. Perhaps, I would not have to lie at all, after all. I would just stand there and shake my head in denials to all quizzing. Say nothing; just twist your head and refute everything.

Hopefully, when it came my turn to address my assigned Customs Agent, my shoe box would remain just as it appeared: A box filled with new shoes, or replaced old ones, and securely protected under my armpit. Hopefully? Yes, that is, of course, for what I prayed. Realistically? Is that what I got? Hardly so...

At the very moment when I took my rightful place at the head of the line, and as the very next US Citizen to be called forth for his "Welcoming Inquisition," *Pompeia* chose to make her presence loudly known to the entire world. She had suffered enough from all the previous manhandling during the prior flights. She had been gorged with food from all directions and stuffed beyond recognition. She had slept for ages in her dark, little chamber, although quite comfortable at that. However, it was time for her to yawn, stretch, move about, and scream to high heavens over her presumed undignified and unwelcome entrapment.

What could I do? *I* was trapped! Everyone everywhere would become precisely aware of what was happening, and I would be immediately discovered as the fraud I was and then be wistfully whisked away and hauled back to *Paris* for Customs' retribution. "Off with his head!" I could almost hear others screaming!

OMG! *Pompeia*? Why now? "Shhhhhh! " I nearly cried. "There, there. Quiet, please! We're almost home! Shhhhhh! Not now, for God's sake, and for my own sake, and for *our own sakes*, and your own!"

Did *Pompeia* listen to me? Did she suddenly become animalistically simpatico to my anxious wishes? Would anyone really think so? Hell, no! That was just her earliest and faintest discomforting warning that she was awakening and immediately wanting out of her mistreated confinement and cramped nesting.

"*Meow*! (Open up this crate!)" she cried out boldly. "*Meow*! (I want out now!) *Meow*! (I'm hungry too!)"

I looked up from my agonized stare at *Pompeia's* highly vocalizing shoe box in total disbelief, and I worried over my serious hint of bad luck from her antics. Then, naturally, an agent at the far end of our next-person, Entry Point was signaling for me to step forth unto his counter's domain. What to do?

Should I turn and make a run for it? Who would care? The Customs line would simply move forward that much faster. Should I just stand there and wait for *Pompeia* to settle down? Hardly. She was just then building up steam. Should I simply tell others to just go on past me while I remained where I was somewhat shielded, distance wise, from the agents? No, again. I would most noticeable attain undesirable attention from every agent then wanting new victims for their citizen inquisitions. No, I had to go forward. Always forward. Never backward. Forward into Hell, itself! "Shut up, *Pompeia*,... please!"

My instincts instantly took over. Without the remotest idea of any realistic plan, all I could do was react to that perverse, present condition and status I was given. I had to cover-up for *Pompeia*. I had to camouflage her defiant screams. I had to distract the Customs Agent away from *Pompeia's* angry and urgent appeals to be released and freed from her present bondage.

"Meow!" Pompeia would begin...

"Aauuurrrghhhh!" I instantly interrupted and screamed as loud as I could as I also began wildly flailing my one free arm and hand which held my passport.

"Meo..." she started up again...

"Aaauuurrrghhh!" I persisted, continuing with my frantically, waving-about free arm and gyrating body.

Shaking my head back and forth, I moved cautiously but steadily toward my assigned Customs Agent. I could tell that I already had his undivided attention. I also observed that I had nearly every other agent's attention too. Oh, well, I determined, "This is the plan I have chosen, and I am already deeply committed to it. Just go with it!"

"Me…," *Pompeia* went again…

"Aaaauuuughhhh!" I let the agent hear my spontaneous, but synchronized, reaction again. I was engrossed in an actor's role, and this charade character became who I was. "Get over it, and deal with me, Customs Agents!"

"Passport, pl…," the agent suspiciously but anxiously began requesting…

"M…!" *Pompeia* began repeating her screaming forth again.

"Aaaaauuuuughhhhh!" I bellowed again as I continued shaking my head profusely, while wobbling my body back and forth, and waving my free arm erratically about me. Fully cognizant of my instructions, though, I respectfully handed over my US Passport to the Customs Agent.

The agent was obviously noticeably shaken by my appearance, thus far. He quickly reviewed my swiftly provided passport, checking its picture with my own face. While haphazardly and sensitively noting my unrestrained wild expressions, movements, and hollering, which effectively coincided precisely with *Pompeia's* own uncontrolled exasperations, the agent rushed through my examination.

The agent then hurriedly, and finally, checked my passport's internal stamps providing some semblance of legality and officiality. He quickly abided by the same sequence of official orientation with a similar series of reentry questions as all other *American Returnees* before me had endured. I shook my head profusely through them all. But *Pompeia* still continued to have other interests soundly interrupting us yet as she attempted getting in the last words:

"M…" she started up again.

"Aaaaaauuuuuughhhhhh!" I co-interrupted again while wildly flapping my free arm about and twisting my head nervously about. What else could I do? I was traveling with an agitated feline who needed precisely attuned affirmations.

The relatively short encounter with Customs finally ended as quickly as it had presumably begun. In swift order, the Customs Agent located and retrieved a precise page of my passport and stamped it vigorously with America's *Welcoming Home* Approval Seal. He then hastily shoved my passport swiftly back to me, to which I just as swiftly snatched up, as he proclaimed and pointed, "Welcome Back! The Exit Gate to all further flights, or Chicago, is that way!"

I could have sworn I also heard him quietly exhale, "Go! Please! Thank God. Yes, he's got to be an American, alright! Crazy. Simply crazy!"

Yet, I wasted not a single second more, and actually for best effects, I continued even more so with my exaggerated gyrations and loud vocalizations. "Aauughh! Thank... you! Aaauuughhh!" I exclaimed joyously as I flailed my arm about and rushed for the exit doors.

A moment later, I was studying overhead signs and retrieving my new travel instructions: "Continuing Passengers for Further Destinations Are to Follow Appropriate Signs to Their Embarkation Zones."

"Thank goodness!" I exhaled from within my completely frayed mind. "Next major hurdle overcome. What in God's good name could possibly come next?" All I could do was attempt to mentally prepare myself for any worse case scenarios. At least I was back in the United States again finally, and as far as I knew, guillotines had been forbidden for a long time. However, I still wasn't sure, for sure, about Chicago or Illinois. "Get onboard your next flight immediately!" I warned myself.

Rushing down a hallway after that previously tumultuous and agonizing affair with O'Hare's International Airport US Customs, I exasperatingly laughed aloud, "Aaauuughhh! Ha! Ha! Ha!" Then reflecting over my circumstances, I noted to myself, "If anything worse was suspect to follow, but nothing except pleasantries come about, it would seem like a miracle."

After *Pompeia's* next feeding, our relaxed interlude between flights came with leisurely and expeditious timing. Once I fed *her* again, she became calmly comforted again, and slept soundly. Going through upcoming US Domestic Travel Control Points was no further issue at all. *Pompeia* slept again through all commotions. I was just like any other US traveler boarding an acceptable airline, and who was also carrying a new pair of shoes along with him. "Or maybe he was even wearing his new shoes already," observers thought. But who cared? Not me...

Several hours later, *Pompeia* and I were once more boarding another flight. That time, however, it was completely a domestic flight and heading for California. I couldn't help but laugh to myself, "We had done it! *Pompeia* and I were nearly home this time. For any interruptions or complications, I could always call my friend in LA to assist with a surprise visit to my girlfriend, which I planned to do anyway, and have her pick me up in San Diego, instead of Los Angeles.

I did not care anymore, and I was equal to any challenges coming from my earlier, Air France Airlines, doomsday-prophet seat companions. I was still absolutely wiling to hitch hike the remaining distance home. But we were still broke and dependent upon airline meals. However, if we had to hitch, *Pompeia* could then regain her prior, rightful position once again on my shoulder, and she would absolutely emphasize my seriousness and our rightful placements among world travelers.

"Criminy!" I bellowed internally, "But we're already leaving Chicago, Illinois, USA! Hop, skip, jump, and we're in San Diego! Then L.A.! Hello, California! Hello, my darling Sue! I'm almost home, and we never even got arrested!"

CHAPTER 20

UNWELCOME HOME PARTY

Lost Luggage

Smooth as silk! That is what our flight to San Diego was like. Once in the air again, and on another Air France aircraft, I felt relaxed enough to bring *Pompeia* back out for viewing. Naturally, once my hands were on her she became wide awake and let everyone know about it. For another hilarious period, she and I were the "talk of the town!" Any child anywhere on the plane squealed with delight in wonderful harmonics to *Pompeia's* screaming bloody murder. She was hungry. No, starving, and she made no bones about it.

I repeated anecdotes of our experiences together again, just as before, and we both garnished more admiration and interest for some of our shared tales. When the airline's cross-country meals were served, once again we both received donated items from so many other passengers' dinners, and I, of course, had to make certain most of the offerings were disposed of appropriately... *Pompeia* had no problems scarfing up the softly crushed meal portions offered her. She still enjoyed her milk servings, but basic, soft-meaty foods were by then easily receiving their share of her eager attention.

Several hours later, and there was yet another touchdown, that time in the beautiful Southern California city of San Diego. According to my flight schedule, I only had about an hour wait there until my next brief flight took me to Los Angeles, literally only minutes away by air. I barely had to move much from one flight gate to the other for my next flight. So, I had time to call a mutual friend and ask her to meet me at Los Angeles International Airport and help with my surprise greeting and reunion with my sweetheart girlfriend, Sue. I found a phone and made a collect call.

"Yes. I'll accept. Hello?" a familiar voice answered on the other line.

"Linda! Hi! It's Danny." I spoke back excitedly. "I'm back and in San Diego right now. I'll be at LA International in less than two hours. Can you pick me up? I want to surprise Sue."

"Uh, hi, Danny!" Linda hesitated. "Wow! This is a surprise! Are you sure you want to come to LA? Sue's parents are gone, but Sue may not be available."

"Oh, wow. Really?" I answered disappointedly. "Is she in town? Can I maybe stay at your place for the night? I really want to see Sue before I leave tomorrow."

"Uh, yeah, sure you can stay here," Linda cautiously added. "In fact, Kay is also down here right now too, and she is going back up to Brownsville herself tomorrow. You can go back home with her if you like."

"That's great!" I got a little more excited. "But do you know if I'll get to see Sue while I'm here?"

"Uh, well, I don't know for sure, but are you sure you want to?" Linda oddly asked.

"Do I want to?" I responded a bit flabbergasted. "Of course, I want to see her. Especially if I have to go back home tomorrow. Find out for me, Linda, please, and pick me up in two hours. I'll be with Air France Arrivals."

"Sure, Danny," Linda responded rather glumly. " I'll try. See you soon. Bye."

That wasn't the exciting surprise announcement for which I had hoped. What did I expect, though? I was two weeks late, and no one had heard a word from me for two and a half months. Naturally, people were surprised. Sue had no idea I'd be there at that time. Even my folks knew nothing about my whereabouts. I knew that I should start letting family know that I was alright. It was just that seeing Sue was my absolute priority. Now that seeing her was at least a possibility, thanks to Linda, I called my folks and let everyone know that I was safe and would be home the very next day.

Shortly thereafter, my flight left San Diego, and literally in only a few minutes, it seemed, the plane was touching down in Los Angeles. Need I mention all the oohs and aahs we received on that short flight too when so many passengers wanted to give oodles of attention to *Pompeia*. She was a big hit wherever we traveled. I began getting anxiously hopeful for my aunt's surprise when I finally and joyously, but wistfully, awarded her *Pompeia* as a thank you gift. It would be difficult to say, "Goodbye" to my little travel mate.

After landing and deboarding the Air France flight in LA, I followed the signs to Baggage Pick-up. I was at last to be reunited with my sea bag for one last time. It would be nice to empty it and finally put the bag away. I didn't want to have to worry about it, or all my stuff anymore. Looking back, it had actually been quite a hardship enduring all the hoisting around of that thing all over Europe. Exhausting, really. Thank goodness, no more. Just one more pick-up, and we would part company for good, hopefully. I followed the signs straight to the large, oval luggage turnstiles and found the one designated for my Air France flight.

Shortly after that, our flight's luggage began arriving and everyone from the flight quickly grabbed their baggage and left. Mine was not yet among the deposited luggage on the conveyor belt. After everyone else's bags, suitcases, and gear and been picked-up by owners, and the belt was completely empty, eventually it stopped rotating.

I became concerned and sought out security. They directed me to a Lost and Found/Missing Baggage office. The personnel officer there informed me that all baggage from my flight had been delivered. He then checked records from San Diego. No luggage was listed as having arrived for me, and nothing was even found as being forwarded to San Francisco the following day. Nothing discovered at all. The agent even called Chicago. Nothing from there to mention either. Nothing.

I explained everything to the officer, and they took down all relevant information from me regarding my flights from *Paris* to Montreal, to Chicago, to San Diego, then to LA, and scheduled flight for San Francisco the next morning. Perhaps, it seemed like a lot to investigate, but I was assured by Los Angeles Airport authorities and Air France officials that they would locate my belongings. My single, navy sea bag, although unlocked or secured, but supposedly aptly tagged for delivery, identification, and confirmation, would be found. Eventually, I was supposed to have them returned to me.

Under those unusual circumstances of overseas and multiple flights, I had to be satisfied with their delayed, luggage-delivery consequence, and simply wait for relief of my bag. But things seemed very odd after two and a half months of carrying that sea bag nearly everywhere with me, and then for it to suddenly be gone from my care. That included three weeks having it hoisted upon one shoulder right along with *Pompeia* resting on my other shoulder.

To be leaving LA Airport, with only myself and a shoe box still tightly tucked under my arm holding *Pompeia*, left me feeling really sort of empty-handed., like a large void was hanging over my shoulder. My travels just didn't seem right anymore... Remnants of my whole adventure in Europe were inside that missing luggage. All evidence of having been anywhere that entire summer, with the exception of my own stories and *Pompeia*, were inside that bag. And naturally, wouldn't you know it, throughout the nearly entire missing sea bag mishap, *Pompeia* had quieted down and had been no bother to anyone. Thanks, *Pompeia*. Finally, some nice, *quiet* time...

Travesty

My friend, Linda, was right on time in her 1961 Ford Fairlane and drove up to the Passenger Pick-up Zone right away and recognized me standing there waiting. Her cute, vivacious, five-foot-two frame with a warming silly attitude made it worthwhile seeing her friendly face again. She, of course, was someone who knew my and Sue's situation and background very well being of one Sue's best friends. Linda, however, was not her typical funny self that afternoon, and she seemed a little hesitant and cautious over my arrival. In fact, our meeting was actually a little awkward.

"Hi, Linda! Great to see you again." I said happily. "Thanks a lot for picking me up. It's the first time I've had a ride waiting for me in ten weeks. Ha! Ha!"

Linda sort of chuckled in response, and after I explained about the absent luggage, a moment later and we were off and running. Then she spoke up again, "Danny, are you sure you want this? It's just sort of difficult with you being here now and all."

"Well, I'm sorry for the surprise visit, Linda. With my new flight home circumstances, though, because of the airline strike, and being dropped off right here in LA, I figured it was fantastic timing. Why? What's going on, Linda?"

"Oh, it's just that everything's all mixed-up and all," Linda pouted. "But you can see Sue, if you really want, and Kay too, and Sue can tell you all about it."

"If I really want…?" I puzzled. "Tell me all about what?" I wondered quietly to myself. But I just shrugged my shoulders instead, opened my shoe box for Linda to meet my little friend and watch them both get excited greeting each other. *Pompeia* had a way of charming anyone. On the other hand, *I* was no longer feeling very *charmed*. Something seemed wrong, and I couldn't tell just what. However, I rationalized that I would be seeing my sweetheart very soon, and then, no matter what, everything would be alright again. Sue also had a way of *charming* anyone too.

Once at Linda's home, I visited with her kind parents who reassured me of a welcomed overnight stay. *Pompeia* and I even had dinner while waiting for Sue and Kay to show up. Typically, I would have gone straight to Sue's house and stayed there with her family, but they were gone apparently, so that was out of the question. Too bad. Sue and I could be trusted,… or maybe not! "What a *Welcoming Home Party* that would be, though!" I thought silently and smiled.

Minutes later, Sue and Kay arrived together at Linda's home. Kay was still driving her faithful and trustworthy, brown, and white, '57 Chevrolet Bel-Aire Station Wagon. Previously, we'd all already had plenty of fun times in that vehicle. We would be riding back in it to our hometown of Brownsville the following day too.

Also, I had fully decided to forsake any further flights with Air France, even if they were taking me back to my original departure point at San Francisco International Airport. After all, if they could lose my luggage, I wasn't about to trust them with me or *Pompeia anymore*. When and if they found my missing sea bag, they would contact me. At least, so I was told. Besides, every flight with *Pompeia* inside her shoe box domicile was still just another chance for exposure and issues. No more chances…

What can I say, however, about what happened next? Once arrived, Sue was immediately stand-offish, distant, and somewhat cool to my excited greeting. First off, though, Kay came rushing over with a very welcoming embrace. By-the-way, Kay was crazy in love with my sailor brother. But I was her second favorite. After excited embracement and warm greetings, I turned to Sue and faced her directly.

"Hi, Sue," I said touchingly and longingly, "I've missed you so much," Then I started feeling a little bit flushed and anxious. "It's so great to see you again."

"Hi, Danny, yeah, it's nice to see you too," she offered back. No kiss, just a modest hug, and then Sue turned away, sort of, and moved to a far part of the home's living room. It suggested a private invitation for me to join her there, which I did, just after noticing embarrassed glances from both Kay and Linda.

"What in the world was wrong?" I wondered. "Has somebody died? No, I had called home, and all was well there. "Maybe something tragic has happened with Sue's family. Afterall, they are gone, and no one has said why." But something was not right. The world suddenly seemed unsynchronized and imbalanced. I was really beginning to feel uneasy about things. I needed to talk to Sue, have her reassure me, and find out what *was wrong.*

I approached Sue closely and longingly, but hesitantly. Her beautiful face, deep brown eyes, darkly golden hair, tanned skin, and, oh, so sexy body urged me forward. "Are you alright, Sue?" I asked. "Is something wrong? You can tell me. I have missed you so much this past summer. Just tell me."

"Danny," Sue blurted out quietly but matter-of-factly, "I am with someone else now. I can't be with you anymore."

"What? Oh, my God!" I reeled in my shoes as my heart skipped a beat. "What do you mean, '...can't be with me anymore?' I don't understand, Sue," I nearly begged, "*Who* is someone else?"

"He's a past boyfriend from school," Sue responded practically whispering, "and we got back together again this summer. I am sorry."

Sorry? Welcome Home, my eye! It was a *Hell Come Home* if anything. It was like having your loving heart burning on fire and then having the blazing flames doused with ice-water. Fire to freeze! I was dumbfounded. Flabbergasted. Upheaved. Turned upside down. Speechless. I, the one who could talk his way out of almost anything, who could use his trusty mouth, voice, and wits to explain away nearly any complication, was without words. Sue's own crushing statement had effectively shut down my vocal cords and left me a helpless mute.

I struggled momentarily for comprehension. Then by truly digging down into the deepest bowels of my assaulted self-confidence and stretching for the last remaining strands of communicative skills, I tried one last time to reassure Sue, change her mind, and bring her solemnly back to my beseeching arms.

"Sue," I began reassuringly, but still pleading, "It's okay. I understand, but I'm back now. Get rid of him and tell him I am here. You and I are back together again now. What do you say? C'mon, Sue."

"Danny, we can't," she disclosed somewhat wistfully. "I am pregnant and going to have his baby. We are getting married next month."

Somewhere deep inside my instantly wrecked and bewildered mind, I burst into unseen tears. My eyes blurred, my head began spinning momentarily, and my entire body flooded with unimaginable sadness. My religious faith temporarily checked-in, and I agonized that the Good Lord, somehow, really did work in mysterious ways. Indeed, I was absolutely baffled. Shocked. Dismayed. Mentally stunned beyond recognition.

My previous fantasy life had been completely flipped topsy-turvy. For a moment, I even anguished over horrifying justifications: Sue and her *past boyfriend* may have likely recommitted themselves at the precise moments as I had backstepped with that temptress, *Monique*. The *Horny Hostel* incident, where she and I had nearly consummated our own faithless relationship, had brought forth that present forsaken love crisis. "God is paying me back for my infidelity. Serves me right!" I struggled…

Life was strange immediately following my *heartbreaking* break-up. Sure, I got sympathetic hugs and well-wishes from my friends and family, but my once typically good mood was terribly shaken. For time being, not much seemed worthwhile after that. Sue was gone, and so was my luggage. I had no one with whom to share all the truly intimate and personal details of my journey. After that amazing yet dreadfully ended summer, my life became a virtual travesty. I had nothing to show for it, anymore. No love. No luggage. No happiness. Nothing, except for *Pompeia*. At least she was gratifying evidence of a summer well spent, and she truly was a marvelous hit with my friends and siblings.

Thus, with a deep sense of shell-shocked sorrow, all my anecdotal storytelling was grotesquely affected, if not negated, by lack of physical evidence, no souvenirs, and melancholia. As I shared a few unique details of my otherwise wonderful, and often exhilarating travels, the private pleasures, and personal rewards I anticipated were undeniably absent. That final evening of reunion time passed casually as I then later slept restlessly on Linda's family couch… alone. The next morning, Kay arrived early for the long trip back to our welcoming homes in the northern mountains of Brownsville, California.

For my summer's trek of hitch hiker trailblazing across an entire foreign continent covering several thousand kilometers, that woeful, last leg of my journey became the loneliest 450 mile stretch of my lifetime. From Burbank, California to Brownsville, it was the longest, quietest, and most subdued portion of my entire summer's journey. Even *Pompeia* must have sensed my helpless sadness by barely rustling and even sleeping most of the way right alongside me.

Yes, sleep has a temporary way of camouflaging pain, and it served me well. Throughout that eight-hour drive, in order to ward off as much discomfort and grief as I could, I did sleep much of the way. I needed to sleep in order to conceal my emotionally drained mind, sudden physically exhausted body, and even stupefied, if not embarrassed, thoughts. After all, I had just received, and had been cruelly taught yet once again, the very same bitter lesson from that chilling summer: *Love and lust are but charades...*

Further Rejections

My arrival home did actually achieve a little fanfare. Enough time had lapsed for several friends and family to come to my family's home and be there when Kay finally dropped me off. Kay and I hugged goodbye, with promises to see each other again soon, and I made my way into the celebratory status of a true *welcoming home*. My elder brother, David, was still out at sea with the US Navy, of course. My dad was also gone away on his work again, as was usual, but I soon learned that his own situation would directly affect my next immediate plans.

My sisters and kid brother were all there, though, and excited to see me, naturally. It was frustrating, however, explaining how they'd all have to wait until my baggage arrived, if ever, before they could receive their souvenirs. However, *Pompeia* rescued me once more by becoming a blessed distraction. After brief hugs and kisses, my siblings began immediately fighting over taking turns to hold her. *Pompeia* seemed to do that to a lot of kids. Good luck to her that time, though. She was finally almost at *home* then, herself.

Mom stood by patiently while everyone else forced themselves all over me. She even allowed neighbors to provide hugs and handshakes for my safe return. Then with open arms she hugged and kissed me tightly and scolded me about not contacting her. All I could do to defend myself was by using teasing lies, "Didn't you get all those letters, and postcards, and phone calls I made every day? What happened? Oh, yeah, no time, no money, and no stamps! But here I am. I did it, Mom! I actually went everywhere, did everything, and I got back safe and sound!"

That coming weekend my heart slowly began climbing back up into its rightful place once again in my chest. It was permanently damaged, of course, but I steadily determined to survive and get on with my life, whatever that mattered anymore. Somehow, someway I knew that I would need to recollect my thoughts and make new plans that only involved my own life from then on, and not Sue's anymore.

My very next train-of-thought, therefore, became resolving *Pompeia's* new home. I needed to contact Aunt Jean, who lived several hours away, and inform her of my safe return and thank her again for sponsoring my European travels. Then, in my classic tone of elation, I would surprise Jean of her new, unique, one-of-a-kind, amazing, and stupendous gift of a baby kitten brought all the way back from *Rome*, itself. No, I would, in fact, *emphasize* to Jean that *Pompeia* had been *snuck* clear into the USA and California just for her as a special *Thank You* present.

Unfortunately, Jean's brusque response, although somewhat defined by her usual terse nature, nevertheless caught me by surprise and brought an unexpected dilemma. She answered, "Hello? Oh, so, you finally made it, huh? Had us worried, but I figured you would. Ron told us he saw you."

After brief salutations, I broke to the news of her gift. Just providing bare minimum details, I explained my surprise present for her. It was always difficult pulling something over on Jean. She typically often responded somewhat rudely.

In short order, though, Jean quickly dispatched of my offering, "What? A cat? Are you kidding? No thanks! Don't want any part of it. Take it back to *Rome* if you don't want it yourself!"

"But I brought it all the way back here just for you, Jean," I began explaining pleadingly. "I even snuck it through US Customs. And it's from *Rome*! Remember your stories about *Rome's* cats? I even named her *Caesar* and then *Pompeia*."

"Don't care. Don't want it!" Jean declared in definitive and emphatic terms. "Give it away or keep it. Anyway, welcome back. Bye for now!"

Rejection again? Poor *Pompeia*. Maybe I should have chosen *Boots* for her name, after all. Or, even kept the name *Caesar*, female or not. I felt sorry for my kitten, Jean's kitten, for some reason. Although, I knew that *Pompeia* was oblivious to any such quandary. In actuality, I also understood, however, that I simply felt sorry for myself even more.

First, my luggage retrieval had been *rejected*. That, in itself, was upsetting beyond explanation. All my personal effects and clothing and shoes were gone, including my blanket and sea bag. My camera and film too, and postcards, and souvenirs. And my trusty map was in that lost bag also. Apparently, Air France Airlines had no records of my bag whatsoever. It was gone. A total *rejection*.

Yet, actually, *Pompeia* had almost been my first *rejection* while at the US Custom's crossing in Chicago. That really would have been a crisis. Basic stuff can be replaced, or not, but not *Pompeia*. She was irreplaceable in thought or deed, and her refusal as a gift, after everything we'd shared, was a surprise.

But then, next did come my lost sea bag. Terrible that was to have traveled so far and then to have to deal with its loss. However, after that came my turn to become utterly *rejected* by my girlfriend. *Pompeia*, my luggage, and then me... And now, *Pompeia* forsaken again? That was almost too much.

It did bind me even more to that little unaware kitten, though. She had been through so much already, and although likely oblivious to it all, she became the source of many hilarious anecdotes to share over time. I believe that in some ways, *Pompeia* had even made history just by surviving and being snuck into the United States, in the *first* place.

Shortly after that debacle rejection by my aunt, however, new plans forced a separation of *Pompeia* from me, after all. My dad had a long-term construction job down on the California coast near the community of Santa Cruz. We had talked, and he knew that I no longer had my heart focused on Sacramento State College as an option nor their offered scholarship.

I decided that I wanted a complete change of scenery from what I was used to, and the beautiful Community College of Cabrillo, nestled right on the gorgeous Aptos coastline, seemed to offer a distant and fresh beginning for me. I would live in a shared apartment with my best friend and one of my dad's coworkers as roommates. *Pompeia* would remain in Brownsville with my sister, Barbara, while she lived with Kay's family and completed her senior year of high school. Mom and the remainder of our family would join Dad near Santa Cruz, and we would all temporarily, at least, be close by to one another.

So, I could say, sort of, that I actually added yet one more *rejection* to the whole list of other rebuffs thus far: *First*, nearly a Customs, legal-kitten denial, then an accidental luggage loss, next, a heartbreaking personal rebuke, followed by poor little *Pompeia's* peculiar unacceptance denial. Finally, then I added, of my own free will and volition, r*ejection* of a college scholarship.

I refused the grant so that I might easier escape my comfort zone and find solace by exploring some new, unseen area with new people, new attractions, and a new environment for which to adjust. Sacramento State was simply too close to home with all those memories I then wished to forget. Santa Cruz offered, hopefully, greater challenges and brighter ideas for me to begin building fresh dreams and a new life upon. I was fairly familiar with Sacramento for its common fields, orchards, interconnecting rivers, and large town atmosphere. So, California's coastline sounded much more different, exciting, and appealing.

And, of course, I must not forget that my initial, summer's-trip plans for Europe had come about in the *first* place because of *rejection*. A military academy had supposedly *rejected* me due to bad eyesight. Perhaps, that had merely been an excuse for them. However, I never would *clearly* see their reasoning (pun intended).

Even then, however, several years later in 1970, having received a low draft number, based on my birthday, for the US Military Selective Service Draft System, it was only a matter of time before I too would be in the military anyway, draft or otherwise. The Vietnam war was raging, and every able-bodied, obligatory young man was required to serve. For me, however, in that September of 1966, my summer's adventure had ended. And surprise endings had by then refocused everything for me. College was just beginning… and so was the rest of my newfound life…

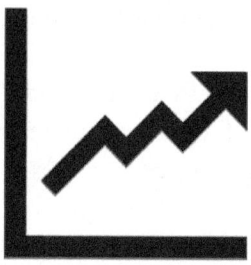

EPILOGUE

S o, there you have it. At the unripe age of eighteen, and fresh out of high school, I received a unique opportunity to *prove* myself trustworthy and earn any unspoken, yet understood and accepted, *manhood* accolades. I was permitted to travel to Europe alone for most of the summer following graduation and to make my own way about the continent essentially on my own merits. Where I went, what I did, and who or what I saw were to be of my own choosing with no specific itinerary or schedule from which to adhere. With such minor, previous experience going anywhere on my own, that challenge for me was expected to be both emotionally taxing and mentally demanding. And most certainly, in varying degrees, it definitely was both. Yet, that summer's trial also became passionately uplifting, developed positive lifetime attitudes, and filled my youth with exuberance, exhilarating experiences, and meaningful life lessons.

To be sure, I did a great deal of growing-up during that *Summer of '66* escapade. If I accomplished anything, however, at least I fulfilled my travel goals and survived to talk about them. Sometime later, after having returned home safely, and having relaxed long enough to take time and reflect upon my summer's adventure, I mentally revisited the initial meaning and purpose of my journey: *To travel the world alone and become an independent man.* Considering all aspects, both good and bad, I felt successful and deserving of having carved out my own berth among our own culture's status of *free* men. *Ideally*, I had shown adult, grown-up *manhood* enough.

Having undergone a variety of unusual circumstances in an assortment of odd, foreign situations, I still arrived home in one piece both mentally and physically fit. I had learned much and brought home with me a few serious lessons about life and myself, and I had lived to laugh, brag, and whine about some details. I had learned from so many experiences noted and shared.

For instance, I successfully assessed myself against unplanned natural extremes which challenged my character and thereby developed personal maturity. In addition, I clearly defined in my mind an ability to look at issues from other, *flip-side* perspectives often allowing for much more positive outlooks on problems. Also, I effectively learned to communicate internationally with all sorts and types of people through willing expressions of humor, appreciation, and apologies.

Additionally, I discovered how to stand-up for myself when challenged or denied by conflicting personalities. I observed and recognized varying governmental and attitudinal differences between nations while noting and addressing shameful barriers separating them. Furthermore, having been initially faithful in love, but after regressing emotionally in dishonored fidelity, I rose again to forgive myself and reaccept personal devotions. Moreover, I discovered, through naïve hardships and difficulties, a recognition of varying humane characteristics while learning to understand different lifestyle-sexualities and develop a mature acceptance of those variances within societies. And certainly, I provided responsible caring for an infant creature's existence while practically placing its own survival above my own. Finally, and overall, I discovered unique examples of worldly and culturally varying attributes yet recognized so many commonalities among nations and their peoples.

I had learned that in our world, some people choose to find conflict within varying, contrary, or contrasting human, social, and cultural characteristics. Yet, in actuality, we all share far more similarities in our lives, beliefs, and natures. Ultimately, I even returned to share some of those unique differences and dynamic similarities several years later with my own, future-classroom students. Given the circumstances, however, in my own mind at least, and perhaps above all else, I had earned and deserved uncelebrated *manhood* status.

In retrospect, though, while closely reexamining that interesting, challenging, meaningful, and enjoyably thoughtful summer's *journey*, I heartily and jovially learned to accept a few conflicting, viewpoints.

For one thing, perhaps I did begin and fulfill my excursion from far too disadvantaged stages. I should have had more funds available for necessary lodging, emergencies, and transportation needs such as the highly desirable Eurail Pass.

It was not prudent to be essentially homeless on too many accounts, and hitchhiking does limit practical safety conditions. Another issue at my journey's initial launching was the point that perhaps I appeared too charming, behaved too confidently, and was cloaked in over eagerness on the outside. Whereas inwardly, however, I was bathed in innocence, ignorance, and naivete. All too often, those circumstances required awkward and occasionally dangerous struggles while defensively forcing me to leap forward experiencing necessary worldly awareness and human understanding.

Looking back, nonetheless, and while factoring in all my voyage's merits and demerits, I came to recognize, accept, understand, and appreciate some viable aspects of myself. I know now, from those transcending 1966 Summer months of mental and physical challenges and maturation, that day-by-day I grew more positively and confidently within my own character. Steadily, I developed valuable lifelong skills of self-reliance, resilience, and worldly communication. For me, ***there and then*** has remained ***a summer to remember.***

Adventure stimulates imagination creating dreams which promote adventure

ABOUT THE AUTHOR

Author, Daniel T. Chapman

A poet at heart, with verse meaningful since his youth, Daniel actually began establishing the poetic phase of his life during his academic career. Initially using poetry in classes to better enhance his students' insight, Daniel later promoted his own, unique poetic style during post-graduate studies to enhance written assignments, projects, and dissertation.

Daniel's poetry and prose career continued comfortably with his first volume of poetry, **Be Not Forgot,'** which introduces connected ideas of attitudes and humor from Daniel's past life as he explores human nature, people's lives, hearts, and conditions. His next effort was the first novel of his *Traveler Series,* **Messages from Vallarta,** a visionary walk of personal and spiritual growth while living within Puerto Vallarta, where he once again utilizes his rich mixture of poetry and prose. Soon following, came Daniel's second volume of poetry, **Poetic Justice,** wherein he examines life with all its curious aspects, strengths, and frailties while deliberately justifying his own unique style of poetry. Then came Daniel's second novel of his *Traveler Series,* **War Torn**, a biography of his struggling, adventurous, and cross-country traveling mother who helped define early, *Me-Too* women's contributions, recognition, and significance such as her experiences from *Rosie the Riveter* fame.

Chapman's latest venture, **There and Then** continues pursuing his personal and unique style-of-writing through his series about *Traveling*. In it, he depicts youthful experiences while seeking adventure and worldly knowledge. And as is his style, he continues sharing mixed storytelling with personal insight while utilizing poetry and language-studies. Descriptions of heart and mind are examined with each new adventure while the author observes people, soul-searches, and occasionally depicts events with personal touches of humor.

"When I am not writing, or traveling, or living-abroad with my 'travel-buddy' wife," Chapman forever quips, "I reside in Suisun City, California with my wife, Angelina, our loving pet Chihuahua, "Mona," and my faithful, loyal, selfless, considerate, industrious, dependable, etc. computer."

www.ingramcontent.com/pod-product-compliance
Lightning Source LLC
Chambersburg PA
CBHW021701120626
46545CB00004B/1341